The Danger of Romance

The Danger of Romance

Truth, Fantasy, and Arthurian Fictions

KAREN SULLIVAN

The University of Chicago Press Chicago and London

The University of Chicago Press, Chicago 60637
The University of Chicago Press, Ltd., London

Published 2018
Printed in the United States of America

27 26 25 24 23 22 21 20 19 18   1 2 3 4 5

ISBN-13: 978-0-226-54012-2 (cloth)
ISBN-13: 978-0-226-54026-9 (paper)
ISBN-13: 978-0-226-54043-6 (e-book)
DOI: https://doi.org/10.7208/chicago/9780226540436.001.0001

The University of Chicago Press gratefully acknowledges the generous support of Bard College toward the publication of this book.

Library of Congress Cataloging-in-Publication Data

Names: Sullivan, Karen, 1964– author.
Title: The danger of romance : truth, fantasy, and Arthurian fictions / Karen Sullivan.
Description: Chicago ; London : The University of Chicago Press, 2018. | Includes bibliographical references and index.
Identifiers: LCCN 2017031778 | ISBN 9780226540122 (cloth : alk. paper) | ISBN 9780226540269 (pbk. : alk. paper) | ISBN 9780226540436 (e-book)
Subjects: LCSH: Arthurian romances—History and criticism. | French literature—To 1500—History and criticism. | Arthur, King—In literature. | Lancelot (Legendary character)—In literature. | Merlin (Legendary character)—In literature. | Arthurian romances—Appreciation.
Classification: LCC PN685.S795 2018 | DDC 809/.93351—dc23
LC record available at https://lccn.loc.gov/2017031778

♾ This paper meets the requirements of ANSI/NISO Z39.48-1992 (Permanence of Paper).

For my aunt,

Mary Jane Sullivan

Contents

Introduction

Over the centuries, the stories have lost none of their old power. The throne of a kingdom has fallen vacant. Following the advice of an enchanter, the people spend Christmas Eve in their church praying for God to reveal who their next ruler should be. When they emerge onto the town square the next morning, they find a mysterious stone with a sword lodged inside it. It is said that only he who can remove this sword from the stone shall rule the kingdom, and only an obscure youth—whom the enchanter reveals to be the late king's son, brought up in ignorance of his identity—is able to do so. After defeating his enemies and establishing himself as sovereign, this young man creates such a court so glorious that all of the best knights from near and far seek to join him and to sit at his Round Table. Among the foreigners who arrive at this court is a knight who surpasses all others in feats of chivalry and, as a result, inspires love in the hearts of all of the ladies and damsels. When the kingdom is still at its height, the knights learn of the existence of a holy vessel that was used during the Last Supper or the Passion of Jesus Christ. They embark on a quest to find this vessel, wandering throughout the land and encountering adventures, though only a few of them ultimately succeed in this endeavor. In the end, after the knights have returned to court, it is revealed that the best of them has long been engaged in a love affair with the queen, and war breaks out between him and his lord. The king pursues this knight to his native land, yet, once there, he learns that his nephew, in whose charge he has left his kingdom, has usurped his throne in his absence. He returns home and confronts this nephew in a battle that ends in the destruction, not only of these two men and their armies, but of the kingdom itself. The queen, who has already withdrawn to a convent, takes the veil. The knight, who hears about the battle only in its aftermath, becomes a hermit. The king, who is mortally wounded, is borne in a boat across the water to a land whence he is expected, one day, to return. Yet while the tales of this enchanter, this king, this knight, and this holy vessel constitute the most enduring literary legacy of the Middle Ages, so too are the debates about the truth value of these works and the genre to which they belong.

In the mid-twelfth century, Arthurian legend began to be written down in the form of what was then becoming known as "romance," though not without misgivings on the part of its first author. Before this time, Arthur had been mentioned in a few Latin chronicles and saints' lives and a few Welsh heroic works,[1] but in both cases only briefly and cryptically. It was not until around 1136 that Geoffrey of Monmouth, a cleric of Breton or Welsh stock who taught at Oxford, provided in his *Historia regum Britanniae* the first lengthy narrative account of this king,[2] and in 1155 that Wace, a cleric from the island of Jersey, translated Geoffrey's Latin prose into the Anglo-Norman French verse of his *Brut*. Until that point, a text that was composed "in romance" (*en romanz*) was simply a text that was written in the romance language, especially Old French, for the benefit of lay readers unfamiliar with Latin.[3] Now, when the *Brut* ends with the declaration "Master Wace made this romance,"[4] it is among the very first few

1. For a useful collection of the Arthurian passages from the early Latin texts, see *Arthur of Britain*, ed. E. K. Chambers (London: Sidgwick and Jackson, 1927; rpt., Cambridge: Speculum Historiale, 1964). For the Welsh materials, see *The Celtic Sources for the Arthurian Legend*, ed. and trans. Jon B. Coe and Simon Young (Burnham-on-Sea, Somerset, UK: Llanerch Publishers, 1995).

2. See Geoffrey of Monmouth, *Historia regum Britanniae*, in *A History of the Kings of Britain: An Edition and Translation of "De gestis Britonum,"* ed. Michael D. Reeve (Woodbridge, UK: Boydell Press, 2009).

3. On the meaning of the word *roman*, see Michel Stanesco, "Chrétien de Troyes et le fondement du roman européen," in *Amour et chevalier dans les romans de Chrétien de Troyes: Actes du colloque de Troyes (27–29 mars 1992)*, ed. Danielle Quéruel (Besançon: Les Belles Lettres, 1995), 361–68; rpt. as "Chrétien de Troyes et la généalogie du roman," in *D'armes et d'amours: Etudes de littérature arthurienne* (Orleans: Paradigme, 2002), 5–14. On the birth of romance, see Jacques Ribard, "Aux Origines du roman français: Le roman au XIIe siècle," in *Le Genre du roman, les genres de romans: Actes de Colloque (Amiens, 25–26 avril 1980)* (Paris: Presses Universitaires de France, 1980), 13–23; Pierre Gallais, "De la naissance du roman: A propos d'un article recent," *Cahiers de civilisation médiévale* 14 (1971): 69–75; and "Recherches sur la mentalité des romanciers français du Moyen Age," *Cahiers de civilisation médiévale* 7, no. 28 (1964): 479–93, and 13 (1970): 333–47.

4. "fist mestre Wace cest romanz," Wace, *Roman de Brut: A History of the British: Text and Translation*, ed. and trans. Judith Weiss (Exeter: University of Exeter Press, 2002), v. 14866. All translations are my own unless otherwise indicated.

works to speak of "romance" as a genre and one to which it belongs.[5] Yet Wace expresses ambivalence about the truth claim he is making in this new category of literature. He addresses his work to those who wish to learn about the history of the kings of Britain, including King Arthur, and he insists, "Master Wace . . . recounts the truth about it."[6] He assumes that it is impossible for so many people to have praised Arthur without there having been a ruler of this name, and one of exceptional greatness. At the same time, he acknowledges that not everything told about this particular king is true. Of the many marvels and adventures attributed to him, he writes, "So much have the storytellers told stories and the fabulators fabled, in order to embellish their stories, that they have made it all seem to be a fable."[7] He responds to the improbabilities in the historical record, not by rejecting the record altogether, as something with no basis in fact, but by wishing that he could separate the historical core from the fictions that have grown up around it,[8] even as he recognizes that this may well be a futile endeavor. When Wace relates the claim that Arthur has survived to this day on the Isle of Avalon—generally regarded as the most fantastical aspect of his story—he refrains from either affirming or denying this legend. He recalls how Merlin is said to have predicted of Arthur that "his death would be doubtful," and he comments, "The prophet spoke the truth. Ever since, people have always doubted—and I believe they always will doubt—whether he is dead or alive."[9] In contrast to readers

5. The classical romances of the Middle Ages antedated the Arthurian romances. The *Roman de Thèbes* (ca. 1150) refers to itself as a romance in some manuscripts. See *Le Roman de Thèbes, publié d'après tous les manuscrits*, ed. Léopold Constans, 2 vols. (Paris: Libraries Firmin Didot, 1890), vol. 1, p. 507. The *Roman d'Eneas* (ca. 1160) refers to itself as a romance as well, but it is posterior to Wace's *Brut*. (See, however, Edna C. Fredrick, "The Date of the *Eneas*," *PMLA* 50, no. 4 [December 1935]: 984–96, which argues for an earlier date.) For general discussion, see Robert Marichal, "Naissance du roman," in *Entretiens sur la Renaissance du 12e siècle (Cerisy-la-Salle, 21–30 juillet 1965)*, ed. Maurice de Gandillac and Emile Jeaneau (Paris: Mouton, 1968), 449–82, at 477n7. Robert d'Orbigny's *Le Conte de Floire et Blanchefleur: Nouvelle édition critique du texte du manuscrit A (Paris, BNF, fr. 375)*, ed. Jean-Luc Leclanche (Paris: Honoré Champion, 2003), has been dated to 1150, but it does not refer to itself as a romance.

6. "Maistre Wace . . . / en conte la verité," Wace, *Roman de Brut*, ed. Weiss, vv. 7–8.

7. "Tant unt li cunteür cunté / e li fableür flablé / pur lur cuntes enbeleter, / que tut unt fait fable sembler," ibid., vv. 9796–99.

8. For the tradition of reading historical texts in this manner, see Paul Veyne, *Les Grecs ont-ils cru à leurs mythes?* (Paris: Editions du Seuil, 1983); and Ad Putter, "Latin Historiography after Geoffrey of Monmouth," in *The Arthur of Medieval Latin Literature: The Development and Dissemination of the Arthurian Legend in Medieval Latin*, ed. Siân Echard (Cardiff: University of Wales Press, 2011), 85–108.

9. "sa mort dutuse serreit. / Li prophetes dist verité; / tut tens en ad l'um puis duté, / e dutera, ço crei, tut dis, / se il est morz u il est vis," Wace, *Roman de Brut*, ed. Weiss, vv. 13286–90. Cf. "exitus eius dubius erit," Geoffrey of Monmouth, *Historia regum Britanniae*, ed. Reeve, VI, 145.

of the modern novel, who have been said to suspend their disbelief in the fictions they encounter in its pages, Wace indicates that the audience of medieval romance was genuinely uncertain as to whether what they found in these narratives had or had not happened.

Despite the claims that had been raised about its veracity, between the late twelfth and mid-thirteenth centuries, Arthurian romance became one of the most popular categories of literature. In the 1170s and 1180s, Chrétien de Troyes, a cleric from Champagne, wrote several Arthurian works in Old French verse that he refers to as "romances," including *Le Chevalier de la charrette*, the first account of the love between Lancelot of the Lake and Guinevere;[10] *Le Conte du Graal*, the first account of Perceval and the Quest of the Holy Grail;[11] and tales of the knights Erec,[12] Yvain,[13] and Cligés.[14] The story of the Grail, left unfinished, inspired a series of lengthy verse continuations—the First Continuation,[15] the Second Continuation,[16] the Third Continuation (by Manassier),[17] and the Fourth Continuation (by Gerbert de Montreuil)[18]—which finally brought the work to a conclusion.[19] From these very early Arthu-

10. See Chrétien de Troyes, *Le Chevalier de la Charrette ou Le Roman de Lancelot*, ed. Charles Méla, in *Romans, suivis des chansons, avec, en appendice, "Philomena,"* ed. Michel Zink, Lettres Gothiques (Paris: Le Livre de Poche, 1994), 495–704, vv. 7113–14, which is based on BN fr. 794.

11. See Chrétien de Troyes, *Le Conte du Graal ou Le Roman de Perceval*, ed. Charles Méla, in *Romans*, ed. Zink, 937–1211, v. 9067, which is based on Bern 354, and *"Le Roman de Perceval" ou "Le Conte du Graal": Edition critique d'après tous les manuscrits*, ed. Keith Busby (Tübingen: Max Niemeyer Verlag, 1993).

12. See Chrétien de Troyes, *Erec et Enide*, ed. Jean-Marie Fritz, in *Romans*, ed. Zink, 56–283, v. 6950, which is based on BN fr. 1376.

13. See Chrétien de Troyes, *Le Chevalier au lion (Yvain)*, ed. David F. Hult, in *Romans*, ed. Zink, 705–936, vv. 6804–5, which is based on BN fr. 1433.

14. See Chrétien de Troyes, *Cligés*, ed. Charles Méla and Olivier Collet, in *Romans*, ed. Zink, 285–494, v. 1, which is based on BN fr. 12560.

15. See *The Continuations of the Old French "Perceval" of Chrétien de Troyes*, 5 vols., ed. William Roach (Philadelphia: University of Pennsylvania Press, 1949–83), which includes vol. 1, *The First Continuation: Mixed Redaction of MSS. TVD*, ed. William Roach (1949); vol. 2, *The First Continuation: Long Redaction of MSS. EMGQU*, ed. William Roach and Robert H. Ivy (1950); vol. 3, pt. 1, *The First Continuation: Short Redaction of MSS. ALPRS*, ed. William Roach (1952); and vol. 3, pt. 2, *A Glossary of the First Continuation*, ed. Lucien Foulet (1955).

16. See *The Second Continuation*, ed. William Roach (Philadelphia: American Philosophical Society, 1971), in *The Continuations of the Old French "Perceval" of Chrétien de Troyes*, vol. 4.

17. See *The Third Continuation by Manessier*, ed. William Roach (Philadelphia: American Philosophical Society, 1983), in *The Continuations of the Old French "Perceval" of Chrétien de Troyes*, vol. 5.

18. See Gerbert de Montreuil, *La Continuation de Perceval*, ed. Mary Williams (vols. 1 and 2) (Paris: H. Champion, 1922–25), and Marguerite Oswald (vol. 3) (Paris: Champion, 1975). Gerbert's Continuation survives in only two manuscripts, namely, BNF fr 12576 and BNF nouv. acqu. fr. 6614.

19. As the Continuators sought to provide an epilogue to Chrétien's romance, the anonymous authors of *The "Elucidation": A Prologue to the "Conte del Graal,"* ed. Albert Wilder Thompson

rian romances, authors represented themselves as conveying the truth about Arthur and his knights, as if that truth were something anterior to their texts. In the thirteenth century, authors shifted from writing about Arthur and his knights in verse to writing about them in prose, a change that made these works seem even more veracious, given the greater historical accuracy associated with the more straightforward style,[20] and even more appealing to their audiences, if we are to judge from the number of surviving manuscripts. Around 1200, Robert de Boron, a cleric (or perhaps a knight) from the Franche-Comté, produced the *Joseph d'Arimathie*,[21] the fragmentary *Merlin*,[22] and perhaps a lost *Perceval*, all in verse; before a quarter century had passed, he or a confederate had composed prose versions of these works, the last of which is known as the *Didot-Perceval*.[23] In doing so, Robert furnished essential information about Merlin's enchantments, Arthur's rise to power, and the Holy Grail's appearance in Britain. Around 1210, an unknown author contributed the prose *Perlesvaus* to this developing Grail tradition.[24] Between 1215 and 1235 or so, a series of anonymous authors composed the Vulgate Cycle,[25] a vast prose compendium of Ar-

(New York: Institute of French Studies, 1931) and *"Bliocadran": A Prologue to the "Perceval" of Chrétien de Troyes: Edition and Critical Study*, ed. Lenora D. Wolfgang (Tübingen: Max Niemeyer, 1976), both writing in the early thirteenth century, sought to provide prologues to this work.

20. See Gabrielle Spiegel, *Romancing the Past: The Rise of Vernacular Prose Historiography in Thirteenth-Century France* (Berkeley: University of California Press, 1993), and "Forging the Past: The Language of Historical Truth in the Middle Ages," *History Teacher* 17, no. 2 (1984): 267–83; and Suzanne Fleischman, "On the Representation of History and Fiction in the Middle Ages," *History and Theory* 22 (1983): 278–310.

21. See Robert de Boron, *Joseph d'Arimathie: A Critical Edition of the Verse and Prose Versions*, ed. Richard O'Gorman (Toronto: Pontifical Institute of Mediaeval Studies, 1995), which provides the verse version of the work (also known as the *Estoire dou Graal or* the *Romanz de l'Estoire dou Graal*), based on Paris, BNF fr. 20047, and the prose version of the work, based on Tours, BM 951.

22. See Robert de Boron, *Merlin: Roman du XIIIe siècle*, ed. Alexandre Micha (Geneva: Droz, 1979), which furnishes the fragmentary verse version of Robert's *Merlin*, based on Paris, BNF fr. 20047, and the prose version of this work, based on Paris, BNF fr. 747.

23. See *The Didot-Perceval, According to the Manuscripts of Modena and Paris*, ed. William Roach (Philadelphia: University of Pennsylvania Press, 1941), which is based on Paris, BNF nouv. acqu. fr. 4166, and Modena, Biblioteca Estense MS 3.30. See also *Le Roman du Graal: Manuscrit de Modène par Robert de Boron*, ed. Bernard Cerquiglini (Paris: Union Générale d'Edition, 1981), which is based on the Modena manuscript.

24. See *Perlesvaus: Le Haut Livre du Graal*, ed. W. A. Nitze and T. Atkinson Jenkins, 2 vols. (Chicago: University of Chicago Press, 1932).

25. Complete editions of the Vulgate Cycle, in its Short Cyclic Version, are provided in *Le Livre du Graal*, ed. Daniel Poirion, Bibliothèque de la Pléiade, 3 vols. (Paris: Gallimard, 2001–9), which is based on Bonn UB 526, and *The Vulgate Version of the Arthurian Romances, Edited from Manuscripts in the British Museum*, ed. Heinrich Oskar Sommer, 8 vols. (Washington, DC: Carnegie Institution, 1908–16), which is based on London, BL Add. 10292–4. A Long Cyclic Version of the text exists as well, which has been published in partial editions, as indicated below.

thurian lore that includes the *Joseph d'Arimathie*,[26] the *Merlin*,[27] the *Suite du Merlin*,[28] the *Prose Lancelot*,[29] the *Queste del Saint Graal*,[30] and *La Mort le Roi Artu*.[31] In the 1230s, another set of anonymous authors produced the Post-Vulgate Cycle, which recasts several of these works.[32] Accounts of Tristan and Iseut, originally separate from Arthurian legend,[33] were now incorporated into this material, to the point where Tristan becomes a knight of the Round Table.[34] Throughout these romances, authors depicted themselves, not as embellishing the stories that had come down to them, as Wace would have it, but merely as filling in the gaps in their plots. Almost all of the stories we now identify with

26. See *Joseph d'Arimathie*, ed. Gérard Gros, in *Le Livre du Graal*, ed. Poirion, vol. 1, 1–567. I will also be citing *L'Estoire del Saint Graal* (as this work is also known), ed. Jean-Paul Ponceau, 2 vols. (Paris: Honoré Champion, 1997), vol. 1 of which is based on Amsterdam BPH 1, i, ff. 1–63 and vol. 2 of which is based on Rennes BM 255; both codices contain the Long Cyclic Version.

27. See *Merlin*, ed. Irene Freire-Nunes, in *Le Livre du Graal*, ed. Poirion, vol. 1, 570–805, and *Lestoire de Merlin*, in *The Vulgate Version*, ed. Sommer, vol. 2, 3–101. This text includes a version of Robert de Boron's *Merlin* and a much longer continuation of this work.

28. See *Les Premiers Faits du Roi Arthur*, ed. Irene Freire-Nunes, in *Le Livre du Graal*, ed. Poirion, vol. 1, 807–1662, which is a retitled version of this text, and the *Suite du Merlin*, in *The Vulgate Version*, ed. Sommer, vol. 2, 101–466. The *Livre d'Artus*, in *The Vulgate Version*, ed. Sommer, vol. 7, which has survived in only one manuscript (BN Fr 337), constitutes an alternate version of the *Suite du Merlin*.

29. I will be citing primarily *Lancelot: Roman en prose du XIIIe siècle*, ed. Alexandre Micha, 9 vols. (Geneva: Droz, 1978–82), which is based on Add. 10293; Cambridge, Corpus Christi College 45; Oxford, Bodl. Rawlinson D. 899; Aberystwyth NLW 5018; and Rawlinson D. 899. The "Cyclic" version of the *Lancelot* anticipates Lancelot's begetting of Galahad and the dominant role of this knight in the Quest of the Holy Grail, as recounted in the *Queste del Saint Graal*. The "Non-Cyclic" version of the text does not head in this direction, concluding, instead, with the death of Galehaut. See *Lancelot do Lac: The Non-Cyclic Old French Prose Romance*, ed. Elspeth Kennedy, 2 vols. (Oxford: Clarendon Press, 1980), which overlaps with Micha's vols. 7 and 8 but is based upon BN fr. 768.

30. See *La Quête du Saint Graal*, ed. Gérard Gros, in *Livre du Graal*, ed. Poirion, vol. 3, 807–1177. I will also be citing *La Queste del Saint Graal*, ed. Albert Pauphilet (Paris: Honoré Champion, 1923), which is based on Bibliothèque Municipale de Lyon, Palais des Arts no. 77.

31. See *La Mort du roi Arthur*, ed. Mary B. Speer, in *Le Livre du Graal*, ed. Poirion, vol. 3, 1179–486. I will also be citing *La Mort le roi Artu: Roman du XIIIe siècle*, ed. Jean Frappier (Geneva: Droz, 1936; rpt., 1964), which provides the Long Cyclic Version, based on Paris, Ars. 3347.

32. The Post-Vulgate Cycle has not survived in entirety in any one manuscript; some of its sections are known only from Portuguese and Castilian translations. For its complex history, see Fanni Bogdanow and Richard Traschler, "Rewriting Prose Romance: The Post-Vulgate *Roman du Graal* and Related Texts," in *The Arthur of the French*, ed. Glyn S. Burgess and Karen Pratt (Cardiff: University of Wales Press, 2006), 342–92. I will be considering primarily *La Version Post-Vulgate de "la Queste del Saint Graal" et de "la Mort Artu": Troisième partie du "Roman de Graal,"* ed. Fanni Bogdanow, 4 vols. (Paris: A. et J. Picard, 1991), which is based on Oxford, Bodleian Library, Rawlinson D 874; Paris Bibliothèque Nationale, fr. 112, 116, 340, 343, and 772; Cologny, Bodmer Library, 105; and the State Archives of Bologna, and *La Suite du Roman de Merlin*, ed. Gilles Roussineau, 2 vols. (Geneva: Droz, 1996), which is based on London, BL Add. 38117, formerly the Huth Collection, and Cambridge, University Library, Add. 7071.

33. See *Early French Tristan Poems*, ed. Norris J. Lacy, 2 vols. (Cambridge: D. S. Brewer, 1998).

34. See *Le Roman de Tristan en prose*, ed. Philippe Ménard, 9 vols. (Geneva: Droz, 1987).

the Arthurian legend originated in French in this manner between the 1170s and the 1240s, but they proved to be so popular that they were quickly translated or adapted into virtually every western European literary language, including Catalan, Dutch, English, German, Norse, Provençal, and Welsh. As beloved as Sir Thomas Malory's *Le Morte D'Arthur* (1485) has become to Anglophone readers, this work was a late addition to Arthurian literature, derived directly or indirectly from what Malory calls "the Frensshe booke."[35] Whether in the original French sources or in these later versions, these works provided a major source of diversion in people's leisure time for centuries.

If Arthurian romance emerged as one of the dominant literary genres of the High Middle Ages, it seems to have been in part because its authors insisted upon its historicity. Though they referred to their works as "romances," they also described them as "stories" (*contes*), recounted in French by the knights who had performed the heroic feats of which they speak. As early as Manassier's Third Continuation,[36] the knights of the Round Table are said to return to Arthur's court to dine with their fellows, especially for the great feast days of Advent, Easter, and Pentecost, and, when they have finished eating, "to recount" (*conter*) under oath what has happened to them since they were last here, whether it be to their honor or to their shame. Because knights are honorable men, there is presumed to be an exact correspondence between the adventures they experience and the account they provide of these adventures. If these works are "stories" (*contes*), they are also "histories" (*estoires*), written down by clerics who heard these knights' testimony. Before the knights begin to speak, four clerics—identified in the *Prose Lancelot* as Arodian of Cologne, Tantalides of Vercelli, Thomas of Toledo, and Sapient of Baghdad[37]—are summoned "to put into writing" (*metre en escript*) what they say, "just as" (*ensi come*) they say it.[38] Because clerics are learned men, there is presumed to be an exact correspondence between what they hear during these sessions and what they write down.[39] Just as the knights function as witnesses to the events they recount, the clerics function as notaries of the words

35. *The Works of Sir Thomas Malory*, ed. Eugène Vinaver, 3 vols. (Oxford: Clarendon Press, 1947), I, vol. 1, p. 7. Malory makes reference to the French book thirty-nine times, often misleadingly. See Bonnie Wheeler, "'As the French Book Seyeth': Malory's *Morte Darthur* and Acts of Reading," *Cahiers de recherches médiévales* 14 (2007): 116–25.

36. See Manassier, Third Continuation, ed. Roach, vv. 42420–25.

37. See *Lancelot*, ed. Micha, vol. 8, 488–89.

38. See, for just a few examples, ibid., vol. 2, 255; vol. 4, 248 and 398; vol. 6, 57.

39. In Robert de Boron's *Merlin*, it is not the knights of the Round Table but Merlin who dictates the work to a cleric, namely, his amanuensis Blaise. Yet it seems clear, Blaise transcribes only

they transcribe: they are not the creators but the transmitters of the tales they produce. As the twelfth- and thirteenth-century authors of Arthurian romances represent the situation, they have consulted the "histories" (*estoires*) of these ancient clerics and have used them as the source of their works. Chrétien de Troyes writes of his *Cligés,* for example, "We find this history, which I want to recount and relate to you, written in one of the books of the treasury of [the Cathedral of] my lord Saint Peter at Beauvais. From there was the story taken out of which Chrétien made this romance."[40] It is because his "story" is based on a written "history" he found in this cathedral, Chrétien asserts, that it is worthy of credence. The author of the Vulgate Cycle is said to be Walter Map, a courtier to King Henry II of England, who supposedly wrote these volumes at the behest of his patron, based upon the lengthy, Latin book he found in the treasury in Salisbury.[41] While the authors of Arthurian romances boast that they have acquired the true and complete version of these tales from these "histories,"[42] they warn that other storytellers have not gone to the same trouble. The author of the Second Continuation protests, "There are now many worthy fellows who go about recounting fables in these courts, who are twisting the good stories, distancing them from the histories, and joining lies to them."[43] From Chrétien's *Conte du Graal,* to the Grail Continuations, to Robert de Boron's *Merlin,* to Wolfram von Eschenbach's *Parzifal,* to the Vulgate Cycle, to the lengthy fourteenth-century *Perceforest,*[44] the authors of the medieval Arthurian corpus insisted that their works were, not fables dreamed up by their own idle powers of invention, but histories, based upon eyewitness testimony as transcribed by reliable clerics.

Merlin's prophecies and the history of the Holy Grail, not the adventures of the knights, which occupy such a prominent role in the Arthurian corpus.

40. "Ceste estoire trovons escrite, / que conter vos vuel et retraire, / en .I. des livres de l'aumaire / mon seignor saint Pere a Beauvez. / De la fu cist contes estrez / dont cest romanz fist Crestiens," Chrétien de Troyes, *Cligés,* ed. Méla and Collet, vv. 18–23.

41. See the *Queste del Saint Graal,* ed. Gros, 1177; *Lancelot,* ed. Micha, vol. 4, 396–97 and vol. 6, 244; and *La Mort le Roi Artu,* ed. Speer, 1181 and 1486. Manassier also claims to write "according to the history [*selonc l'estoire*]" he found in Salisbury (Third Continuation, ed. Roach, vv. 42659–68).

42. As Richard Barber points out in *The Holy Grail: Imagination and Belief* (Cambridge, MA: Harvard University Press, 2005), authors of Arthurian romance tended to appeal to source texts when they were introducing elements of the narrative that might strain the audiences' credulity (161).

43. "il sont ore maint vasal / qui vont fabloient par ces cors, / qui les bons contes font rebors / et des estoires les esloignent / et les mançonges i ajoignent," Second Continuation, ed. Roach, vv. 26086–90.

44. See *Le Roman de Perceforest,* ed. Jane H. M. Taylor (Geneva: Librairie Droz, 1979), which includes the first part of this work, and *Perceforest,* ed. Gilles Roussineau, 3 vols. (Geneva: Librairie Droz, 1993–98), which includes the third part.

Yet if Arthurian romance proved to be as popular as it did, it also seems to have been in part because its authors implicitly acknowledged its fictionality. Though these romances were "stories" (*contes*), supposedly based on oral tales recounted by the knights of the Round Table at court, they included material that could not possibly have been related under such circumstances. In the *Prose Lancelot*, Arthur asks Lancelot to recount, under oath, all of the adventures he experienced since he left court. Yet it is said, "[Lancelot] recounted many of them, and many of them he concealed."[45] On another occasion, after the Daughter of the Fisher King has tricked Lancelot into sleeping with her, he omits this incident from the story he gives to the court. We are told, "He did not recount to them how he had been deceived by the beautiful damsel, the Daughter of the Fisher King. He failed to tell it, not on account of the shame he would have incurred because of it, but, rather, on account of his lady the queen, whose love he thought he would lose if she knew the truth."[46] One of the most important themes of Arthurian romance—Lancelot's liaison with Guinevere and the complications it brings about—is thus something that the text admits never could have been spoken of before an audience and therefore never could have been written down in the way in which these stories were said to have been recorded. Not only Lancelot but numerous knights are described in the romances as embarking on love affairs that, according to the conventions of courtly love, should have remained hidden from others. By the same token, though the romances were "histories," supposedly based on oral testimonies transcribed by clerics at court, they could have been derived from no such sources. As far as we know, there was never an archive of Arthurian manuscripts at Beauvais or Salisbury. Even if there had been, the Vulgate Cycle could not possibly have been prepared by Walter Map, who died between 1208 and 1210, years before this collection began to be composed, let alone for the benefit of Henry II, who had passed away in 1189.[47] Even apart from the circumstances of

45. "il l'en conta pluisors et pluisors l'en cela," *Lancelot*, ed. Micha, vol. 2, 110–11.

46. "il ne lor conte pas conment il avoit esté deceuz de la bele damoisele, la fille au Roi Pescheor, ne il ne lor laissa mie a dire por honte qui avenue l'an fust, mais por sa dame la roine cui amor il cuidoit perdre, s'ele en seust la verité," ibid., vol. 4, 395.

47. The archive of Salisbury has been associated with that of the Benedictine abbey at Amesbury, but there is no evidence that any Arthurian histories survived in this locale. See Joshua Byron Smith, *Walter Map and the Matter of Britain* (Philadelphia: University of Pennsylvania Press, 2017), 151, for discussion. Though Map was a well-known figure, the only written work ascribed to him is *De nugis curialium*, a Latin collection of anecdotes from folklore and history. Smith argues that Map was identified as the author of the Vulgate Cycle because it was someone like him—that is, an educated, Latinate cleric, familiar with the monastic archives of southern Wales

the romances' composition, the fantastical nature of their tales, with their fairies, enchantments, and mythical beasts, would normally prevent them from being accepted as true. Confronted with the contradiction between the works' claims to historicity and the evidence of their fictionality, audiences of medieval romance were faced with a fiction that refuses to admit its fictionality and is thus doubly fictional.

The supposed veracity of Arthurian romance has perplexed some modern critics, especially those of a historicist bent, who deplore what they see as the credulousness of this genre's original audience. In the seventeenth century, the French bishop and scholar Pierre-Daniel Huet depicted Arthurian romances as products of "the Dark Ages, full of ignorance,"[48] a time, he writes, when "people made fabulous histories because, failing to know the truth, they could not make true ones."[49] The authors of these works composed fictions, Huet alleged, not because they intended to do so, but because they mistook fiction for fact. In the eighteenth century, the Scottish novelist Tobias Smollett attributed romance not just to the Dark Ages but to the Catholic clergy, who, as he saw it, fostered the ignorance and obscurantism of this time. He writes, "When the minds of men were debauched by the imposition of priestcraft to the most absurd pitch of credulity, the authors of romance arose and, losing sight of probability, filled their performances with the most monstrous hyperboles."[50] The authors of these works composed not only fictions but absurd fictions, Smollett insisted, because, under the influence of their priests, they confused what could and could not happen. In the nineteenth century, the anonymous author of an article in the *Westminster Review* (who may have been George Eliot) traced romance not to Catholicism but to a more general superstitiousness. In contrast to readers of the present day, who live in "a scientific, and somewhat skeptical age,"[51] the reviewer contends, readers of the past, who lived in "an unlettered age," welcomed romance because they subsisted under

and western England, and not an illiterate Breton minstrel, as is often assumed—who brought about the transmission of Brythonic legends into continental romance.

48. "des temps obscurs, pleins d'ignorance," Pierre-Daniel Huet, *Lettre-traité de Pierre-Daniel Huet sur l'origine des romans: Edition du tricentenaire (1669–1969)*, ed. Fabienne Gégou (Paris: Editions A.-G. Nizet, 1971), 133–34.

49. "on fit alors les histoires fabuleuses parce qu'on n'en pouvait faire de véritables, faute de savoir la vérité," ibid., 111–12.

50. Tobias Smollett, "Preface to *Roderick Random*, 1748," in *Novel and Romance, 1700–1800: A Documentary Record*, ed. Ioan Williams (New York: Barnes and Noble, 1970), 119–21, at 120.

51. Anonymous, "The Progress of Fiction as an Art," *Westminster Review* 60 (October 1855): 342–74; rpt., *The Victorian Art of Fiction: Esssays on the Novel in British Periodicals, 1870–1900*, ed. John Charles Olmsted (New York: Garland, 1979), 73–105, at 74.

the power of a "magician's wand, or enchanter's spell";[52] they believed in romance for the same reason that they "believe[d] . . . in witches [and] fairies."[53] In the twentieth century, the German sociologist Max Weber made no reference to romance per se in his writings, but he famously contrasted the magical and religious worlds before the Protestant Reformation with what he called the "disenchanted world"[54] that came after it. While more recent scholars have contested Weber's characterization of the modern era as disenchanted,[55] they have not challenged his assumption that the medieval world existed under a kind of spell. In a similar manner, the American Marxist scholar Fredric Jameson connected romance to ways of thinking in the Middle Ages that he sees as rendered obsolete in our modern era. In an economy dominated by agriculture, he argues, people believed in magic, which we now know not to exist. In a society afflicted by barbarian invasions, they believed in evil, which we now know to be just a name we give an "other." While some readers may continue to be attracted to romance, out of nostalgia for a lost, theistic epoch, Jameson comments, most are not, recognizing that its way of thinking has been replaced by what he calls "the secularized world of modern capitalism."[56] Whether these historians believe medieval ignorance to have been superseded by modern learning, medieval superstition to have been superseded by modern reason, or medieval religiosity to have been superseded by modern secularism, they all subscribe to a view of literary history as a linear trajectory, progressing from error to truth and, by extension, from romance to realism.[57]

52. Ibid., 75.

53. Ibid., 76.

54. "entzauberten Welt," Max Weber, "Wissenschaft als Beruf," in *Schriften, 1894–1922*, ed. Dirk Kaesler (Stuttgart: Alfred Kröner Verlag, 2002), 474–511, at 501. Weber seems to have been inspired by Friedrich Schiller's poem "Die Götter Griechenlands" (1788) and Heinrich Heine's similarly titled "Die Götter Griechenlands" (1827) and his Les Dieux en exil (1853). Weber does not reject all of the medieval tradition as antirational. As he sees it, Benedictine monks, Franciscan tertiaries, and béguines observed rules that anticipated those of the modern factory. Still, he argues that these groups' practices did not affect the medieval population in general.

55. See Jason A. Josephson-Storm, *The Myth of Disenchantment: Magic, Modernity, and the Birth of the Human Sciences* (Chicago: University of Chicago Press, 2017); Jonathan Sheehan, "When Was Disenchantment? History and the Secular Age," in *Varieties of Secularism in a Secular Age*, ed. Michael Warner and others (Cambridge, MA: Harvard University Press, 2010), 217–42; Michael Saler, *As If: Modern Enchantment and the Literary Prehistory of Virtual History* (Oxford: Oxford University Press, 2012); *The Re-enchantment of the World: Secular Magic in a Rational Age*, ed. Joshua Landy and Michael Saler (Palo Alto, CA: Stanford University Press, 2009); and Jane Bennett, *The Enchantment of Modern Life: Attachments, Crossings, and Ethics* (Princeton, NJ: Princeton University Press, 2001).

56. Fredric Jameson, "Magical Narratives: Romance as a Genre," *New Literary History* 7 (1975): 135–63, at 146.

57. Peter Haidu writes, in "Romance: Idealistic Genre or Historical Text?," in *The Craft of Fiction: Essays in Medieval Poetics*, ed. Leigh A. Arrathoon (Rochester, MI: Solaris, 1984), 1–46,

In these pages, I would like to show that virtually all of the supposedly modern objections historicist critics raise about romance had already been raised in the Middle Ages, including in the romances themselves. Authors of learned works did not write extensively about this genre, which they seem to have regarded as unworthy of their attention, but some of them—Aelred of Rievaulx, Caesarius of Heisterbach, William of Newburgh, Gerald of Wales, Dante Alighieri, and Jacob van Maerlant, to name a few—did discuss it briefly, in passages of great interest. Authors of Arthurian romances celebrated the values of their aristocratic patrons in their works, but, as Douglas Kelly, Sarah Kay, and Simon Gaunt have addressed in different ways,[58] they also acknowledged the criticisms that were being made about this body of literature by their learned peers, especially, I will argue, through the voices of certain puzzled or hostile characters. First, learned authors questioned how Merlin could engineer "marvels" (*merveilles*), that is, natural phenomena that flout the laws of Nature without any evident assistance from God. In romances, many of Merlin's peers express doubt that he really can perform such feats and fear that, if he really can do so, it must be with the help of the nether forces. While these learned authors and these literary characters recognize the existence of supernatural powers in a way in which modern critics do not, their point is to prove that phenomena that appear to contradict the laws of Nature actually conform to them and, in doing so, to distinguish "marvels" from what we might call science. Second, learned authors questioned how Arthur could have ruled Britain for many years, conquered thirty kingdoms and established a glorious court, though he goes virtually unmentioned in the chronicles of his day. In these romances, many of the British barons fail to recognize the greatness of Arthur's reign, to the point where, under Mordred's leadership, they rise up against this king. While these learned authors and literary characters generally acknowledge that a historical, fallible Arthur once lived, in a way in

"The medieval text . . . functions as a binary opposite to the modern, defining it oppositionally, arrogating to itself those traits that are negatively marked . . . and, by implicational devolution, assigning to the modern text those traits that are positively marked in his scale of literary value" (1).

58. See Douglas Kelly, "Romance and the Vanity of Chrétien de Troyes," in *Romance: Generic Transformation from Chrétien de Troyes to Cervantes*, ed. Kevin Brownlee and Marina Scordilis Brownlee (Hanover, NH: University Press of New England, 1985), 75–90; Sarah Kay, "Courts, Clerks, and Courtly Love," in *The Cambridge Companion to Medieval Romance*, ed. Roberta L. Krueger (Cambridge: Cambridge University Press, 2000), 81–96, and *Courtly Contradictions: The Emergence of the Literary Object in the Twelfth Century* (Stanford, CA: Stanford University Press, 2001); and Simon Gaunt, "Romance and Other Genres," in *The Cambridge Companion to Medieval Romance*, ed. Krueger, 45–59.

which modern critics do not, their point is to expose that the legendary, infallible "Arthur" never existed and, in doing so, to distinguish history from fiction. Third, learned authors expressed incredulity that there can ever be a knight as perfect as Lancelot, who is said to have never been defeated in battle and to have never been unfaithful to his lady, either in deed or in desire. In these romances, King Yder, a knight of the Round Table, and Morgan Le Fay, Arthur's sister, plot to demonstrate that Lancelot is fallible on both counts. For these learned authors and these literary characters, it is impossible for anyone to be the best of men, let alone for someone to enjoy this status who, through his affair with his king's wife, is guilty of the crime of treason and the sin of adultery. Finally, learned authors expressed skepticism that there ever was a Holy Grail, given that this vessel was never recognized as a Christian relic, nor were the knights who sought it ever recognized as saints. In the romances, from the castle that houses the Grail, to the maidens who carry it, to the knights who embark on the quest for it, the Grail is consistently located in a secular rather than an ecclesiastical context, as if in recognition of its secular rather than ecclesiastical status. With its account of natural phenomena that defy the laws of Nature; of historical events that never occurred in history; of virtuous people who do not act virtuously; and of sacred objects that are only ambiguously Christian, Arthurian romance was, as many medieval people saw it, bad science, bad history, bad morality, and bad religion.

Yet even as medieval authors, including authors of Arthurian romance, raised objections about this genre, the romances defended themselves against these charges. In response to complaints that Merlin could not possibly thwart the laws of Nature, the romances represent this enchanter as effecting, not miracles, which only God can bring about, and not magic, which only the devil and his minions can effect, but "marvels," a third category of supernatural—or, rather, preternatural—phenomena whose origin can never entirely be explained. In response to complaints that someone as obscure as Arthur could not possibly have ruled Britain, conquered so many lands, and established such a magnificent court, the romances propose that there are rulers, like Arthur, whose greatness is recognized, not at the time by their contemporaries, but only retrospectively, by those who come after them. Faced with charges that there cannot be a perfect knight, let alone a perfect knight who is engaged in a liaison with his king's wife, they demonstrate that there are knights so excellent that that which would be a vice in ordinary men becomes, in them, a virtue. To those who insist that there cannot be a sacred object that exists wholly in a secular realm, the romances show that the sacred is that which, by definition, cannot be confined within the categories we devise. With its account of marvels that can indeed be seen as having occurred, if one opens one's eyes to them; of historical figures who can indeed be seen as having lived, if one knows how to appreciate their greatness; of virtuous people who can indeed be recognized as virtuous, if one expands one's notion of virtue; and of a sacred object that can indeed be perceived as sacred, if one expands one's notion of Christianity, Arthurian romance represents itself as good science, good history, good morality, and good religion, though in a way that demands we reconceptualize each of these categories.

While the supposed truth value of Arthurian romance has puzzled some modern critics, it has made sense to others, especially those of essentialist inclinations, who have shared the enthusiasm of its original audience for this genre. Under the influence of Carl Jung's theory of archetypal images,[59] the American mythographer Joseph Campbell argued that, in all time and in all places, stories recount how a hero (like Arthur), destined for greatness but reared in obscurity, separates himself from his society; how, with the assistance of a guardian (like Merlin), he enters into battle and achieves a great victory; and how he then returns to the realm in which he lives (like the Kingdom of Logres) with power to aid his fellow humans. Far from viewing such stories as misguided, Campbell saw them as giving "symbolic expression . . . to the unconscious desires, fears, and tensions that underlie the conscious patterns of human behavior."[60] Like Jung and Campbell, the Canadian literary critic Northrop Frye (whom we will have occasion to consider more later on) approached romance as a universal category rather than a historical construct. In contrast to the novelist, he states, "The romancer does not attempt to create 'real people' so much as stylized figures which expand into psychological archetypes"[61]—archetypes that he goes on to define with reference almost exclusively to postmedieval English and American texts. As Frye sees it, romance characterizes the

59. C. G. Jung describes the powerful effect the Grail legend had upon him in *Erinnerungen, Träume, Gedanken* (Zurich: Rascher, 1962), 169. If his wife, Emma, had not devoted her life's work to the Grail legend—a project that culminated in her posthumous *Die Graalslegende in psychologischer Sicht* (Zurich: Rascher, 1960)—he states, he would have addressed it in his study of alchemy (ibid., 218).

60. Joseph Campbell, *The Hero with a Thousand Faces*, 3rd ed. (Novato, CA: New World Library, 2008), 23.

61. Northrop Frye, in *Anatomy of Criticism: Four Essays* (Princeton, NJ: Princeton University Press, 1957), 304.

hero as a simple paragon of virtue,[62] and it recounts how he falls in love with a maiden[63] and ultimately succeeds in winning her hand in marriage,[64] in accordance with this genre's "conventional happy ending."[65] For that reason, he writes, "The romance is nearest of all literary forms to the wish-fulfillment dream."[66] The American novelist Marion Zimmer Bradley did not interpret Arthurian legend through the lens of "archetypes" per se, but she did read it through the categories of comparative religion. Her best-selling *The Mists of Avalon* (1983) retells these stories from the point of view of Morgaine, Arthur's sister ("who was in later days called Morgan le Fay"[67]), now envisioned as a priestess to the Great Goddess. The stories thus give voice, not to the collective unconscious of human society in general, but to the feminine principle of pagan society, driven underground by the new Christian religion. Though Bradley's audience is popular rather than academic, many scholars, especially in France, have likewise interpreted Arthurian romance as illustrating psychoanalytic and often feminist truths.[68] Whether these mythic writers speak of archetypes, of gods and goddesses, or of a feminine *anima*, they conceive of literary history not as a linear trajectory from past to present, but, instead, as the circular spiral of eternity, though one where romance needs to be viewed from a sufficient distance for it to seem to conform to a predetermined pattern.

In these pages, I would like to show that the seemingly traditional defenses essentialist critics have mounted in favor of Arthurian romance were never advanced in the Middle Ages, including in the romances themselves. These works do not feature "the hero" in any archetypal sense. Arthur, that most celebrated of kings, makes a series of misjudgments, waging war against the most powerful of his knights, entrusting his realm to the most treacherous of his vassals, and refusing to seek the aid that could have helped him in the battle against this usurper. Instead of a happy ending, his tale concludes with defeat and

62. Ibid., 151, 195; and Frye, *The Secular Scripture: A Study of the Structure of Romance* (Cambridge, MA: Harvard University Press, 1976), 50, 195.

63. Frye, *Secular Scripture*, 183.

64. Ibid., 54 and 134.

65. Ibid., 134.

66. Frye, *Anatomy of Criticism*, 186.

67. Marion Zimmer Bradley, *The Mists of Avalon* (New York: Knopf, 1982), x.

68. See, for example, Pierre Gallais, *La Fée à la fontaine et à l'arbre: Un archetype du conte merveilleux et du récit courtois* (Amsterdam: Rodopi, 1992); Jean-Claude Aubailly, *La Fée et le chevalier: Essai de mythanalyse de quelques lais "féeriques" des XIIe et XIIIe siècles* (Paris: Honoré Champion, 1986); and Charles Méla, *La Reine et le Graal: La "conjointure" dans les romans du Graal de Chrétien de Troyes au "Livre de Lancelot"* (Paris: Editions du Seuil, 1984).

destruction. Lancelot, that most celebrated of lovers, is enamored, not with a maiden he might marry, but with the wife of his lord. In contrast to the marriage-plot novels of later centuries, his story concludes, not with a wedding, but with eremitical seclusion. Though from a modern, postfeudal perspective, a king may be a king and a knight a knight, in the romances themselves these figures are not types, but individuals—and tragic ones at that. As these works do not forefront "the hero," neither do they forefront pre-Christian religious practices. Far from promoting magic, they make clear that human beings who cast such spells do so with the assistance of the devil. They contrast necromancers who contract such illicit alliances with Merlin, who never commits such a sin. Far from promoting an indigenous "Celtic" tradition, they identify the "fairies" (*faes*) who populate their pages as Roman gods and goddesses, and they interpret these supposed deities as human beings worshiped by their foolish contemporaries. From a modern, post-Christian perspective, the Quest of the Holy Grail may seem mythic, but in the romances themselves, this vessel recalls a container of the Eucharist, and the journey the knights embark on to find it resembles a pilgrimage. As we shall see, in the late twelfth and early thirteenth centuries, when Arthurian romances were being composed, the clerical culture in which its authors participated was experiencing a shift toward rationalization—in its demand for historical evidence, especially that based on eyewitness testimony and authoritative written sources; in its articulation of moral norms, especially those based in an intentionalist ethics; in its investigation of scientific laws, especially those grounded in Aristotelian theories of causation; and in its elaboration of a sacramental theology, especially one focused on Holy Communion and penance—and the romances acknowledged that shift. These works do not stand apart from the intellectual currents of their time and place but, on the contrary, immerse themselves in them.

Yet even as medieval authors refrained from championing Arthurian romance on essentialist grounds, the romances themselves put forth what they represent as lasting truths. Though these works do not feature "the hero," they do feature models of people who strive to exemplify certain codes of behavior. With Arthur, romance evokes the possibility of a king who, despite the mistakes he makes, unites his people, enables them to live in peace and prosperity, and makes his court a place to which all knights from far and wide seek to belong. In doing so, it demonstrates that there exist great leaders who merit later generations' admiration. With Lancelot, romance evokes the possibility of a knight who, however scandalous his ardor, is devoted to his lady with his whole heart and for his whole life. In doing so, it demonstrates that there exist great suitors who, loving unconditionally, deserve to be loved unconditionally in return. While these works do not forefront pre-Christian religious practices, they do forefront a model of the natural world that transcends the laws of Nature in a manner not reducible to any Catholic doctrine. Through its portrait of Merlin, romance proposes the possibility of a seer who, though performing neither miracles nor magic, harnesses the marvelousness latent within creation for his own purposes. Through its account of the Holy Grail, romance proposes the possibility of a vessel that, while neither simply a Christian container of the Eucharist nor a Celtic cauldron of abundance, is imbued with a power that exceeds its physical parameters. Even as Arthurian romance recognized the shift toward rationalization that was occurring at this time, it insisted that there exists a historical reality that cannot be established, in every situation, by eyewitness testimony and authoritative written sources; a moral reality that cannot be adjudicated, in each individual case, by general rules; a scientific reality that cannot be accounted for, in each individual instance, by the laws of causation; and a spiritual reality where the sacred cannot always be confined to the sacramental. In its resistance to rationalization, romance can be identified, to some extent, with the contemplative traditions of the Cistercian monasteries and the School of Saint-Victor, as opposed to the logical traditions of the cathedral schools and universities, yet it demonstrates the irreducibility of reality to any such systematic thought. In the end, even as these works immerse themselves in the intellectual currents of their time and place, they present an alternative to those currents that ultimately can be located only in their own pages.

In chapter 1, I show how, from the birth of romance in the twelfth century to the present day, works categorized under this genre have consistently been accused of posing a danger to their readers and have consistently defended themselves against this accusation. It is important not to conflate objections raised against Arthurian literature in the Middle Ages with those raised against romance in later centuries. Though the authors—or at least the copyists—of medieval Arthurian literature referred to their works as "romances,"[69] as well as "stories"

69. The Third Continuation is referred to as "The Romance of Perceval [*li romans de Percheval*]" (ed. Roach, 344); *Joseph d'Arimathie* as "The Romance of the History of the Grail [*li romanz de l'estoire dou Graal*]" (ed. O'Gorman, 339n1); the *Didot-Perceval* as "The Romance of the Prophecies of Merlin [*le romanz des prophecies Merlin*]" or "The Romance of Merlin and the Grail [*li roman de Merlin et del Graal*]" (ed. Roach, 279); and the Vulgate Cycle as "The Romance of Lancelot [*LI*

(*contes*) and "histories" (*estoires*), critics of this literature from this time identified the problem, not with its form, but with its content. It was only after the Middle Ages had come to a close that Arthurian literature came to be conceptualized as a genre, that that genre came to be construed as "romance," and that the epistemological perils it threatened came to be identified with that genre instead of with the tales themselves. It was only in the seventeenth and eighteenth centuries, when the novel emerged as the dominant form of prose, narrative fiction, that the fantastical scenarios of romance came to stand out, unfavorably, in contrast to the everyday settings of this new type of literature. And it was only in the nineteenth century, when realism emerged as the dominant mode of the novel, that the "idealism" of romance came in for blame. I will refer to "Arthurian romance" throughout this book, given the phrase's usefulness in designating this body of literature, but it is with the caveat that it is retrospective to the time when this corpus was composed. While, in continental Europe, the word "romance" (*roman, romanzo, Roman*, and so on) has persisted in various languages as the primary term for lengthy, fictional, prose narratives,[70] in England, the word "novel" has become the term for that category of literature, perhaps because "romance" remained so strongly associated with its French, Italian, and Iberian progenitors.[71] For that reason, it has been primarily Anglophone literary critics who have contrasted these two genres, with some insisting upon the originality of the English novel[72] and others stressing its continuity with its continental predecessors.[73]

ROMANS DE LANSELOT]" (*La Mort du roi Arthur*, ed. Speer, 1486). It is often a scribe—and not, apparently, the author himself—who refers to the work in this manner in an incipit or explicit.

70. The major exception is Spain. As in other European languages, the "novel" (*novela*) in Spanish was originally a tale, like Miguel de Cervantes' *Novelas ejemplares* (1613), and not a lengthy, fictional, prose work, like this author's *La Historia del famoso don Quijote de la Mancha* (1605–15), which was known as a "history" (*historia*). It is only over the course of the eighteenth century, under the influence of English, that the Spanish began to consider *Don Quixote* and other similar works "novels." From the mid-fifteenth century on, a "romance" (*romance*) in Spanish is a ballad.

71. On the evolution of the word *roman* in the eighteenth century, see Jean Sgard, "Le Mot *roman*," *Eighteenth-Century Fiction* 13, nos. 2–3 (2001): 183–95, and Edith Kern, "The Romance of Novel/Novella," in *The Disciplines of Criticism: Essays in Literary Theory, Interpretation, and History*, ed. Peter Demetz, Thomas Greene, and Lowry Nelson Jr. (New Haven, CT: Yale University Press, 1968), 511–30.

72. See Ian Watt, *The Rise of the Novel: Studies in Defoe, Richardson, and Fielding* (Berkeley: University of California Press, 1957); Nancy Armstrong, *How Novels Think: The Limits of British Individualism, 1719–1900* (New York: Columbia University Press, 2005); and Lennard J. Davis, in *Factual Fictions: The Origins of the English Novel* (New York: Columbia University Press, 1983).

73. See English Showalter Jr., *The Evolution of the French Novel, 1641–1782* (Princeton, NJ: Princeton University Press, 1972), 3, and "Prose Fiction: France," in *The Cambridge History of Literary Criticism*, vol. 4, *The Eighteenth Century*, ed. H. B. Nisbet and Claude Rawson (Cambridge:

Yet as important as it may be to distinguish medieval condemnations of Arthurian literature from modern, especially Anglophone condemnations of romance, it is also necessary to recognize the continuity of this criticism. Over time, the novel inherited much of the onus of romance, yet it was always the "romantic" aspect of the novel—its idealized heroes and heroines, its great passions and adventures, its disconnection from everyday reality—that came in for condemnation. While this book is focusing upon the danger associated with Arthurian romance during the first and most formative stage of its development, it is also necessarily addressing the danger associated with romance, as a genre or a mode, across history.

In chapters 2, 3, 4, and 5, I demonstrate how the authors of medieval French Arthurian romance, in particular, responded to the criticisms levied against it, whether from the point of view of science, history, morality, or religion, and, in doing so, redefined each of these categories of knowledge in ways that I have already suggested. The authors of these romances presented themselves, not as singular geniuses (or *auctores*, as they would have put it), like Homer, Virgil, or Dante Alighieri, but as contributors to an ongoing literary tradition. Like members of online fan fiction communities today,[74] one of these authors would read or hear a version of an Arthurian tale and be inspired to continue it, to rewrite it, or to amplify it, without claiming any personal credit for what he wrote aside from, on occasion, a mention of his name. As a result, romances stand out, not as singular works of genius but, as parts of a continuing literary tradition where the boundaries between one work and the other are blurred. In the manuscripts, a scribe would copy Chrétien de Troyes' *Conte du Graal* and its Continuations or the various sections of the Vulgate Cycle one after the other, without interruption, giving precedence to the integrity of the story over the identity of its authors or their creations. If Arthurian romance has seemed trivial compared to "great" works of literature, whether during the centuries that saw its creation or today, it is in large part because, as an ill-defined series of texts of varying quality and interest, it allows the hero and his story to usurp the place of the author and his work and, by extension, the fiction to usurp the place of the individual sup-

Cambridge University Press, 2005), 210–37; Margaret Anne Doody, *The True Story of the Novel* (New Brunswick, NJ: Rutgers University Press, 1996); Thomas DiPiero, *Dangerous Truths and Criminal Passions: The Evolution of the French Novel, 1549–1791* (Stanford, CA: Stanford University Press, 1992); and Michael McKeon, *The Origins of the English Novel, 1600–1740* (Baltimore: Johns Hopkins University Press, 1987).

74. See Anne Jamison, *Fic: Why Fanfiction Is Taking Over the World* (Dallas: Smart Pop, 2013).

posed to have created it. Given the absence of self-defined "great" authors of "great" works in the medieval Arthurian corpus,[75] when other medieval authors referred to these texts, they tended to cite them, not by their authors or their titles, but by their principal character or (in the case of the Holy Grail) their principal theme. It is for that reason that, old-fashioned as it may seem today, I organize these chapters, not around authors or titles, but around characters, such as Merlin, Arthur, and Lancelot,[76] and around the theme of the Holy Grail, together with the epistemological issues they bring to the fore. At times, I will focus upon one text when its treatment of a topic is especially original or influential (such as the *Prose Lancelot*'s account of Lancelot's love of Guinevere or *La Mort le Roi Artu*'s account of the death of King Arthur). At other times, I will focus on multiple texts when their discussions of a topic overlap (such as Chrétien de Troyes', the Continuators', and the Vulgate Cycle's descriptions of the Holy Grail). Because I am concerned as much with the reception of Arthurian romance as with the romances themselves, I am privileging those works that medieval authors themselves privileged—namely, those of Chrétien, his Continuators, Robert de Boron, the *Didot-Perceval*, and the Vulgate and Post-Vulgate Cycles—over the ancillary Arthurian romances of the late twelfth and thirteenth centuries,[77] and, within these works, I am highlighting those story lines that have proved most popular, both in the medieval and the postmedieval periods. As delightful as these romances

75. Chrétien de Troyes may seem to be a partial exception to this rule, given the tendency of romance manuscripts to identify him as an author, yet, after the Middle Ages come to a close, even his name is eclipsed in favor of that of his characters. The preeminence of Malory's *Le Morte D'Arthur* in the English literary tradition despite this book's dependence upon French and English sources may reflect a desire to ground the Arthurian tradition in a single, named author and a single, unified book.

76. If I am concentrating on male characters as opposed to their female counterparts, it is because the texts themselves do so. Arthurian romance sees itself as the history of the Kingdom of Logres, and, because men have played disproportionately important roles in the history of such realms, male characters play disproportionately important roles in these works. That being said, women like Morgan Le Fay, Guinevere, and the Lady of the Lake remain significant figures in these works, in a way in which women are not, say, in the *chansons de geste*, and I discuss them at length in the relevant chapters.

77. Many of these other Arthurian romances, including Renaut de Beaujeu's *Le Bel Inconnu* (ca. 1190), *La Mule sans frein* (1190–1210), *Le Chevalier à l'épee* (early 1200s), and Raoul de Houdenc's *La Vengeance Raguidel* (ca. 1210), have to do with Gawain. There were, of course, important non-Arthurian romances as well, such as Robert d'Orbigny's *Le Conte de Floire et Blanchefleur* (1150), Guillaume de Lorris and Jean de Meun's *Le Roman de la Rose* (1225–75), and Jakemés' *Le Roman du Chastelain de Couci et de la Dame de Fayel* (late 1200s). For the genre of romance in general at this time, see my "Romance, *Roman*, and the Novel: The Problem of Medieval French Narrative," in *The Cambridge Companion to French Literature*, ed. John D. Lyons (Cambridge: Cambridge University Press, 2015), 3–17.

have seemed for centuries of readers, they have always been tales about the reading of romance and especially about the controversial pleasure such a reading can arouse.

Finally, in chapter 6, I consider how the debate over the truth claims of romance continues to play out in the twentieth and now twenty-first centuries. While many forms of "genre" fiction may be considered heirs of romance in our day, fantasy plays this role most of all, to the point where its characters are often knights and ladies, their residences towers and castles, and their lands inhabited by mythical beasts of medieval origin. In *The Chronicles of Narnia* (1949–54), C. S. Lewis has his four modern, middle-class protagonists become knights and ladies who, when raised to the thrones of Narnia, speak in a Malory-inflected English. In her *Harry Potter* books (1997–2007), J. K. Rowling situates Hogwarts School of Witchcraft and Wizardry in a castle filled with marvels, and she sends her hero on a Grail-like quest for "Horcruxes" and "Deathly Hallows" with supernatural powers. Just as medieval romance was scorned by the learned readers of its time, modern fantasy has largely been disdained (for good or for bad) by the academic and literary establishments of our day. And just as the authors of medieval romance responded, in their works, to the criticisms that were being levied against this form of literature, Lewis and Rowling have responded in their novels to the current prejudice against fantasy. They know well that, for centuries, philosophers have expressed suspicion of ideas that are based, not in observation of the sensorily perceptible world, but in the inventions of the imagination, and that fantasy literature has been considered dubious because of its dependence upon that faculty. They respond to this concern by contrasting characters (like Edmund Pevensie or the Dursleys) who reject imagination and, in doing so, avert their eyes from the reality around them, and characters (like Lucy Pevensie and Harry Potter) who embrace imagination and, as a result, see and understand what their peers cannot. In what is called "portal-quest" fantasy, like Lewis's and Rowling's series, the hero or heroine enters, physically, into a strange and marvelous land in a way that mirrors how the reader of these works enters, imaginatively, into a strange and marvelous work.

If this book differs from its predecessors, it is because its interest lies not in the literary history of these romances,[78] in the political or

78. Thomas Hinton, *The "Conte du Graal" Cycle: Chrétien de Troyes's "Perceval," the Continuations, and French Arthurian Romance* (Cambridge: D. S. Brewer, 2012); Matilda Tomaryn Bruckner, *Chrétien Continued: A Study of the "Conte du Graal" and Its Verse Continuations* (Oxford: Oxford

social history to which these romances refer,[79] or in the structure of these romances' narrations,[80] but in the epistemological issues these works raise. Analytic philosophers have long pondered the problems of fictionality,[81] as have literary scholars,[82] including a few who have considered fictionality in medieval literature[83] and in romance in par-

University Press, 2009); and *The Manuscripts of Chrétien de Troyes / Les manuscrits de Chrétien de Troyes*, ed. Keith Busby, Terry Nixon, Alison Stones, and Lori Walters, 2 vols. (Amsterdam: Rodopi, 1993) address the creation and transmission of Arthurian manuscripts.

79. Erich Köhler, in *Ideal und Wirklichkeit in der höfischen Epik: Studien zur Form der frühen Artus- und Graldichtung* (Tübingen: Max Niemeyer Verlag, 1956; rpt., 2002), and R. W. Southern, in *The Making of the Middle Ages* (New Haven, CT: Yale University Press, 1953), especially the final chapter, which charts the progression "From Epic to Romance," contrast the age of the *chanson de geste* and the age of romance. Sarah Kay complicates this picture in *The "Chansons de Geste" in the Age of Romance: Political Fictions* (Oxford: Clarendon Press, 1995). Robert M. Stein, in *Reality Fictions: Romance, History, and Governmental Authority, 1025–1180* (Notre Dame, IN: University of Notre Dame Press, 2006), connects the development of fictionality with the transformation of sociopolitical conditions after the Norman Conquest, as do Michelle L. Warren, in *History on the Edge: Excalibur and the Borders of Britain, 1100–1300* (Minneapolis: University of Minnesota Press, 2000), and Susan Crane, in *Insular Romance: Politics, Faith, and Culture in Anglo-Norman and Middle English Literature* (Berkeley: University of California Press, 1986). Geraldine Heng, in *Empire of Magic: Medieval Romance and the Politics of Cultural Fantasy* (New York: Columbia University Press, 2006), connects the development of romance with western European incursions in the East. Peggy McCracken, in *The Romance of Adultery: Queenship and Sexual Transgression in Old French Literature* (Philadelphia: University of Pennsylvania Press, 1998); Roberta Krueger, in *Women Readers and the Ideology of Gender in Old French Verse Romance* (Cambridge: Cambridge University Press, 1993); and E. Jane Burns, in *Bodytalk: When Women Speak in Old French Literature* (Philadelphia: University of Pennsylvania Press, 1993), address the increasing importance of women patrons and readers at this time.

80. Jean Frappier, in "Plaidoyer pour l' 'Architecte' contre une opinion d'Albert Pauphilet sur le *Lancelot en prose*," *Romance Philology* 8 (1954–55): 27–33, argues persuasively that one "architect" united the various books of the Vulgate Cycle. For other treatments of narrative structure in this series of works, see *A Companion to the Lancelot-Grail Cycle*, ed. Carol Dover (Cambridge: D. S. Brewer, 2003); Elspeth Kennedy, *Lancelot and the Grail: A Study of the "Prose Lancelot"* (Oxford: Clarendon Press, 1986); Douglas Kelly, *The Art of Medieval French Romance* (Madison: University of Wisconsin Press, 1992); E. Jane Burns, *Arthurian Fictions: Re-reading the Vulgate Cycle* (Columbus: Ohio State University Press, 1985); Charles Méla, *La Reine et le Graal: La conjointure dans les romans du Graal de Chrétien de Troyes au "Livre de Lancelot"* (Paris: Editions du Seuil, 1984); and Eugène Vinaver, *The Rise of Romance* (Oxford: Oxford University Press, 1971).

81. See Marie-Laure Ryan, *Possible Worlds, Artificial Intelligence, and Narrative Theory* (Bloomington: Indiana University Press, 1992); Ruth Ronen, *Possible Worlds in Literary Theory* (Cambridge: Cambridge University Press, 1994); and Thomas G. Pavel, *Fictional Worlds* (Cambridge, MA: Harvard University Press, 1986).

82. See Richard Walsh, *The Rhetoric of Fictionality: Narrative Theory and the Idea of Fiction* (Columbus: Ohio State University Press, 2007); Catherine Gallagher, "The Rise of Fictionality," in *The Novel*, ed. Franco Moretti, vol. 1, *History, Geography, and Culture* (Princeton, NJ: Princeton University Press, 2006), 336–63; and Michael Riffaterre, *Fictional Truth* (Baltimore: Johns Hopkins University Press, 1990). Nicholas D. Paige, in *Before Fiction: The Ancien Régime of the Novel* (Philadelphia: University of Pennsylvania Press, 2011), argues interestingly that fiction as we know it did not exist prior to the turn of the eighteenth and nineteenth centuries.

83. See Virginie Greene, *Logical Fictions in Medieval Literature and Philosophy* (Cambridge: Cambridge University Press, 2014), which considers the philosophical roots of fictionality in the twelfth and thirteenth centuries, and Monika Otter, *Inventiones: Fiction and Referentiality in Twelfth-Century English Historical Writing* (Chapel Hill: University of North Carolina Press, 1996), which considers a series of medieval Latin works on the border of fiction and history.

ticular.[84] In order to understand how learned audiences of the Middle Ages responded to the truth claims of Arthurian literature, we will be considering didactic writings outside this literature, whether about romance (brief and scattered as they may be) or about topics that have bearing upon how romance was read. In order to understand how popular audiences of the time responded to these truth claims, we will be considering the romances themselves, as they constitute our primary source on this topic. As we shall see, Arthurian texts are filled with "readers," that is, with people, like Merlin's fellow courtiers, Arthur's last surviving retainer, ladies enamored with Lancelot, and almost all the Grail knights, who observe the extraordinary actions occurring around them and try to make sense of what they see. In contrast to the learned authors, these "readers" are aristocratic instead of middle class, lay instead of clerical, and female as well as male. It is from the texts' depiction of these characters, I would argue, that we can ascertain how they expect their readers to react to these same remarkable phenomena. It would be possible to write a cultural history of the reading of Arthurian romance in the Middle Ages, and, in chapter 1, we will make reference to several scholars who have done exactly that. Yet in this study, it is my aim to approach the question of how this literature was received, not from outside the text, but from inside, through a close reading of its major tales. While scholars have addressed the history of romance before, it has been only in brief, general overviews of the genre, without sustained attention to individual works of the kind I wish to pursue here,[85] or in specialized studies of the English literary tradition and, hence, of the Late Middle Ages,[86] without con-

84. See Dennis Howard Green, *The Beginnings of Romance, 1150–1220* (Cambridge: Cambridge University Press, 2002), and Gertrud Grünkorn, *Die Fiktionalität des höfischen Romans um 1200* (Berlin: Erich Schmidt Verlag, 1994), which focus upon the German context. Jean M. Dornbush argues in *Pygmalion's Figure: Reading Old French Romance* (Lexington, KY: French Forum, 1990) that Old French romance dramatizes concerns about interpretation at the time they were being composed, though she traces these concerns to discussions of rhetoric and, by extension, the arts of memory. Patricia A. Parker, in *Inescapable Romance: Studies in the Poetics of a Mode* (Princeton, NJ: Princeton University Press, 1979), discusses romance as the genre that at once seeks and defers a particular end. Ben Ramm's *A Discourse for the Holy Grail in Old French Romance* (Woodbridge, UK: Boydell and Brewer, 2007) approaches the romance of the Grail from the perspective of writings by Jacques Lacan and Slavoj Žižek.

85. See Barbara Fuchs, *Romance*, The New Critical Idiom (New York: Routledge, 2004); Michel Stanesco and Michel Zink, *Histoire européenne du roman médiéval: Esquisse et perspectives* (Paris: Presses Universitaires de France, 1991); and Gillian Beer, *The Romance* (London: Methuen, 1970).

86. See Melissa Furrow, *Expectations of Romance: The Reception of a Genre in Medieval England* (Rochester, NY: D. S. Brewer, 2009). K. S. Whetter's *Understanding Genre and Medieval Romance* (Aldershot, UK: Ashgate, 2008) addresses discussions of romance in the context of Sir Thomas Malory's *Le Morte D'Arthur.* Many works whose titles indicate a general treatment of romance, such as *A Companion to Romance: From Classical to Contemporary*, ed. Corinne Saunders (Malden,

sideration of the Old French works of the High Middle Ages. Insofar as this study will be of interest to readers, it will be, not simply insofar as they are students of Old French literature, but insofar as they are readers of romance who presumably take pleasure in this genre and who wish to understand why they enjoy texts that have historically been so dispraised.

"But you are romanticizing!" the reader of this book may protest, and it is to that reader that I wish to appeal. Since the seventeenth and eighteenth centuries, it has often been assumed that literature should represent life "as it truly is," in its everyday reality. If it takes us away from our world through its fictions, it should do so only in order to bring us back to this world with an improved understanding of the environment in which we live. Romance, it is argued, by depicting situations in which characters feel wonder, admiration, love, or reverence, depicts, not what people actually feel in their quotidian existence, but what they *wish* they felt, thanks to the books they read. We should reject this genre, it seems, for making us expect more of life than it can offer, for setting us up for disappointment, and for causing us, in the end, to prefer literature to our own existence. Yet if romance is responding to this assumption (as I am arguing that it is), it is saying that it does, in fact, represent life "as it truly is," not, perhaps, in its everyday reality, but in its exceptional aspect. If romance takes us away from our world through its fictions, it does so in order to bring us back to this world with an improved ability to recognize and appreciate its most intense and heightened moments. It depicts the wonder people feel when they are traveling to a foreign country; the admiration they feel when they are inspired by a political leader's inaugural address; the ardor they feel when they meet a new person with whom they are falling in love; or the reverence they feel when they behold a precious object, perhaps today an artistic masterpiece or a historical artifact. Far from rejecting romance, we should embrace it for awakening us to that in life we would not have noticed were it not for its sake, and for confirming the reality of what we have perceived, however ephemeral it may have seemed. If "to romanticize" refers to the way in which we distort reality in order to make it resemble the conventions of romance, the term "to realicize" could be coined to refer to the way in which we also distort reality in order to make it adhere to the conventions of the realist novel. While it is true that we may experience such exalted moments only because ro-

MA: Blackwell, 2007), and Derek Pearsall, *Arthurian Romance: A Short Introduction* (Malden, MA: Blackwell, 2003), restrict themselves to the English context.

mance has taught us that such moments can occur, it is also true that, if we did not believe such moments to be possible, thanks, in part, to romance, we would likely never experience them.

I am grateful for the assistance of a fellowship from the John Simon Guggenheim Memorial Foundation in writing this book. At various stages, Sarah Kay, R. Howard Bloch, and Mark Lambert provided valuable responses to what I was writing. Conversations with Michael Staunton, Francine Prose, Cami Townsend, and Lindsay Watson helped to clarify my arguments. Carolyn Dewald shared important thoughts about the classical romance and novel, and Lydia Davis helped me with the Dutch translations. Richard Aldous inspired me to add one crucial paragraph. Omar Encarnación encouraged me to consider more the Spanish tradition. And Leon Botstein was a great support, as always. I am thankful for Lory Gray for her reliable assistance with my research, to Dawn Hall for her careful copyediting of the manuscript, and to Randy Petilos for his shepherding through of this project.

ONE

Romance and Its Reception

Over the course of its history, the scene in which romance was received moved from public recitations to private readings. Between the mid-twelfth and mid-thirteenth centuries, when romances were first being composed, jongleurs or minstrels sang them to the accompaniment of stringed instruments, along with songs and lays.[1] Numerous texts from these years recount how, after the evening meal in a castle, the servants would dismantle the tables and push them against the walls of the great hall, and members of the household would then use this open space to amuse themselves in various ways, including by listening to such tales. Even as romances were being performed for large assemblies, they were also being recited to small gatherings. Texts describe a lady or damsel reading a romance to her companions outdoors[2] or a

1. See John W. Baldwin, "The Image of the Jongleur in Northern France around 1200," *Speculum* 72, no. 3 (1997): 635–63; Christopher Page, *The Owl and the Nightingale: Musical Life and Ideas in France (1100–1300)* (Berkeley: University of California Press, 1989), 85–109; and Joseph J. Duggan, "Oral Performance of Romance in Medieval France," in *Continuations: Essays on Medieval French Literature and Language, in Honor of John L. Grigsby*, ed. John L. Grigsby, Norris J. Lacy, Gloria Torrini-Roblin (Birmingham, AL: Summa Publications, 1989), 51–61. For other references to performances of romances, see Gerbert de Montreuil, *La Continuation de Perceval*, vol. 1, ed. Williams, vv. 6702–8; Raimon Vidal, "Abril issia," in *Raimon Vidal: Poetry and Prose*, ed. W. H. W. Field, 2 vols. (Chapel Hill: University of North Carolina Press, 1971), vol. 2, vv. 38–40; *De deus bordeors ribaus*, in Edmond Faral, *Mimes français du XIIIe siècle: Contribution à l'histoire du théâtre comique au Moyen Age* (Paris: Honoré Champion, 1910), vv. 56–98; and *The Romance of Flamenca*, ed. E. D. Blodgett (New York: Garland, 1995), vv. 665–99.

2. See Chrétien de Troyes, *Le Chevalier au lion*, ed. Hult, vv. 5360–62; *Li Chevalier aux deus épées*, ed. Wendelin Foerster (Halle: M. Niemeyer, 1877), vv. 4255

young man and woman reading a romance together under a tree.[3] The insomniac narrator of Geoffrey Chaucer's *The Book of the Duchess* turns to a romance "to rede and drive the night away"[4] because he believes it will distract him better than playing chess or another board game. Whereas families tended to gather by the hearth to listen to moral or religious works together, beginning in the sixteenth century, young people preferred to retreat to their bedrooms or boudoirs to read romances and, later, novels by themselves.[5] Alone, they experienced their encounter with these works as unmediated, to the point where they could become entirely absorbed into their world and their characters' minds.[6] Both men and women read novels, but women were seen as especially susceptible to this private, inward-directed state and to the amorous fantasies to which it could lead.[7] In Gustave Flaubert's *Madame Bovary* (1856), Emma Bovary spends her days in her room, half dressed, burning Turkish pastilles and devouring "extravagant books where there were orgiastic tableaux and thrilling situations."[8] Having shut out her husband, her daughter, and her servants, she pursues a sol-

---

and 8952–53; *The Romance of Hunbaut: An Arthurian Poem of the Thirteenth Century*, ed. Margaret Winters (Leiden: Brill, 1984), vv. 3052–53; Robert d'Orbigny, *Le Conte de Floire et Blanchefleur*, ed. Leclanche, vv. 49–55; and *Florence de Rome: Chanson d'aventure du premier quart du 13ᵉ siècle*, ed. A. Wollensköld (Paris: Firmin-Didot, 1907), vv. 3053–54. Even when men and women could read, they seem to have found it more enjoyable to have romances read aloud to them. In the early thirteenth-century *Galeran de Bretagne*, ed. Lucien Foulet (Paris: Honoré Champion, 1925), the heroine Fresne is said "to read [her] Psalter [*lire mon saultier*]" (v. 3880), but "to hear of Thebes or Troy [*oÿr de Thebes ou de Troye*]" (v. 3882).

3. Robert de Blois, *Floris et Liriopé: Altfranzösischer Roman*, ed. Wolfram von Zingerle (Leipzig: O. R. Reisland, 1891), vv. 971–73. See Evelyn Birge Vitz, "Erotic Reading in the Middle-Ages: Performance and Re-Performance of Romance," in *Performing Medieval Narrative*, ed. Evelyn Birge Vitz, Nancy Freeman Regalado, and Marylyn Lawrence (Rochester, NY: D. S. Brewer, 2005), 73–88, which emphasizes the connection between devotional and erotic reading, both of which are designed to arouse emotion.

4. Geoffrey Chaucer, *The Book of the Duchess*, in *The Riverside Chaucer*, ed. Larry D. Benson (Oxford: Oxford University Press, 2008), 339–46. v. 49.

5. See Marguerite de Navarre, *L'Heptaméron*, ed. Michel François (Paris: Bordas, 1991), 164, and Blaise de Montesquiou de Lasseran-Massencôme, *Commentaires de Messire Blaise de Montluc*, ed. Paul Courteault (Paris: Bibliothèque de la Pléiade, 1968), 346.

6. On "absorbtive" reading, see William Warner, *Licensing Entertainment: The Elevation of Novel-Reading in Britain, 1684–1750* (Berkeley: University of California Press, 1998), 225–26, and Rebecca Tierney-Hynes, *Novel Minds: Philosophers and Romance Readers, 1680–1740* (Basingstoke: Palgrave Macmillan, 2012), 3–4.

7. See Thomas Laqueur, *Solitary Sex: A Cultural History of Masturbation* (New York: Zone Books, 2003), 247–358, which traces the increasing prohibition against onanism in the eighteenth century to the increasing popularity of the novel. Northrop Frye also makes the connection between reading and masturbation in *The Secular Scripture*, 24.

8. "des livres extravagants où il y avait des tableaux orgiaques avec des situations sanglantes," Gustave Flaubert, *Madame Bovary*, in *Oeuvres*, ed. Albert Thibaudet and René Dumesnil, Bibliothèque de la Pléiade, 2 vols. (Paris: Gallimard, 1951–52), vol. 1, pp. 293–610, at pt. 3, chap. 6, p. 554.

itary infidelity with these books, in addition to the more conventional infidelity she pursues with her lovers. Even in the twentieth century, housewives left alone during the day frequently distracted themselves from their chores with Harlequin or Mills & Boon–style romances.[9] As varied as these scenarios may be, the reading of romance has always been regarded as a pleasurable activity, yet also as a potentially pernicious one insofar as it removes readers from their actual day-to-day lives.[10]

If it is necessary for our purposes to consider the history of romance, not only in the Middle Ages but in the postmedieval period, it is because this genre had not yet acquired its definition during the time of its creation.[11] In the Middle Ages, as we have seen, Arthurian romances were referred to as "romances" (*romans*), but also as "stories" (*contes*) and "histories" (*estoires*), especially as the verse narratives of the twelfth century gave way to the prose accounts of the thirteenth century. Yet when people of this time referred to these texts, they tended to cite not the genre to which they belong but the "subject matter" or "matter" (*matiere*) they treated. Jean Bodel, a poet from Arras writing at the turn of the twelfth and thirteenth centuries, famously declares, "There are only three subject matters to any knowledgeable man: that of France, that of Britain, and that of Rome the Great."[12] The "Matter of Rome" to which Bodel alludes included stories about Aeneas and his men, the destruction of Troy, and the foundation of Rome, such as Benoît de Sainte-Maure's *Roman de Troie* (1155–60) and the anonymous *Eneas* (ca. 1160). The "Matter of France" included stories—also known as "songs of

9. See Janice A. Radway, *Reading the Romance: Women, Patriarchy, and Popular Literature* (Chapel Hill: University of North Carolina Press, 1984; rev. ed., 1991).

10. On responses to romance, see Stanesco and Zink, *Histoire européenne du roman médiéval: Esquisse et perspectives*, 175–84.

11. The classical world produced five complete lengthy, prose, fictional works between the first and the third century AD, including Heliodorus's *Aethiopica*, Petronius's *Satyricon*, and Apuleius's *Golden Ass*, as well as fragments of several other such works. Never given a generic label in their time, these works have in recent centuries been assimilated to "romances" or "novels." As Ben Edwin Perry, in *The Ancient Romances: A Literary-Historical Account of Their Origin* (Berkeley: University of California Press, 1967); J. R. Morgan, "Make-Believe and Make Believe: The Fictionality of the Greek Novels," in *Lies and Fiction in the Ancient World*, ed. Christopher Gill and T. P. Wiseman (Austin: University of Texas Press, 1993), 175–229; D. C. Feeney, "Epilogue: Toward an Account of the Ancient World's Concepts of Fictive Belief," in ibid., 230–44; and John J. Winkler, "The Invention of Romance," in *The Search for the Ancient Novel*, ed. James Tatum (Baltimore: Johns Hopkins University Press, 1994), 23–38, represent its history, this literature, like its medieval and modern heirs, was always seen as pleasurable and as dangerous to its readers.

12. "N'en son que trois materes a nul home vivant: / De France et de Bretaigne et de Ronme la grant," *La Chanson des Saisnes de Jehan Bodel*, ed. Annette Brasseur, 3 vols. (Geneva: Librairie Droz, 1989), vol. 1, 1, vv. 6–7. See also Robert Guitte, "Li Conte de Bretaigne sont si vain et plaisant," *Romania* 88 (1967): 1–12.

deeds" (*chansons de geste*)—about Charlemagne and his knights, such as Roland, Oliver, and Ogier the Dane, including the *Chanson de Roland* (ca. 1100) and *Huon de Bordeaux* (ca. 1215–40). The "Matter of Britain," finally, consisted of tales about King Arthur and his knights, such as Lancelot of the Lake, Gawain, and Perceval, as well as other legendary kings of Britain. While Bodel categorizes the three "matters" according to the nations they address, both he and other authors more commonly categorize these lengthy, narrative literary works according to their central character.[13] In the opening of the second branch of the *Roman de Renart* (1175–90), the narrator recalls how his listeners have heard stories from the Matters of Rome and Britain: "Lords, you have heard recounted many a story . . . about how Paris ravished Helen, . . . about Tristan, . . . romances about Yvain and his beast."[14] Renart himself, in the guise of a Breton jongleur, boasts to a potential client that in addition to good "song[s]"[15] about Roland, Oliver, and Ogier, "I know good Breton lays about Merlin and Noton, King Arthur and Tristan."[16] Jean Renart writes of a courtly gathering in his *Roman de la Rose* (ca. 1210), "Then entered the minstrels. This one played one piece, that one another. This one recounted the story about Perceval, that one the one about Roncevaux, among the rows of barons."[17] As these examples reflect, performers commonly referred to Arthurian romances not only as "romances," but as the "stories," "songs," or "lays" about a British hero or even simply as "the one about" (*cil de*) such a person, and they grouped them together with similar accounts of classical and French figures. As tales from the Matter of Britain were not always termed "romances," tales from the Matters of Rome and France[18]

13. In the *ensenhamens*, troubadours speak of the need for jongleurs to know tales from the Matter of Britain (about King Arthur, Merlin, Gawain, Erec, Tristan, and Lancelot) as well as from the Matter of Rome (about Daedalus, Aeneas, and Alexander the Great). See Martín de Riquier, "*L'Ensenhamen* de Guiraut de Cabrera," in *Les Chansons de gestes françaises*, ed. Irénée Cluzel, 2nd ed. (Paris: Nizet, 1967), 332–51, and François Pirot, *Recherches sur les connaissance littéraires des troudabours occitans et catalans des XIIe et XIIIe siècles* (Barcelona: Memorias de la Academia de Buenas Letras de Barcelona, 1972), 563–614.

14. "Signor, oï avés maint conte, / . . . / coment Paris ravi Helainne, / . . . / de Tristan, . . . / . . . / romanz d' Yvain et de sa beste," *Roman de Renart*, ed. Armand Strubel Bibliothèque de la Pléiade (Paris: Gallimard, 1998), Branch VIIa, vv. 1–8.

15. "chanson," ibid., v. 2853.

16. "Ge fot savoir bon lai breton / et de Merlin et de Noton, / del roi Artu et de Tristan," ibid., Branch 1b, vv. 2389–91.

17. "ors vindrent li menesterel. / i uns note un li autres el / il conte ci de Perceval, / il raconte de Rainceval / ar les rens devant les barons," Jean Renart, *Roman de la rose*, in *"The Romance of the Rose" or of Guillaume de Dole*, ed. and trans. Regina Psaki (New York: Garland, 1995), vv. 1745–49.

18. *Renaut de Montauban*, ed. Jacques Thomas (Geneva: Droz, 1989) (v. 14309); *Daurel et Beton: Chanson de geste provençal*, ed. Paul Meyer, Société des Anciens Textes Français (Paris: Firmin Didot, 1880), 1; *Aiol: A Chanson de Geste*, ed. Sandra C. Malicote and Richard A. Hartman (New

were occasionally labeled in this manner, as were fabliaux,[19] beast epics,[20] and allegories.[21] Medieval authors, though eloquent in theorizing biblical, patristic, and classical literature as texts worthy of study, never theorized romance as a genre. The Latin term for "romance" (*romanus* or *romancius*), though attested to from the twelfth century on, is seldom used.[22] In its capacity to encompass a multitude of different texts, the word "romance" at this time signified any lengthy fictional narrative, just as the word "novel" does today. It was not the form of Arthurian romance—which passed unremarked—but its subject matter that inspired disdain.

It was only in the sixteenth and seventeenth centuries that romance was first conceptualized as a literary genre, and one in which Arthurian works assumed pride of place.[23] In the sixteenth century, what were now called the "old romances" (*vieux romans*) of *Lancelot du Lac, Perceval,* and *Tristan* remained popular,[24] especially when they were rewritten to conform to modern tastes,[25] and they were seen as an inspi-

York: Italica, 2014), BN Ff 25516, folio 173; *Fierabras: Chanson de geste du XIIe siècle,* ed. Marc Le Person (Paris: Honoré Champion, 2003) (vv. 6216–17) all refer to themselves as *romans.*

19. The author of a fabliau in a manuscript at the University of Cambridge, Corpus Christi Coll., 50, fol. 91a–94c, refers to his work as a "romance about a knight, his lady, and a cleric [*romanz de un chivaler et de sa dame et de un clerk*]," in *Nouveau recueil complet des fabliaux,* ed. Willem Noomen, 10 vols. (Assen: Van Gorcum, 1998), vol. 10, Fabliau 123, p. 121.

20. The author of *Le Couronnement de Renard: Poème du treizième siècle,* ed. Alfred Foulet (Paris: Presses Universitaires de France, 1929) refers to his work as "this romance [*icest roumant*]" (v. 140) and compares it positively to stories about Lancelot, Tristan, Gawain, Bors, and Yvain.

21. Guillaume de Lorris identifies *Le Roman de la Rose,* ed. Daniel Poirion (Paris: Garnier-Flammarion, 1974) as a *roman* from the outset (vv. 34–38).

22. Lambert of Ardres, in his *Historia comitum Ghisnensium* (1194–98), ed. Johann Heller, in MGH Scriptores 24, pp. 550–642, refers to old people at court recounting "adventures, fables, and histories [*eventuras et fabulas et historias*]" (96, p. 607) about Constantine, Charlemagne, Roland, Oliver, and Arthur of Britain, Merlin, and Tristan and Iseut. He mentions the "*Romanum de Silentio*" (81, p. 598) composed by Walter Silens, who was in service to his patron, Baldwin of Guines. See also Jean Gerson, "Contra superstitionem sculpturae Leonis," in *Oeuvres complètes,* ed. Palémon Glorieux, 10 vols. (Paris: Desclée, 1960), vol. 1, 227–32, at 231.

23. See Michael McKeon, in *The Origins of the English Novel, 1600–1740* (Princeton, NJ: Princeton University Press, 1987; rpt., 2002), 45.

24. In 1549, Joachim du Bellay refers, in *La Deffense et Illustration de la Langue Françoyse,* in *"The Regrets"; with, "The Antiquities of Rome," "Three Latin Elegies," and "The Defense and Enrichment of the French Language,"* ed. Richard Helgerson (Philadelphia: University of Pennsylvania Press, 2006), 317–417, to "those beautiful old French romances, like *Lancelot, Tristan,* or others [*ces beaux vieulx romans Françoys, comme un "Lancelot," un "Tristan," ou autres*]" (bk. II, chap. 5, p. 379). Rita Copeland, in "Between *Romans* and Romantics," *Texas Studies in Literature and Language* 33, no. 2 (1991): 215–24, considers how romance, though originally identified with modernity (that is, with the ascendency of the vernacular over Latin and the written text over the oral tale), by the sixteenth and seventeenth century became identified with the archaic.

25. For a full listing of Arthurian and non-Arthurian romances published in France during the late fifteenth and the sixteenth centuries, see Jane H. M. Taylor, *Rewriting Arthurian Romance in Renaissance France: From Manuscript to Printed Book* (Cambridge: D. S. Brewer, 2014), 217–22.

ration for new heroic works. By the 1540s, the vogue for "old romances" was replaced by that for new, hybrid genres that combined an interest in feats of arms inherited from the Matter of France with an interest in love affairs and enchantments inherited from the Matter of Britain. In Italy, "heroic poems" (*poemi eroici*), such as Luigi Pulci's *Morgante* (1483), Matteo Boiardo's *Orlando inammorato* (1495), and Ludovico Ariosto's *Orlando furioso* (1516–32), celebrated French paladins in Italian *ottava rima*, while, in Spain, "books of chivalry" (*libros de caballerías*), including, most importantly, *Amadís de Gaula* (1508), sang of heroes from Iberian legends in Castilian prose. It is often remarked that even as humanists were promoting the value of the classical tradition, the most popular literary works were these rewritings of medieval legends.[26] In the seventeenth century, the genre of romance came to include multi-volumed prose "heroic romances" (*romans héroïques*), such as Madeleine de Scudéry's *Artamène, ou, le Grand Cyrus* (10 vols., 1648–53) or *Clélie* (10 vols., 1654–61)[27] and La Calprenède's *Cassandre* (10 vols., 1642–50), where impossibly brave heroes and beautiful heroines fall in love in ancient and exotic settings, are cruelly separated by war, shipwreck, and abduction by pirates, and strive to reunite.[28] In the first edition of the *Dictionnaire de Académie Françoise* (1694), the entry under "romance [*roman*]" includes both "old romances [*vieux romans*]," such as *Lancelot du Lac*, and "modern romances [*romans modernes*]," such as *Amadís, Cyrus*, and *Cassandre*.[29] The Matter of Britain and of France from the Middle Ages were thus progressively joined together with heroic works from this later period.

26. The criticism of sixteenth-century chivalric romance is enormous and rich. See, for just a few examples, see Daniel Javitch, "The Disparagement of Chivalric Romance for Its Lack of Historicity in Sixteenth-Century Italian Poetics," in *Romance and History: Imagining Time from the Medieval to the Early Modern Period*, ed. Jon Whitman (Cambridge: Cambridge University Press, 2015), 187–99; Virginia Krause, *Idle Pursuits: Literature and "Oisiveté" in the French Renaissance* (Newark: University of Delaware Press, 2003); and Nicole Cazauran, "Les Romans de chevalerie en France: Entre 'exemple' et 'récréation,'" in *Le Roman de chevalerie au temps de la Renaissance*, ed. Marie-Thérèse Jones-Davies (Paris: Jean Touzot, 1987), 29–45.

27. The attribution of the Scudéry's works has long been a source of contestation. The romances were commonly said to be written by Madeleine de Scudéry, but the original title pages tend to cite her brother Georges' name.

28. For criticism of seventeenth-century heroic romance, see Amelia A. Zurcher, *Seventeenth-Century English Romance: Allegory, Ethics, and Politics* (New York: Palgrave Macmillan, 2007); Roger Chartier, "Lectures et lecteurs 'populaires' de la Renaissance à l'âge classique," in *Histoire de la lecture dans le monde occidental*, ed. Guglielmo Cavallo and Roger Chartier (Paris: Seuil, 1997), 337–54; and Alain Niderst, "Le Danger des romans dans les romans du XVIIe siècle," in *L'Epreuve du lecteur: Livres et lectures dans le roman d'ancien régime; Actes du VIIIe Colloque de la Société d'analyse de la topique romanesque, Louvain-Anvers (19–21 mai 1994)*, ed. Jan Herman and Paul Pelckmans (Louvain: Société pour l'information grammaticale, 1995), 52–58.

29. *Dictionnaire de l'Académie françoise*, 2 vols. (Paris: J.-B. Coignard, 1694), vol. 2, 415.

While romance was first conceived as a genre of literature in the sixteenth and seventeenth centuries, it was reconceived in the eighteenth and nineteenth centuries, when it took on a new look in contrast to the novel. Already in the 1660s, in France, the "short romance" (*petit roman*) or "novel" (*nouvelle*) was replacing the heroic romance. In works such as Madame de Villedieu's *Cléonice* (1669) and Madame de Lafayette's *La Princesse de Clèves* (1678), heroes and heroines from the recent past and nearby locales struggled, no longer with external adventures in the world, but with internal affairs of the heart. In the early 1700s, in England, Daniel Defoe, Samuel Richardson, and Henry Fielding (who would be remembered, retrospectively, as the first English novelists) likewise strove to make their characters accessible to their readers, though, in contrast to their French contemporaries, they emphasized their outer, social conditions rather than their inner, moral states. In his preface to *Moll Flanders* (1722), Defoe acknowledges that his works may not be "public histories," that is, accounts of well-known personages, already familiar to his readers, but, he contends, they are "private histories,"[30] or accounts of obscure but no less real people. In their efforts to make their works seem like histories rather than romances, these authors typically presented them as historical documents, such as collections of letters, travel memoirs, or journalistic reports. By the end of the eighteenth century, the novel had definitively supplanted romance in the literary marketplace in England, but Romanticism had by that point infiltrated the novel, making its characters, once more, very good or very evil, its plots twisted and supernatural, and its settings dark and exotic. Gothic novels like Ann Radcliffe's *The Mysteries of Udolpho: A Romance* (1794) and M. G. Lewis's *A Monk: A Romance* (1796) advertised their affiliation with this alternate genre in their titles. By the middle of the nineteenth century, the realist novel had taken the place of its Romantic predecessor,[31] but romance continued to make itself felt in works with heroic protagonists and action-packed plots. In the 1880s and 1890s, in what is called the "Romance

30. Daniel Defoe, "Preface to *Moll Flanders*, 1722," in *Novel and Romance, 1700–1800*, ed. Williams, 75–78, at 75.

31. In England, William Harrison Ainsworth is the major exception of an author who continued to call his works "romances." In America, authors preserved this nomenclature. Herman Melville calls *Typee: A Romance of the South Seas* (1846), and Nathaniel Hawthorne writes *The House of the Seven Gables: A Romance* (1851) and *Marble Fawn, or the Romance of Monte Beni* (1860). See G. R. Thompson and Eric Carl Link, *Neutral Ground: New Traditionalism and the American Romance Controversy* (Baton Rouge: Louisiana State University Press, 1999); Nina Bayn, "Concepts of Romance in Hawthorne's America," *Nineteenth-Century Fiction* 38 (1984): 426–43; and Michael Davitt Bell, *The Development of American Romance* (Chicago: University of Chicago Press, 1980).

Revival"[32] or "New Romance,"[33] travel stories, like Jules Verne's *Vingt mille lieues sous les mers* (1870); adventure stories, like Robert Louis Stevenson's *Treasure Island* (1883); detective stories, like Arthur Conan Doyle's Sherlock Holmes tales (1887–1927); horror stories, like Bram Stoker's *Dracula* (1897); fantasy, like William Morris's *The Wood beyond the World* (1894); and science fiction, like H. G. Wells's *The War of the Worlds* (1897), united the rigorous scientific observation of realism with the fantastical imagination of romance in a way that would provide the foundation of popular, genre fiction as we know it today.[34] Whether romance was considered to be a genre similar to the novel, a genre different from the novel, or a mode within the genre of the novel, it remained a cumulative tradition where new contributions were periodically added to the existing corpus and where the entire category was periodically reconceptualized to encompass its expanded membership.

Though the category of romance as we know it, including Arthurian romance, is posterior to the Middle Ages, it remains essential for interpreting Arthurian literature of the twelfth and thirteenth centuries for two reasons. First, it is difficult, if not impossible, to read this literature unmediated by these subsequent generations of readers. Insofar as we perceive "Arthurian romance" as a category of literature at all, it is worth reiterating, it is only because this subject matter became identified with this genre in centuries after the Middle Ages. And if we understand the word "romance" to have the connotations it does, it is only because this relatively neutral term in Old French became identified with a set of characteristics, in a series of stages, well after Arthurian romances had ceased to be composed. Second, even if one could read medieval Arthurian literature unmediated by later debates about romance, it is not clear that one should want to do so. While the sophisticated language postmedieval critics employ when speaking of romance is absent from this earlier time period, given the relatively impoverished state of its literary theory, the traits these critics attribute to this genre are nonetheless present in these works. A consideration of the reception of romance thus provides us with a critical vocabulary

32. On the evolution of the word "romantic," see Raymond Immerwahr, "The Word *romantisch* and Its History," in *The Romantic Period in Germany: Essays by Members of the London University Institute of Germanic Studies*, ed. Siegbert Prawer (New York: Schocken Books, 1970), 34–63.

33. In *Modernism, Romance, and the Fin de Siècle* (Cambridge: Cambridge University Press, 1999), Nicholas Daly argues for the modernity of this "romance revival." See also Armstrong, *How Novels Think*, and Saler, *As If*, 57–104.

34. See Andrew Lang, "Realism and Romance," *Contemporary Review* (November 1887): 683–93.

that can help us understand, in retrospect, what these works had been doing all along. As we shall see, for its opponents, romance imparts no useful lesson; it fails to represent people as they are; and it "idealizes" or "romanticizes" the world in its pages. Instead of helping us to function better in the outer world, it draws us in to a world of its own making. For its defenders, however, romance does teach a useful lesson, though one not reducible to moral truisms; it represents people, not as they are, but as they aspire to be; and it reveals the world, outside its pages as well as inside, to be more "ideal" or "romantic" than realists take it as being. In doing so, it enables us to function in this alternate world, even if this is a world not everyone can apprehend.

The Case against Romance

If learned men of the Middle Ages and later eras criticized romance, as we shall see that they did, it is because they were trained to be suspicious of a literature that did not transcend literature. In Late Antiquity, certain types of fiction were considered untrue because of their lack of utility. Augustine of Hippo, writing at the turn of the fourth and fifth centuries, argues that signs are "to be used" (*uti*) in order to accede to the thing signified by the sign and not "to be enjoyed" (*frui*) in and of themselves.[35] If one dwells upon images from fictional works, enjoying them in and of themselves, he maintains, one mistakes the sign for the thing, that is, that which signifies the truth for the truth itself. Even if one is not genuinely deceived by these texts, as Augustine acknowledges that he is not,[36] one does not learn the truth from them either. "When we fabricate something which signifies nothing," he writes, "then it is a lie."[37] Macrobius, writing in the early fifth century, similarly repudiates fictions "[that] are invented . . . to win over the ears with pleasure."[38] In the Middle Ages, when "romances" per se were first being composed, they were regarded as useless, if pleasurable. Though

35. Augustine, *De doctrina Christiana*, ed. Joseph Martin, CCSL, vol. 32, pp. 1–167, at I, 4, 8.

36. Of the "fables of the poets [*poetarum fabellae*]," Augustine writes in his *Confessiones*, ed. Lucas Verheijen, CCSL, vol. 27, "Though I sang them, I did not assert them; though I heard them sung, I did not believe them [*etsi cantabam, non asserebam; etsi cantari audiebam, non credebam*]" (III, 11, p. 32).

37. "quando id fingimus quod nihil significat, tunc est mendacium," Augustine, *Quaestiones Evangeliorum*, ed. Almut Mutzenbecher, CCSL, vol. 44B, II, 51, p. 116. Cf. Lk 24.28.

38. "Fabulae . . . conciliandae auribus voluptatis . . . repertae sunt," Macrobius, *Commentarii in somnium Scipionis*, ed. J. Willis, BSGRT (Leipzig: G. Teubner, 1963), I, 2, 7–8, p. 5.

they attracted people's attention more than the Gospel, they taught no lesson. Though they stirred people's emotions, they had no effect upon their actions. As occasions for idleness, they did nothing to improve their audiences and thus nothing to contribute to their salvation. In the sixteenth and seventeenth centuries, romances were regarded as untrue, not because of their lack of utility, but because of their lack of verisimilitude. They depicted, not credible characters, with whom we can identify, but incredible figures, who perform feats that no one, however valorous, could ever achieve and who are, as a result, entirely foreign to us. In the eighteenth and nineteenth centuries, romances were regarded as untrue because of their lack of "realism." They portrayed, not the common and ordinary people who fill our world, but, rather, rare and extraordinary individuals who exist seldom, if at all. While critics of romance from these later periods expressed themselves differently from Augustine and Macrobius, they agreed that the problem with romance is that it is a sign that asks, idolatrously, to be enjoyed as an end in and of itself. Useful, verisimilar, or realist literature helps readers by giving them a heightened access to the world in which they live, but romance, it is alleged, harms them by inviting them to enter into an alternate, fantasy realm. Insofar as all fiction to some extent draws the audience into its own world, the danger of romance is also necessarily the danger of fiction itself.[39]

When learned men of the Middle Ages refer to Arthurian literature, they do so, most commonly, to criticize the fact that it is false and useless, yet strangely more attractive to listeners than texts that are true and useful. Caesarius, the prior of the Cistercian abbey of Heisterbach, recounts in his *Dialogus miraculorum* (1219–25) how the former abbot Gevard was once preaching to the monks in their chapterhouse on a feast day when several of the monks fell asleep and even began to snore. He cried out, "Listen, brethren, listen! I will propose something new and important to you. There was once a king who was called Arthur . . ."[40] When the monks immediately awoke at this interjection, the abbot remarked sorrowfully, "See, brethren, our great misery. When I was speaking to you about God, you fell asleep, but as soon as I introduced frivolous words, you all began to listen, awak-

39. On the way in which criticism of romance is ultimately a criticism of fiction in general, see Beer, *Romance*, 5; Fuchs, *Romance*, 2; and Bell, *Development of American Romance*, xii.

40. "Audite, fratres, audite, rem vobis novam et magnam proponam. Rex quidam fuit, qui Artus vocabatur," Caesarius of Heisterbach, *Dialogus miraculorum*, ed. Joseph Strange, 2 vols. (Cologne: J. M. Heberle, 1851), vol. 1, chap. 36, p. 205.

ened, with erect ears."[41] In the thirteenth century, it becomes a commonplace in devotional texts that audiences pay greater attention to stories about King Arthur and his knights or Charlemagne and his paladins than they do to the Gospels. In the *Evangile de l'Enfance*, for example, the anonymous author announces, "You have often enough heard romances about different people, the lies of this world, and the great Round Table, which King Arthur maintained, which had no truth and which pleased you. Listen now devoutly to this, which is entirely about Jesus Christ, for you will have great profit from it, and there will be great benefit to all as long as the world lasts."[42] The English casuist Thomas Chobham,[43] the theologian and prelate Odo of Châteauroux,[44] the Anglo-French writer Chardri,[45] a certain Brother Angier,[46] and the anonymous authors of the *Miroir du monde*[47] and the *Vie des pères*[48] echo this text's appeal. In the fourteenth century, the Flemish layman Jacob van Maerlant complains, "I know hardly anyone alive today who loves truth, but Tristan and Lancelot, Perceval and Galahad—made-up names and other unborn heroes—this is what the people want to hear about. Trifles of love and fighting are read throughout the world; the Gospel is too hard for us because it is righteous and true."[49] If these men

41. "Videte, fratres, miseriam magnam. Quando locutus sum de Deo, dormitastis; mox ut verba levitatis inservi, evigilantes erectis auribus omnes auscultare coepistis," ibid.

42. "S'avés oï aséz souvent / les romans de diverse gent / et des mençongez de cest monde, / et de la grant Table Roonde, / que li rois Artus maintenoit / ou point de verité n'avoit, / qui vous venoient a talent. / Cestui öés devotement, / que tout est fet de Jesu Crist, / car vous i avréz grant profit; / et grant bien a tous cex sera, / tant con ceste siecle durera," *The Old French "Evangile de l'Enfance,"* ed. Maureen Barry McCann Boulton (Toronto: Pontifical Institute of Mediaeval Studies, 1984), 23, vv. 13–24.

43. Thomas Chobham, *Summa Confessorum*, ed. F. Broomfield (Louvain: Editions Nauwelaerts, 1968), Articulus 6, Quaestio IIa, p. 242.

44. Odo of Châteauroux, *Sermones de tempore et de sanctis et de diversis casibus*, in *Analecta novissima spicilegii solesmensis, altera continuatio*, ed. Jean-Baptiste Pitra, 2 vols. (Paris: Typis Tusculanis, 1885–88), vol. 2, *Tusculana*, from Sermo XVI, p. 227.

45. Chardri, *La Vie de set dormanz*, ed. Brian S. Merilees (London: Anglo-Norman Text Society, 1977), vv. 51–61.

46. Frère Angier, "La Vie de saint Grégoire le Grand traduite du latin par frère Angier, religieux de Sainte-Frideswide," ed. Paul Meyer, *Romania* 12 (1883): 145–208, at 146–47. For discussion of this text's contrast of Christian and chivalric ideals, see Simon Gaunt, *Gender and Genre in Medieval French Literature* (Cambridge: Cambridge University Press, 1995), 185–97.

47. *Miroir du monde*, BNP, fr. 1109, fol. 203, cited in C. V. Langlois, *La Vie en France au Moyen Age de la fin du XIIe au milieu du XIVe siècle*, 4 vols. (Paris: Hachette, 1924–28), vol. 4, *La Vie spirituelle: Enseignements, méditations et controverses d'après les écrits français à l'usage des laïcs*, 150n2.

48. *Vie des pères*, ed. Paul Meyer, in *Histoire littéraire de la France: Ouvrage commencé par les religieux bénédictins de la congrégation de Saint-Maur et continué par les membres de l'Institut* (Académie des Inscriptions et Belles-Lettres), vol. 33, *Suite du quatorzième siècle* (Paris: Imprimerie nationale, 1906), 293–94, at vv. 30–35.

49. "Cum es hi van mi bekent, / die nu leest ende waerheit mint; / maer Tristram ende Lanceloot, / Perchevael, ende Galehoot, / Ghevensde namen ende ongeboren, / hier of willen de lieden

object to stories about Arthur or his knights, it is because these stories are false, not only in the sense that they are about people who never existed but also in the sense that they are useless. Humbert of Romans, a thirteenth-century Dominican friar and master general of his order, expects that an audience should want to listen to a preacher's sermon because his words are important and beneficial in a way in which other speeches are not. He writes, "The utility of the Word should move us to listen to the Word of God. . . . If people listen willingly to teachings that confer health of the body, how much more ought they listen to those that are effective for the salvation of souls."[50] If people are more drawn to light, entertaining works, like Arthurian literature, which do them no good, these authors suggest, it is because they shrink from serious, salutary works, which would challenge them and urge them to improve their lives.

False and useless as it is, these authors observed, romance appeals strongly to audiences' emotions and, indeed, does so more than works that are true and useful. Aelred, the abbot of the Cistercian abbey of Rievaulx, recounts a conversation between an abbot and a novice in his *Speculum caritatis* (1141–42) where this literature comes into question. The novice is troubled that while he was still in the world, he used to weep freely for Christ, but, now that he is a monk, he can barely squeeze out one tear on his behalf. Consoling the novice, the abbot compares the tears the youth shed for Christ, when he was still in the world, to the tears people shed for fictional characters. He refers to how audiences can be affected emotionally when, "in tragedies and vain songs, someone, whose loveable handsomeness, marvelous courage, or gracious affect is proclaimed, is depicted as wronged or oppressed."[51]

---

horen; / truffe van minnen ende van stride / leestemen dor de werelt wide; / die ewangelie es ons te zwaer. / Om dat soe rechte seit ende waer," Jacob van Maerlant, *Leven van Sint Franciscus*, in *Dboec vanden Houte* (Leiden: D. du Mortier en Zoon, 1844), 3–353 at 4, vv. 31–40. See Geert H. M. Claassens and David F. Johnson, "Arthurian Literature in the Medieval Low Countries: An Introduction," in *King Arthur in the Medieval Low Countries*, ed. Geert H. M. Claassens and David F. Johnson (Leuven: Leuven University Press, 2000), 1–34, at 2.

50. "ad audiendum verbum Dei debet movere . . . utilitas verbi . . . Ideo si auditur libenter documentum quod confert salutem corporis, quanto magis ista quae valent ad salutem animae!" Humbert of Romans, *De eruditione predicatorum*, in *Opera: De vita regulari*, ed. J. J. Berthier, 2 vols. (Rome: Typis A. Befani, 1888–89; rpt., Turin: Marietti, 1956), vol. 2, pp. 373–484, at VI, 29, p. 445.

51. "in tragoediis vanisue carminibus quisquam injuriatus fingitur, vel oppressus, cuius amabilis pulchritudo, fortitudo mirabilis, gratiosus praedicetur affectus," Aelred of Rievaulx, *Liber de speculo caritatis*, ed. C. H. Talbot, in *Opera omnia*, ed. A. Hoste and C. H. Talbot, CCCM, vol. 1, 2.17.50, p. 90. With the word "tragedies," the abbot refers not to classical Greek and Roman drama, to which medieval people had no access, but to narratives, like those about Arthur, in which noble characters meet with misfortune. See Henry Ansgar Kelly, *Ideas and Forms of Trag-*

The novice blushes, bows his head, and fixes his eyes on the ground. He acknowledges that he himself has had this reaction to such fictions: "I remember being moved by fables in the vernacular which depict a certain Arthur—I know not exactly who—sometimes to the point of shedding tears."[52] As the abbot sees it, the secular person may weep for Arthur, but his emotion is transitory and meaningless. He may weep, similarly, for Christ, the abbot adds, but he then returns to "his vain, ludicrous, and base former ways, after those sterile tears and momentary attachments."[53] Though these affected individuals pride themselves on their sensibility, their tears are "sterile," he claims, because they result in no action. In contrast, a monk in a religious order may not weep for Christ, but his emotion is lasting and meaningful. He has abandoned the world and dedicated himself to the service of God. Though this monk does not weep, he acts, committing himself, fully, rationally, and intentionally, to serve God in the monastery. What matters, the abbot argues, is, not a passing sensation of love, however intense, but the unwavering commitment to that which one loves over the course of one's life. What matters is, not "these momentary attachments which are not at all dependent on our will, but, rather, . . . the continuous quality of the will itself."[54] Peter of Blois, an archdeacon and secretary to King Henry II of England and Eleanor of Aquitaine and a supporter of the Cistercians, develops this passage from Aelred in his *De confessione* (1190). Citing again "the tragedies, the other songs of the poets, and the verses of the jongleurs,"[55] he writes, "Minstrels relate certain fabulous things about, say, Arthur, Gawain, and Tristan, by which the hearts of those hearing are aroused to compassion and are pricked even to tears."[56] Like Aelred, Peter calls into question the value

---

edy from Aristotle to the Middle Ages (Cambridge: Cambridge University Press, 2005), 86–87, and M. Victoria Guerin, *The Fall of Kings and Princes: Structure and Destruction in Arthurian Tragedy* (Stanford, CA: Stanford University Press, 1995).

52. "in fabulis, quae vulgo de nescio quo finguntur Arthuro, memini me nonnunquam usque ad effusionem lacrimarum fuisse permotum," Aelred of Rievaulx, *Liber de speculo caritatis*, vol. 1, 2.17.51, pp. 90–91.

53. "ad vana et ludicra et sordes pristinas . . . secundum steriles has lacrimas ac momentaneos affectus," ibid., vol. 1, 2.17.50, p. 90.

54. "hos momentaneos affectus, quos minime nostrae subesse voluntati, . . . sed potius secundum continuam ipsius voluntatis qualitatem," ibid., vol. 1, 2.17.53, p. 91.

55. "tragoediis et aliis carminibus poetarum, in joculatorum cantilenis," Peter of Blois, *Liber de confessione sacramentali*, in PL, vol. 207, cols, 1077–92, at col. 1088. On Peter's dependance upon Aelred, see Peter von Moos, *Consolatio: Studien zur mittellateinischen Trostliteratur über den Tod und zum Problem der Christlichen Trauer*, 4 vols. (Munich: Wilhelm Fink Verlag, 1971), vol. 2, 213–14.

56. "sicut de Arturo et Gaugano et Tristanno, fabulosa quaedam referunt histriones, quorum auditu concutiuntur ad compassionem audientium corda, et usque ad lacrimas compunguntur,"

of the tears people shed for God, when they shed tears for fictional characters as well. "You have compassion for God," he observes. "You also have compassion for Arthur."[57] Like Aelred, Peter suggests that these tears of sympathy for Christ's Passion will be for naught if one does not also shed tears of devotion and penitence, out of faith, hope, and charity. While Aelred and Peter do not condemn the stories about Arthur and his knights—on the contrary, they acknowledge the attractive qualities of these characters—they see these stories as stirring, not genuine love and pity, but false and counterfeit sentiments. Emotion is valuable, they suggest, not if it leads one to take pleasure in another person's sorrows, but only if it leads one to grieve for one's own sins and take action to reject them. Emotion is valuable, in other words, not if it causes aesthetic pleasure, but only if it causes penitential pain, and this is what Arthurian romance fails to do.

As critics condemned Arthurian romances, they also condemned the jongleurs who performed these works to popular acclaim. In the twelfth century, ecclesiastical authorities renewed the criticisms that had been levied against performers in Late Antiquity and the Early Middle Ages.[58] Around 1159, John of Salisbury, a secretary to the archbishop of Canterbury and bishop of Chartres, condemns the mimes, magicians, wrestlers, jugglers, and jongleurs active at his time. Though John praises classical, Latin literature, such as the plays of Plautus and Terence, which instructs as well as entertains, he disparages medieval, vernacular literature, which merely amuses. He writes, "Our age, descending to fables and similar empty things, not only prostitutes the ear and heart to vanity but also encourages idleness through the pleasures of eye and ear."[59] Because idle people today cannot bear to be entirely idle, he states, they busy themselves with "the solace of some pleasure,"[60] including "the pleasure in tellers of fables."[61] In the late twelfth and early thirteenth centuries, Peter the Chanter, a master of theology at the cathedral school of Paris, likewise raises concerns

Peter of Blois, *Liber de confessione sacramentali*, col. 1088. "Histriones" could be translated as "actors," but the context here suggests that "minstrels" is more appropriate.

57. "Qui compateris Deo, compateris et Arturo," ibid.

58. See *Corpus iuris canonici*: *Decretum Magister Gratiani*, ed. Aemelius Ludwig Richter and Emil Friedberg, 2 vols. (Leipzig: B. Tauchnitz, 1879; rpt., Graz: Akademische Druck- u. Verlagsanstalt, 1959), vol. 1, Prima Pars, distinctio 86, c. 7, p. 299.

59. "At nostra aetas prolapsa ad fabulas et quaevis inania, non modo aures et cor prostituit vanitati, sed oculorum et aurium voluptate suam mulcet desidiam," John of Salisbury, *Policraticus I–V*, ed. K. S. B. Keats-Rohan, CCCM, I, 8, p. 53. Cf. J. D.

60. "voluptatis solatio," ibid., I, 8, p. 54.

61. "fabulantium gratia," ibid., I, 8, p. 53.

about jongleurs that were reiterated by Thomas Chobham[62] and other academic colleagues.[63] In 1213 and 1214, Robert of Courson, the chancellor of the University of Paris and a papal legate, convened a series of local councils in Paris and other towns in France in order to prepare his fellow clerics for the Fourth Lateran Council, and he drew heavily upon the reforms proposed by these Parisian clerics, including their criticisms of jongleurs.[64] The first three Lateran Councils, in 1123, 1139, and 1179, had made no mention of these performers, yet the Fourth Lateran Council of 1215—convened after the first outpouring of Arthurian romances—declares, "Clerics . . . should not attend the performances of mimes, jongleurs, and actors."[65] By banning clerics from listening to jongleurs at a time when vernacular literature was still primarily something one would have heard rather than read, the council effectively banned them from having access to these literary works at all. Though the Church never prohibited authors from composing Arthurian romances, its prohibition on clerics attending performances of these works made clear that it regarded them as a frivolous and possibly vicious use of their time.

While Renaissance humanists continued to disparage the "old romances" of Arthurian literature, together with heroic poems and books of chivalry, because of their uselessness, they objected to them even more because of their lack of verisimilitude. From Aristotle, these writers knew that poetry (or literature, as we would put it now) was concerned with the "imitation" or the "representation" (*mimēsis*) of reality. Poetry may not *be* true, in the way in which history is true, Aristotle had said, but it should *seem* true.[66] It does not portray people who existed or events that occurred, as history does, but it portrays characters who may exist, and "It relates . . . things that may happen."[67] The pleasure we take in poetry is the pleasure of recognizing that which is being depicted, and this can transpire only if the representation resembles the original. Juan Luis Vives, in his *De institutione feminae christianae* (1524; rev., 1538), complains of "pestiferous books like those in

62. See Thomas Chobham, *Summa confessorum*, ed. Broomfield, 292.

63. See John W. Baldwin, *Masters, Princes, and Merchants: The Social Views of Peter the Chanter and His Circle*, 2 vols. (Princeton, NJ: Princeton University Press, 1970), vol. 1, 198–204.

64. See Robert of Courson, *Summa*, bk. 10, chap. 10. There is no critical edition of this text. See Page, *The Owl and the Nightingale*, 195.

65. "Clerici . . . mimis, ioculatoribus et histrionibus non intendant," *Decrees of the Ecumenical Councils*, ed. Norman P. Tanner, 2 vols. (Washington, DC: Georgetown University Press, 1990), vol. 1, Nicaea I to Lateran V, "Lateran IV," pp. 227–71, canon 16, p. 243.

66. Aristotle, *Poetics*, trans. Richard Janko (Indianapolis: Hackett, I, 3 (ix), (51b5), p. 12.

67. Ibid.

Spain—*Amadís, Esplandián, Florisando, Tirant, Tristán*—in which there is no end of absurdities,"[68] of *Lancelot du Lac* in France, and of similar books in Flanders and other countries. In such works, he protests, knights perform feats that would be impossible for any man to accomplish. He writes of such heroes, "This one killed twenty by himself, that one thirty; another, pierced with six hundred wounds and left for dead, immediately rose up and, restored the next day to health and strength, prostrated two giants in single combat."[69] Readers of these works claim to take delight in the accounts of such feats of arms, but Vives asks, "What pleasure can there be in the things they invent with such manifest foolishness?"[70] He denies that anyone who has ever read good books, such as the writings of Cicero and Saint Jerome, could enjoy such material.[71] Desiderius Erasmus[72] and Michel de Montaigne[73] both echo Vives's point, comparing legends about King Arthur and Lancelot unfavorably to classical literature. If one is to read literature, these humanists agree, one should devote one's time to serious, learned works, satisfying to scholarly audiences, rather than to idle, frivolous texts, appealing to the ignorant.

Given its lack of verisimilitude, many authors of the seventeenth and eighteenth centuries warned that romance would lead its readers astray. Young men, it was feared, would fail to be content with the careers to which they are destined.[74] Most famously, the hero of Miguel

68. "de pestiferis libris, cuiusmodi sunt in Hispania Amadisus Splandianus, Florisandus, Tirantus, Tristanus, quarum ineptiarum nullus est finis," Juan Luis Vives, *De institutione feminae christianae*, ed. C. Fantazzi and C. Matheeussen (Leiden: E. J. Brill, 1996), 44.

69. "Hic occidit solus viginti, ille triginta; alius sexcentis vulneribus confossus ac pro mortuo iam derelictus, surgit protinus et postridie sanitati viribusque redditus, singulari certamine duos Gigantes prosternit," ibid., 46.

70. "quae potest esse delectatio in rebus quas tam aperte et stulte confingunt?" ibid.

71. For similar remarks, see André de Rivaudeau, *Aman, de la perfidie* (1561), in *Aman, tragédie sainte*, ed. Keith Cameron (Geneva: Droz, 1969), 58, and François de Belleforest, *L'Histoire des Neuf Rois Charles* (Paris: impr. par F. Le Blanc pour P. L'Huillier, 1568) (cited in Michel Simonin, "La Disgrâce d'Amadis," *Studi Francesi* 28 [1984]: 1–35, at 25–26).

72. Desiderius Erasmus, *Institutio principis Christiani*, in *Opera omnia*, ed. Jean Leclerc, 10 vols. (Ludguni Batavorum: Impensis Petri Vander, 1703; rpt., London: Gregg Press, 1961–62), vol. 4, pp. 561–612, at chap. 2, p. 587.

73. Michel de Montaigne, "De l'institution des enfants," in *Essais*, ed. Jean Balsamo, Michel Magnien, and Catherine Magnien-Simonin, Bibliothèque de la Pléiade (Paris: Gallimard, 2007), 150–84, at 182, and "Des livres," ibid., 427–41, at 430. See Rothstein, *Reading in the Renaissance: Amadis de Gaule and the Lessons of Memory* (Newark: University of Deleware Press, 1999), 121–23 for discussion. See also Francesco Montorsi, "'Un fatras de livres a quoy l'enfance s'amuse': Lectures de jeunesse et romans de chevalerie au XVI siècle," *Camenulae* 4 (February 2010): 1–10.

74. See Georges May, *Le Dilemme du roman au XVIIIe siècle: Etude sur les rapports du roman et de la critique, 1715–1761* (New Haven, CT: Yale University Press, 1963); Françoise Weil, *L'Interdiction du roman et de la librarie, 1728–1750* (Paris: Presses Universitaires de France, 1986); and Henri Coulet, "Le Topos du roman corrupteur dans les romans français du XVIIIe siècle," in *L'Epreuve du*

de Cervantes Saavedra's *El ingenioso hidalgo don Quijote de la Mancha* (1605–15), having immersed himself in books of chivalry, dons an old suit of armor and sallies forth on his nag to become a knight errant, to disastrous results. His niece suggests, "Señor uncle, . . . would it not be better to stay peacefully in your house and not wander around the world searching for bread made from something better than wheat?"[75] Would it not be better, she proposes, to be satisfied with a humble but good situation in life and not to seek a superior, but elusive role? The novelist Charles Sorel, in his *De la connoissance des bons livres* (1671), bemoans the fate of young men who, as a result of reading books of chivalry, like Don Quixote, lose their minds, abandon their studies, and fail to choose "some useful profession,"[76] instead believing "that the most beautiful life is that of knights errant."[77] Given that young men cannot have lives like Amadís of Gaul, he asks, "What is the good of representing that which is not and cannot be? What good examples does one find in that which cannot happen?"[78] By the same token, young women readers of romance, it was thought, would fail to be content with the marriages arranged for them.[79] In his *Traité de l'education des filles* (1687), François Fénelon, the archbishop of Cambrai and tutor in the royal household, writes that, in romances, women are like "imaginary princesses, . . . always charming, always adored, always above all

lecteur: Livres et lectures dans le roman d'ancien régime; Actes du VIIIe Colloque de la Société d'analyse de la topique romanesque, Louvain-Anvers (19–21 mai 1994), ed. Jan Herman and Paul Pelckmans (Louvain: Société pour l'information grammaticale, 1995), 175–90.

75. "¿señor tío, . . . No será mejor estarse pacífico en su casa y no irse por el mundo a buscar pan de trastrigo?" Miguel de Cervantes, *Don Quijote de la Mancha*, ed. John Jay Allen, 2 vols., 6th ed. (Madrid: Edicions Cátedra, 1984), I, 7, p. 129. I am following, with alterations, Edith Grossman's translation of this work in *Don Quixote* (New York: Ecco, 2003; rpt., New York: Harper Perennial, 2005).

76. "quelque profession utile," Charles Sorel, *De la connoissance des bons livres; ou, Examen de plusieurs auteurs*, ed. Lucia Moretti Cenerini (Rome: Bulzoni, 1974), 96.

77. "que la plus belle vie est celle des Chevaliers Errans," ibid., 98–99.

78. "A quoi sert de representer ce qui n'est point et ce qui ne peut estre? Quels bons exemples trouve t'on en ce qui ne peut arriver?" ibid., 98.

79. On this concern, see Vives, *De institutione feminae christianae*, ed. Fantazzi and Matheeussen, vol. 1, p. 44; François de la Noue, *Discours politiques et militaires*, ed. F. E. Sutcliffe (Geneva: Librairie Droz, 1967), sixième discours, p. 169; Pierre de Bourdeille, seigneur de Brantôme, *Vies des Dames galantes*, ed. Pascal Pia (Paris: Gallimard, 1981), 535; Roger Ascham, *The Schoolmaster*, in *English Works of Roger Ascham*, ed. William Aldis Wright (London: Cambridge University Press, 1904), 171–303, at 80; Sorel, *De la connoissance des bons livres*, ed. Moretti Cenerini, 97–98; Morvan de Bellegarde, *Deuxième lettre curieuse de littérature et de morale*, 124; and Armand-Pierre Jacquin, *Entretiens sur les romans: Ouvrage moral et critique* (Paris: Chez Duchesne, 1755), 337. For discussion, see Carla Peterson, *The Determined Reader: Gender and Culture in the Novel from Napoleon to Victoria* (New Brunswick, NJ: Rutgers University Press, 1986), and Kate Flint, *The Woman Reader, 1837–1914* (Oxford: Clarendon Press, 1993).

necessities."[80] In real life, however, they are wives, occupied not with the rapturous love of men around them but with the domestic management of their homes. He exclaims of a young female reader of romance, "What disgust for her to descend from heroism to the lowest detail of the household!"[81] Having read works that promise a more exalted life than that in store for them, young women were said to enter into love affairs, imagining themselves to be Ariosto's Angelica and their lovers Angelica's handsome Medoro.[82] As the abbé Armand-Pierre Jacquin sees it, in his *Entretiens sur les romans* (1755), romances not only encourage readers to enter into love affairs, but they teach them how to love. He writes, "A still-novice heart learns in these romances the theory of love, that is, learns to sigh, to formulate desires, and to conduct intrigues of gallantry. . . . The first object will soon fix this still-floating heart."[83] As our emotions are naturally inchoate, it is romances that teach us to call a certain emotion "love" and to fix that "love" upon whomever one happens to meet, even in the absence of a marital tie. For that reason, in *La Nouvelle Héloïse* (1761), Jean-Jacques Rousseau proclaims, "Never has a chaste girl read romances."[84] According to these critics, romances not only mislead readers as to the nature of reality, but, by filling them with ideas about chivalry and courtly love, encourage them to neglect their duties in society.

If authors of the nineteenth century continued to disdain romance, it was not because they perceived this genre as lacking verisimilitude, as critics of earlier centuries had done, but because they perceived it as lacking what was now called "realism." In 1835, the art historian Gustave Planche used this term for the first time when he expressed admiration for "the realism of Rembrandt,"[85] whose "human truth"[86] he

80. "ces princesses imaginaires, . . . toujours charmantes, toujours adorées, toujours audessus de tous les besoins," François Fénelon, *Traité de l'éducation des filles*, ed. Bernard Jolibert (Paris: Klincksieck, 1994), chap. 2, p. 40.

81. "Quel dégoût pour elle de descendre de l'héroïsme jusqu'au plus bas détail du ménage!" ibid.

82. See Etienne Bonnot de Condillac, *Essai sur l'origine des connoissances humaines*, in *Oeuvres philosophiques de Condillac* (Paris: Chez les Librairies Associés, 1793), vol. 1, 85.

83. "Un coeur encore novice apprend dans ces Romans la théorie de l'amour; c'est-à-dire apprend à soupirer, à former des désirs et à conduire des intrigues de galanterie . . . [L]e premier objet fixera bientôt ce coeur encore flottant," Jacquin, *Entretiens sur les romans*, bk. 4, pp. 318–19.

84. "Jamais fille chaste n'a lu de Romans," Jean-Jacques Rousseau, *La Nouvelle Héloïse*, in *Oeuvres complètes*, ed. Bernard Gagnebin and Marcel Raymond, Bibliothèque de la Pléiade, 5 vols. (Paris: Gallimard, 1969), vol. 3, Preface, p. 6.

85. "le réalisme de Rembrandt," Gustave Planche, "L'Ecole anglaise en 1835: Exposition de Somerset-House," *Revue des deux mondes* 2 (1835): 675–76.

86. "verité humaine," ibid.

contrasted positively to the "poetic ideality"[87] of neoclassical painters. The art critic Fernand Desnoyers, in an article called "Du Réalisme," likewise praises the tendency of artists like Gustave Courbet to paint, not goddesses or nymphs, who have by now become tired commonplaces, but something that they have in fact beheld, such as "a country scene, something ordinary, of an everyday sort."[88] To represent the "real" world of our day, as one sees it, as opposed to the "ideal" world of an earlier time, is to represent middle-class and lower-class people, as opposed to royal and divine personages, and to accord these commoners a dignity that they have not been granted before. For realist literary critics as well as realist art critics, the novel was the genre best suited to report what society is actually like. In *Adam Bede* (1859), George Eliot expresses her preference for the Dutch masters, with their depictions of homely old women by their flower pots or awkward bridegrooms at a village wedding, over neoclassical painters inclined to depict "cloud-borne angels . . . prophets, sibyls, and heroic warriors."[89] Like these Dutch masters, she resolves to depict "real breathing men and women," as opposed to "things as they never have been and never will be."[90] Honoré de Balzac similarly determines to represent people as they truly are, by which he means as they are situated in their society. In the "Avant-propos" to his *Comédie humaine* (1842), he keeps in mind that while "Romance ought to be the 'better world,'"[91] namely, that of the "beautiful ideal,"[92] "history is—or should be—that which is."[93] While romance represents the ideal, as imagined by the author, he indicates, history (or the "realist" novel) reflects the real, as it has imposed itself on this author. It was only in the late eighteenth and early nineteenth centuries that "the real," as Eliot and Balzac resolve to depict it, began to be construed in opposition to "the ideal," that the one came to be understood as existing in the world and the other as existing only in one's mind, and that the one therefore came to be understood as possessing an ontological validity that the other did not. It was only at this

87. "idéalité poétique," ibid.

88. "une scène de campagne, quelque chose d'ordinaire, de l'espèce quotidienne," Fernand Desnoyers, "Du Réalisme," *L'Artiste* (December 9, 1855): 197–200; rpt. in Fernand Desnoyers, *Salon des refusés: La Peinture* (Paris: Azur Dutil, 1863), 108–27, at 123.

89. George Eliot, *Adam Bede*, ed. Margaret Reynolds (Harmondsworth: Penguin Classics, 2008), book II, chap. 17, p. 197.

90. ibid.

91. *"le roman doit être 'le monde meilleur,'"* Honoré de Balzac, *La Comédie humaine*, ed. Pierre-Georges Castex, 12 vols., Bibliothèque de la Pléiade (Paris: Gallimard, 1976–81), vol. 1, foreword, 7–20, at 9. Balzac is quoting Madame de Staël here.

92. "le beau idéal," ibid.

93. "L'histoire est ou devrait être ce qu'elle fut," ibid.

time that someone who represented a man or woman who surpasses other people would be reproached as having "idealized" or even "romanticized" that individual.

Even in the twentieth century, critics have continued to denigrate romance for failing to represent everyday reality. In his celebrated *Mimesis: The Representation of Reality in Western Literature* (1946), Erich Auerbach observes that in the *chansons de geste*, a knight functions as a member of his society, whether by advising his lord or by protecting his lands against invaders, but in a romance, like Chrétien de Troyes' *Yvain*, he functions as an autonomous individual. After riding about all day on his horse, Chrétien's knight Calogrenant is said to arrive at a castle, where he receives hospitality for the night. Auerbach remarks, "About the practical conditions and circumstances which would make the existence of such a castle in complete isolation possible and compatible with common experience, nothing is said."[94] We do not hear about the king reigning over the lands, who would have granted the castle to this lord or his family in exchange for their military service. We do not hear about the peasants toiling in the fields, who would have provided the food that Calogrenant later eats for dinner. "Such an idealization leads us very far from the imitation of reality,"[95] Auerbach states. When a knight like Calogrenant sets forth, he does so not to serve any purpose for those around him, but merely to seek adventures. Insofar as romance elevates the pursuit of honor as a value unto itself, separate from any positive effect knightly deeds might have upon society, he writes, "the contact with the reality of the world [*Weltwirklichkeit*] becomes ever more fictitious and devoid of purpose."[96] With reality defined as the outer world, in its political, economic, and social specificity, romance, which privileges the inner world, encourages what he calls a "turning away from reality"[97] and a "flight into fairy-tale."[98] Ian Watt, in his influential 1957 study *The Rise of the Novel*, raises similar objections to romance. As Auerbach objects to knights who pursue adventures outside of society, Watt objects to knights who pursue

94. "von allen praktischen Bedingungen und Umständen, die die Existenz eines solchen Schlosses in völliger Einsamkeit möglich und mit der gewöhnlichen Erfahrung vereinbar machen könnten, wird nichts gesagt," Erich Auerbach, *Mimesis: Dargestellte Wirklichkeit in der abendländischen Literatur* (Bern: A. Francke: 1946), 134–35.

95. "Eine solche Idealisierung führt weit fort von der Nachahmung des Wirklichen," ibid., 135.

96. "die Berührungen mit der Weltwirklichkeit immer fictiver und immer zweckfreier wurden," ibid., 138.

97. "der Abwendung von Wirklichen," ibid.

98. "ein Ausweichen ins Märchen," ibid., 136.

love affairs outside of marriage. He writes, "It is not surprising that a knight errant should typically postpone marriage, which would root him in society, requiring him to play the role of husband and father, in favor of courtly love, which allows him to continue to function autonomously in the world."[99] It was only when literary heroes began to marry and have families, as they did first in Puritan England, he believes, that "the code of romantic love began to accommodate itself to religious, social, and psychological reality."[100] There is only one reality, these critics assume, and romance neglects to depict it.

In the present day, what is known as "literary fiction," whose roots lie in the realist novel, has triumphed over romance from a critical perspective. While the fantastical literary tradition of continental Europe (E. T. A. Hoffmann, Nikolai Gogol, Guy de Maupassant, Franz Kafka, and Italo Calvino) and the magical realist traditions of Latin America and other non-Western countries (Gabriel García Márquez, Jorge Luis Borges, and Salman Rushdie) remain respected,[101] this esteem has done little to lift the fortunes of fantasy or other genre fiction elsewhere in the world. The mainstream novels that are reviewed in prominent newspapers, that are taught in colleges and universities, and that receive prestigious literary prizes still focus disproportionately on the everyday reality of ordinary people and events. Modernist and postmodernist novelists may set themselves against their realist peers, but they insist even more vehemently upon the quotidian aspect of existence. The frustration of many academics and critics with romance was perhaps best expressed years ago by Henry James, who writes in his essay on "The Art of Fiction" (1884) that he can evaluate what one might call a realist novel, but not a romance. With a realist novel, he states, he can compare its depiction of the world in which he lives to his own observation of this world, saying, "at successive steps, . . . Yes or No, as it may be, to what the artist puts before me."[102] With a romance, he cannot do so because it makes no effort to depict that world in the first place. Without any standard by which the veracity of its account can be judged, James writes, romance resembles a hot-air balloon when the cable tying it to the ground has been cut. Though the passenger in the

99. Watt, *Rise of the Novel*, 136.

100. Ibid.

101. See Tzvetan Todorov, *Introduction à la littérature fantastique* (Paris: Editions du Seuil, 1970) for this version of the fantastic.

102. Henry James, "The Art of Fiction," *Longman's Magazine* 4 (September 1884): 502–21; rpt., *The Victorian Art of Fiction*, ed. Olmsted, 287–306, at 303.

balloon may be exhilarated by the ascent into the sky, he warns, "it is by the rope we know where we are, and from the moment that cable is cut we are at large and unrelated."[103] Because romance is based on what the author has invented, and not on what he or she has observed, it causes the reader to lose his or her bearings. The danger of romance remains, as it always has been, the danger of leaving this world and drifting, as in a balloon, into another realm.

The Case for Romance

Even as medieval clerics and their successors criticized romance, defenders of this genre insisted that it did, in fact, transcend literature, though in a manner different from what one might expect. It is not that late antique and medieval thinkers ever condemned fiction entirely. Augustine maintains that when Horace represents mice, weasels, and foxes as speaking to each other,[104] no one is so foolish as to believe that such creatures actually communicate in this way and, hence, no one is deceived by such a fiction. "For not everything that we fabricate is a lie,"[105] he writes. He who lies intends to lie, and the author of such fictions has no such intention in mind. In depicting something that did not and could not happen, this type of fiction not only does not deceive, Augustine acknowledges, but it signifies something true: "When . . . our fiction refers to some signification, it is not a lie but a kind of figure of truth."[106] Men attribute human deeds and words to irrational animals, he explains, "so that, with fictitious narrations of this kind but true significations, they may intimate what they wish in a more commending manner."[107] As much as Macrobius disapproves of fictions that are invented to give pleasure to their audiences, he approves of "fables . . . [that] are invented . . . for the sake of exhorting

103. Henry James, preface to *The American: An Authoritative Text, Backgrounds, and Sources*, ed. James W. Tuttleton (New York: Norton Critical Editions, 1978), 10–11.

104. See Horace, *Sermones* II, 6, vv. 77–115 and *Epistola* I, 7, vv. 29–33.

105. "Non enim omne quod fingimus mendacium est," Augustine, *Quaestiones Evangeliorum*, ed. Mutzenbecher, II, 51, p. 116.

106. "Cum . . . fictio nostra refertur ad aliquam significationem, non est mendacium sed aliqua figura veritatis," ibid.

107. "ut eius modi fictis narrationibus, sed veracibus significationibus quod vellent commendatius intimarent," Augustine, *Ad Consentium contra mendacium*, in *Sancti Aureli Augustini "De fide et symbolo," "De fide et operibus,"* CSEL, vol. 41 (sect. 5, pars. 3), ed. Joseph Zycha (Prague: F. Tempsky, 1900), 467–528, at XIII, 28, pp. 508–9.

people to fruitful action."[108] Though learned men of the Middle Ages did not champion Arthurian literature per se, many among them acknowledged that fiction could be beneficial to readers if it illustrated a moral principle; if it appealed to their reason rather than to their emotion; and if it restored the listless, so they could prove useful once more. In the sixteenth and seventeenth centuries, in response to the charge that romance lacks verisimilitude, its defenders argued that it aims to represent people, not as they are, in all of their moral failings, but as they should be and, in doing so, inspires readers to want to imitate them. In the eighteenth and nineteenth centuries, in response to the charge that romance is not realistic, its defenders asserted that romance strives to depict people, not as they are, in the sense of beings defined by the society in which they live, but as they yearn to be, that is, as beings capable of far more than their environments allow. While romance represents the danger of fiction, it represents the promise of fiction as well.

Even as learned men regretted the way in which stories about Arthur could overshadow those about Christ, they themselves used illustrative anecdotes (*exempla*) to enliven their sermons. Since the Church Fathers,[109] it had been recognized that Christ taught the people, not just by providing precepts for them to obey, but by recounting parables for them to use as models for their behavior. As Gregory the Great had stated, "Examples of the faithful convert many more minds of listeners than words of teaching."[110] It was during the late twelfth and early thirteenth centuries that preachers began to use exempla on a regular basis in their sermons.[111] Caesarius of Heisterbach's abbot may lament the fact that he could only awaken his sleeping audience with a reference to Arthur, but Jacques de Vitry, one of the most celebrated preachers of the thirteenth century, recommends that one awaken such an audience with an exemplum. He observes of preachers, "They know

108. "Fabulae adhortantis . . . in bonam frugem gratia repertae sunt," Macrobius, *In somnium Scipionis*, ed. Willis, I, 2, 7–8, p. 5.

109. See Saint Jerome, *Commentarium in Esiam Libri I–XI*, CCSL, vol. 73, prologue, 1–4.

110. "nonnunquam mentes audientium plus exempla fidelium quam docentium verba convertunt," Gregory the Great, *Homiliae in Evangelia*, ed. Raymond Etax, CCSL, vol. 141, Homilia XXXVIII, 15, p. 373.

111. On the usefulness of exempla, see also Gerald of Wales, *Gemma ecclesiastica*, in *Opera*, ed. J. S. Brewer, 8 vols. (London: Longmans, 1861–91; rpt., Nendelm: Kraus Reprints, 1964–66), vol. 2, I, p. 6; Alan of Lille, *Summa de arte praedicatoria*, PL 210, cols. 111–98, at cols. 113–14; and Stephen of Bourbon, *Tractatus de diversis materiis praedicabilibus*, in *Anecdotes historiques, légendes et apologues, tirés du recueil inédit d'Étienne de Bourbon, Dominicain du XIIIe siècle*, ed. A. Lecoy de La Marche (Paris: Librairie Renouard, 1877), I, pp. 3–4.

through experience how much fruit will come forth from this manner of fictitious examples [*fabulosis exemplis*] to lay and simple people, not only for their edification but also for their recreation, especially when they are tired and, overcome by tedium, begin to nod off."[112] So effective were exempla in attracting the attention of audiences that preachers were apparently tempted to recount tales that would delight them without offering instruction. Jacques warns, "We must banish fruitless fables and the curious songs of poets from our sermons,"[113] especially, he adds, "scurrilous . . . and indecent words."[114] Humbert of Romans inveighs against "preachers who speak vain things in familiar speech, in the manner of secular people,"[115] and who proffer "trifles or fables,"[116] so that people attend their sermons, not to profit from them, but solely for the pleasure of listening. Preachers occasionally drew their exempla from literary works, such as classical fables or the *Roman de Renart*,[117] but they were advised to draw them, instead, from pious works, such as the *Vitae fratrum*, patristic writings, and saints' lives, in order to avoid making sermons excessively diverting. When a preacher finds it necessary to resort to "some very edifying fable,"[118] Humbert recommends that he do so carefully: "These secular words . . . should be uttered rarely, and, when they are uttered, something spiritually useful should be mixed in with them."[119] By joining the precept and the exemplum, Humbert states, the preacher makes his sermon resemble a dish that is at once nutritious and, hence, "useful"[120] to its audience and tasty, "so that it will be consumed more willingly and will be digested better."[121]

112. "Per experientiam noverunt quantus fructus proveniet ex hujusmodi fabulosis exemplis proveniat laicis et simplicibus personis, non solum ad aedificationem, sed ad recreationem, maxime quando fatigati et taedio affecti incipiunt dormitare," Jacques de Vitry, *Sermones vulgares*, in *Analecta novissima spicilegii solesmensis, altera continuatio*, ed. J. B. Pitra, 2 vols. (Paris: Roger et Chernowitz, 1885–88), vol. 2, *Tusculana*, 189–93, at 192.

113. "infructuosas enim fabulas et curiosa poetarum carmina a sermonibus nostris debemus relegare," ibid.

114. "scurrilia . . . aut obscaena verba," ibid., 193.

115. "praedicatores qui in familiaribus colloquutionibus loquuntur vana, ad modum saecularum," Humbert of Romans, *De eruditione praedicatorum*, ed. Berthier, VII, 39, p. 463.

116. "nugas vel fabula," ibid., VII, 39, p. 465.

117. See John Flinn, *"Le Roman de Renart" dans la littérature française et dans les littératures étrangères au Moyen Age* (Toronto: University of Toronto Press, 1963), 485–528.

118. "fabula aliqua multum edificatoria," Humbert of Romans, *De dono timoris*, ed. Christine Boyer, CCCM, vol. 218 (Turnhout: Brepols, 2008), prologue, 6.

119. "verba saecularia . . . rara dicantur, et cum dicuntur, aliqua spiritualis utilitas admisceatur eisdem," Humbert of Romans, *De eruditione praedicatorum*, ed. Berthier, VII, 40, p. 467.

120. "utile," ibid., I, 7, p. 395.

121. "ut libentius sumantur, et melius incorporentur," ibid., I, 7, p. 396.

So long as preachers aimed to instruct their audiences, they were allowed to tell them entertaining tales.

While learned men criticized stories about Arthur that appealed to audiences' emotions, they praised illustrative stories about animals and human beings that appealed to their reason. Fables, the twelfth-century philosopher William of Conches affirms, convey factual falsehoods, designed to delight readers, but also moral truths designed to instruct them. He writes of Aesop, "Through the fables that he composed, we are exhorted to some instruction in morals. . . . Even if the fable signifies nothing true, by way of it he indicates a moral point."[122] In Late Antiquity, when Augustine was reading the *Aeneid*, he famously wept for Dido and forgot about his own erring self. Yet commentators like Fulgentius and Macrobius argued that Virgil's great poem, if approached properly, can lead the reader not to weep for its characters, but to think about his own soul. In the twelfth century, members of the so-called School of Chartres revived this allegorical reading of the *Aeneid* and of fiction in general. Pseudo-Bernardus Silvestris writes that when Aeneas succumbs to "Dido, that is, Lust,"[123] "we are recalled from the appetite for illicit things."[124] When Dido, abandoned by Aeneas, consigns herself to the pyre, he states, we learn that "abandoned, Lust ceases and, consumed by the heat of manliness, passes into ashes, that is, into solitary thoughts."[125] According to Pseudo-Bernardus's interpretation, Dido and Aeneas are, not real people to whom one responds emotionally, but allegorical personifications to which one responds rationally. Insofar as poetry conveys a truth, like the necessity of forsaking Lust, he affirms, it constitutes not just poetry but philosophy. "To the extent that he writes about the nature of human life," he states of Virgil, "he is a philosopher."[126] While, as poetry, the *Aeneid* causes delight in its reader through its verbal ornaments, he asserts, as philosophy, it also brings him profit through its moral lessons. The classical tradition of the "introductions to authors" (*accessus ad auctores*), which

122. "Per fabulas enim, quas ille composuit, ad aliquam morum instructionem exortamur. . . . Per hanc igitur fabulam, etsi veri nichil significeret, per eam tamen innuit hanc moralitatem," William of Conches, *Excursus*, quoted in Peter Dronke, *Fabula: Explorations of the Uses of Myth in Medieval Platonism* (Leiden: Brill, 1974), 17. William's text remains unedited.

123. "Dido, id est libido," *Commentum Quod Dicitur Bernardi Silvestris Super Sex Libros "Eneidos" Virgilii / The Commentary on the First Six Books of the "Aeneid" of Virgil Commonly Attributed to Bernardus Silvestris*, ed. Julian Ward Jones and Elizabeth Frances Jones (Lincoln: Univeristy of Nebraska Press, 1977), bk. 1, chap. 13, p. 12.

124. "ab appetitu illicitorum revocamur," ibid., preface, 3.

125. "Desueta enim libido defficit et fervore virilitatis consumpta in favillam, id est in solas cogitationes, transit," ibid., bk. 4, p. 25.

126. "scribit ergo in quantum est philosophus humane vite naturam," ibid., preface, p. 3.

were composed either as prefaces to the authors' writings or as independent treatises, was renewed in the twelfth century. These introductions had traditionally cataloged the basic facts about the authors, including their names and the titles and subjects of their works, but they now increasingly identified, in addition, the "intention of the writer" (*intentio scribentis*), the "utility" (*utilitas*) of the work, and the "part of philosophy to which it belongs" (*cui parti philosophiae supponatur*).[127] As the medieval masters of the *accessus ad auctores* saw it, a poem is composed with a conscious intention; it serves a useful purpose by helping the reader to understand human beings and to learn how he should best act; and, in doing so, it can be considered a form of philosophy (especially practical philosophy, or ethics). Even in the fourteenth century, Dante Alighieri will ascribe a utilitarian purpose to his *Commedia*. "The end . . . is to remove those living in this life from the state of misery and to lead them to the state of happiness,"[128] he writes, for which reason, "The genus of philosophy under which we here proceed . . . is the business of morals or ethics."[129] Giovanni Boccaccio states more generally, "Fiction [*fabula*] is a form of discourse, which, under a figure, provides examples or demonstrations of a point. Its outward covering having been removed, the intention of the author is exposed. If then from under the veil of fable, something wise is discovered, it will not have been superfluous to compose fables."[130] So long as authors appealed to their audience's reason and not to their emotion (or at least not *just* to their emotion), in order to urge them to amend their lives, they were allowed to tell entertaining stories.

While learned men never argue that Arthurian romance leads to the truth, as they maintain that classical epic does, they do occasionally defend what appears to be romance for providing respite to a weary mind. Even the clerics who condemned jongleurs acknowledged that

127. See Bernard of Utrecht, *Commentum in Theodolum*, in *Accessus ad auctores, Bernard d'Utrecht, Conrad Hirsau: Dialogus super auctores*, ed. R. B. C. Huygens (Leiden: Brill, 1970), 55–69, at 59 and 66–67. This seems to have come from the first version of Boethius's commentary on Prophyry's *Isagoge*. See also Edwin A. Quain, *The Medieval "Accessus ad auctores"* (New York: Fordham University Press, 1986).

128. "finis . . . est removere viventes in hac vita de statu miserie et perducere ad statum felicitatis," Dante Alighieri, *Epistola a Cangrande*, ed. Enzo Cecchini (Florence: Giunti, 1995), 15, p. 16.

129. "Genus vero phylosophie sub quo hic . . . proceditur, est morale negotium sive ethica," ibid.

130. "Fabula est exemplaris seu demonstrativa sub figmento locutio, cuius amoto cortice, patet intentio fabulantis. Et sic, si sub velamento fabuloso sapidum comperiatur aliquid, non erit supervacaneum fabulas edisse," Giovanni Boccaccio, *Genealogie deorum gentilium*, ed. Vittorio Zaccaria, in *Tutte le opere di Giovanni Boccaccio* (Milan: Mondadori, 1998), vols. 7–8, pt. 2, bk. XIV, chap. 9, p. 1412.

their performances could be helpful in teaching people about the deeds of princes and the lives of saints and in comforting them when they are ill or depressed. John of Salisbury may be making a concession to contemporary vernacular literature when he writes, "It is pleasant and it does not depart from decency for a worthy man to delight occasionally in modest mirth. . . . Truly, the mind of a wise man notices that which is profitable or fitting in individual cases, nor does he flee tales, narrations, or spectacles in general, so long as they have the requirements of virtue and honorable utility."[131] Thomas Chobham writes of jongleurs that, "If . . . they sing the deeds of princes and other useful things with their instruments in order to provide solace to people, . . . they can be tolerated."[132] It was generally recognized that just as the body needs rest, so does the mind need recreation in order to restore itself. In the *Tacuinum sanitatis*, a fourteenth-century handbook on health, it is said that "a reciter of fictions [*recitator fabularum*]"[133] will know how to bring pleasure to an audience, "which in turn will purify people's blood, enhance digestion, and promote untroubled sleep."[134] Physiological and psychological theories of the time acknowledged the usefulness of "solace" (*solatium*) in enabling people to function well and even, on occasion, the usefulness of delight simply in improving their lives.[135] While some secular rulers, like Philip Augustus, shunned jongleurs, others, such as Eleanor of Aquitaine, Richard the Lion-Heart, and even the sainted Louis IX, openly provided patronage to them. Despite the Fourth Lateran Council's prohibition against clerical support for jongleurs, bishops numbered among their most important patrons.[136] Thomas Aquinas asserts that mirth is useful insofar as it affords us pleasure and relaxation, though he adds, "Pleasure and relaxation are sought in human life, not for their own sake, but for the sake

131. "Iocundum quidem est et ab honesto non recedit virum probum quandoque modesta hilaritate mulceri, sed ignominiosum est gravitatem huiuscemodi lascivia frequenter resolve. . . . Verumtamen quid in singulis prosit vel deceat, animus sapientis advertit, nec apologos refugit, aut narrationes, aut quaecunque spectacula, dum virtutis, aut honestae utilitatis habeant instrumentum," John of Salisbury, *Policraticus*, ed. Keats-Rohan, bk. 1, chap. 8, p. 55.

132. "Si . . . cantant instrumentis suis gesta principum et alia utilia ut faciunt solatia hominibus, . . . bene possunt sustineri tales," Thomas Chobham, *Summa confessorum*, ed. Broomfield, 292.

133. Quoted in Glending Olson, "The Profits of Pleasure," in *The Cambridge History of Literary Criticism*, vol. 2, *The Middle Ages*, ed. Alastair Minnis and Ian Johnson (Cambridge: Cambridge University Press, 2005), 275–87, at 278.

134. Ibid.

135. See Glending Olson, "The Medieval Theory of Literature for Refreshment and Its Use in the Fabliau Tradition," *Studies in Philology* 71, no. 31 (1974): 291–313.

136. See Peter the Chanter, *Verbum abbreviatum*, quoted in Baldwin, *Masters, Princes, and Merchants*, vol. 2, 140.

of operation."[137] Jongleurs were allowed to tell amusing stories, if only to enable people to return, restored, to their useful business.

In the sixteenth century, even as some humanists criticized the "old romances," heroic poems, and books of chivalry for their failure to represent people as they are, others among them praised these genres for their success in representing people as they should be. While Aristotle had affirmed that poetry should imitate reality, he had also affirmed that "the characters should be good"[138] and that the poet, like a good portrait painter, should depict people "as finer than they are."[139] It is clear that the reality he believed the poet should imitate is not that of an everyday individual in his or her daily life, but that of an exemplary type undertaking extraordinary and admirable feats. Though Vives and his cohort complain that contemporary heroic works represent knights more valiant than any knight could ever be, other humanists contend that in doing so they propose exemplary models of chivalry. Torquato Tasso, in his *Discorsi dell'arte poetica e in particolare sopra il poema eroico* (1562–65, published 1587), finds the epitome of courage in Achilles, of prudence in Ulysses, of piety in Aeneas, "and, to come to our times, of loyalty in Amadís, [and] of constancy in [Ariosto's] Bradamante."[140] Sir Philip Sidney inquires rhetorically in his *Defence of Poesy* (written ca. 1579–80, published 1595), if Nature has ever brought forth so right a prince as Xenophon's Cyrus, so excellent a man as Virgil's Aeneas, or "so valiant a man as Orlando."[141] Precisely the heroes whom some humanists criticize on account of the exaggerated quality of their virtues, these authors defend on account of their perfections. Lodovico Castelvetro suggests in his *Poetica d'Aristotele vulgarizzata e sposita* (1570), "When a poet has not represented things as they are or were, the poet can defend himself by responding that they are represented as they ought to be."[142] The purpose of such literary

137. "delectatio autem et quies non propter se quaeruntur in humana vita, sed propter operationem," Thomas Aquinas, *Summa theologiae*, 61 vols. (Cambridge: Blackfriars, 1964–78), vol. 44, II^a–II^{ae}, qu. 168, art. 4.

138. Ibid., I, 4 (xv), 54a15, p. 19.

139. Ibid., I, 4 (xv), 54a10, p. 20.

140. "e per venire a i nostri, della lealtà in Amadigi; della constanza in Bradamante," Torquato Tasso, *Discorsi dell'arte poetica e in particolare sopra il poema eroico* (1562–65, pub. 1587), in *Scritti sull'arte poetica*, ed. Ettore Mazzali, 2 vols. (Milan: Riccardo Ricciardi, 1959; rpt., Turin: Giulio Einaudi, 1977), vol. 1, Discorso I, p. 14.

141. Sir Philip Sidney, *The Defence of Poesy*, in *Sidney's "Defence of Poesy" and Selected Renaissance Literary Criticism*, ed. Alexander Gavin (Harmondsworth: Penguin Classics, 2004), 1–54, at 7.

142. "quando alcun poeta non ha prese le cose tali quali sono o erano, il poeta si può salvare rispondendosi che si sono prese tali quali dovrebbono essere," Lodovico Castelvestro, *Poetica*

works is not just to illustrate certain virtues by representing characters who exemplify them, but also to inspire readers to imitate these characters. In his *Della nuova poesia* (1596), Giuseppe Malatesta claims that, in the heroic poem, "We are presented with so many and such diverse images of qualified and virtuous persons that it is impossible that we should not all burn with a desire to resemble them."[143] Instead of restricting itself to abstract principles, attractive to our reason alone, as moral philosophy does, Malatesta suggests, the heroic poem provides concrete examples of virtuous people, appealing to our imagination as well. In representing people not as they are but as they should be, these critics insist, romance tells the truth, but a truth not about who we are but about who we should aspire to become.

Because romances provide models of exemplary behavior, these critics argued, they do not lead their readers astray, but, on the contrary, guide them down the best path. Readers of the first volume of the history of Don Quixote may find its hero to fall short of the models of chivalry to which he aspired, this hero himself acknowledges, but this is only because the author of this work has fallen short of his literary predecessors. Don Quixote states, "By my faith, Aeneas was not as pious as Virgil depicts him, nor Ulysses as prudent as Homer describes him."[144] Because Homer and Virgil knew what their heroes should have been like, he hypothesizes, they edited out episodes where they had failed to achieve this standard of perfection. In doing so, he asserts, they portrayed these heroes, "not as they were, but as they should have been, to serve as examples of virtue to men who came after them."[145] As it does not matter if ancient epic heroes occasionally failed to be heroic because they establish a standard of excellence to which modern knights errant can aspire, it does not matter if modern knights errant—even Don Quixote himself—occasionally fail to match this standard of excellence because their efforts to match it are, in and of themselves, admirable. The narrator refers to "Don Quixote of La Mancha, . . . about

d'Aristotele vulgarizzata e sposta, ed. Werther Romani, 2 vols. (Rome: Gius. Laterza, 1978–79), vol. 2, V, 3, p. 265.

143. "ci si offeriscono tante & di diverse immagini di personaggi qualificati & virtuosi che non potemo non arder tutti di desiderio d'assomigliarci a loro," Giuseppe Malatesta, *Della nuova poesia, overo Delle difese del "Furioso," rationamento secondo . . . Della difese del "Furioso" ragionamento terzo*, cited in Bernard Weinberg, *A History of Literary Criticism in the Italian Renaissance*, 2 vols. (Chicago: University of Chicago Press, 1961), vol. 2, 1065.

144. "A fee que no fue tan piadoso Eneas como Virgilio le pinta, ni tan prudente Ulises como le describe Homero," Cervantes, *Don Quijote de la Mancha*, ed. Allen, II, 3, pp. 48–49.

145. "como ellos fueron, sino como habían de ser, para quedar ejemplo a los venideros hombres de sus virtudes," ibid., I, 25, p. 291.

whom it will be said . . . that, if he did not achieve great things, he died in the effort to perform them."[146] As literary works provide models of chivalry to which a young man can aspire, they provide models of love to which a young woman can aim. In *Emile, ou l'éducation* (1762), Rousseau represents his heroine Sophie as having read Fénelon's lengthy and immensely popular "fabulous narration in the form of an epic poem,"[147] *Les Aventures de Télémaque* (1699), as falling in love with its hero, and as resolving to marry only a man who resembles him. As Rousseau sees it, such a literary work not only teaches the reader what the ideal young man or woman would look like, but it kindles that reader's emotions, so that he or she is able to love this person. He explains, "There is no true love without enthusiasm, and no enthusiasm without an object of perfection, real or chimerical, but always existing in the imagination."[148] He acknowledges that the young woman who believes her lover to be such an "object of perfection" may be deluded, but he defends the value of such an error: "Everything in love is only an illusion, I admit, but what is real are the feelings with which love animates us for the true, beautiful thing that it makes us love. This beautiful thing is not in the object that one loves; it is the work of our errors. Eh! What does that matter?"[149] If one feels love for someone, he asserts, it is because one apprehends a certain fictional perfection in one's imagination, which one then transposes onto that real person. If Sophie ultimately feels love for Emile, it is because she perceives resemblances between "that model of the loveable man"[150] she had come to know in fiction and the actual loveable man she now comes to know in real life. For these authors, romance may fill its readers with ideas about chivalry and courtly love, but literature in general enables them to become better men and better women than they would have been otherwise.

Insofar as Romantic and Romantic Revival critics of the eighteenth and nineteenth centuries championed romance, it was because they

146. "don Quijote de la Mancha, . . . del cual se dirá lo . . . que si no acabó grandes cosas, murió por acometellas," ibid., I, 26, p. 307.

147. In an undated letter to Fr. Le Tellier, cited in *Les Aventures de Télémaque*, ed. J.-A. Adry (Paris: Adrien Egron, 1840), Fénelon refers to *Télémaque* as "une narration fabuleuse, en forme de poëme épique" (liii).

148. "Il n'y a point de véritable amour sans enthousiasme et point d'enthousiasme sans un objet de perfection réel ou chimérique, mais toujours existant dans l'imagination," Rousseau, *Emile*, in *Oeuvres complètes*, ed. Gagnebin et Raymond, vol. 4, bk. 5, p. 743.

149. "Tout n'est qu'illusion dans l'amour, je l'avoüe; mais ce qui est réel ce sont les sentiments dont il nous anime pour le vrai beau qu'il nous fait aimer. Ce beau n'est point dans l'objet qu'on aime, il est l'ouvrage de nos erreurs. Eh! qu'importe?," ibid.

150. "ce modèle de l'homme aimable," ibid., bk. 5, p. 761.

saw it as representing something no less real than the novel. In *The Prelude* (1798–1850), William Wordsworth praises medieval romance as the genre of literature that cultivates our aspiration to such a higher existence. He describes himself as a child reading, "romances; legends penned / For solace by dim light of monkish lamps; / Fictions, for ladies of their love, devised / By youthful squires."[151] He was attracted to romances because, as a child, he existed in a state "ere we learn to live / In reconcilement with our stinted powers"[152] and because he therefore still believed that people can be greater than they seem to be. Though Wordsworth does not affirm that our powers are, in fact, unstinted, he does argue that the desire for such powers is a good thing. Whereas realist authors proclaim the ordinariness of our everyday lives, Romantic authors insist upon their occasional extraordinariness. In his *Diamond Necklace* (1837), Thomas Carlyle affirms that "Romance exists."[153] Skeptics claim that the Age of Romance never occurred and that Roland had to fight in rainy weather, saddle-sore and constipated, with worn-out hose to wear and tough beef to chew, but he assures us, "Depend upon it, for one thing, good Reader, no age ever seemed the Age of Romance to *itself*. . . . Only in long subsequent days, when the tough beef, the constipation and the calumny had clean vanished, did it all begin to seem Romantic, and your Turpins and Ariostos found music in it. So, I say, is it *ever*!"[154] To those who claim that the Age of Romance does not occur today, Carlyle gestures to the sky, with its constellations and lightning, and to the earth, with its snowstorms. He asks, "O Brother! is *that* what thou callest prosaic; of small interest? . . . This is God's Creation; this is Man's Life!"[155] Anyone who has ever looked at these phenomena cannot fail to have witnessed, he proclaims, "much that could be called romantic, even miraculous."[156] Anthony Hope Hawkins, the author of *The Prisoner of Zenda* (1893), likewise views romance as an expression, not only of readers' desire to perform exciting deeds, but of their unrealized potential to do so. "Romance," he declares in an 1897 lecture, "can give to love an ideal object, to ambition a boundless field, to courage a high occasion."[157] Human beings feel love, ambition,

151. William Wordsworth, *The Prelude: The Four Texts (1798, 1799, 1805, 1850)*, ed. Jonathan Wordsworth (Harmondworth: Penguin Classics, 1995), bk. 5, vv. 497–500.

152. Ibid., vv. 516–17.

153. Thomas Carlyle, *The Diamond Necklace* (Boston: Houghton Mifflin, 1913), 15.

154. Ibid., 9–11.

155. Ibid., 13–14.

156. Ibid., 11.

157. Anthony Hope Hawkins, quoted in *The Prisoner of Zenda*, ed. Tony Watkins, Oxford World Classics (Oxford: Oxford University Press, 2009), ix.

and courage, but the lives that most of them lead do not give them full scope to act upon these emotions. When romance invites them into an exciting story of love or adventure, he affirms, "It shows them what they would be if they could, if time and fate and circumstances did not bind, what in a sense they all are, and what their acts would show them to be if an opportunity offered."[158] While the realist novel may represent the world as it is, in its manifest actuality, romance, these authors affirm, represents the world as it can be, once we open ourselves up to its latent potentiality.

In the twentieth century, critics on occasion praised romance for recognizing that everyday reality is not all that there is. In *The Secular Scripture: A Study in the Structure of Romance* (1978), Northrop Frye writes that all fiction is characterized by "symbolic spread," that is, by "the sense that a work of literature is expanding into insights and experiences beyond itself."[159] Insofar as a realist novel seems to be giving us access to a truth outside its own pages, he argues, it is because its "symbolic spread" moves from the fictional story into the world around it. By urging us to awaken and to observe this world, Frye writes, "many literary critics today . . . attach what are for them the real values of literature to something outside literature which literature reflects."[160] Insofar as romance does not seem to give us access to a truth outside its own pages, Frye argues, it is because its "symbolic spread" moves, not from the fictional text to the extraliterary context, but, rather, from the fictional text to "its literary context, to other romances that are most like it in the conventions adopted."[161] While readers of the realist novel take satisfaction in the sensation that the text is teaching them about a world outside the novel, readers of romance take pleasure in the sensation that the text is resonating with other texts. If Frye, as a New Critic, celebrates literature in general, he makes clear, it is because it functions not as a means to illustrate something outside itself, but, instead, as an end in itself. He writes, "My proposal [is] to take literature itself as the area of critical investigation, without granting anything else priority to it."[162] If he celebrates romance, in particular, he explains, it is because, in this mode of literature, the story is not told for the sake of something else; rather, "the story is told primarily for the sake of the story."[163]

158. Ibid.
159. Frye, *Secular Scripture*, 59.
160. Ibid., 25.
161. Ibid., 59.
162. Ibid., 25.
163. Ibid., 41.

While what Frye calls "the guardians of taste and learning"[164] have traditionally condemned romance for its failure to transcend itself—to convey a useful lesson, to seem true to reality, to be true to reality—popular audiences have always delighted in this genre for the autotelic pleasure it provides. In contrast to Auerbach and Watt, who argue that there is only one reality, contrary to romance, Frye contends that romance too is a reality, sufficient unto itself.

In the present day, even as literary fiction has triumphed over romance from a critical perspective, genre fiction has claimed victory from a commercial point of view. Whatever admiration the winner of the Man Booker International Prize or National Book Award may inspire among a small academic or intellectual readership, the teller of stories about witches and wizards, vampires and werewolves, Mothers of Dragons and rulers of the Iron Throne, have proved vastly more appealing to mass, popular audiences, especially when their movie and television spin-offs are taken into consideration.[165] The enthusiasm of many writers and readers for romance may have been best expressed by Robert Louis Stevenson, who defends this category of literature against Henry James's critique. While James stated that he could not evaluate Stevenson's *Treasure Island* (1883) because he himself had never sought buried treasure, Stevenson affirms that Master James must never have been a child, because all children have looked for lost gold, just as all children have been pirates, bandits, and military commanders. It is the common experience of children, he writes, to "have ardently desired and fondly imagined the details of such a life in youthful day-dreams."[166] It is the task of the creative writer, he asserts, not to obey the real laws of waken consciousness, but "to obey the ideal laws of the day-dream."[167] It is his or her obligation, not just to represent the world in which we live, so that we can find our observations to be confirmed, but to invent a world in which we might prefer to live, so that we can feel our fantasies to be satisfied. The promise of romance, here, as else-

164. Ibid., 23.

165. See Ken Gelder, *Popular Fiction: The Logics and Practices of a Literary Field* (London: Routledge, 2004), 38.

166. Robert Louis Stevenson, "A Humble Remonstrance," *Longman's Magazine* 5 (December 1884): 139–47; rpt., *The Victorian Art of Fiction*, ed. Olmsted, 341–49, at 346. For discussion of the conflict between Robert Louis Stevenson and James on this topic, see George Dekker, "James and Stevenson: The Mixed Current of Realism and Romance," in *Critical Reconstructions: The Relationship of Fiction and Life*, ed. Robert M. Polhemus and Roger B. Henkle (Stanford, CA: Stanford University Press, 1994), 217–49.

167. Robert Louis Stevenson, "A Gossip on Romance," *Longman's Magazine* 1 (November 1882): 69–79; rpt., *The Victorian Art of Fiction*, ed. Olmsted, 189–99, at 192.

where, is the promise that we can experience, at least vicariously, an alternate existence.

The debate about the value of romance has always been a debate about the value of a literature that enables us to exit our world and to enter, imaginatively, another one. For critics of romance, this flight from one world to another is to be repudiated. In the final chapter of Charlotte Lennox's *The Female Quixote* (1752) (which may have been composed by Samuel Johnson), a doctor attempts to persuade the heroine Arabella to give up her attachment to French romances by warning her, "Your Writers have instituted a World of their own."[168] In this world, he protests, her writers have established kings and queens to rule over imaginary nations, and they have distributed mountains, deserts, and forests wherever they wished. They have erred in creating such a world, he informs Arabella, because "the only Excellence of Falsehood . . . is its Resemblance to Truth."[169] The more in which fiction departs from fact, replacing the world we observe with a world it has invented, he contends, the more it leads its reader astray. Yet even as critics of romance have reproached this genre for transporting us from our own world into another, its defenders have praised it for facilitating this journey. As Giuseppe Malatesta puts it, romance does not imitate the world Nature has created, but, rather, imitates Nature herself by creating "a little world"[170] of its own. On reading such a work, he writes, "Human minds marvel to see in a poem . . . many different things unlike one another come together to produce so well disciplined and well organized an entirety."[171] Far from scorning the "little world" for not resembling the big one, he suggests, we should feel amazement at the self-contained organization of this microcosm. For the authors of romance and their supporters, the fact that the human mind is capable of creating an alternate world is not something to deplore, but, on the contrary, something to celebrate. The danger of romance, in the past as in the present, is the danger of delight, independent of any political, social, or moral consequence.

168. Charlotte Lennox, *The Female Quixote; or, the Adventures of Arabella*, ed. Margaret Dalziel (Oxford: Oxford University Press, 2008), 378.

169. Ibid.

170. "un picciol mondo," Malatesta, *Della nuova poesia overo delle difese del Furioso* (Verona: Per Sebastiano dalle Donne, 1589),1, quoted in Weinberg, *A History of Literary Criticism*, vol. 2, 1062.

171. "gli humani ingegni, si ammirassero di vedere in un Poema . . . molte cose diverse non conformi tra loro concorrere à produrre un tutto cosi bene disposto & ordinato," ibid.

TWO

Merlin: Magic, Miracles, and Marvels

Throughout the first narrative accounts of him, in the twelfth and the early thirteenth centuries, Merlin, more than any other character in the Matter of Britain, is characterized as someone who speaks and performs "marvels" (*mirabilia* in Latin or *merveilles* in French).[1] At this time, "marvels" were considered to be phenomena so new, rare, or extraordinary that they caused those who behold them "to marvel" (*mirari* or *admirari* in Latin or *merveiller* in

1. My thoughts about the marvelous are most influenced by Lorraine Daston and Katharine Park, *Wonders and the Order of Nature, 1150–1750* (New York: Zone Books, 2001). See also Michelle Karnes, "Marvels in the Medieval Imagination," *Speculum* 90, no. 2 (2015): 327–65; Laurent Guyénot, *La Mort féerique: Anthropologie du merveilleux, XIIe–XVe siècle* (Paris: Gallimard, 2011); Robert Barlett, *The Natural and the Supernatural in the Middle Ages: The Wiles Lecture Given at the Queen's University of Belfast, 2006* (Cambridge: Cambridge University Press, 2008); Caroline Walker Bynum, "Wonder," *American Historical Review* 102 (1997): 1–26; Jacques Le Goff, "The Marvelous in the Medieval West," in *The Medieval Imagination*, trans. Arthur Goldhammer (Chicago: University of Chicago Press, 1988), 27–44, and "Le Merveilleux scientifique au Moyen Age," in *Zwischen Wahn, Glaube, und Wissenschaft: Magie, Astrologie, Alchemie, und Wissenschaftsgeschichte*, ed. Jean-François Bergier (Zurich: Verlag der Fachvereine, 1988), 87–113; Michel Meslin and Nicole Bériou, eds., *Le Merveilleux: L'Imagination et les croyances en Occident* (Paris: Bordas, 1984); and Claude Lecouteux, "Introduction à l'étude du merveilleux médiéval," *Etudes germaniques* 36 (1981): 273–90. On the marvelous in medieval French literature, in particular, see Daniel Poirion, *Le Merveilleux dans la littérature française du Moyen Age*, Que sais-je? (Paris: Presses Universitaires de France, 1982); Claude Lecouteux, "Introduction à l'étude du merveilleux médiéval," *Etudes Germaniques* 36 (1981): 273–90; and Edmond Faral, "Le Merveilleux et ses sources dans les descriptions des romans français du XIIe siècle," in *Recherches sur les sources latines des contes et romans courtois du Moyen Age* (Paris: Honoré Champion, 1913), 307–88.

French). Whether they were a salamander, which survives in the fire; an eclipse, which darkens the sun at midday; or the Dead Sea, which causes heavy objects to float on its waters, marvels were seen as contradicting the laws of Nature in ways that were both mysterious and meaningful. As Gervase of Tilbury puts it, "We generally call those things miracles [*miracula*] which, being beyond Nature, we ascribe to divine power . . . while we call those things marvels [*mirabilia*] which are beyond our comprehension, even though they are natural; in fact, the inability to explain why a thing is so constitutes a marvel."[2] Yet how is it possible, medieval thinkers debated, that a part of the natural world cannot be understood according to the laws of Nature? In the context of Christianity, which typically assigns supernatural abilities only to God, if a marvel is not a miracle and, hence, not a product of divine power, does it not necessarily follow that it must be a product of diabolical illusion? In all of the texts written about him in the Middle Ages, Merlin causes those around him to wonder because, in contravention of the laws of Nature, he knows the secrets of the past, the present, and the future and because he can transform his shape and that of those around him at will.[3] Yet how can a mere human being, without illumination from heaven, perform such feats? Given that Merlin is never described as a saint, from whom such miracles might be expected, does it not necessarily follow that he must be a limb of the devil? In both scholarly, Latin treatises and literary, vernacular romances of these years, medieval thinkers argued about marvels and about Merlin, the foremost producer of marvels, at once agreeing that there were people, like this seer, who seemed to possess preternatural gifts and disagreeing as to how one should make sense of them.

2. "miracula dicimus usitatius que preter naturam divine virtuti ascribimus . . . Mirabilia vero dicimus que nostre cognicioni non subiacent, etiam cum sunt naturalia; sed et mirabilia constituit ignorantia reddende rationis quare sic sit," Gervase of Tilbury, *Otia Imperialia: Recreation for an Emperor*, ed. and trans. S. E. Banks and J. W. Binns (Oxford: Clarendon Press, 2002), bk. 3, preface, p. 558.

3. Recent general studies of Merlin include Anne Lawrence-Mathers, *The True History of Merlin the Magician* (New Haven, CT: Yale University Press, 2012); Stephen Knight, *Merlin: Knowledge and Power through the Ages* (Ithaca, NY: Cornell University Press, 2009); Geoffrey Ashe, *Merlin: The Prophet and His History* (Stroud, Gloucestershire: Sutton Publishing, 2006; rpt., Stroud, Gloucestershire: History Press, 2008); *Merlin: A Casebook*, ed. Peter H. Goodrich and Raymond H. Thompson (London: Routedge, 2003); Carol E. Hardling, *Merlin and Legendary Romance* (New York: Garland, 1988); Jean Markale, *Merlin l'enchanteur, ou, l'éternelle quête magique* (Paris: Retz, 1981); A. O. H. Jarman, *The Legend of Merlin* (Cardiff: University of Wales Press, 1970). Paul Zumthor, *Merlin le prophète: Un thème de la littérature polémique, de l'historiographie et des romans* (Lausanne: Payot, 1943; Geneva: Slatkine Reprints, 1973) is also very useful.

In the twelfth and the thirteenth centuries, clerics invested in rationalistic traditions, such as philosophy or theology, tended to reject the notion of marvels because they rejected the possibility that anything natural was beyond human comprehension. Aristotle cited "wonder"[4] (*thámbos* in Greek or *admiratio* in the medieval Latin translation) as the origin of philosophy, given that, as soon as man sees that he does not understand something, he wants to understand it. While Aristotle perceives wonder positively, as an incitement to learning, because it makes one want to know the cause of what one is beholding, other philosophers perceive it negatively, as a deterrent to rigorous thought, because it makes one think that no such cause is to be found. Cicero,[5] Boethius,[6] Isidore of Seville,[7] John of Salisbury,[8] and the scholastics who follow them all insist that creatures exist in harmony with the laws of Nature and, by extension, with God, who has established those laws. If we perceive something as contrary to these laws, they reason, it is only because we do not yet understand how it adheres to them. When a nephew asks Adelard of Bath about thunder, "an object of wonder to all peoples,"[9] Adelard reproaches him for remaining at the level of wonderment instead of proceeding to knowledge. "Look more closely!" he urges. "Consider the circumstances! Lay down the causes first, and you will not be surprised by the effect."[10] If he considered the matter more closely and came to understand it better, he would not allow his mind to be "veiled by the marvelousness and unusualness of the matter."[11] In order fully to comprehend phenomena like thunder, medieval thinkers believed, it is necessary to grasp both their "manifest" properties, such as hotness or coldness, wetness or dryness, which

4. "admirationem," Aristotle, *Metaphysica, Lib. I–X, XII–XIV: Translatio Anonyma sive "Media,"* ed. Gudrun Vuillemin-Diem, in *Aristoteles Latinus*, ed. G. Verbeke, 27 vols. (Leiden: Brill, 1970; rpt., 1976), vol. 25.2, I, 2, p. 10.

5. Cicero, *De divinatione*, in *"De divinatione," "De fato," "Timaeus"* ed. Remo Giomini, BSGRT (Stuttgart: Teubner, 1975), II, 28, 60, p. 105.

6. Boethius, *Consolatio Philosophiae*, ed. Ludwig Bieler, CCSL, vol. 94 (Turnhout: Brepols, 1957), IV, 5, p. 78.

7. Isidore of Seville, *Etymologiae*, in *Isidore Hispalensis episopi Etymologiarum sive Originum*, ed. W. M. Lindsay, 2 vols. (Oxford: Clarendon Press, 1911), XI, 3, 1–2 (no page numbers).

8. John of Salisbury, *Policraticus I–IV*, ed. Keats-Rohan, II, 12, p. 91.

9. "omnibus populis mirandum," Adelard of Bath, *Questiones naturales*, in *Conversations with His Nephew: "On the Same and Different"; "Questions on Natural Science"; and "On Birds,"* ed. and trans. Charles Burnett (Cambridge: Cambridge University Press, 1998), 202.

10. "Propius intuere, circumstantias adde, causas prepone, et effectum non mirabere," ibid., 202–4.

11. "ammiratione enim insolentiaque indutus," ibid., 202. Avicenna makes a similar claim in *De viribus cordis* I, 10, in *Canon medicinae*, trans. Arnold of Villanova (Venice: Dionysius Bertochus, 1489–90) (no page numbers).

are perceptible to our senses, and their "occult" or hidden properties, which are not perceptible in the same way. Insofar as demons are able to produce marvels, it is not because they are able to break the laws of Nature but, rather, because they are able to access these occult properties through their own skill and to use them to produce the effects they seek. Like farmers, who know the occult properties of the seeds they plant, Peter Lombard writes, "Evil angels . . . know by virtue of the subtlety of their sense and body the seeds of these things which are more concealed from us,"[12] and they manipulate those seeds in order to delude human beings. If one wishes not to be deceived by demons or by people allied with demons, such thinkers maintained, one must learn to trace the supposedly marvelous qualities of certain phenomena to their occult properties. So skeptical were rationalist thinkers of marvels that the author of the thirteenth-century *De mirabilibus mundi* ascribed to Albertus Magnus encourages his readers to seek out natural explanations for marvelous phenomena and promises that, if they do so, "[they] will see that nothing is marvelous."[13] If these readers then publicize these explanations, he states, they will fulfill their duty as wise men, which is "to make all marvels cease."[14] As these thinkers saw it, the world must be disenchanted, that is, ridded of the marvels that, as the result of diabolical delusion or human ignorance, make the unified, coherent, and centralized natural order seem scattered, contradictory, and multipolar.

For clerics writing in accordance with this rationalistic tradition, Merlin does not really perform marvels, but, with the assistance of demons, merely deceives people into thinking he is doing so. From their reading of patristic literature, Christian thinkers were aware that, though only God knows all things, demons know far more than human beings, whether because of the keenness of their intelligence, which is not weighed down by a corporeal body; because of the extensiveness of their experience, which is not limited to a mortal lifespan; or because of the illuminations they have received from good angels, on God's command.[15] In accordance with the Book of

12. "mali angeli . . . pro subtilitate sui sensus et corporis, semina istarum rerum nobis occultiora noverunt," Peter Lombard, *Sententiae in IV Libris Distinctae*, 3rd ed., 2 vols. (Grottaferrata: Ed. Collegii S. Bonaventurae Ad Claras Aquas, 1971–81), vol. 1, II, ii, 7, 8, p. 363.

13. "tu vides quod nihil est mirabile," Pseudo-Albertus Magnus, *Liber de mirabilibus mundi*, published with the *Liber secretorum Alberti magni de virtutibus* (Amsterdam: n.a., 1760), 187.

14. "facere quod cesset omne mirabile," ibid.

15. See Augustine, *De Genesi ad litteram*, ed. Zycha, II, 17, pp. 59–62, and *De divinatione daemonum*, III, 7 in PL 40, cols 581–92, at VII, cols 587–88, and Isidore of Seville, *Etymologiae*, ed. Lindsay, VIII, 11, 15–16.

Deuteronomy,[16] Augustine,[17] Isidore of Seville,[18] and Hugh of Saint-Victor[19] held that diviners, who claim to see the future, enter into compacts with the devil, either implicitly or explicitly, and learn what they know from this association. William of Newburgh, an Augustinian canon writing sometime before 1198, argues that because Merlin did not receive his faculty of prophecy from God, he must have received it from the devil. Though Geoffrey of Monmouth ascribed more prophecies to Merlin than we do to Isaiah, William complains, "He did not dare to introduce these vaticinations by saying, 'Thus spoke the Lord,' and he was ashamed to introduce them by saying, 'Thus spoke the devil.'"[20] However veracious Merlin's prophecies are deemed to be, he warns, they can only be false because demons can conjecture, but not actually know the future. Though William is the most vehement of Merlin's critics, he is far from the only person to express qualms about the validity of this seer's prophecies at this time. Gerald of Wales, the Norman-Welsh chaplain to King Henry II of England, acknowledges in 1191 that while biblical prophets attributed their words to God, Merlin did not do so. "However faithful [to Christianity] he may have been, there is little to be read about his sanctity or devotion,"[21] he states. Instead of having spoken through "the spirit of God,"[22] he writes, Merlin is thought to have spoken through "a Pythonic spirit"[23]—that is, a demonic spirit like that which inspired the Pythia, the priestess who transmitted Apollo's oracles at Delphi. The author of a commentary attributed to Alan of Lille likewise raises the question, "whether [Merlin] was Christian or a pagan and whether the spirit in which he prophesied

16. Deut. 18:10–11.

17. See Augustine, *De Genesi ad litteram*, ed. Zycha, II, 17, pp. 59–62, and *De doctrina Christiana*, ed. Martin, II, 23, pp. 57–58.

18. See Isidore of Seville, *Eymologiae*, ed. Lindsay, VIII, 9, 31.

19. Hugh of Saint-Victor, *Didascalion de studio legendi: A Critical Text*, ed. Charles Henry Buttimer (Washington, DC: Catholic University Press, 1939), VI, 15, 132–33.

20. "ejus vaticiniis non audet inserere, 'haec dicit Dominus,' et erubuit inserere, 'haec dicit diabolus'; quippe hoc debut congruere vati, incubi daemonis filio," William of Newburgh, *Historia rerum Anglicarum*, in William of Newburgh, *The History of English Affairs*, ed. P. G. Walsh and M. J. Kennedy, 2 vols. (Warminster, Wiltshire: Aris and Phillips, 1988–2007), vol. 1, preface, 14, p. 34.

21. "sanctitate ipsius vel devotione, quanquam fidelis fuerit, minime legitur," Gerald of Wales, *Descriptio Kambriae*, in *Opera*, 8 vols., ed. J. S. Brewer, vol. 6, ed. James F. Dimock, Rolls Series (London: Longmans, 1861–91; rpt., Nendeln: Kraus Reprint, 1964), vol. 6, 155–227, at I, 16, p. 198.

22. "spiritu Dei," ibid., I, 16, p. 197.

23. "pithonico spiritu," ibid., I, 16, p. 198.

was divine or pythonic."[24] John of Salisbury,[25] William the Breton,[26] Peter of Blois,[27] Gervase of Canterbury,[28] Alexander Neckam,[29] and Thomas Wykes[30] were other clerics of the twelfth and thirteenth centuries who denied and even ridiculed the validity of Merlin's prophecies. By the late sixteenth century, the English remained attached to what they now regarded as their national seer, but people outside their island had ceased to take Merlin's prophecies seriously. The Council of Trent placed his book of prophecies on the Index, one anonymous commentator of this period explains, because "it was not filled with the Holy Spirit of God, but, rather, stirred by an evil demon."[31] For William and his fellow critics of Merlin, there are biblical and Christian prophets who are inspired by God and who therefore speak the truth, and there are pagan sorcerers who are inspired by the devil and who therefore speak falsehoods. If Merlin is not a biblical or a Christian prophet, as he clearly is not, he must therefore be a pagan sorcerer, allied with the devil.

During these same centuries, however, clerics invested in contemplative traditions, such as monastic spirituality, accepted the notion of marvels because they viewed the natural as a mirror of the divine, which is indeed outside our grasp. To those skeptics who would deny the existence of Christian miracles because they thwart attempts at rational explanation, Augustine points out the existence of mar-

24. "utrum Christianus fuerit, an gentilis: et quo nam spiritus prophetaverit, phytonico an divino?" Pseudo-Alan of Lille, *Explanationum in prophetiam Merlini Ambrosii Britani libri VII* (Frankfurt: Typis Ioachimi Bratheringij, 1603), 3.

25. *The Letters of John of Salisbury*, ed. W. J. Millor and H. E. Butler, rev. C. N. L. Brooke, 2 vols. (Oxford: Clarendon Press, 1979), vol. 2, Letter 292, p. 668. Cf. Deut. 34:9. Yet John also cites Merlin with approbation in a letter of July 1166 to Thomas Becket, in *The Correspondence of Thomas Becket, Archbishop of Canterbury, 1162–1170*, ed. Anne Duggan, 2 vols. (Oxford: Clarendon Press, 2000), vol. 1, 453.

26. William the Breton, *Philippidos*, in *Oeuvres de Rigord et de Guillaume le Breton*, ed. H.-François Delaborde, 2 vols. (Paris: Librairie Renouard, 1882–85), vol. 2, at VIII, 905.

27. Peter of Blois, *Invectiva in depravatorem operum*, in PL, vol. 207, cols. 1113–26, at col. 1124.

28. Gervase of Canterbury, *Mappa Mundi*, in *The Historical Works of Gervase of Canterbury*, ed. William Stubbs, Rolls Series, 2 vols. (London: Longman, 1879–80; rpt., Wiesbaden: Kraus Reprint, 1965), vol. 2, 414–49, at 414.

29. Alexander Neckam, *De Laudibus divinae sapientiae*, ed. Thomas Wright, Rolls Series (London: Longman, 1863), 457.

30. Thomas Wykes, *Annales Monastici*, ed. Henry Richard Luard, Rolls Series, 5 vols. (London: Longman, 1864–69), vol. 4, 59–60.

31. "non cum Spiritu Dei plenum, sed potius malo daemone agitatum," an anonymous commentator of Vincent of Beauvais, *Speculum historiale* (Douai, France: Ex officina typographica Baltazaris Belleri, 1624), rpt., *Speculum historiale*, in *Speculum quadruplex; sive, Speculum maius* (Graz: Akademische Druck- u. Verlaganstalt, 1964–65), vol. 4, XX, 30, pp. 791.

vels around us—such as asbestos, which once set afire, cannot be put out—which also frustrate such efforts. Ultimately, for Augustine, marvels include not just "those things for which a reason cannot be given, and yet seem to be contrary to the laws of Nature,"[32] but any part of Creation, whose inherent wondrousness we overlook once we have grown used to it, though it should still cause us to marvel at the unfathomable nature of God as reflected in his creatures. He writes, "God, who made the visible heaven and earth, does not disdain to make visible miracles in heaven or on earth, by which he excites the soul, immersed in visible things, to worship him, the invisible."[33] The *Navigatio sancti Brendani*, the account of the travels of Saint Brendan of Clonfert and his months in the North Atlantic, which was composed in Latin in the sixth century and translated into Anglo-Norman French in the twelfth, illustrates this Augustinian tendency to marvel at the created world and, in doing so, to appreciate the Creator who fashioned it. One day during their journey, in the Latin text, Brendan and his monks come across a column of clear crystal (presumably an iceberg) so high that its summit cannot be glimpsed. When the abbot beholds this column, he orders the monks to steer their boat through an opening in it, "so that we may see carefully the wonderful works of our Creator."[34] Elsewhere in the French text, he explains to his monks why it is important that they behold marvels like the birds or the iceberg: "God wanted to lead you here because he wanted to instruct you. The more you see his marvels, the more you will believe in him."[35] Contemplatives like Brendan try to deepen their appreciation of a transcendent, spiritual reality through their meditation upon an immediate, physical reality. Far from being disenchanted, such clerics held, the world must retain its marvels, which continually remind us of the irreducible mysteriousness of Creation and of the God who made it.

32. "ista . . . de quibus ratio reddi ab homine non potest, et tamen sunt, et ipsi rationi naturae videntur esse contraria?" Augustine, *De civitate Dei*, ed. Bernard Dombart and Alphonsus Kalb, CCSL, vol. 48, XXI, 5, p. 766.

33. "Deus, qui fecit visibilia caelum et terram, non dedignatur facere visibilia miracula in caelo vel terra, quibus ad se invisibilem colendum excitet animam adhuc visibilibus deditam," ibid., X, 12, p. 287.

34. "ut videamus diligenter magnalia creatoris nostri," *Navigatio Sancti Brendani Abbatis: From Early Latin Manuscripts*, ed. Carl Selmer (Notre Dame, IN: University of Notre Dame Press, 1959), 22, p. 59.

35. "Pur ço vus volt Deus ci mener / que il vus voleit plus asener: / ses merveilles cum plus verrez, / en lui puis mult mieulx crerrez," Benedeit, *The Anglo-Norman Voyage of St. Brendan*, ed. Ian Short and Brian Merrilees (Manchester: Manchester University Press, 1979), vv. 473–76.

For clerics writing in accordance with the contemplative tradition, Merlin genuinely does perform marvels.[36] From their reading of classical literature, Christian thinkers were familiar with the popular view that a certain mysterious spirit, neither good nor evil, could enable seers, sibyls, and soothsayers to foretell the future. In Cicero's dialogue *De divinatione*, for example, Cicero's brother Quintus asserts that "there is a certain natural power [*vis . . . natura*], which . . . through some divine excitement and inspiration, makes prophetic announcement of the future."[37] While this power lies latent within the individual, it is triggered when a god enters into that person and inspires a kind of prophetic madness. Quintus explains, "Frenzy [*furor*] . . . occurs when the soul is withdrawn from the body and is aroused by a divine impulse."[38] In his *De Genesi ad litteram*, Augustine similarly acknowledges that "there are some who hold that the human soul has within itself a certain power of divination."[39] As Quintus spoke of a "natural power" that enables certain people to prophesy, Augustine speaks of a "spiritual vision" (*visio spiritualis*) that enables them to know through the imagination matters they could not know through their senses or their mind. Gregory the Great likewise writes, "sometimes the soul, by its own subtle powers, has knowledge of the future."[40] Under the influence of this classical and patristic tradition, medieval thinkers maintained that people could receive divine illumination though they were not saints or even Christians.[41] While it is typically biblical or

36. Historians of magic, such as Edward Peters, in *The Magician, the Witch, and the Law* (Philadelphia: University of Pennsylvania Press, 1978), xii and 52–53, and Richard Kieckhefer, in *Magic in the Middle Ages* (Cambridge: Cambridge University Press, 1989), 109 and 113, have argued that the treatment of Merlin in medieval romances bears little relation to the treatment of magicians in the theological and pastoral writings at this time, where they were unequivocally condemned. Kieckhefer observes that romancers suggest, if one uses the occult arts for good ends, as Merlin does, one does not necessarily enter into the devil's power, and that, in doing so, they differ from the theologians of their time, but he does not elaborate upon this point.

37. "est enim vis et natura quaedam, quae . . . tum aliquo instinctu inflatuque divino futura praenuntiat," Cicero, *De divinatione*, ed. Giomini, 1, 6, 12, p. 7.

38. "furor . . . cum a corpore animus abstractus divino instinctu concitatur," ibid., 1, 31, 66, p. 40.

39. "Nonulli quidem volunt animam humanam habere vim quandam divinationis in se ipsa," Augustine, *De Genesi ad litteram*, ed. Zycha, XII, 13, p. 397.

40. "Ipsa aliquando animarum vis subtilitate sua aliquid praevidet," *Li Dialoge Gregoire lo Pape: Altfranzösische Uebersetzung des XII. Jahrhunderts der Dialogen des Papstes Gregor, mit dem lateinischen Original*, ed. Wendelin Foerster, 2 vols. (Halle: Max Niemeyer, 1876), vol. 1, IV, 27, p. 225.

41. In the *Posterior Analytics* I, 34, Aristotle asserted that some people are capable of grasping the middle term of a syllogism immediately. In his *Kitāb al-Najāt*, in *Avicenna's Psychology: An English Translation of "Kitāb al-Najāt," Book II, Ch. VI, with Historico-Philosophical Notes and Textual*

Christian figures of the highest probity who can tell the future, Gerald of Wales points out that the Chaldean wise men, who interpreted Nebuchadnezzar's dream, Calchas and Cassandra, who predicted the fall of their city of Troy, and the Cumean Sibyl, who predicted the coming of Jesus Christ, also did so, though they were unbelievers. Even today, he testifies, certain Welshmen known as "those who are inspired" (*awenyddion*) fall into trances, babble incoherently, and yet speak the truth to those who question them. He states, "If you should ask, scrupulous reader, by what spirit such prophecies are brought forth, I do not necessarily say that it is pythonic or demoniacal."[42] If it is not their Christian religiosity that attracts the Holy Spirit to speak through these seers, Gerald hypothesizes, it may be their Trojan or, by extension, British nationality. Just as Calchas and Cassandra foretold its destruction and the coming of the Greeks, "at a time when the Kingdom of Britain still existed, Merlin . . . declared prophetically its destruction and the coming first of the Saxons and then of the Normans."[43] Because Britons can prophesy and because Merlin was a Briton, Gerald concludes, Merlin too could foretell the future. Despite the qualms some clerics expressed about them, Merlin's prophecies were already available in Welsh at least by the early twelfth century.[44] The Anglo-Norman chronicler Orderic Vitalis writes shortly before Geoffrey drafts the *Historia regum Britanniae*, "The prophet Merlin predicted the course of things to come in the northern isles and preserved it in writing in figurative language. . . . Some part of the book of Merlin . . . has, I know, already been fulfilled in past events, and, unless I am mistaken, more will be proved true, with sorrow or with joy, by future generations."[45]

Improvements on the Cairo Edition, ed. and trans. F. Rahman (Oxford: Oxford University Press, 1952), Avicenna connects this "intuition" to prophetic power, which he deems "the highest human faculty" (36–37).

42. "Sin autem quo spiritu proferantur hujusmodi, scrupulosus lector inquiras, non dico quod pithonico, non daemoniaco," Gerald of Wales, *Itinerarium Kambriae*, ed. Dimock, I, 16, p. 197.

43. "extante adhuc Britonum regno, gentis excidium, et tam Saxonum primo, quam etiam Normannorum post adventum, Merlinus . . . vaticinando declaravit," ibid., I, 16, p. 196. Pseudo-Alan of Lille, in *Explanationum in prophetiam Merlini Ambrosii Britani libri VII*, pp. 4–6, echoes Gerald's defense of Merlin, noting that Job, Balaam, the Cumaean Sibyl, and Virgil were all allowed by God to foresee the coming of Jesus Christ.

44. The surviving Welsh lyrics about Merlin cite his prophecies, though these works are difficult to date. In his *Expugnatio Hibernica*, in *Opera*, ed. Brewer, vol. 5, ed. Dimock, III, preface, pp. 401–3.

45. "Iamdictus vates seriatim quae futura erant insulis septemptrionis predixit, tipicisque locutionibus memoriae litterarum tradidit. . . . Merlini libello . . . cuius aliquam partem in rebus gestis intellexi, plura vero ni fallor cum merore seu gaudio experientur adhuc nascitur," *The Ecclesiastical History of Orderic Vitalis*, ed. and trans. Marjorie Chibnall, 6 vols. (Oxford: Clarendon Press, 1969–80), XII, 47, pp. 384 and 386.

While no *Prophetiae Merlini* has survived as an independent work, Geoffrey incorporates these prophecies into Book VII of his *Historia regum Britanniae*,[46] and Gerald cites them in other writings.[47] Once these prophecies were available in Latin, they became wildly popular and, indeed, the subject of five commentaries between the 1130s and 1170s. From Henry I's ascent to the throne of England in 1100 to Joan of Arc's appearance on the French political stage in 1429, observers interpreted current events as a fulfillment of Merlin's predictions.[48] For supporters of Merlin, there are true, biblical and Christian prophets and false, pagan sorcerers, but there are also profane people, like Cassandra, the Sibyl, and Merlin, who utter prophetic truths.

Even as rationalistic clerics rejected marvels and Merlin as contrary to Christian theology and contemplative clerics embraced them as orthodox, the authors of the earliest narrative accounts of Merlin—Geoffrey of Monmouth, Wace, and Robert de Boron—suggest that they occupy a third category, fundamentally unassimilable into the binary structures of medieval theologico-scientific ways of thinking. Certain individuals, they indicate, receive a "spirit" that enables them to gain an insight into Creation that other people do not possess. While most people understand the world as defined by causation, where effects are produced by causes, these prophets understand it as defined by signification, where things are indicated by signs. While most people conceive of time as a linear sequence of points, where the past gives way

46. See Geoffrey of Monmouth, *Historia regum Britanniae*, ed. Reeve, VII, p. 142. See also Caroline D. Eckhardt, "The *Prophetia Merlini* of Geoffrey of Monmouth: Latin Manuscript Copies," *Manuscripta* 26 (1982): 167–76. While William of Newburgh accuses Geoffrey of having added to Merlin's prophecies with his own inventions, he does not accuse him of having invented them all together. See also Julia Crick, "Geoffrey and the Prophetic Tradition," in *The Arthur of Medieval Latin Literature*, ed. Echard, 67–82, and R. W. Southern, "Aspects of the European Tradition of Historical Writing, 3: History as Prophecy," *Transactions of the Royal Historical Society* 22 (1972): 159–80.

47. Gerald of Wales claims to have finally found a copy of Merlin's prophecies in Nefyn, in Gwynned, Wales, and to have translated it into Latin. See *Expugnatio Hibernica*, ed. Dimock, III, preface, pp. 401–3, and *Itinerarium Kambriae*, ed. Dimock, II, 6, p. 124. Though neither this original Welsh book nor Gerald's Latin translation has survived, Gerald does refer to nineteen of Merlin's prophecies, none of which overlap with those transcribed by Geoffrey. John of Cornwall similarly cites Merlin's prophecies in his *Prophetia Merlini* (1141–55). In "A New Edition of John of Cornwall's *Prophetia Merlini*," *Speculum* 57, no. 2 (1982): 217–49, Michael J. Curley maintains that only thirty-eight out of the 139 prophecies John lists can be traced back to Geoffrey of Monmouth; the others derive from Welsh or perhaps, intriguingly, Cornish sources.

48. For discussion of medieval historians who who cited Merlin's predictions, see Zumthor, *Merlin le prophète*, 82–85. On the *Prophetiae Merlini* and its commentaries, see *Moult obscures paroles: Etudes sur la prophétie médiévale*, ed. Richard Trachsler (Paris: Presses de l'Université Paris-Sorbonne, 2007), including Géraldine Veysseyre, "*Metre en roman*: Les prophéties de Merlin; Voies et détours de l'interprétation dans trois traductions de *l'Historia regum Britannie*," 107–66, and Claire Wille, "Le Dossier des commentaires latins des *Prophetie Merlini*," 167–83.

to the present and the present gives way to the future, these prophets conceive of it as a web of correspondences, where portents anticipate the future and memorials recall the past. Finally, while most people attempt to obtain the truth and whatever else they desire by actively inquiring into it, Merlin teaches that those who passively await assistance are sometimes rewarded. As Geoffrey and these vernacular authors see it, in order to grasp the truths that Merlin offers, one must be able to conceive of truth the way this mysterious figure does.

The Madman and the Seer

In the first tradition we have about him, Merlin is an ambiguous figure, not because he is diabolical, but because he is mad. Around 1150, Geoffrey of Monmouth was inspired by an existing Welsh tradition about "Myrddin," reflected in a half-dozen surviving Welsh poems from the ninth, tenth, and eleventh centuries, to compose his 1,529-line Latin poem, the *Vita Merlini*. In this poem, "Merlinus," as Geoffrey now named him, is the king of the South Welsh at the turn of the sixth and seventh centuries and an ally of Peredur, the king of the North Welsh, who is waging war on Gwendelau ap Ceidio, the ruler of Scotland. In the course of a battle between these two camps, Merlin witnesses the death of three close companions fighting at his side. In his grief, he loses his mind and, given the typical medieval conflation of madness and wildness, retreats to the Caledonian Forest, which stretched over much of what is now southern Scotland. On one level, the *Vita Merlini* represents this madman as a wretched creature who lives in alienation from his true, rational self; in alienation from the true, rational companionship of other human beings; and in alienation from the true, rational order of Creation. On another level, however, the poem represents this madman as a strangely blessed creature who possesses access, if not to reason, then to a certain "spirit"; if not to other human beings, then to fauna and flora; and, if not to the rational order of Creation, then to the transitory nature of earthly existence. If Merlin is marvelous, it is insofar as he is a human being who exceeds the boundaries of what it means to be a human being, whether by losing his human rationality or by gaining a superhuman spirituality.[49]

49. As Jacques Le Goff has argued in "The Marvelous in the Medieval West," in *The Medieval Imagination*, trans. Arthur Goldhammer (Chicago: University of Chicago Press, 1985), 27–44, "the official ideology of Christianity" (32) propounded a certain humanism in the Middle Ages, exalt-

The *Vita Merlini*, existing as it does in only one complete manuscript, seems to have been little distributed and little read during the Middle Ages,[50] but the influence of the Merlin it depicts should not be underestimated.[51] While the wild man of the woods would be eclipsed by the advisor of British courts, the later Merlin would continue to withdraw periodically into a forest; would continue to possess secret knowledge about both human and nonhuman creatures; and would continue to have access to a "spirit"[52] that could not be identified clearly with either a demon or an angel. Though Merlin ceases to be a madman or a wild man in the romances, other major Arthurian figures, such as Lancelot of the Lake, Tristan, and Yvain, lose their minds and retreat to the woods; even when sane, the knight errant is, like Merlin "Silvester," a solitary figure, wandering about the forest and living in estrangement from society.[53] In French romance, as in this Latin poem, the madman demonstrates that truth can be found, not only or even primarily in a rational, human discourse, but also in an inspired, extrahuman experience.

When Merlin becomes mad in the *Vita Merlini*, he loses his reason and, as a result, his capacity for rational speech. He is represented as suffering from "frenzy [*furor*],"[54] "fury [*furia*],"[55] and "raving [*rabies*],"[56] all words for a specific kind of madness, which, at this time, was con-

ing man as the image of God and, by the same token, God as the image of man, yet the marvelous offered an alternative to this ideology, emphasizing animals, minerals, and plants in human beings' stead. It is in his antihumanism that the Merlin of the *Vita Merlini* becomes marvelous.

50. There exists only one complete manuscript of the *Vita Merlini* (Cotton Vespasian E iv, fol. 112b–138b), from the late thirteenth century; four collections of extracts, covering all together about half the text of the full manuscript; and two manuscripts that have shorter extracts from the prophetic parts of the *Vita Merlini*. Given this limited manuscript evidence, Clarke has speculated that Geoffrey composed this poem for a small group of friends.

51. Gerald of Wales, in *Descriptio Kambriae*, ed. Dimock, I, 16, p. 196, refers not only to the more familiar Welsh or "Cambrian Merlin," but also to the Scottish or "Calidonian Merlin" of this poem.

52. Merlin refers to "the spirit that teaches me [*spiritus qui me docet*]," Geoffrey of Monmouth, *Historia regum Britanniae*, ed. Reeve, VIII, p. 173, and to "the spirit I possess, from whom I know what I know [*li espirites que jo ai, / par ki jo sai ço que jo sai*]," Wace, *Roman de Brut*, ed. Weiss, vv. 8031–32.

53. Judith S. Neaman, in *Suggestion of the Devil: The Origins of Madness* (Garden City, NJ: Anchor Books, 1975), speculates that if the madman (and the maniac in particular) became such an important figure in romance, it was because he epitomized the new, romance hero, who is an individual alienated from society and even from himself, in contrast, perhaps, to the old, epic hero, who was an integral member of his society (141). See also Sylvia Huot, *Madness in Medieval French Literature: Identities Lost and Found* (Oxford: Oxford University Press, 2003).

54. "furores," Geoffrey of Monmouth, *Vita Merlini*, in *The Life of Merlin*, ed. Basil Clarke (Cardiff: University of Wales Press, 1973), v. 226.

55. "furias," ibid., vv. 72, 190, and 223.

56. "rabiem," ibid., v. 1; "rabiem," ibid., 1150.

trasted with other forms of madness, such as stupor or melancholy,[57] on account of the irrationality into which its sufferer descends. Some of Merlin's previous companions who happen to eat poisoned apples similarly succumb to "miserable raving,"[58] we are told. Losing their reason, these companions lose the ability to speak, as human beings do, and they cry and howl instead, like wild beasts (or, perhaps more precisely, like rabid wild beasts): "Lacking reason, . . . they screamed, foamed at the mouth, and rolled on the ground, demented. Then they dispersed and went off, filling the empty air with their pitiful howlings, like wolves."[59] Merlin differs from these other madmen because he retains the capacity for speech, but his utterances seem to bear no relation to reality. He laughs when he sees Rodarch, king of the Cumbrians and husband of his sister Ganieda, brush a leaf from his wife's hair, when he sees a doorkeeper beg outside the palace gates, and when he sees a young man buy patches for his new shoes, incidents in which no one else discerns any humor. Ganieda reproaches her husband for listening to her brother. "Why do you believe a madman [*furenti*] who, lacking reason, mixes lies and truths?"[60] she demands. Deprived of reason, as expressed in rational utterances, Merlin is deprived of his very self. "For a whole summer," it is said, "he stayed hidden in the woods, discovered by none, forgetful of himself."[61]

Losing his reason, Merlin loses his feeling for other human beings. When he is mad, it is said, "Feeling [*sensus*] [was] long dormant in him."[62] Of Merlin's maddened companions, we are told, "Lacking reason, they lacerated each other, biting each other, like dogs."[63] Though they were friends a moment before, now that they are mad they perceive each other as strangers, and threatening ones at that. Again, Merlin differs from these other madmen because he retains the capacity to recognize people he previously held dear, but he too has lost the capacity to sympathize with them. He abandons Ganieda, who, a min-

57. Neaman writes in *Suggestion of the Devil*, "*Furor* was rage or mania. . . . Those suffering from *mens alienata* were comparable to our schizophenics and were out of touch with social reality or estranged" (90).

58. "rabies miserabilis," Geoffrey of Monmouth, *Vita Merlini*, ed. Clarke, v. 1417.

59. "ratione carentes / . . . / Stridunt et spumant et humi sine mente volutant. / Denique digressi sunt illinc, more lupino / complentes vacuas miseris ulalatibus auras," ibid., vv. 1418–22.

60. "credisque furenti / qui ratione carens miscet mendacia veris?" ibid., vv. 300–301.

61. "Inde per estatem totam nullique repertus / oblitusque sui," ibid., vv. 82–83.

62. "torpuerat per longum tempus in illo / sensus," ibid., vv. 1150–51.

63. "ratione carentes / more canum sese lacerant mordendo vicissim," ibid., vv. 1418–19.

strel recounts, "grieves for her lost brother, comfortless."[64] He abandons his wife Gwendoloena, who, the minstrel also reports, sheds "piteous tears."[65] He abandons his subjects, who beseech him to return to them. "I will not reign again,"[66] he tells them. In his madness, Merlin forgets all attachments, whether familial, marital, or feudal, which had once bound him to other human beings, and he ceases to feel the compassion he would have once felt for those close to him and in distress. Fleeing his sister, his wife, and his subjects, Merlin flees human contact altogether. When a traveler encounters him in the forest, we are told, "Merlin saw him and was off. The traveler followed, but could not keep up with the fugitive."[67] At one point, Merlin is lured back to court, but he is overwhelmed by the sight of all the people in the palace: "When Merlin saw such crowds of people there, he could not bear them. He went mad, and once more his derangement filled him with a desire to go off to the forest, and he longed to slip away."[68] Deprived of feeling, Merlin becomes "forgetful," not only "of himself," but, we are told, "of his people as well, . . . lurking like a wild thing."[69]

Losing his feeling for human beings, Merlin loses, finally, his reverence for God. In the beginning of the poem, summer turns to winter, and the nineteen apple trees that had once nourished him cease to bear fruit. He protests, "They stand so no longer. . . . Where have they gone so suddenly? Now I see them, now I do not."[70] If he reproaches this divinity, it is because he grasps only one part of Creation—one place, namely, the forest where he is living, and one time, namely, the winter, which is now upon him. If he grasps only part of Creation, it is because he uses only his senses, which allow him to comprehend only what he experiences in the present. He states, "I see there is nothing here to eat—no grass on the ground, no acorns on the tree."[71] As a result, he feels bitterness toward God, who has neglected him. "O King of all, how happens it that all the seasons are not the same?" he asks him. "Would

64. "dolet sine consolamine fratrum," ibid., v. 186.

65. "miseras lacrimas," ibid., v. 171.

66. "Rursus regnare recuso," ibid., v. 1280.

67. "Quo viso Merlinus abit sequiturque viator, / nec retinere virum potuit sic diffugientem," ibid., vv. 117–18.

68. "At postquam tantas hominum Merlinus adesse / inspexit turmas, nec eas perferre valeret. / Cepit enim furias iterumque furore repletus / ad nemus ire cupit furtimque recedere querit," ibid., vv. 221–24.

69. "cognatorumque suorum / . . . obductus more ferino," ibid., vv. 81–83.

70. "nunc non stant . . . / Quo devenere repente? / Nunc illas video, nunc non," ibid., vv. 92–94.

71. "nil quo vescar adesse / inspicio, nec gramen humi nec in arbore glandes," ibid., vv. 96–97.

there were no winter, no white frost!"[72] Merlin is distressed, not only because he is hungry, but because he does not understand how it can be that the world functions in such a way as to leave him hungry. At the end of the poem, when Merlin regains his reason, he praises this deity. Lifting his face toward the heavens, he extols the Lord, "by whom the frame of the starry sky stands established; through whom the earth with happy seed and the sea give forth and cherish their children and provide for man repeatedly out of their abundant fertility."[73] If he praises God, it is because he is able to grasp the whole of his Creation, from its "starry sky," to its "earth with happy seed," to its "sea." And if he is able to grasp the whole of Creation, it is because he is able to use his intellect, which allows him to comprehend a totality that his senses could not encompass. Because he perceives the whole of Creation in this manner, he feels gratitude toward God, who provides for that which he has made in general, if not at every time and place. When Merlin is free, as a human being, to consider all times and places, as he perceives them with his intellect, he knows God to care for his creatures, but when he is confined, like an animal, to one time and place, as he perceives it with his senses, he believes him to be indifferent to his plight, and he is wretched as a result. The text relates, "When winter came and took all the plants and the fruit on the trees and left him nothing to live upon, he poured out these complaints in a pitiful voice."[74] Forgetful of himself and his people, Merlin is forgetful of God as well.

Yet the poem makes clear, as Merlin loses reason and the capacity for rational speech, he gains access to spirit and the capacity for prophecy.[75] As he later recalls, when he became mad, "I was taken up out of myself [*raptus eram michimet*], like a spirit [*quasi spiritus*]. I knew the acts of people long past, and I could predict those of the future."[76] At

72. "O qui cuncta regis, quid est cur contigit ut non / tempora sint eadem numeris distincta quaternis? / . . . / O utinam non esset hiems aut cana pruina!" ibid., vv. 146–55.

73. "siderei quo constat machina celi, / quo mare quo tellus leto cum germine fetus / dantque foventque suos crebroque juvamine prosunt / human generi profusa fertilitate," ibid., vv. 1156–59.

74. "At cum venit yems herbasque tulisset et omnes / arboreos fructus nec quo frueretur haberet, / diffudit tales miseranda voce querelas," ibid., vv. 84–86.

75. See Jan Ziolkowski, "The Nature of Prophecy in Geoffrey of Monmouth's *Vita Merlini*," in *Poetry and Prophecy: The Beginnings of a Literary Tradition*, ed. James L. Kugel (Ithaca, NY: Cornell University Press, 1990), 151–62. Neil Thomas argues, in "The Celtic Wild Man Tradition and Geoffrey of Monmouth's *Vita Merlini*: Madness or *Contemptus Mundi*?" *Arthuriana* 10, no. 1 (2000): 27–42, that Geoffrey brought together the figure of the wild man from world literature with the figure of the saint from Cambrian historiography, thus rendering the wild man holy.

76. "Raptus eram michimet quasi spiritus acta sciebam / preteriti populi predicebamque futura," Geoffrey of Monmouth, *Vita Merlini*, ed. Clarke, vv. 1161–62.

the same time that he becomes "forgetful of himself," by losing his reason, he gains a new faculty of perception, through rapture. At the end of the work, Ganieda undergoes a similar transformation. The poem reports, "Her spirit [*suus . . . spiritus*] took her up out of herself [*rapiebat*] so that she would often sing of the future of the kingdom."[77] "The spirit" is here an entity in and of itself, which brings these siblings outside of themselves and, in doing so, enables them to predict what is to come.[78] When the text describes Merlin as "taken up out of [himself], like a spirit," or when it states that Ganieda's "spirit took her up out of herself," it evokes Saint Paul's depiction of the Holy Spirit, one of whose charisms is the gift of prophecy, and the Apostle's description of himself as "taken up [*raptum*] to the third heaven"[79]—a state that Augustine identifies as the intellectual vision of God. Yet even if this spirit were assumed to be the Holy Spirit, there is no indication that the purposes for which it has inspired Merlin or Ganieda are holy, given the purely secular nature of their predictions. Like the seers recognized in classical philosophy, Merlin succumbs to "frenzy," he is overtaken by a higher force when he is in this state, and he acquires the ability to prophesy, yet, unlike the inspired figures of Christian theology, he does not identify this higher force as good or evil, godly or diabolical. If Merlin's utterances when he is mad seem to bear no relation to reality, it is only because they express hidden truths, which those around him cannot appreciate. He laughs when Rodarch brushes a leaf from his wife's hair because the leaf became entangled in her locks when she crept into the underbrush to lie with her lover. He laughs when the doorkeeper begs by the palace gate because a hoard of coins lies buried underneath the spot where he is standing. He laughs when the young man buys patches for his new shoes because he will drown before he has the chance to use them. Ultimately, it is not Merlin's laughter, but people's actions, which provoke this laughter, that make no sense. Juxtaposing Rodarch's loyalty to his wife with his wife's disloyalty to him, the doorkeeper's poverty with the wealth lying beneath him, and the

77. "Hanc etiam quandoque suus rapiebat ad alta / spiritus ut caneret de regno sepe futura," ibid., vv. 1469–70.

78. While the *Vita Merlini*, ed. Clarke, makes periodic reference to the Christian God, Geoffrey appeals to the Muses in his dediction; Ganieda, at one point, takes leave of her "household gods [*lares*]" (v. 715); and Taliesin delivers a discourse, "Minerva teaching him [*dictante Minerva*]" (v. 736). It is customary for medieval Latin authors to incorporate their writings into the classical Latin literary tradition by citing these pagan deities—who typically function as superficial literary devices—but this poem is clearly evoking a genuine supernatural force when it speaks of the spirit.

79. "raptum hujusmodi usque ad tertium caelum," 2 Cor. 12:2. See also 1 Cor. 12:10.

young man's prudence in buying patches with the disaster that awaits him, Merlin shows how human beings' ignorance of the past, the present, and the future leads them to act in foolish ways. It takes a madman to see the truth because only a madman can appreciate the essential absurdity of the human condition and can give voice to the dark comedy in which we live. The loss of reason, that is, of that which distinguishes a human being as a human being, is what enables Merlin to become like a spirit and, hence, to look upon other human beings from a superior perspective.

As Merlin loses his feeling for human beings, he gains feeling for fauna and flora. He observes these nonhuman creatures. At the onset of his madness, the text recounts, "He went into the forest, glad to lie hidden beneath the ash trees. He marveled at [*miratur*] the wild creatures grazing on the pasture of the glades."[80] Settling down next to a spring bordered by hazels and thorn bushes, the text continues, "He would watch [*spectabat*] the whole woodland and the running and gamboling of the creatures of the wild."[81] "Watching [*spectans*]," "inspecting [*inspiciens*]," or "seeing [*videns*]" these fellow denizens of the forest, he learns about them, so that, later, when some chieftains ask him about the cranes they see flying in long lines across the sky, he is able to teach them how they maintain order during their flight. As he dwells among these creatures, he becomes sensitive to what they are suffering, and he identifies with these sensations. He addresses a wolf who inhabits the woods with him: "Wolf, dear companion, you used to wander along the byways of the forest and through the glades with me; now you scarcely get across the field. Harsh hunger has weakened both you and me. You lived in these woods before me, and age has turned you grey first."[82] If the wolf is Merlin's companion, in a way in which other human beings are not, it is because they live together in this forest; because they are aging together in this inhospitable place; and because they suffer the pangs of hunger together, unable to find nourishment in this locale. Merlin speaks with similar feeling of an oak tree that he has seen develop from an acorn, to a sapling, to a fully grown tree and that he is now seeing die. Immediately after recalling how the oak has lived long, he adds, "I have lived long, then, and by

80. "ingreditur . . . nemus gaudetque latere sub ornis / miraturque feras pascentes gramina saltus," Geoffrey of Monmouth, *Vita Merlini*, ed. Clarke, vv. 75–76.

81. "inde per omnes / spectabat silvas cursusque jocosque ferarum," ibid., vv. 140–41.

82. "Tu lupe care comes, nemorum qui devia mecum / et saltus peragrare soles vix preteris arva, / et tur dura fames et me languere coegit. / Tu prior has silvas coluisti, te prior etas / protulit in canos," Geoffrey of Monmouth, *Vita Merlini*, ed. Clarke, vv. 102–6.

now the weight of my years has told upon me."[83] As he identified with the wolf, who has become weak and unable to hunt in his old age, he identifies with the oak, which is losing its sap and beginning to rot. Whether animal or vegetable, Merlin suggests, in accordance with the tradition of Welsh poetry,[84] that all mortal creatures live and, at a certain point, decline. Though Merlin forgets human beings, this forgetting enables him to feel a kinship with other creatures he had not felt before.

As Merlin loses one kind of reverence for God, he gains another. If Merlin goes mad, it is because he perceives the part, disconnected from the whole, in all of its intensity. He focuses upon one place, the battlefield where he and his three companions have been fighting, and upon one time, when those companions are struck down. He laments, "Brave youths, . . . a moment back, and you were tearing through the formations in battle array, striking down all the opposition. Now you lie heavy on the earth, red with fresh blood."[85] The violence that appalls him is not the violence of the battle itself but the violence of fate, which, in an instant, can make that which is active, mobile, and alive passive, inert, and dead. Yet even though these thoughts precipitate Merlin into his madness, the problem seems to be not that he fails to grasp the truth of Creation but that he grasps it all too well. Later in the poem, when Rodarch dies, Gaienda deplores the loss of the husband who had one moment been so fair, reclining on luxurious sheets, and who the next is decomposing under the cold stone. She mourns, "There is no profit in the intermittent glory of the passing world, a painful deception even for the great. . . . What if the rose blushes? What if white lilies bloom? What if a man, a horse, or all the rest be fair?"[86] The violence that appalls her is, once more, the violence of fate, which ensures that everything that is living on earth will one day die, no matter how noble or how beautiful it may be. While Merlin is descending into madness as he mourns his three companions, Ganieda is perfectly sane as she utters these words. And while Merlin echoes other

83. "Ergo diu vixi, mea me gravitate senectus / detinuit dudum," ibid., vv. 1277–78.

84. See Kenneth Jackson, *Studies in Early Celtic Nature Poetry* (Cambridge: University Press, 1935). The affinity between the hermit and the animals among whom he lives is evident in many of these works.

85. "Audaces juvenes, . . . / Qui modo per cuneos discurrebatis in armis / obstantesque viros prosternebatis ubique / nunc pulsatis humum rubeoque cruore rubetis!" Geoffrey of Monmouth, *Vita Merlini*, ed. Clarke, vv. 49–53.

86. "nichil prodest pereuntis gloria mundi / que fugit atque redit fallit leditque potentes / . . . / Quid rosa si rutilet, si candida lilia vernent, / si sit pulcher homo vel equus vel cetera plura?" ibid., vv. 710–18.

Celtic warriors, both historical[87] and literary,[88] who lost their minds as a result of battle, Ganieda echoes the conventional trope of *sic transit gloria mundi*. Though Merlin forgets God, as the Arbiter of the universe, this forgetting enables him to remember how transitory our existence is, with its cycle of birth, decline, and death, and, in doing so, to enter into a long-standing Christian discourse.

As the poem recalls in the end, there are two kinds of people who inhabit the forest—mad or wild men and holy men—and these two populations overlap more than it might seem. According to one medieval tradition, the man who loses his reason, flees to the forest, and despairs of Creation is a wretched soul, tormented by the devil. In two short twelfth-century texts,[89] Saint Kentigern, the legendary sixth-century founder of Geoffrey's eventual see at Asaph, encounters Lailoken, a madman and wild man who lives in the Caledonian Forest in Scotland and who is loosely identified with Merlin,[90] and he perceives him as one such miserable creature. Considering how Lailoken lives, without the food, clothing, and shelter necessary for human beings, Kentigern deems him to be "the most wretched of wretched men . . .

87. It appears to have not been uncommon for men to become "mad" (*gelt* in Irish or *gwyllt* in Welsh) in battle: the Irish *Mirabilia* in the thirteenth-century Old Norse *Kongs Skuggsjo* (*Speculum Regale*) relates, "It happens . . . that cowardly men run wild and lose their wits from the dread and fear which can seize them. And then they run into a wood away from other men and live there like wild beasts and shun the meeting of men like wild beasts," *Kongs Skuggsjo* (*Speculum Regale*), in *Ériu* 4 (1910): 11. In *Yr Afallennau*, Merlin is said not only to become a madman but to join the company of "the wild men" (*gwyllon*).

88. In the twelfth-century *Buile Suibhne* (*Suibhne's Frenzy*), "Mad Sweeney" (*Suibhne Geilt*), a legendary king of Dál nAraidi in Ulster, is said to have lost his mind, fled into the forest, and lived high in trees. See *"The Banquet of Dún na nGédh" and "The Battle of Mag Rath,"* ed. and trans. J. O. Donovan (Dublin: Irish Archaeological Society, 1848), and *"Buile Shuibhne (The Frenzy of Suibhne)," Being the Adventures of Suibhne Geilt, A Middle-Irish Romance*, ed. and trans. J. G. O'Keeffe (London: D. Nutt, 1913).

89. The two accounts of Lailoken precede the *Vita Kentigerni* (1147–64) in the manuscript Titus A xix in the British Library. The first account, which was given the title *Vita Merlini silvestris* by a later writer, takes up folios 74–75. It was edited by H. L. D. Ward as "St. Kentigern and Laikoken" in "Lailoken (or Merlin Silvester)," *Romania* 22 (1893): 504–26, at 514–21, parallel to Walter Bower's fifteenth-century abridgement of this text in his *Scotichronicon*. Ward's edition of the twelfth-century text was reprinted and annotated by Christine Bord and Jean-Claude Berthet in *Le Devin maudit: Merlin, Laikloken, Suibhne; Textes et étude*, ed. Philippe Walter (Grenoble: Ellug, 1999), 176–91. The second account of Laikoken, which has no title, continues on folio 75 of Titus A xix. It was edited by Ward as "King Meldred and Lailoken" in "Lailoken (or Merlin Silvester)," 522–25, and reprinted by Bord and Berthet, in *Le Devin maudit*, 192–202. Though these texts clearly overlap with Geoffrey of Monmouth's *Vita Merlini*, it is not clear which text influenced which.

90. "St. Kentigern and Laikoken," ed. Ward, refers to Lailoken as someone "whom some say to have been Merlin, who was an extraordinary prophet among the British, but this is not known to be certain [*quem quidam dicunt fuisse Merlynum, qui erat Britonibus quasi propheta singularis, sed nescitur*]" (515).

like a beast among beasts, a naked fugitive feeding only on plants."[91] For a human being to live in the woods is for him to live, not like a human being, but like an animal. And for a human being to live like an animal, the account makes clear, is for him to suffer divine punishment. Lailoken explains to Kentigern that a celestial voice condemned him to live with the beasts of the woods: "I was torn out of my own self, . . . I am unworthy to meet the punishment for my sins among men."[92] A human being is essentially different from a beast, given that he, alone among these creatures, has been made in the image of God and has been endowed with reason and speech. For that reason, for him to be living among beasts, instead of among his fellow human beings, can only be a punishment by demons or, at best, a penance from God. So alienated has Lailoken become from his natural, God-given condition that when Kentigern first addresses him, he adjures him to speak, "whatever creature of God you are . . . if you are in any degree of God and believe in God."[93] Kentigern is not sure if Lailoken is a human being or a beast, let alone if he is conscious of the Creator who has made him. According to another medieval tradition, however, the man who is inspired by divine grace, who retreats to the woods to become a hermit, and who places hope in the Creator is a saint, blessed by God.[94] Gildas, the sixth-century British saint and historian, is said to have retired to the solitary life on the island of Houet, off the coast of Brittany. In his *Vita Gildae,* Caradoc of Llancarfan, a friend of Geoffrey of Monmouth, writes, "He warned men to despise, he advised them to scorn mere transitory things."[95] In another *Vita Gildae,* from the eleventh century, the Monk of Rhuys recounts how two of Gildas's brothers and his sister retreated to "the remotest part of that region,"[96] apparently near Quiberon Bay. There, it is said, "Despising all the wealth

91. "miserorum miserrimus hominum, . . . inter bestias ut bestia nudus et profugus et herbarum tantum pabulo pastus," ibid., 516.

92. "Unde extra meipsum conversum, . . . non sum dignus inter homines mea punire peccamina," ibid., 515–16.

93. "qualiscunque es creatura dei . . . si ex parte dei es et in deum credis, ut mecum, loquaris," ibid., 515.

94. On the connection between the retreat to the forest and early medieval eremetical spirituality, see Jean Leclercq, "L'Erémitisme en Occident jusqu'à l'an mil," *L'Eremitismo in Occidente nei secoli XI e XII. Atti della seconda Settimana internazionale di studio, Mendola (30 agosto–6 settembre 1962)* (Milan: Società Editrice Vita e Pensiero, 1965), 27–44.

95. "Praecipiebat spernere, ammonebat despicere quae transeunt in momento," Caradoc of Llancarfan, *Vita Gildae,* in *Gildae "De excidio Britanniae," "Fragmenta," "Liber de Paenitentia," accedit et "Lorica Gildae" / Gildas: "The Ruin of Britain," "Fragments from the Lost Letters," "The Penitential," Together with "The Lorica of Gildas,"* ed. and trans. Hugh Williams (London: David Nutt, 1899), 394–413, at 396.

96. "in extrema parte regionis illius," Monk of Ruys, *Vita Gildae,* in ibid., 322–89, at 326.

and luxuries of the world, [they] strove with the whole bent of their soul to reach the celestial country and devoted their lives to fasting and prayers."[97] It was commonly recognized that when people like Gildas and his siblings withdraw from physical possessions, they become more open to receiving spiritual illuminations.[98] At the end of the *Vita Merlini*, Merlin regains his wits, but, instead of returning to society, as one might expect, he remains in the woods, together with Ganieda, Taliesin, the celebrated British bard, and Maeldin, another recovered madman. He justifies his decision with a new, eremitical language: "Here I will be while I live, happy with fruit and herbs, and I will purify my flesh with pious fasting, to enable me to enjoy everlasting life."[99] Just as Merlin possesses a natural spirit, independent of the Holy Spirit, which enables him to prophesy, and a natural affinity to fauna and flora, independent of any rational human capacity, which enables him to comprehend these creatures, he possesses a natural holiness, independent of Christian doctrine, which enables him to spurn material goods. Once he regains his sanity—that is, once he remembers his self, his fellow human beings, and God—he is able to put this natural spirit to good use and to transform his woodland home into an anchoritic retreat, which other human beings wish to join.

The Engineer and the Prophet

In the second tradition we possess about him, Merlin is an ambiguous figure, not because he is mad, but because he is skillful, in a way that is at once natural and supernatural. Around 1136, Geoffrey represents Merlin in his *Historia regum Britanniae* as a grandson of the king of Dyfed in southwest Wales who becomes a counselor to three consecutive kings of the British—Vortigern, Aurelius Ambrosius, and Aurelius's brother Uther—in the mid- to late fifth century. Over the next seven decades, Wace and then Robert de Boron recast his account into French. At the time when Merlin enters into this political stage, the Britons are at war with the Saxons, who have invaded their country,

97. "spretis opibus et deliciis toto nisu mentis ad supernam tendentes patriam in ieiuniis et orationibus suam commendantes," ibid., 16.

98. See Plato, *Phaedo*, XXVII; Augustine, *De Genesi ad litteram*, ed. Zycha, XII, 13, p. 397; and Thomas Aquinas, *Summa theologiae*, Blackfriars, vol. 45, II, II[ae], qu. 172, art. 4.

99. "Hic ero dum vivam pomis contentus et herbis, / et mundabo meam pia per jejunia carnem / ut valeam fungi vita sine fine perhenni," Geoffrey of Monmouth, *Vita Merlini*, ed. Clarke, vv. 1289–91.

and Vortigern has agreed to meet with them near Salisbury in order to work out a reconciliation. Though both sides agree to leave their weapons at home, the Saxons conceal long knives in their boots and, when given a signal by their leader, draw them out, grab the Briton next to them, and slit his throat. Four hundred and sixty British barons and earls are put to death that day. While Vortigern survives this massacre, he retreats to Mount Snowdon in Wales, where he attempts to build a fortress to defend himself against these foreigners, with Merlin's help. After Vortigern has died and Aurelius has ascended to the throne, the new king visits the cemetery at a monastery near Salisbury where these British noblemen have been buried, and he is troubled by the thought of their deaths. In order to commemorate these men, he resolves to build a monument on this site, "a new structure that would stand forever in memory of so many men,"[100] for which he too requires Merlin's assistance. On one level, Geoffrey's *Historia* represents Merlin as advising these kings on their construction projects through a kind of natural, scientific insight. During the time when Geoffrey was writing, an "engineer" (*ingeniator* in Latin or *engigneour* in French) was a constructor of "military engines" or other such "contrivances" (*machinationes* or *machinations*) who relied upon his "skill," "intelligence," or "wit" (*ingenium* or *engin*) in the completion of this task. The skill that Merlin shows in establishing a foundation for Vortigern's fortress and in transporting great stones for Aurelius's monument is that of such a workman. On another level, however, Geoffrey's history represents Merlin as advising these kings through a kind of supernatural, magical power. An "engineer" was not only a constructor but also potentially a deceiver, and his "skill" could be his deceit or even his magical power. At a time when "craft" (*ars* in Latin) could refer to either technical or magical ability, the man who could identify and make use of the occult virtues in physical entities in either way was thought to be of great assistance to his lord.

Merlin helps Vortigern in a manner that seems, at least at first, more natural than supernatural. In an episode lifted from the *Historia Brittonum*, a ninth-century chronicle attributed, in one manuscript line, to the Welsh monk Nennius, Geoffrey relates that every day, after the stonemasons working on Vortigern's tower have completed their work, the building is swallowed up by the earth. At a loss over what to

100. "novam . . . structuram adinvenire quae in memoriam tantorum virorum in aevum constaret," ibid., VIII, 128, p. 171.

do, Vortigern consults with what are called his "magicians [*magis*]."[101] (Robert de Boron will refer to these men as clerics specializing in "astronomy,"[102] a word used interchangeably with "astrology" at this time.) These men recommend that he find a fatherless child, kill him, and sprinkle his blood on the site where the tower is being built, as only by doing so, they maintain, will he be able to make this building stand. In proposing this solution, the magicians suggest that their king offer what is known in anthropology as a "foundation sacrifice,"[103] that is, the ritual murder of a human being (often a child) whose death was believed necessary in order to ensure the stability of a fortress, a bridge, or a church. Vortigern sends envoys throughout his kingdom to find such a youth, but, in Geoffrey's account, the boy they discover turns out to be Merlin, who chastises the magicians for speaking without knowing what they are talking about. He demands, "Tell me what lies hidden underneath the foundation. There is something beneath that does not permit it to stand."[104] When the magicians fail to answer him, Merlin instructs Vortigern to have his workmen dig into the earth, where, he promises, they will find a pool that is undermining his tower's stability. Merlin's words are justified when Vortigern's workmen do, in fact, uncover the pool. During these interactions with Vortigern, the magicians, and the workmen, Merlin seems to assume that a structure of a certain weight, like this tower, will need a foundation of a certain firmness to support it. If that structure keeps collapsing, he seems to think, it stands to reason that the foundation is not as sturdy as it should be—perhaps on account of a body of water lying underneath where it is being set. Because Merlin has discerned the presence of the pool underneath the tower's foundation, though

101. "magis," Geoffrey of Monmouth, *Historia regum Britanniae*, ed. Reeve, VI, 106, p. 136 passim. Cf. "magos suos," *Historia Brittonum*, in Nennius, *"British History" and "The Welsh Annals,"* ed. John Morris (London: Phillimore, 1980), 40, p. 70.

102. "astronomie," Robert de Boron, *Merlin*, ed. Micha, 20, p. 88. See Charles Burnett, "Astrology," in *Medieval Latin: An Introduction and Bibliograpical Guide*, ed. Frank Anthony, Carl Mantello, and A. G. Rigg (Washington, DC: Catholic University of America Press, 1996), 369–82, at 372.

103. On foundation sacrifices in the British Isles, see Leslie Forbes, *The Early Races of Scotland and Their Monuments*, 2 vols. (Edinburgh: Edmonston and Douglas, 1866), vol. 1, 149; Edward Burnett Tylor, *Primitive Culture*, 2 vols. (London: John Murray, 1871), vol. 1, 16; and M. MacLeod Banks, "A Hebridean Version of Colum Cille and St. Oran," *Folklore* 42, no. 1 (1931): 55–60. "Devil's Bridges" (which supposedly required such sacrifices) exist in numerous places in Wales, including Ceredigion; Pontwalby, Glynneath; Cardiganshire; and Worms Head, Rhossili, Pembrokeshire. In general, see Paul G. Brewster, "The Foundation Sacrifice Motif in Legend, Folksong, Game, and Dance," *Zeitschrift für Ethnologie* 96, no. 1 (1971): 71–89.

104. "Dicite michi quid sub fundamento latet. Nam aliquid sub illo est quod ipsum stare non permittit," Geoffrey of Monmouth, *Historia regum Britanniae*, ed. Reeve, VI, 108, p. 141.

he had not seen it, it is said, "All those who were present marveled at his wisdom."[105] While Geoffrey depicts Merlin as instructing the workmen to drain the pool with channels, Robert de Boron, in his version of the episode, emphasizes even more the technical assistance Merlin provides them as he shows them how to remove the soil, with the help of yoked buckets, horses, and carts, and how to drain the water, with the help of ditches. Insofar as Merlin does something worth marveling at, it is because he possesses an occult knowledge—that a pool is undermining the foundation and that it needs to be removed—but this knowledge seems, to us at any rate, entirely natural, based as it is upon physical laws.

As Merlin seems to rely upon natural rather than supernatural means in aiding Vortigern, he seems to rely upon the same methods in aiding Aurelius later on. When Aurelius embarks on his plan to construct a memorial on Salisbury Plain, Tremorius, the archbishop of Caerleon, suggests, "Bid [Merlin] to come and to use his skill [*ingenio*] to build the work you desire. . . . I do not deem anyone in your kingdom to be more distinguished in the skill [*ingenium*] . . . of the operation of contrivances [*in operationibus machinandis*]."[106] Carpenters and stonemasons, "uncertain of their skills [*ingeniis*],"[107] had already refused to accept this task. Summoned before the king, Merlin proposes that he bring what he calls "the Giants' Ring,"[108] a cluster of massive stones on Mount Killaraus in Ireland, to Britain. (Geoffrey later refers to the Giants' Ring, in a manner more familiar to us, as "the stone structure . . . which is known in the language of the English as 'Stonehenge.'"[109]) When the expeditionary force arrives before the Giants' Ring in Ireland, it might seem that the workmen among them possess "strength" (*vis*), namely, the brute force that enables them to move heavy objects, like stones, but they fail at this undertaking as well. Merlin taunts them, saying, "Use your strength [*viribus*], men, to take down the stones, and we shall see whether skill [*ingenium*] will yield to strength

105. "Ammirabantur etiam cuncti qui astabant tantum in eo sapientiam," ibid.

106. "Iube eum venire atque ingenio suo uti ut opus quod affectas constet . . . non existemo alterum esse in regno tuo cui sit clarius ingenium . . . in operationibus machinandis," ibid.

107. "ingeniis suis diffidentes," ibid.

108. "chorea gigantum," Geoffrey of Monmouth, *Historia regum Britanniae*, ed. Reeve, VIII, 128, p. 173.

109. "lapidum structuram . . . quae . . . Anglorum lingua Sanheng nuncupatur," ibid., XI, 180, p. 255. On Geoffrey of Monmouth's account of the construction of Stonehenge, see Stuart Piggott, "The Sources of Geoffrey of Monmouth. II: The Stonehenge Story." *Antiquity* 15, no. 60 (1941): 305–19, which is refuted by J. P. S. Tatlock in *The Legendary History of Britain*, 40–42.

or strength to skill."[110] With these words, he identifies the workers' approach to these stones—which involves ropes, pulleys, and ladders—with "strength," presumably because it relies upon the application of a superior physical force, and his own approach to these stones with "skill," presumably because it does not depend upon such power. When the workmen cannot move the stones, the text relates, "Merlin dissolved into laughter and prepared contrivances [*machinationes*] of his own"[111] with which he has the stones easily carried to the water and loaded onto the ships. It is thus, the text observes, that "he proved skill to prevail over strength."[112] In Wace's version of this episode, after the workmen fail to move the stones, Merlin tells them, "Rise, . . . you will do no more by force [*force*]. Now you shall see how knowledge and skill [*engin et saveir*] are better than bodily power [*vertue de cors*]."[113] As Merlin seems to know that a tower can be made to stand only through the reinforcing of its foundation, he seems to know that heavy stones can be transported for long distances only through similar techniques of engineering. Insofar as Merlin does something worth marveling at, it appears, it is, again, because he possesses an occult knowledge, but one entirely natural, based upon physical laws.

Yet the way in which Merlin helps Vortigern is, ultimately, at least as supernatural as it is natural. After Merlin has the workmen uncover the pool, he turns again to the king's magicians and bids them, "Tell me . . . what is beneath the pool."[114] When the magicians make no reply, he informs them, "You will see at the bottom two hollow rocks, and in them two sleeping dragons."[115] Those in attendance see his words to be confirmed when they behold two dragons emerge from the pool, one white and one red, and engage each other in a terrible battle. It may seem that it is one thing to know that a collapsing tower may have a pool underneath it and quite another thing to know that there are dragons in that pool. Yet Merlin knows not only that the dragons are there but what they mean as they enter into combat. As

110. "Utimini viribus vestris, iuvenes, ut in deponendo lapides istos appareat utrum ingenium virtuti an virtus ingenio cedat," Geoffrey of Monmouth, *Historia regum Britanniae*, ed. Reeve, VIII, 130, p. 175.

111. "solutus est Merlinus in risum suasque machinationes confecit," ibid.

112. "ingeniumque virtuti praevalere comprobavit," ibid. In addition to meaning "skill," *engin* also suggests at this time an inborn talent or intelligence, cleverness, deceitfulness, ingenuity, and even magical ability.

113. "Traiez vus . . . en sus, / ja par force nen ferez plus. / Or verrez engin e saveir / mielz que vertu de cors valeir," Wace, *Roman de Brut*, ed. Weiss, vv. 8143–46.

114. "Dicite michi . . . quid sub stagno est," Geoffrey of Monmouth, *Historia regum Britanniae*, ed. Reeve, VI, 108, p. 141.

115. "videbis in fundo duos concavos lapides et in illis duos dracones dormientes," ibid.

he sees how the red dragon is driven by the white dragon to the edge of the pool, he laments, "Alas for the red dragon, for its end is hastening. Its caverns will be occupied by the white dragon, who signifies [*significat*] the Saxons. . . . The red dragon designates [*designat*] the people of Britain, who will be oppressed by the white."[116] When he then sees how the red dragon rallies and drives the white dragon back, he comments, "At last the oppressed will prevail and resist the foreigners' savagery."[117] It may seem that it is one thing to know that there are dragons in the pool and quite another thing to know that these dragons stand for the Saxons and the Britons in their wars. Yet if Merlin is able to make such prognostications, the text states, it is because "the spirit of prophecy [*spiritum . . . prophetiae*] swept him up."[118] It makes no distinction between the reason that enables Merlin to discern the existence of the pool and the "spirit" that enables him to discern the future. Even when he was announcing the presence of the pool, the people are depicted, not only as marveling at his human insight, but as "deeming divine power [*numen*] to be in him."[119] If the people connect what might seem to be Merlin's natural and supernatural abilities, it is because they perceive him, not just as an engineer who can discern what lies underground, but as a prophet who can discern what lies in the future. Insofar as Merlin does something worth marveling at in this continuation of the episode, it is, again, because he possesses an occult knowledge—now, that two dragons lie in the pool and that these dragons represent these two warring nations—but this knowledge seems, at least to us, marvelous, based as it is upon a metaphysical inspiration.

Merlin stands out from other people, it is clear, because he knows not only how to excavate earth and drain water but how to interpret signs of future events. He is not interested in the cause of the dragons' behavior. He does not tell Vortigern why the dragons lie in two hollow rocks in the pool, why they are sleeping, or why, when awakened, they engage in combat, though the Welsh tale *Lludd a Llefelys* from the *Mabinogion* (which may have influenced or been influenced by the *Historia regum Britanniae*), answers all of these questions. Instead of the cause, Merlin is interested in the meaning of the dragons' behavior. In the

116. "Vae rubeo draconi: nam exterminatio eius festinat. Cavernas ipsius occupabit albus draco, qui Saxones . . . significat. Rubeus vero gentem designat Britanniae, quae ab albo opprimetur," ibid., VII, 112, p. 145.

117. "Praevalebit tantem oppressa et saeviciae exterorum resistet," ibid.

118. "spiritum hausit prophetiae," ibid., VII, 111, p. 145.

119. "existimantes numen esse in illo," ibid., VI, 108, p. 141.

Book of Revelations,[120] the dragon is a figure of Satan, and in the legends of Perseus, Hercules, Sigurd, Beowulf, and Peredur, he is a hoarder of gold.[121] Yet the red dragon who emerges from the drained pool is a warrior.[122] With this image, Geoffrey evokes "the Red Dragon" (*Y Ddraig Goch*) of British tradition who was carried on the military standards of the British king Cadwaladr in the seventh century,[123] as well as the word *draig* or *dragon* in Welsh, which refers to a warrior, a chieftain, or a military leader. (Geoffrey terms Uther "Pendragon," or "Dragon's Head."[124]) Should the skeptical reader of this text, medieval or modern, question whether there ever really were dragons and what these dragons were like, the dragons in this story provide ocular proof of an alternate population, distinct from ours in its reptilian form but identical to it in its opposition to foreign invaders, that functions as a mystical counterpart to the British. For the Britons watching the dragons' combat, this double acts out what they had not yet experienced but would experience before long. While patristic and medieval thinkers had long condemned magicians and astrologers, who read the movement of stars and the flight of birds, they had defended other interpreters, who made sense of the "signs" (*signa*) and "portents" (*portenta*) God sends the human race. As much of a rationalist as John of Salisbury believed that, just as God sends certain signs, such as the appearance of clouds or the behavior of birds, to inform farmers and sailors about immanent storms, so does he send other such signs to inform human beings about other matters: "At times, out of divine compassion, [God]

120. "Et projectus est draco ille magnus, serpens antiquus, qui vocatur diabolus, et Satanas, qui seducit universum orbem," Rev. 12:9.

121. Dragons protect treasure as well in Macrobius, *Saturnalia* I, 20, 3; Prosper of Aquitaine, PL 51, cols. 835–36; Martial, XII, 53, 3; and Isidore of Seville, *Etymologiae*, ed. Lindsay, XIV, 3, 7 and XIV, 6, 9. The Anglo-Saxons referred to their burial mounds (which contained gold) as "hills of the dragon."

122. Red and white are colors traditionally associated with otherwordly creatures in Celtic mythology. See Jessica Hemming, "*Bos Primagenius* in Britain: Or Why Do Fairy Cows Have Red Ears?" *Folklore* 113, no. 1 (2002): 71–82.

123. On the Roman use of the dragon standard, see Vegetius, *De Re Militari*, II, 13, and Ammianus Marcellinus, *Rerum gestorum libri*, XVI, 10, 7 and XVI, 12, 39. Isidore of Seville, in *Etymologiae*, ed. Lindsay, XVIII, 3, 1 and 3, lists dragons among the common images on military standards. See Carl Lofmark, *A History of the Red Dragon* (Llanrwst: Gwasg Carreg Gwalch, 1995). For the dragon's relevance to Merlin, see Michael J. Curley, "Animal Symbolism in the Prophecies of Merlin," in *Beasts and Birds of the Middle Ages: The Bestiary and Its Legacy*, ed. Willene B. Clark and Meradith T. McMunn (Philadelphia: University of Pennsylvania Press, 1989), 150–63, at 158–60.

124. The phrase "dragon's head" occurs several times in Scripture (such as in Ps. 17:13). Geoffrey tells us of Uther, "He was known as Uther 'Pendragon,' which means 'dragon's head' in British [*vocatus fuit Uther 'Pendragon,' quod Britannica lingua 'caput draconis' sonamus*]" (*Historia regum Britanniae*, ed. Reeve, VIII, 135, p. 181). *Pendraig* or *Pendragon* in Welsh means, not "dragon's head," but "chief dragon."

forearms our ignorance with the evidence of his signs."[125] Vortigern's advisors counsel him badly because they do not know how to interpret signs, and yet they attempt to do so nonetheless. In Robert's version, they are explicitly deceived by demons as a punishment for their curiosity. In contrast, Merlin counsels him well because he does know how to interpret signs, which are sent to his nation to brace them for what is to come.[126] Whether they are storm clouds gathering in the sky or dragons rising up into combat, the creatures of this world are all conveying messages about what is about to occur, for the benefit of those, like Merlin, who are capable of reading them.

As flawed a king as he is otherwise shown to be, Vortigern knows how one should respond to portents. It is striking that this ruler does not show any fear of the dragons, even when they rise up and enter into battle, belching forth flames and driving each other in turn to the edge of the pit. On the contrary, reference is made to "Vortigern . . . sitting . . . on the bank of the drained pool."[127] Later authors were intrigued by this image of the king sitting on the bank of the pool and beholding the battle. Gerald of Wales alludes to "Dinas Emrys, that is, the promontory of Ambrosius, where Merlin made his prophecies, Vortigern sitting on the bank."[128] Robert de Boron cites Vortigern as declaring of the dragons, "However much it costs, I will do whatever [Merlin] tells me to, so that I might find them."[129] He represents this leader as inviting all the worthy men of the land to watch the spectacle of the dragons' combat, and these men as exclaiming, "This should be worth seeing!"[130] If Vortigern can sit so close to the combat between these dragons and remain unthreatened by them, it may be because he knows them to be less things than signs. In Geoffrey's account, as the dragons fight, "The king ordered . . . Merlin to say what the battle of the dragons portended [*portendebat*],"[131] and he accepts Merlin's ac-

125. "Hoc quoque divinae miserationis est quod signorum suorum indicio ignorantiam nostram quandoque praemunit," John of Salisbury, *Policraticus*, ed. Keats-Rohan, II, 13, p. 92.

126. In the *Historia Brittonum*, ed. Morris, Ambrosius, the counterpart of Merlin, describes what he exposes, not only as a "marvelous . . . sign [*mirabile . . . signum*]" (42, p. 71) but as a "figure [*figura*]," ibid., like the "figures" (or "types") of Scripture.

127. "Sedente itaque Vortegirno . . . super ripam exhausti stagni," Geoffrey of Monmouth, *Historia regum Britanniae*, ed. Reeve, VII, 111, p. 145.

128. "Dynas Emereis, id est, promontorium Ambrosii, ubi Merlinus prophetizativit, sedente super ripam Vortigerno," Gerald of Wales, *Itinerarium Kambriae*, ed. Dimock, II, 8, p. 133.

129. "il ne me savra ja tant coster que je ne face quanque il me dira, tant que je les truisse," Robert de Boron, *Merlin*, ed. Micha, 28, p. 112.

130. "Ce fera molt bon veoir," ibid., 28, p. 113.

131. "praecepit rex . . . Merlino dicere quid proelium draconum portendebat," Geoffrey of Monmouth, *Historia regum Britanniae*, ed. Reeve, VII, 111, p. 145.

count of what this conflict foreshadows. He does not express incredulity or even skepticism that the dragons represent the Britons or the Saxons, that the battles between the dragons anticipate the battles that will take place between the Britons and the Saxons, or that any of the other events Merlin predicts will come to pass. On the contrary, when Merlin utters his predictions, we are told, "Vortigern, marveling even more than the others, praised the youth's sense and his predictions."[132] Whereas modern meteorological prophets claim to foresee the future because they believe they know what causes will produce what effects, Vortigern accepts that Merlin foresees the future because he knows what signs correspond to what things. In doing so, he grasps not the relation of cause and effect but the relation of signifier and signified. In all of this, the king represents the readers of this text, who also watch the combat between the dragons, who also feel unthreatened by these dragons' violence, and who also want to know the meaning of what they see. If we are to read the prophecies of Merlin that are inserted at this point in the text the right way, we should imitate Vortigern by marveling at these prophecies, as he marvels at the dragons, and by learning from this spectacle, as he learns from it.

As with Vortigern, Merlin helps Aurelius in a manner that may seem ultimately at least as supernatural as it is natural. Though Merlin succeeds in constructing the memorial that Aurelius had requested, it is not clear, at first, in what way his skills are superior to those of the workmen who had failed to accomplish this task. Geoffrey tells us that Merlin builds "contrivances" (*machinationes*) with which he transports the stones, but he never tells us what exactly these contrivances are. They clearly do not involve ropes, pulleys, or ladders, as these are the devices with which the workmen try and fail to move the stones. When Merlin first tells Aurelius about these stones, he explains, "The Giants' Ring . . . is a structure of stones which no man of this era could erect except by skill [*ingenium*] and craft [*artem*] combined. Great are the stones; they will not yield to the strength [*virtuti*] of any man."[133] With these words, Merlin suggests that while the giants of the past could transport these stones with "strength," the men of the present, given their weakness, must rely upon "skill." While Geoffrey does not explain with what "skill" Merlin transported these stones, he cites

132. "Vortegirnus vero prae ceteris ammirans et sensum iuvenis et vaticinia collaudat," ibid., VIII, 118, p. 161.

133. "chorea gigantum . . . [e]st etenim ibi structura lapidum quam nemo huius aetatis construeret nisi ingenium artem subvectaret. Grandes sunt lapides, nec est aliquis cuius virtuti cedant," ibid., VIII, 128, p. 173.

Tremorius as declaring that he knew no one in the kingdom to be more distinguished, not only "in the operation of contrivances," but "in the skill . . . of telling the future."[134] Wace makes clear that Merlin was able to move the stones, not by inventing machines, but by speaking certain words: "He looked around, and he moved his lips like a man saying his prayers. I do not know if he said a prayer or not."[135] Once Merlin has spoken these words, he recounts, the workmen are able to load the stones easily into the boats. As Wace hints that Merlin transported the stones by using an incantation, Robert states that he did so "by force of craft,"[136] which also indicates magic. After Merlin has brought the stones to Salisbury, he proposes that they be set upright, "for they would be far more beautiful standing up than lying down."[137] Before he erects the stones in their famous trilithons, he makes everyone withdraw, seemingly because his methods in raising them are not something to be witnessed by others. As Geoffrey and his successors make no distinction between Merlin's natural ability to ascertain a weak foundation and his supernatural ability to ascertain future events, they make no distinction between the ordinary skill with which any builder might construct a memorial and the extraordinary skill with which Merlin transports these stones. The reconstruction of the Giants' Ring thus lies at the border between what is based on physical laws and what exceeds these laws, though exactly how it does so we are not told.

Merlin stands out from other people because he knows not only how to transport heavy stones but how to use these stones to create a sign of past events. In Geoffrey's history, he promises Aurelius, "If you wish to mark their graves with a lasting work, send for the Giants' Ring. . . . If you set up in the stones in the same pattern around the burial-place, they will stand forever."[138] Though he claims that "the stones are magical [*mistici*]"[139] in their power to cure those who come in contact with them, the occult power he attributes to them is not their ability to cure

134. "ingenium . . . sive in futuris dicendis sive in operationibus machinandis," ibid., VIII, 128, p. 171. Wace will cite Tremorius as saying, "d'ovrer ne de deviner / ne poeit l'um trover sun per" (*Roman de Brut*, ed. Weiss, vv. 8009–10).

135. "entur guarda, les levres mut / comë huem ki dit oreisun; / ne sai s'il dist preiere u nun," Wace, *Roman de Brut*, ed. Weiss, vv. 8146–50.

136. "par force d'art," Robert de Boron, *Merlin*, ed. Micha, 47, p. 180.

137. "car eles seroient molt plus beles que gisanz," ibid., 47, p. 181.

138. "Si perpetuo opere sepulturam virorum decorare volueris, mitte pro chorea gigantum. . . . Qui si eo modo quo ibidem positi sunt circa plateam locabuntur, stabunt in aeternum," Geoffrey of Monmouth, *Historia regum Britanniae*, ed. Reeve, VIII, 128, p. 173.

139. "Mistici sunt lapides," ibid., VIII, 129, p. 173.

the ailing but their ability to recall the dead. If the Giants' Ring will stand for eternity, as Merlin promises that it will do, it is because it already serves as a memorial for the giants, who alone could have moved such great weights with their strength. Up to this point, the giants who appear in Geoffrey's text have been hostile creatures. Though of roughly human shape, they are bigger, stronger, and more brutal than human beings, so that they can lift heavy objects, like trees and boulders, that human beings could not begin to shoulder and so that they engage in acts of rape and cannibalism that human beings disdain as outside their law. Yet when Merlin tells Aurelius that about the Giants' Ring, he depicts the giants who constructed this complex as gentle. He relates that the giants long ago brought the stones from Africa to Ireland and that they did so because the stones have medicinal powers: water that had been washed over them could be used in baths "when they were afflicted with illness"[140] or in poultices "from which their wounded would be healed."[141] Whereas elsewhere in Geoffrey's text the giants are stupid, here they are intelligent. Whereas elsewhere they attack others, here they are victims of attack, and they are nursed by their fellows.[142] In Merlin's depiction of their creation of the Giants' Circle, we see the giants not just from the outside, as creatures opposed to us, but from the inside, as creatures similar to us. Should a skeptical reader of this text, medieval or modern, question whether there ever really were giants and what these giants were like, the Giants' Ring provides ocular proof of an earlier population, different from ours in strength but similar to ours in intelligence, who lived in Britain before we do. As such, the Giants' Ring is, literally, a *lieu de mémoire* where one sees evidence of a past population in the present day and where one is thus assured of the historical reality, otherwise uncertain, of this past population. A few years after Geoffrey composed the *Historia regum Britanniae*, Henry of Huntingdon writes of Stonehenge, one of "four marvels [which] are to be seen in England,"[143] "No one can find out by what art such great stones have been elevated to such a height or why

140. "cum infirmitate gravarentur," Geoffrey of Monmouth, *Historia regum Britanniae*, ed. Reeve, VIII, 129, p. 173.

141. "unde vulnerati sanabantur," ibid.

142. If anything, these giants resemble the giants of Gottfried von Strassburg's *Tristan*, who create the Cavern of the Lovers to which first they and then Tristan and Isolde retire for their dalliances.

143. "Quatuor autem sunt que mira videntur in Anglia," Henry of Huntingdon, *Historia Anglorum / The History of the English People*, ed. and trans. Diana Greenway (Oxford: Clarendon Press, 1996), I, 7, p. 22.

they were constructed there."[144] It is because the Giants' Ring is a marvel, that is, something we cannot fully understand, that it succeeds as a memorial. In its ability to make us pause and wonder how and why it was built, the Giants' Ring arrests the movement of time and makes us turn from the present to the past. The carpenters and stonemasons failed to construct the memorial Aurelius proposed to them not because they lacked the skills to construct a building, but because they lacked the skill to make people remember, which Merlin possesses. In Robert's version of the story, Merlin urges, "Let us undertake to make something that no one has ever known before, and it will be spoken of forever after."[145] Robert himself remarks, "The stones are still in the cemetery at Salisbury, and they will be there for as long as Christianity lasts."[146] While for those who grasp only the manifest properties of entities, the stones are just stones, like any one could find in Britain; for those who can grasp occult properties, the stones possess a magical or mystical ability to make us recall their history.

Like Vortigern, Aurelius illustrates that one should respond to memorials not by trying to understand them, through determining their cause, but by marveling at them, through contemplating their meaning. At first, Aurelius does not appreciate Merlin's proposal to transport the Giants' Ring to Britain because he conceives of the stones functionally. When Merlin makes this proposal to him, the text relates, "Aurelius dissolved into laughter, asking how it should be that such great stones should be brought from such a distant kingdom, as if Britain lacked stones that would suffice for this operation."[147] He assumes that stones are stones, whether they are in Ireland or in Britain, and that as a result, if one has sufficient stones in one's own country to complete a project, it is foolish to transport them from another land. Yet Aurelius comes to appreciate Merlin's proposal because he comes to conceive of the stones not in terms of their use value, but in terms of their intrinsic worth. He had decided to construct the memorial to begin with because he recognized the way in which a

144. "nec potest aliquis excogitare qua arte tanti lapides deo in altum elevati sunt, vel quare ibi constructi sunt," ibid.

145. "Enprenons a faire tel chose que ja ne soit seu et si en sera mes toz jors parlé," Robert de Boron, *Merlin*, ed. Micha, 47, p. 179.

146. "les pierres . . . encor sont au cimentire de Salebires et i seront tant come crestientez dura," ibid., 47, p. 181.

147. "solutus est Aurelius in risum, dicens qualiter id fieri posset ut tanti lapides ex tam longinquo regno adveherentur ac si Britannia lapidibus careret qui ad operationem sufficerent," Geoffrey of Monmouth, *Historia regum Britanniae*, ed. Reeve, VIII, 129, p. 173.

place could evoke a past. When he had visited the monastery cemetery near Salisbury, we are told, "Looking round at the place where the dead lay, Aurelius dissolved into tears of pity. Afterwards, having been drawn into diverse meditations, he deliberated how to make the place memorable. For he considered the turf that protected so many noblemen who had died for their country to be worthy of memory."[148] Instead of attempting to understand these men's deaths, Aurelius recognizes that the failure to understand is central to mourning. To mourn is not to explain why a death has happened, by tracing it to its cause, but to recognize that a death, especially the death of hundreds of one's countrymen, defies such explanation. To mourn is to wonder because wonder is the recognition that some events can never be fully accounted for. When Aurelius learns about the Giants' Ring from Merlin, he recognizes that it is precisely the apparent impossibility of transporting the stones from Ireland to Britain that will make them a marvel and, hence, a memorial, prompting anyone who sees it to wonder how and why it was constructed. He assembles an army of fifteen thousand men, he places his brother Uther at the head of this army, and he has the army defeat the Irish in battle in order to gain possession of the stones. When the army returns from Ireland with the Giants' Ring, Aurelius summons the bishops, the abbots, and the clergy from all of Britain to join him at the monastery, where he wears his crown, bestows bishoprics, and leads his people in three days of celebration in commemoration of this structure. Later, when Aurelius himself dies, having been poisoned by a Saxon, the bishops, abbots, and clergy gather again at Winchester to conduct his funeral, but the king is buried in the Giants' Ring. It is noted, "Before his death, Aurelius had instructed that he was to be buried in the cemetery he himself had built, so they took his body there and gave it a royal burial."[149] In all of this, Aurelius represents the readers of this text, who to this day see Stonehenge, who to this day reflect upon how and why this monument was constructed, and who to this day want to know the meaning of what they see. If we are to read the Giants' Ring the right way, we should imitate Aurelius by marveling at these stones and by

148. "Ut igitur locum quo defuncti iacebant circumspexit, motus pietate in lacrimas solutus est. Postremo, in diversas meditationes inductus, deliberavit apud se qualiter locum faceret memorabilem. Dignam namque memoria censebat caespitem quae tot nobiles pro patria defunctos protegebat," ibid., VIII, 127, p. 171.

149. "Et quia videns adhuc praeceperat ut in cimiterio quod ipse paraverat sepeliretur, tulerunt corpus eius ibidem atque cum regiis exequiis humaverunt," ibid., VIII, 134, p. 181.

remembering the British noblemen, as well as the British king, who are buried here.

If, in accounts about Merlin, the categories of engineer and magician are ultimately difficult to distinguish, it is because the categories of the natural and the supernatural were also hard to separate at this time. It is not that people were incapable of critical thought. It was a commonplace that one should not put credence in what one is told unless one had read about it in authoritative books or observed it in one's own experience. Yet it was precisely because of these criteria that people could not dismiss the existence of marvels like dragons, descriptions of which they had read in so many esteemed works, or giants, evidence of which they believed they had seen at Stonehenge, the Giants' Causeway, and Danish burial mounds, among other places.[150] Augustine relates what he acknowledges to be incredible accounts of marvels, but he does so, he insists, "without affirming or denying them."[151] Given the uncertain truth value of these accounts, he concedes, "It is permitted to anyone, without reproach, not to believe them."[152] Gerald of Wales, following Augustine, passes on reports of marvels as well, and he claims that he does so "neither denying those things, in such a way that I am placing a limit on God's power, nor affirming them, in such a way that extends beyond the bounds of credibility."[153] Human beings should not expect to understand everything that exists, he suggests, because the power of the Creator is, by definition, far greater than the comprehension of his creatures. When Wace arrives at the point in his romance where his source lists Merlin's prophecies, he states that he will not translate this part of the book, "since I do not know how to interpret it."[154] It is in the capacity of authors like Augustine, Gerald, and Wace to entertain the possibility of marvels, like dragons, giants, and prophecies, without affirming or denying that of which they speak, that we can find a major source of the fictionality of medieval romance.

150. Saxo Grammaticus, the late twelfth- and early thirteenth-century Danish historian, asserts in his *Gesta Danorum*, in *The History of the Danes*, ed. Hilda Ellis Davidson, 2 vols. (Rochester, NY: D. S. Brewer, 1980; rpt., 1996), that the ancient burial mounds of his country testify to the fact that Denmark was once settled by "a civilization of giants [*giganteo quondam cultu*]" (vol. 1, p. 3), who were then replaced by "magicians [*magi*]" expert in "the Pythonic art [*artem . . . Pythonicam*]" (I, 5, pp. 2–4).

151. "neque neganda neque affirmanda," Augustine, *De civitate Dei*, ed. Dombart and Kalb, XXI, 7, p. 770.

152. "licet cuique sine recta reprehensione non credere," ibid.

153. "nec ego negando divinae potentiae terminos pono, nec affirmando eam quae extendi non potest insolenter extendo," Gerald of Wales, *Itinerarium Kambriae*, ed. Dimock, I, 8, p. 78.

154. "quant jo nel sai interpreter," Wace, *Roman de Brut*, ed. Weiss, vv. 7540.

The Devil and the Enchanter

In the final tradition we possess about Merlin, the issue is not just who Merlin is but also how one should respond to him. Around 1200, Robert de Boron composed his Old French *Merlin*, in which he enabled this figure to make the transition from prophet to enchanter, a role he would continue to occupy throughout later vernacular works, including the Vulgate and Post-Vulgate Cycles. In this text, Robert depicts the people who spurn Merlin along the lines of the rationalist thinkers of his time. While all Catholics of these years recognized that the ultimate mysteries of the faith, such as the nature of the Godhead, the Trinity, and the Incarnation of Jesus Christ, are beyond human comprehension, rationalists, trained in the cathedral schools or the universities, emphasized the degree to which human beings could understand the world around them and even the God who had created this world. Peter Abelard had famously affirmed that "something cannot be believed unless it is first understood."[155] At the same time, however, Robert depicts people who embrace Merlin along the lines of the contemplative thinkers of his period. In contrast to rationalists, contemplatives, trained in monastery schools, stressed the degree to which human beings could not understand the world around them, let alone the God who had created that world. Anselm of Canterbury had declared, "I do not seek to understand in order that I may believe, but I believe in order that I may understand."[156] In Robert's *Merlin*, some people refuse to believe that Merlin possesses the powers he seems to possess because they cannot understand where these powers come from. In courts at this time, it was not uncommon for high noblemen to bring accusations of necromancy against courtiers of lower birth, like Merlin, whom they perceived as having gained an inordinate influence over their lord.[157] Merlin anticipates this situation, warning Aurelius (or Pendragon, as Robert calls him), "Sire, your men . . . will be angry . . .

155. "Nec credi posse aliquid nisi primitus intellectum," Peter Abelard, *Historia calamitatum*, ed. J. Monfrin (Paris: Librairie Philosophique J. Vrin, 1959; rpt., 1967), 83.

156. "Neque enim quaero intelligere ut credam, sed credo ut intelligam," Anselm of Canterbury, *Proslogion*, in *Opera omnia*, ed. Franz Sales Schmitt, 2 vols. (Stuttgart: Friedrich Fromann Verlag, 1968), vol. 1, 89–122, at I, 100. Cf. Isa. 7:9 (Vulg: "Si non credideritis, non permanebitis"). Cf. Augustine, *Tractatus in Evangelium Johannis CCXIV*, ed. Radbodus Willems, CCSL, vol. 36, XXIX, 6, pp. 286–87.

157. See Richard Kieckhefer, *Witchcraft in Medieval Europe* (Cambridge: Cambridge University Press, 1989), 96–97.

when you trust me."[158] Meanwhile, Pendragon and Uther believe that Merlin possesses these powers, and, because they believe in them, they understand that the source of their powers is good, whatever it may be. Over the course of this text, Merlin teaches those around him that they should respond to him as they should respond to the marvels he performs: they should not attempt to fathom what he does, but, instead, they should take delight in it. Instead of approaching Merlin or the romances in which Merlin appears with skepticism, the text suggests, one must approach them with trust, as it is only by doing so that one will be rewarded.

There is reason to believe, in Robert's *Merlin* and in its vernacular successors, that Merlin is a devil or someone associated with the devil.[159] In Geoffrey's *Historia regum Britanniae,* one of Vortigern's counselors speculates that he is the son of a demon. When Merlin's mother was asked how it was possible that he could have no father, she explained that no man had lain with her, but only someone in the form of a man, and that he had begotten this child upon her. The counselor offered the opinion that this apparition was one of the "incubus demons"[160] described in Apuleius's *De deo Socratis,*[161] who, he recalled, "assume human figures and lie with women."[162] In *Merlin,* Robert represents it as a fact that Merlin is the son of a devil. When Merlin's mother failed to cross herself one night before going to bed, he recounts, a demon came to her and sired this child. Frustrated that the prophets had brought so many people to the truth and, in doing so, had removed them from their power, the demons conspired to create their own version of a prophet, who would deceive human beings and, in doing so, restore them to their dominion. As the son of a devil, Merlin possesses

158. "Sire, . . . se corroceroient vostre home . . . quant vos me creez," Robert de Boron, *Merlin,* ed. Micha, 35, p. 137.

159. Even insofar as Merlin is identified with the devil in the Vulgate and Post-Vulgate *Merlins,* it is not always clear that the devil is a negative figure. See *Les Premiers Faits du Roi Arthur,* ed. Freire-Nunes, 606, p. 1403, and *La Suite du Roman de Merlin,* ed. Roussineau, vol. 1, IX, 142, pp. 107–8. The authors of the Vulgate and Post-Vulgate Merlins suggest that these knights are perceived as diabolical because they possess extraordinary, inexplicable, and, therefore, marvelous gifts, seemingly beyond those of ordinary men.

160. "incubos daemones," Geoffrey of Monmouth, *Historia regum Britanniae,* ed. Reeve, VI, p. 139.

161. See Apuleius, *De deo Socratis,* in *De Philosophia libri,* ed. C. Moreschini, BSGRT (Stuttgart: Teubner, 1991), 7–38, esp. XIII, 15, p. 23. Apuleius's views of *daemones* were shaped by Plato's *Apology* 31 c–d and *Symposium* 202d–203e.

162. "assumunt sibi humanas figuras et cum mulieribus coeunt," Apuleius, *De deo Socratis,* p. 139. On demons who copulate with women, see Geoffrey of Monmouth, *Vita Merlini,* ed. Clarke, vv. 779–84 and Augustine, *De civitate Dei,* ed. Dombart and Kalb, XV, 23, p. 489.

traits recognizable to anyone familiar with medieval demonology. Like a demon, he knows hidden matters of the past, such as the content of people's private conversations and the nature of their secret sins. Like a demon, he can transform his and others' appearance at will. Like a demon, he can move from one place to another without traversing intermediate space. Merlin himself avers, "I have not lost [the devils'] skill or their craft."[163] While in Robert's text Merlin reproaches those, like Vortigern's advisors, who dabble in astrology and necromancy, in the Vulgate and Post-Vulgate Cycles, he himself becomes an expert in those fields. In the Post-Vulgate *Merlin*, for example, he boasts, "I have been the wisest in necromancy of all who have ever been seen in the Kingdom of Logres."[164] So well known does Merlin become for his magical abilities that he becomes the tutor, first, to Morgan Le Fay, Arthur's sister, and, then, to Ninianne, the daughter of the vavasor Dyonas, who becomes known as the Lady of the Lake. If these women become proficient in these forms of magic, it is because of the assistance they receive from the devil and from pagan gods. Though Morgan had been a beautiful girl before she began to learn spells and enchantments, "ever since the Enemy was placed inside her,"[165] we are told, she has been hideous and lecherous. Ninianne is not associated with Satan in the same way Morgan is, but she is nonetheless linked with Diana, her father's godmother, a mortal woman who is said to have lived in pagan times and who was believed to be "the goddess of the wood."[166] As the supreme master of these magical arts, it seems, Merlin must have allied himself with the devil or with a pagan god, like other practitioners of these arts with whom he is affiliated.

Because of Merlin's diabolical origins and diabolical skills, many people in Robert's text express anxiety about this figure. Some suspect he is a devil himself. When the young Merlin reveals knowledge that no human being could possess, they cry out, "We have spoken with a devil,"[167] and "this is no child but a demon, who knows what we have said."[168] Others suspect that even if he is not a devil, he acquires his knowledge and his powers from the dark side. An unnamed

163. "Je n'ai pas perdu lor enging ne lor art," Robert de Boron, *Merlin*, ed. Micha, 16, p. 72.

164. "j'ai esté li plus sages de nigromanchie de tous cheus qui onques fuissent ou roiame de Logres," *La Suite du Roman de Merlin*, ed. Roussineau, vol. 1, XIV, 341, p. 296.

165. "puis que li anemis fu dedens li mis," ibid., vol. 1, I, 27, p. 20.

166. "la divesse del bois," *Les Premiers Faits du Roi Arthur*, ed. Freire-Nunes, 253, 1055.

167. "Nos avons parlé a un deable," ibid., 32, 126.

168. "Ce n'est pas enfes, ains est deables qui set ce que nos avons dit," Robert de Boron, *Merlin*, ed. Micha, 11, p. 55.

baron in Pendragon's court warns his king, "Sire, it is a wonder that you trust this man, for you know well that that which he tells you and that which you believe . . . comes to him from the devil."[169] These characters know that if Merlin were to be placed in a category, based upon his skill set, it would have to be that of demons, who alone in the medieval imaginary share his talents. Confronted with Merlin's marvelous words and deeds, many make the sign of the cross in order to protect themselves against his diabolical power. When Merlin's mother first sees him, we are told, "She crossed herself and said, 'This child gives me great fear.'"[170] When Merlin appears to some of Pendragon's messengers and then vanishes from their sight, the text relates, "They crossed himself and said, 'We have spoken to a devil.'"[171] When he appears to Uther first in one guise and then in another, we are told, "Uther raised his hand, crossed himself, and said, 'Sire, God help me, I am all enchanted.'"[172] In all of these cases, people cross themselves because they do not understand how Merlin is able to say and do what he says and does and because they worry—though they do not know for sure—that he is able to perform such marvels because he is linked to the nether powers.[173] That which is marvelous, that which one cannot, by definition, comprehend, produces unease.

Yet even as there is reason to believe that Merlin is a devil or someone associated with the devil, there is also reason to believe that his identity is not quite so clear-cut. In Geoffrey's text, Merlin's mother does not herself testify that an incubus demon has come to her. Instead, she states that "someone in the form of a most beautiful youth often appeared to me, holding me tight in his arms and kissing me. After remaining with me for a while, he would suddenly disappear from my sight. Often he would talk to me without appearing, while I sat alone."[174] Her lover appears to be, not seducing her in order to bring

169. "Sire, vos faites merveilles de cest home que vos creez, quar bien sachiez que ce que il vos dit et que vos creez . . . il li vient de deable," ibid., 41, 155.

170. "si se seingna et dist, 'Cist enfes me fait grant paor,'" ibid., 10, 51.

171. "cil se seingnet et dient, 'Nos avons parlé a un deable,'" ibid., 32, 126.

172. "Et Uitiers si lieve sa main, si se seingne et dist, 'Sire, si m'aïst Diex, je sui touz enchantez,'" ibid., 38, 144.

173. In the Vulgate and Post-Vulgate Cycles, we see people cross themselves out of wonder as well. See *Les Premiers Faits du Roi Arthur*, ed. Freire-Nunes, 11, p. 819; ibid., 789, p. 1608; *La Suite du Roman de Merlin*, ed. Roussineau, vol. 1, III, 86, p. 62; ibid., vol. 1, X, 223, p. 80; and ibid., vol. 2, XXIII, 464, p. 419.

174. "apparebat michi quidam in specie pulcherrimi iuvenis et saepissime amplectens me strictis brachiis deosculabatur. Et cum aliquantulum mecum moram fecisset, subito evanescebat ita ut nichil ex eo viderem. Multociens quoque alloquebatur dum secreto sederem nec usquam comparebat," Geoffrey of Monmouth, *Historia regum Britanniae*, ed. Reeve, p. 139.

about her and others' damnation, as one would expect a demon to do, but engaging with her in an amorous dalliance, with loving foreplay or even mere conversation. Indeed, if Merlin's father resembles a character from Apuleius, it is not so much the *daimon* of *De deo Socratis* as the Cupid of the *Asinus aureus*, a handsome youth who often appeared to Psyche, holding her, kissing her, and conversing with her, but whose identity was genuinely godlike and whose attentions were genuinely amorous. What seemed to a learned man to be a *daimon* or a demon seems to this woman to be what one might call, perhaps, a courtly lover. In Robert's text, Merlin's mother is clearly impregnated by an incubus demon, but it is left uncertain to what extent this parentage affects his identity. Despite his mother's momentary infraction, she is a holy woman. Having received from the demons the power to know the past, Merlin receives from God, thanks to his mother's holiness, the power to know the future. With both the devil and God having participated in Merlin's generation, the text states that "it remained to be seen to which one he would hold."[175] His free will governs him, as it governs all rational creatures. In the Vulgate and Post-Vulgate *Merlins*, other enchanters are referred to as "enemies"[176] and "princes and ministers of Hell,"[177] but Merlin, whose skills appear no different from theirs, is never referred to in such a manner. Morgan is linked with the devil and Ninianne with a pagan deity, but their master is never characterized in this way. The texts never explain why the enchanters' and Morgan's use of astrology and necromancy should be diabolical and Merlin's use of the same skills should not be so, but that is the case. In a movement typical of romance, even as each succeeding text clarifies obscure aspects of its predecessor, by establishing that Merlin is, in fact, the son of a devil and a practitioner of the arts traditionally traced to the devil, it opens up more ambiguities, by refusing to tar him through these associations.

Because of Merlin's irreducibly indeterminate nature, many people express delight at him. Every good person in the Kingdom of Logres, including Pendragon, Uther, and ultimately, Arthur himself, ends up loving and admiring this seer. These people do not know, as we too do not know, who Merlin truly is, but they trust that if he possesses skills outside any category of creatures aside from demons, it may be because he is uncategorizable. Faced with Merlin's marvelous deeds

175. "Si savra or bien au quiel il se devra tenir," Robert de Boron, *Merlin*, ed. Micha, 10, 50–51.
176. "anemis," *La Suite du Roman de Merlin*, ed. Roussineau, vol. 1, XIV, 339, 295.
177. "les prinches et les menistres de infier," ibid., XIV, 338, 294.

and words, they do not cross themselves out of fear, but, rather, laugh out of pleasure. After Pendragon learns of Merlin's capacity to shapeshift, he hears his men insisting that they will recognize him when he appears, and we are told, "He laughed and said, 'Be sure that you know him well.'"[178] When he sees Merlin confound Uther, appearing to him now in one guise, now in another, it is said, "the king and Merlin began to laugh and to have great joy between the two of them."[179] Still later, when Uther hears from his companion Ulfin that an old man in the road claims to know Uther's secrets and to know someone who could offer him good counsel, it is said, "He laughed and appeared to be happy."[180] In all of these cases, people laugh because they recognize Merlin and the marvels he can perform, especially if someone else is present who does not recognize them. Accustomed as they are to Merlin and his antics, they do not try to understand how he can say and do such things. That which is marvelous, that which one cannot, by definition, comprehend, may produce fear, but it may also produce delight, depending upon whether one is outside or inside Merlin's circle of knowledge.

If Pendragon comes to meet Merlin, it is not because he seeks him out, actively and masterfully, but because he learns to await him, passively and receptively. This king has been besieging the fortress of the Saxon chieftain Hengest for many months, and he wants to know whether he will ever succeed in taking it. Five of his counselors had belonged to Vortigern's council, and they recommend that he track down Merlin, who had predicted the future for his predecessor and who may be able to do the same for him. As a king, Pendragon assumes that if he applies sufficient resources to the task, he will be capable of finding Merlin or whatever he seeks. He resolves, "If he is in this country, I will find him."[181] He musters a large number of men and sends them throughout his realm to look for this enchanter, and he himself ultimately joins them on this quest. In Northumbria, they meet a fierce-looking woodcutter with a great ax over his shoulder, who, when asked about Merlin, states, "He knows well that you are looking for him, but you will not find him if he does not wish you to."[182] Later, the king

178. "si s'en rist et demande, 'Gardez que vos le conoissoiez bien,'" Robert de Boron, *Merlin*, ed. Micha, 34, 134.

179. "le roi et Merlin comencerent a rire et a avoir molt grant joie entre els .II.," ibid., 38, p. 145.

180. "si rist et fist molt grant semblant qu'il en fust liez," ibid., 61, 219.

181. "S'il est en cest païs, dont le troverai je bien," ibid., 31, 125.

182. "Il set bien que vos le querez, mais vos n'en trouverez point, se il ne viaut," ibid.

meets an ugly herdsman, who advises him that should he wish to see Merlin, he should settle down in one of the nearby towns. "He will come to you when he knows that you are waiting for him,"[183] he tells him. As these strangers' words reflect, despite Pendragon's determination to find Merlin, it will be Merlin, ultimately, who finds him. When the king takes lodgings in the town, a handsome gentleman with elegant clothes visits him in his rooms and informs him: "If you had need of [Merlin], he would come to you very willingly."[184] Confronted with this gentleman's words, Pendragon protests, "I have need of him every day. Never have I had such desire to see a man as I have to see him."[185] It is only at this moment, when the king shifts from insisting that he has a right to see Merlin to acknowledging that he needs and desires to see him, that the gentleman reveals himself—and the woodcutter and the herdsman—to be this enchanter. Pendragon later says to Merlin, "I would like to beseech you, if it would be possible, that you love me and that I may be acquainted with you, because worthy men told me that you are very wise and of very good counsel,"[186] and it is to this polite appeal that Merlin responds. It is not Pendragon's exercise of royal authority, but his expression of heartfelt love and appreciation that attracts Merlin. In order to find this seer, it seems, one must not seek him, outside oneself, but merely want him, inside oneself, because, like God responding to a prayer, he will know of that desire and grant it. As Pendragon's counselors had warned him about Merlin from the very beginning, "He knows well when he is being spoken of, and . . . if he wished, he would come."[187] And, as Merlin himself tells Pendragon and Uther, wherever they may be, he will know of what they are doing, and he will come to their aid: "I will not know that you are troubled by anything without coming to help and counsel you in all ways."[188] It is not through the assertion upon one's own will over another, but through the submission of one's will to another that one will obtain what one wishes.

After Pendragon meets Merlin for the first time, he learns that he

183. "il vendra a vos, quant il savra que vos l'atandez," ibid., 33, 129.

184. "Se en avoies mestier, il venroit molt volentiers a toi," ibid., 33, 131.

185. "Je ai mestier de lui toz jorz ne onques n'oi si grant envie d'ome veoir come j'ai de lui," ibid.

186. "Je vos voudroie molt prier, se estre pooit, que vos m'amesoiez et que je fusse molt acointes de vos, que cist prodome m'ont dit que vos estes molt saiges et molt de bon conseil," ibid., 34, 134.

187. "Il set bien quant l'en parole de lui et . . . s'il vouloit, il venroit bien," ibid., 31, 124–25.

188. "je ne savrai que vos soiez encombrez de nule chose que je ne vos en veigne aidier et conseillier en toutes manieres," ibid., 39, 149–50.

will be able to recognize him in subsequent encounters, not if he considers his appearance but if he considers his "quality of heart" (*corage*). Originally, as Pendragon had expected his men to find Merlin, he had expected the counselors who had known him in Vortigern's court to be able to recognize him when they found him. When the gentleman visits him in the Northumbrian town, the stranger proposes, "Sire, . . . call those whom you have brought here who should know Merlin, and ask them if I could be this Merlin."[189] Summoned to the king's presence, the counselors affirm, "Sire, . . . we would recognize well his appearance, if we saw him."[190] As they see it, each person possesses an "appearance" (*semblance*) by which he can be known to be who he is. In part, this appearance reflects the social category to which the person belongs. Someone who looks like a woodcutter, with his ax, a herdsman, with his flock, or a gentleman, with his fine clothes, one can assume, is a woodcutter, a herdsman, or a gentleman. In part, this appearance reflects individual identity within this social category. Someone who looks old or young, crippled or healthy, one can assume, is, in fact, old or young, crippled or healthy. Defined by these social and individual categories, a person's appearance is assumed to be stable across time, so that these counselors, who had known Merlin during Vortigern's reign, should be able to recognize him under Pendragon's rule as well. Yet despite these counselors' confidence in their ability to recognize Merlin on the basis of his "appearance," they fail to do so. Confronted with this failure, they excuse themselves by pointing out that Merlin, unlike other men, can transform himself, so that he seems to be a woodcutter at one moment, a herdsman at another, and a gentleman at still another; as we see later, he can assume the semblance of an old man or a young man and, then, of a cripple or a healthy person. Yet, as Merlin reminds Pendragon, it is not only tricksters like himself but all human beings whose physical appearance changes over time. In one manuscript of this text, he avers, "The things of this world are never always in one state. Thus, as Saint John says, they are mutable, for sometimes people are white and, at other times, black, for it happens that a man who is white at one time becomes black at another because of heat, as is customary for those who go on pilgrimage."[191] As people can become tan from the heat, Merlin continues, they can

189. "Sire, . . . apelez cels que vos avez amenez qui devoient conoistre Merlin et si lor demandez se je porroie ja icil Merlins estre," ibid., 132.

190. "Sire, . . . nos conoistrom bien sa samblance, se nos la veom," ibid., 34, 132–33.

191. "Les chouses de cest ciecle ne sunt mies adés an un estait. Ensi comme dist sainz Jehainz, sont muaubles, car aucune foiz est on blanc et aucune foiz noir, car il avient bien k'uns honz qui

also become green from fear or yellow from jaundice. Young people can become old, and healthy people can become sick. "And because of this," he concludes, "it is not enough to know no more than the appearance of the man, for he does not know him who knows his appearance alone."[192] If one means to recognize someone, Merlin makes clear, one must rely not upon appearance, but, instead, upon what he calls "quality of heart" (*corage*). An unnamed baron presents himself to Merlin in three different guises, asking him each time to predict the manner in which he will die, in order to debunk his claims to prophetic insight. While the counselors are deceived as to who Merlin is because they assume that what one appears to be, one is, Merlin is not deceived by this baron because he does not take this for granted. He declares of the baron, "I know well all that is in his heart [*corage*] and all that his foolish, wicked heart thinks."[193] Like God, who, according to the First Book of Kings, "alone know[s] the hearts of the sons of men,"[194] Merlin grasps not just what men look like, on the outside, but who they are, on the inside. Though Merlin reproaches Pendragon's counselors for relying upon appearance instead of upon the "quality of heart" in knowing people, his point is not that they, or any human beings, should be expected to discern people's identity, but, rather, that they should admit to themselves that they cannot discern who people truly are and that they must depend upon God—or upon a seer like himself—to expose that identity to them.

Finally, when Pendragon is persuaded of someone's words, he learns that it is not because the other person persuades him, but because he agrees to put faith in what he is told. When he is questioning the herdsman, he asks him, "Can it be true what you tell me?"[195] and "How will I know that you are telling me what is true?"[196] He assumes that the burden of proof lies with his interlocutor, who will want to overcome any skepticism he may have about what he is saying. Yet the herdsman replies, "If you do not believe me, do not do what I tell you,

---

est blanz en un tanz devient noir en un autre per challour, si comme suelent estre cil qui vont es pellerinaignes," ibid., 34, 133. Micha is citing Vatican Library, Reg. 1517 here.

192. "Et pour ce ne soufist il mie a connoistre sanz plus la samblance de l'omme, car il ne le connoist mie qui ne connoist que sa samblance," ibid., 34, 133–34. The base manuscript states simply, "Ne conoist pas bien home qui ne conoist que la samblance," ibid., 34, 133.

193. "Je sai tout son coraige et tot ce que son fol mauvais cuer pense," ibid., 42, 160.

194. "Tu nosti solus cor omnium filiorum hominum," 1 Kings 8:39. See also Luke 16:15 and Acts 1:24.

195. "Puet ce estre voirs que tu me diz?" Robert de Boron, *Merlin*, ed. Micha, 33, 131.

196. "Coment savrai ge que tu me dies voir?" ibid., 33, 129.

for it is madness to believe bad advice."[197] The king concludes, "I will believe you."[198] If Pendragon decides to believe what Merlin says, it is not because Merlin provides evidence to support his words—he never does this—but because he decides to trust him. The unnamed baron who asks Merlin to predict his death when he is wearing three different disguises feels that he has proven Merlin's mendaciousness when the seer predicts, first, that he will fall from his horse and break his neck, then, that he will be hanged, and, finally, that he will be drowned.[199] Because it is self-evident that someone who has died one way cannot die a second, let alone a third way, it is self-evident that Merlin's predictions are contradictory and, hence, untrue. According to Aristotle's law of noncontradiction, "Opposing statements cannot be true at the same time."[200] As the Philosopher recommends, the baron relies upon his determination of whether someone's words are internally consistent in order to ascertain their veracity. Yet Pendragon replies to the baron's demand that he cease to give credence to Merlin's words by stating, "I will not disbelieve them until I know from what death you die,"[201] and his hesitation to accept the initial results of the baron's test is ultimately vindicated. Some time later, when the baron is crossing a bridge, his palfrey stumbles, so that he is thrown forward onto the ground, breaking his neck; he rolls off the bridge, but in such a way that a post catches his mantle and he dangles, upside down, over the river below, and his head and shoulders are plunged in the water. He thus breaks his neck, he hangs, and he drowns. Truth is revealed here, not through the baron's test of Merlin's prophetic ability, which seemed so damning when he administered it, but through the passage of time, which made the test's failings become apparent. It is because the baron is sure that what seems to be the truth is, in fact, the truth that he rushes to judgment and rejects, precipitously and erroneously, the validity of Merlin's predictions. It is because Pendragon does not share the baron's exces-

197. "Se vos ne me creez, si ne faites pas ce qui je vos di, quar il est folie de croire mauvais consoil," ibid., 33, 129–30.

198. "Je te crerai," ibid., 33, 130.

199. The tale of the threefold death appears in Geoffrey of Monmouth's *Vita Merlini*. For its precedent, see Jocelin of Furness, *Vita Kentegerni*, in *Lives of S. Ninian and S. Kentigern*, ed. A. P. Forbes (Edinburgh: Edmonston and Douglas, 1874), 522–25, at 524. For discussion of earlier versions of this episode, see the *Vita Merlini*, ed. Clarke, 12.

200. "Non esse simul veras oppositas dictiones," Aristotle, *Metaphysica*, ed. Vuillemin-Diem, IV, 6, p. 88.

201. "Je nou mescrerai ja tant que je saiche de quel mort vos morroiz," Robert de Boron, *Merlin*, ed. Micha, 42, 161.

sive confidence in an ordinary, human understanding but, instead, waits to see if someone with extraordinary, superhuman insight may be right that he does not make the same mistake.

In the end, Robert's Merlin teaches us how to read marvels by teaching us how to read himself and, by extension, how to read the type of text in which he appears. At the beginning of the work, the wise cleric Blaise, like other contemporaries of Merlin, wants to understand how this seer can perform marvels, and he tests him for that purpose. Yet Merlin informs Blaise, "The more you test me, the more you will marvel."[202] Instead of subjecting him to such examinations, he advises, "Do what I beseech you to do, and believe a great part of what I tell you."[203] With these words, which the author seems to second, Merlin suggests that one should respond to him, not as Blaise has been doing, with a desire to understand how he is able to perform marvels, but, rather, with a willingness simply to believe that he performs them. One should not test but, rather, trust him, because any effort to make the inexplicable explicable will only make it more perplexing. At the beginning of the work, Blaise, like his peers, worries about Merlin's diabolical affiliation. He begs him to swear "that [he] not trick nor deceive [him], nor do anything that is not to the pleasure of Our Lord."[204] Yet later, we are told, "Blaise marveled greatly many times at the marvels Merlin told him. Nevertheless, these marvels always seemed to him good and fair, and he heard about them very willingly."[205] If Blaise ultimately ceases to worry about Merlin's diabolical origins, it is not because he has been persuaded that his marvels are from God, but merely because he has observed that his marvels are good. He does not understand; he merely observes, and this observation leads to a kind of understanding. Merlin asks Blaise to take up ink and parchment and to write down the stories he tells him, which include the stories of Joseph of Arimathea, the coming of the Holy Grail to Britain, and the reign of King Arthur. As Blaise was at first wary of Merlin because of the uncertain source of the marvels he performs, Merlin warns, people will be wary of the book he writes because of the uncertain source of

202. "Tant com tu plus m'essaieras, et tu plus te merveilleras," ibid., 16, 71.

203. "Mais fai ce que je te prierai et croi grant partie de ce que je te dirai," ibid. The text gives no explanation as to why Blaise should believe only a "grant partie" of that which Merlin tells him.

204. "Tu ne me puisses engingnier ne decevoir ne faire chose qui au plaisir Nostre Seingor ne soit," ibid., 16, 73.

205. "Molt se merveilla Blaises par plusors foiz des merveilles que Mellins li disoit et toutes voies ces merveilles li sembloient a estre bonnes et beles, si i entendoit molt volenteirs," ibid., 16, 74.

the wonders he recounts: "I will tell you many things that you will not believe that a man could say."[206] Yet even as Robert's Merlin anticipates the hostility with which these stories will be met, he also anticipates the rejoicing with which they will be greeted. The authority of Blaise's book may be doubted, but, Merlin predicts, the affection people feel for it will be no less profound. As he assures his amanuensis, "Know that your book will be greatly loved and greatly prized by many people who have not seen it. . . . And know well that no one's life will have ever been heard so willingly, by fools and by wise men, as will be that of the king who will have the name 'Arthur' and other people who will rule at this time."[207] He predicts, "The work will be retold and willingly heard for as long as the world shall last."[208] If the tales about Arthur, with the marvels they contain, were beloved at the time of their composition—and if they remain beloved today, one might add—it is because they contain truths that surpass our own understanding but are no less valid because of their incomprehensibility.

206. "je te dirai maintes choses que tu ne cuideroies que nus hom poïst dire," ibid., 72.

207. "Et saiches que tes livres sera encores molt amez et molt prisiez de maintes genz qui ja ne l'avront veu. . . . Et saiches bien que onques nule vie de genz ne fu plus volontiers oïe de fols ne de saiges que sera cele dou roi qui avra non Artus et des genz qui a ce tens regneront," ibid., 100–101.

208. "Et t'oevre sera toz orz mais, tant come le siecle durra, retraite et volantiers oïe," ibid., 23, 99.

THREE

King Arthur: History and Fiction

As Merlin draws into question the relation between Nature and marvels, Arthur draws into question the relation between history and fiction. A few early historical accounts, including the *Historia Brittonum* (800), the *Annales Cambriae* (900s), and the *Legenda Sancti Goeznovii* (1019), make tantalizingly brief allusions to a British military leader or king by his name who, during the Saxon invasions of the fifth and sixth centuries, arose and rallied his people for a time to withstand these invaders. In the High Middle Ages, the descendants of the Britons were said to have believed that this Arthur had lived, that he had been a great and glorious king, and that, never having died, he would one day return to restore his kingdom. So passionately were they said to hold to this view that they entered into brawls with foreigners who dared to contradict it.[1] In Cornwall, some canons traveling from Laon in 1113 are said to have met a man in a church "saying that Arthur was living."[2] When one of the canons' servants

1. Virginie Greene, in "Qui croit au retour d'Arthur?" *Cahiers de civilisation médiévale* 45 (2002): 321–40, expresses doubt that the belief in Arthur's return was ever genuinely held; in the medieval sources, it is always someone else who is said to hold it. See also Roger Sherman Loomis, "The Legend of Arthur's Survival," in *Arthurian Literature in the Middle Ages*, ed. Loomis, 64–71.

2. "dicens adhuc Arturum vivere," Herman of Tournai, *De Miraculis S. Mariae Laudunensis*, PL 156, cols. 963–1018, at col. 983. See J. S. P. Tatlock, "The English Journey of the Laon Canons," *Speculum* 8, no. 4 (1933): 454–65.

dared to differ, the man's countrymen rushed up to defend his point of view, and it was only with difficulty that they were deterred from bloodshed. In Brittany, a gloss of Merlin's prophecies written sometime between 1167 and 1174 warns that travelers who go to villages and marketplaces and proclaim that Arthur is dead, "in the manner of other dead men,"[3] would be lucky to escape without being cursed or pelted with stones.[4] In Wales, the Gwentian code, composed in the tenth century and revised through the thirteenth century, advises that if a bard is to sing a song about the Battle of Camlann, in which Arthur fell, he should do so in a low voice, "lest the hall be disturbed."[5] Learned clerics, while they did not deny that Arthur existed, expressed doubt that he was as magnificent a king as popular legend indicates and, even more, that he could possibly return after all these years to his people. As they note, if Arthur did exist, it is curious that none of the chroniclers of the time, including the British Gildas (d. 570) and the Anglo-Saxon Bede (d. 735), whom one might expect to be most apprised of his accomplishments, make mention of them. The discrepancy between the popular, Brythonic tradition about Arthur and the learned, Latin tradition provoked consternation among clerics. William of Malmesbury, writing around 1125, refers to "Arthur, about whom the trifles of the Bretons rave even in our own day, who is assuredly deserving, not of being dreamed of in fallacious fables [*fallaces . . . fabulae*], but of being proclaimed in veracious histories [*veraces . . . historiae*]."[6] As William sees it, Arthur was a historical figure and, in-

3. "more ceterum mortuorum," Pseudo-Alan of Lille, *Explanationum in prophetiam Merlini Ambrosii Britani libri VII*, vol. 1, quoted in Chambers, *Arthur of Britain*, 110 and 265. Cf. also William of Newburgh, *Historia rerum Anglicarum*, ed. Walsh and Kennedy, vol. 1, I, preface, 15, p. 36.

4. Herman of Tournai also observes, in *De Miraculis S. Mariae Laudunensis*, that "Bretons are accustomed to get into fights with the French about King Arthur [*Britones solent iurgari cum Francis pro rege Arturo*]" (col. 983). When Jacques de Vitry is making a list of the disputes that arise among the different nations at the University of Paris between 1216 and 1224, he observes of students, "Judging the Bretons to be frivilous and rambling, they frequently taunt them with the death of Arthur [*Britones . . . leves et vagos iudicantes, Arturi mortem frequenter eis obiciebant*]," *The "Historia occidentalis" of Jacques de Vitry: A Critical Edition*, ed. John Frederick Hinnebusch (Fribourg: University Press, 1972), 92.

5. "rac teruysgu yny neuad," Cyvreithiau Hyoel DDA ar Ddull Guent [The Laws of Howel DDA, according to the Gwentian Code], in *Ancient Laws and Institutes of Wales, Comprising Laws Supposed to be Enacted by Howel the Good*, ed. Aneurin Owen, 2 vols. (London: G. E. Eyre and A. Spottiswoode, 1841), vol. 1, 618–797, I, 37, no. 7, p. 678. Constance Bullock-Davies, in "*Exspectare Arthurum*: Arthur and the Messianic Hope," *Bulletin of the Board of Celtic Studies* 29 (1982): 432–40, connects the legend of Arthur's return to the struggle for Welsh independence under Owain Gwynedd and Rhys ap Gruffydd.

6. "Artur de quo Britonum nugae hodieque delirant, dignus plane quem non fallaces somniarent fabulae sed veraces predicarent historiae," William of Malmesbury, *Gesta regum Anglorum:*

deed, a great historical figure, but his story has been corrupted by fictional embellishments.[7] If there is anything that makes Arthurian legend and, by extension, Arthurian romance disturbing to its critics, even in the Middle Ages, it is the confusion it creates between a king and a secular messiah,[8] between history and fable, and between what is true and what is make-believe.

Medieval learned men expressed great respect for "histories" (*historiae*). From classical rhetoricians like Cicero,[9] Quintilian,[10] and the author of the *Rhetorica ad Herennium*,[11] they knew that "History consists of deeds performed [*gesta res*], removed from the recollection of our own age." Echoing these rhetoricians, Isidore of Seville writes, "Histories consist of true deeds that have happened."[12] It is not that medieval historians were under any impression that they were giving their readers unmediated access to what happened in the past. When recounting a historical event, they would not just report the facts, such as the number of men killed in a battle, but draw out the meaning of these facts, by imagining, for example, a speech the commander gave before leading these men into combat. While readers would know that the commander had not spoken these exact words, they would take pleasure in reading them so long as they seemed like the words that such a leader would be likely to speak in such circumstances. As medieval authors sought to fill in gaps in the historical record with rhetorical set pieces, they sought to demonstrate, in their writing, the workings of God in the world and the moral lessons that could be learned from such inter-

---

The History of the English Kings, ed. and trans. R. A. B. Mynors, R. M. Thomson, and M. Winterbottom (Oxford: Clarendon Press, 1998), vol. 1, 27. When a twelfth-century author uses the word *Britones*, he is typically refering to the British of Britain, if he is speaking of the time when Arthur was ruling, and to the Bretons who descended from them, if he is speaking of the time when he is writing. In contrast, when such an author uses the word *Britanni*, he is typically referring to the Welsh and the Cornish.

7. See also Wace, *Roman de Brut*, ed. Weiss, vv. 9793–98, and *Layamon's Arthur*, ed. Barron and Weinberg, vv. 11471–75.

8. On the resemblance between Arthur and the Jewish Messiah, see Gerald of Wales, *Speculum Ecclesiae*, ed. Brewer, II, 9, p. 49, and Walter of Châtillon, *Tractatus sive Dialogus . . . contra Judaeos*, PL, vol. 209, cols. 423–53, at col. 423.

9. "Historia est gesta res, ab aetatis nostrae memoria remota," Cicero, *Rhetorici Libri duo qui vocantur "De inventione,"* ed. E. Stroebel, BSGRT (Stuttgart: Teubner, 1977), I, 19, pp. 24–25.

10. "historiam, in qua est gestae rei expositio," Quintilian, *Institutio oratoria*, ed. M. Winterbottom, 2 vols. (Oxford: Clarendon Press, 1970), vol. 1, II, 4, 2, p. 80.

11. "Historia est gesta res, sed ab aetatis nostrae memoria remota," *Rhetorica ad Herennium*, ed. Friedrich Marx and Winfried Trillitzsch, BSGRT (Leipzig: Teubner, 1964), I, 8, p. 10.

12. "historiae sunt res verae quae factae sunt," Isidore of Seville, *Etymologiae*, ed. Lindsay, I, 44, 5.

vention. Bede,[13] Orderic Vitalis,[14] Henry of Huntingdon,[15] and John of Salisbury[16] all agree that history is valuable, not just because it provides us with particular knowledge about this or that ruler's fate, but because it furnishes us with universal truths that one can see reflected in his destiny. At the same time, however, these historians held that they were giving their readers access to the truth of what happened. As part of the revival of Roman law in the twelfth century, jurists were moving from a reliance upon "witnesses of truth" (*testes de veritate*), who possess knowledge about the character of the accused party, to "witnesses of sight and hearing" (*testes de visu et auditu*), who possess knowledge about the facts of the case, thanks to what they had themselves seen and heard. In canon law, Gratian insists that "witnesses are not to give testimony except about those things which they know from being present."[17] In civil law, the *Coutumes de Beauvaisis* asserts, "A person who wants to say, 'I know it for certain' cannot do so unless he says, 'I was present and I saw it.'"[18] Like these jurists, historians emphasize anew the importance of depending upon one's own firsthand observation of these events or, if that is not possible, upon consultation of well-informed and trustworthy sources. John of Salisbury announces, in beginning his *Historia pontificalis* (1164), that he will write "nothing except that which I know to be true, by sight and by hearing [*visu et auditu*] or, what is supported in the writings or by the authority of reliable men."[19] It is insofar as history was able to represent what truly occurred, especially through the testimony of eyewitnesses and through authoritative sources, that it was esteemed at this time.

Medieval historians tended to regard Arthur, at least in part, as a

13. See Bede, *Ecclesiastical History of the English People*, ed. Bertram Colgrave and R. A. B. Mynors (Oxford: Clarendon Press, 1969), preface, 3.

14. See Orderic Vitalis, *Historia ecclesiastica*, ed. Marjorie Chibnall, 6 vols. (Oxford: Clarendon Press, 1990), vol. 1, prologue, 130.

15. See Henry of Huntingdon, *Historia Anglorum: The History of the English People*, ed. and trans. Diana Greenway (Oxford: Clarendon Press, 1996), prologue, 5, 4–5.

16. See John of Salisbury, *Historia Pontificalis / Memoirs of the Papal Court*, ed. and trans. Marjorie Chibnall (London: Thomas Nelson and Sons, 1956), 2. Cf. Cato, *Disticha* III, 13.

17. "Testes non dicant testimonium, nisi de his, que presentialiter noverunt," *Corpus iuris canonici: Decretum Magister Gratiani*, ed. Richter and Friedberg, Secunda pars, Causa III, Quaest. 9, c. 15, col. 532.

18. "qui veut dire, 'Je le sai de certain,' il ne puet dire s'il ne dit, 'Je fui presens et le vi,'" *Coutumes de Beauvaises*, ed. Amédée Salmon, 2 vols. (Paris: A. Picard et fils, 1899–1900), vol. 2, n. 1234, p. 138.

19. "nichil . . . nisi quod visu et auditu verum esse cognovero, vel quod probabilium virorum scriptis fuerit et auctoritate subnixum," John of Salisbury, *Historia Pontificalis*, ed. Chibnall, 2–4. Cf. Isidore of Seville, *Etymologiae*, ed. Lindsay, I, 41, 1–2.

figure out of history.[20] Though early Latin authors had made brief references to Arthur, it was Geoffrey of Monmouth, in his *Historia regum Britanniae*, who established him as the preeminent king of the Britons. While Geoffrey's work covered the British kings from Brutus to Cadwaladr, the last, seventh-century king of Britain, it was the pages he devoted to Arthur—with his conquest of thirty kingdoms, his defeat of the Romans, and his betrayal by Mordred—that aroused the greatest interest. Geoffrey acknowledges that in researching this book, he had found little about Arthur and many other British rulers in the standard histories, "even though their deeds . . . are proclaimed by many people, as if they had been entertainingly and memorably written down."[21] He was able to write so much about these rulers despite the lack of evidence about them, he explains, because he had consulted a previously unknown source. As he tells the story, Walter, an archdeacon at Saint George's convent of Augustinian canons at Oxford and an associate of his, lent him "a very old book in the British tongue,"[22] and he told him stories that amplified what the book said.[23] After Geoffrey's history began to circulate in the 1130s, it aroused an excitement that is difficult to overstate. Henry of Huntingdon had been working on his *Historia Anglorum* since 1129, yet feeling frustrated by the dearth of information he had been able to retrieve about the early British monarchs. In a letter to a certain Warin the Breton, he writes that when traveling through Normandy in 1139, "I discovered to my amazement

20. On Geoffrey of Monmouth's conception of history, see, in addition to the studies of twelfth-century English historiography already mentioned, Helen Fulton, "History and Myth: Geoffrey of Monmouth's *Historia regum Britanniae*," in *A Companion to Arthurian Literature*, ed. Helen Fulton (Chichester, UK; Malden, MA: Wiley-Blackwell, 2009), 44–57; Martin B. Shichtman and Laurie A. Finke, "Profiting from the Past: History as Symbolic Capital in the *Historia regum Britanniae*," *Arthurian Literature* 12 (1993): 1–35; Julia C. Crick, "Geoffrey of Monmouth, Prophecy, and History," *Journal of Medieval History* 18 (1992): 357–71; and Christopher Brooke, "Geoffrey of Monmouth as a Historian," in *Church and Government in the Middle Ages: Essays Presented to C. R. Cheney on His 70th Birthday*, ed. Christpher Brooke et al. (Cambridge: Cambridge University Press, 1976), 77–91.

21. "cum et gesta eorum . . . a multis populis quasi inscripta iocunde et memoriter praedicentur," Geoffrey of Monmouth, *Historia regum Britanniae*, prologue, 5.

22. "quendam Britannici sermonis librum vetustissimum," ibid., 5. Robert A. Caldwell has argued interestingly that what is normally interpreted as the variant version of Geoffrey's *Historia*—Geoffrey of Monmouth, *Historia regum Britanniae: A Variant Edition Edited from Manuscripts*, ed. Jacob Hammer (Cambridge: Medieval Academy of America, 1951)—is, in fact, the original upon which Geoffrey based his *Historia*. The absence of references to Walter the Archdeacon and the ancient book upon which the text depends supports Caldwell's thesis; the fact that the book is in Latin, rather than Welsh, weakens it.

23. Geoffrey of Monmouth, *Historia regum Britanniae*, ed. Reeve, XI, 249.

a written account of those very matters at the abbey of Le Bec."[24] After summarizing the contents of Geoffrey's book, including his life of Arthur, he urges Warin to track the volume down. So widely and so quickly did news of Geoffrey's book spread that as far away Yorkshire, Alfred of Beverley reports around 1149, "Narratives of the history of the Britons were borne in the mouths of many at that time, and he who did not have knowledge of such narratives was looked upon as a rustic."[25] Not only Henry and Alfred but virtually all medieval historians of Britain make use of Geoffrey's volume. The over two hundred surviving manuscripts of this work, in addition to its numerous translations and adaptations into vernacular tongues, testify to its popularity. In the thirteenth century, Jacob van Maerlant expresses skepticism about many Arthurian figures, including Lancelot and Perceval, but he does not doubt the existence or the greatness of Arthur: "Although there exist many fabricated stories about Arthur, which are written by minstrels and goliards who lie to invent nonsensical stories, the truth about the king should not be despised."[26] If the people of the Middle Ages embraced Arthur as historical to the extent that they did, it is often thought, it is because Geoffrey's account of this story corresponds to history as they were already predisposed to understand it.

Though learned men regarded "histories" with respect, they looked upon "fables" or "fictions" (*fabulae*) with suspicion. Classical rhetoricians, like Cicero,[27] Quintilian,[28] and the author of the *Rhetorica ad Herennium*,[29] affirm that "a fable [*fabula*] is that in which statements are expressed which are neither veracious nor verisimilar." While history

24. "apud Beccensem abbatiam scripta rerum predictarum stupens inveni," Henry of Huntingdon, "Letter to Warin the Breton," in *Historia Anglorum*, ed. Greenway, 559–83, at I, 559.

25. "Ferebantur tunc temporis per ora multorum narrationes de historia Britonum, notamque rusticitatis incurrebat, qui talium narrationum scientiam non habebat," Alfred of Beverley, *Annales*, quoted in Chambers, *Arthur of Britain*, 260. Alfred's work was published in 1716 by Thomas Hearne but still has not received a modern edition.

26. "Ende al es van hem achterbleven / boerden vele, die sijn bescreven / van menestrelen, van goliarden, / die favelen visieren begaerden, / dies en salmen niet ommare," Jacob van Maerlant, *Spiegel historiael*, ed. Philip Utenbroeke and Lodewijc van Velthem, 2 vols. (Leiden: Brill, 1863), vol. 2, Part III, Book V, chap. 48, vv. 67–71. See Bart Besamusca, "The Medieval Dutch Arthurian Material," in *The Arthur of the Germans: The Arthurian Legend in German and Dutch Literature*, ed. W. H. Jackson and S. A. Ranawake (Cardiff: University of Wales Press, 2000), 187–228, at 189.

27. "Fabula est, in qua nec verae nec veri similes res continentur," Cicero, *De inventione*, ed. Stroebel, I, 19, p. 24.

28. "fabulam, quae versatur in tragoediis atque carminibus non a ueritate modo sed etiam a forma veritatis remota," Quintilian, *Institutio oratoria*, ed. Winterbottom, vol. 1, II, 4, 2, p. 80.

29. "Fabula est, quae neque veras neque veri similes continet res," *Rhetorica ad Herennium*, ed. Marx, I, 8, p. 10.

signifies things that exist beyond the words in which they are uttered, Isidore of Seville indicates, fables signify things that exist only in those words: "Poets named 'fables' [*fabulas*] from 'speaking' [*fando*] because they are not events that happened, but are fabricated in speech."[30] As we have seen, it is not that medieval authors saw no value in fables. What makes a lie, a lie, Augustine had long since made clear, is not the utterance of an untruth per se, but the intention to deceive through that untruth.[31] Yet while medieval authors acknowledged that some poetical texts, such as parables and allegories, though false in and of themselves, could lead their audiences to the truth, they insisted that other such works, which fail to acknowledge their fictionality, mislead them as to what really happened. Given the privilege of history over fable, contributors to the Matter of Rome regularly expressed a preference for the accounts of the Trojan War attributed to Dictys Cretensis, a Cretan ally of the Greeks, and Dares Phrygius, a Trojan priest, who were believed to be eyewitnesses to the conflict, over those provided by Homer and Virgil, who wrote centuries later on the basis of hearsay and invention. (Dictys' and Dares' accounts were later proven to be forgeries from the fourth and fifth centuries AD.) In *De bello Troiano* (ca. 1188), Joseph of Exeter, for example, asks, "Should I admire Homer, that old man of Maeonia, Virgil from Latium, or Dares, the Phrygian master who was present as an eyewitness—a surer witness to describe the war that fable does not really know?"[32] In his *Roman de Troie* (1155–60), Benoît de Sainte-Maure likewise declares his intention to adhere exactly to Dares' text: "I shall follow the Latin source to the letter. I do not want to put in anything other than as I find it written down."[33] These authors' claims are not necessarily to be taken at face value, especially given their own tendency to interpolate invented narratives, such as the story of Troilus and Cressida, into their texts. By writing fables that they claim to be histories, these authors partake in a long-standing medieval tradition that passes off fictions as true accounts. In the fabliaux (a genre whose very name derives from "fable"), we read,

30. "Fabulas poetae a fando nominaverunt, quia non sunt res factae, sed tantum loquendo fictae," Isidore of Seville, *Etymologiae*, ed. Lindsay, I, 40, 1.

31. See Augustine, *De mendacio*, 3.

32. "Meoniumne senem, mirer, Latiumne Maronem / an vatem Phrygium Martem cui certior index / explicuit presens oculus, quem fabula nescit?" Joseph of Exeter, *Trojan War I–III*, ed. A. K. Bate (Bristol: Bolchazy-Carducci, 1986), 31, vv. 24–26.

33. "Niul autre rien n'i voudrai metre / s'ensi non com jel truis escrit, / le latin sivrai e la letre," Benoît de Sainte-Maure, *Roman de Troie: Extraits du manuscrit Milan, Bibliothèque ambrosienne, D 55* (1165), ed. Emmanuèle Baumgartner and Françoise Vielliard, Lettres Gothiques (Paris: Livre de Poche, 1998), vv. 139–41.

"I will tell you in place of a fable, an adventure that happened. . . . I will tell you the truth about it,"[34] "Lords, after having recounted fables, I would like to apply myself to telling the truth,"[35] and "I will tell, in the place of fables, the truth."[36] History may represent what happened, through eyewitness testimony and through reliable sources based upon eyewitness testimony, but there is nothing that prevents fiction from claiming to do so as well.[37]

Even as learned men acknowledged Arthur's historical basis, they tended to regard him, at least in part, as a figure out of fiction. At the end of the twelfth century, William of Newburgh once again provides the harshest denunciation of Geoffrey's veracity. How is it possible, he demands, that an obscure British chieftain could have conquered more land, more quickly, than Alexander the Great or Julius Caesar? How is it possible that a man who accomplished such great deeds should go unmentioned by early British and English historians, such as Gildas and Bede? The problem is not so much that Geoffrey writes fables, William states, but that he attempts to pass off these fables as history. He writes of its author, "Having taken up fables about Arthur drawn from the ancient fictions of the Britons and having added those of his own to them, he cloaked them, through the coloring of Latin words, with the honorable name of 'history.'"[38] To pass off fables as history, he alleges, is to pass off falsehood as truth and, thus, to lie. He declares, "It is plain that whatever this man published by writing about Arthur . . . was invented by liars."[39] While William is the most vehement of Geoffrey's critics, other historians of the twelfth and thirteenth centuries, though accepting Arthur's existence, refrain from repeating the more fabulous stories told about him.[40] In writing his *Annales*, Alfred of Beverley reports, "I applied myself to pluck out from

34. "je vous dirai en lieu de fable / une aventure qui avint; / . . . / vous en dirai bien verité," *Les .II. changeors*, in *The Fabliaux*, ed. Nathaniel E. Dubin (New York: Liveright, 2013), 244–60, at vv. 2–5.

35. "Seignor, aprés le fabloier, / me vueil a voir dire apoier," Jean Bodel, *Du Covoiteus et de l'envieus*, in ibid., 930–37, at vv. 1–2.

36. "dirai, en lieu de fable, voir," *La Dolente qui fu fotue sur la tombe*, in ibid., 324–31, v. 3.

37. See Frank Brandsma, "The Eyewitness Narrator in Vernacular Prose Chronicles and Prose Romances," in *Text and Intertext in Medieval Arthurian Literature*, ed. Norris J. Lacy (New York: Garland, 1996), 57–70.

38. "fabulas de Arturo ex priscis Britonum figmentis sumptas et ex proprio auctas per superductum Latini sermonis colorem honesto historiae nomine palliavit," William of Newburgh, *Historia rerum Anglicarum*, ed. Walsh and Kennedy, vol. I, preface, 3, p. 28.

39. "liquet a mendacibus esse conficta quaecunque de Arturo . . . homo ille scribendo vulgavit," ibid., I, preface, 14, p. 34.

40. See Robert H. Fletcher, *The Arthurian Material in the Chronicles, Especially Those of Great Britain and France* (Boston: Ginn, 1906; rpt., New York: B. Frankin, 1966), 179–80.

the said history those things which did not exceed the faith . . . and whose truthfulness is confirmed by consultation of other histories."[41] Those aspects of his work that he did not find to be theologically justified or historically verified, he indicates, he omitted. Of all the episodes in Arthur's life, the legend that this king never died and will one day return to his native land provoked the most incredulity among such historians. Not only William of Newburgh[42] and Gerald of Wales,[43] but Henry of Huntingdon,[44] Walter of Châtillon,[45] Joseph of Exeter,[46] Peter of Blois,[47] and Gervase of Tilbury,[48] among others, explicitly repudiate this story as absurd. In the sixteenth century, at the same time that authors were beginning to discount Merlin's prophecies, Raphael Holinshed, in his *Chronicles of England, Scotland, and Ireland* (1577–87), begins to discount Arthur's heroic feats. Though he accepts that someone by Arthur's name, "hardie and valiant in armes,"[49] had lived, he suspects that he was "not in diverse points so famous as some writers paint him out."[50] As a reflection of the disfavor into which this monarch had fallen, William Shakespeare devotes no play to King Arthur, despite his evident tragic potential, or to any other Arthurian figure. It is not only medieval historians who express indignation with Geoffrey's work. Christopher Brooke asserts, for example, "There has scarcely, if ever, been a historian more mendacious than Geoffrey of Monmouth."[51] Antonia Grandsen protests, "Geoffrey was a romance writer masquerading as a historian. No historian today would object to him if he had avowedly written a historical novel (like Sir Walter Scott) or a romance-epic (like Malory). But on the contrary he pretended to

41. "De praefata historia quaedam deflorare studui, ea videlicet quae fidem non excederent, et legentem delectarent, et memoriae tenacius adhaererent, et quorus veritatem etiam ceterarum historiarum collatio roboraret," Alfred of Beverley, *Annales*, 260.

42. William of Newburgh, *Historia rerum Anglicarum*, ed. Walsh and Kennedy, vol. 1, I, 15, pp. 34–36.

43. Gerald of Wales, *Descriptio Kambriae*, ed. Dimock, II, 7, p. 216; Gerald of Wales, *Speculum Ecclesiae*, ed. Brewer, II, 9, pp. 48–49.

44. Henry of Huntingdon, "Letter to Warin the Breton," ed. Greenway, IX, p. 580.

45. Walter of Châtillon, *Tractatus sive Dialogus . . . contra Judaeos*, col. 424.

46. Joseph of Exeter, *De Bello Trojano*, ed. Bate, III, vv. 472–73.

47. Peter of Blois, *Contra clericos voluptati deditos, sive de vita clericorum in plurimis reprobata*, PL, vol. 207, cols. 1129–36, at col. 1134, v. 28.

48. Gervase of Tilbury, *Otia Imperialia*, ed. Banks and Binns, II, 17, 67, p. 428.

49. Raphael Holinshed, *Chronicles of England, Scotland, and Ireland*, ed. Henry Ellis, 6 vols. (London: J. Johnson, 1807–8), vol. 1, V, 14.

50. Ibid.

51. Christopher Brooke, "Geoffrey of Monmouth as a Historian," 78.

be writing history."[52] For both these medieval and modern historians, "histories" that represent fictions about Arthur as true do their readers a disservice.

As we will see, vernacular accounts of Arthur in the Middle Ages recognize the concerns contemporary historians raised about whether this figure ever existed and whether he was as great as he is said to be, yet they respond to these concerns by showing that the definition of what happened in the past is more complicated than one might assume. If learned men doubted that Arthur ever existed, let alone as the celebrated "Arthur" of legend, it is worth remembering that the barons of the Kingdom of Logres and even Arthur himself doubt that the seemingly low-born youth who draws the sword from the stone is their rightful king. If learned men questioned whether Arthur's court ever existed, let alone as the famed "Camelot" of legend, it is, again, worth remembering that some of Arthur's vassals fail to recognize the greatness of his rule, to the point where they ally themselves with the traitor Mordred, rebel against their lord, and bring about the destruction of the kingdom. If learned men mocked suggestions that Arthur did not die, but, rather, still lives and will one day return, it is worth remembering that, according to the most influential account of this king's last days, the one eyewitness of these last days fails to make sense of what he observed. A great ruler, a great court, a great kingdom, these texts suggest, never exist unto themselves, as stable, fully actualized entities, and, therefore, are never experienced in their plenitude in the present. Instead, they are always remembered as something that occurred in the past or anticipated as something that will reoccur in the future. Insofar as they are experienced in the current time, it is only for a brief and evanescent moment, which is overshadowed by the knowledge that it will soon vanish. For a realist, the fact that the excellence of a person, a place, or a time is not appreciated in its own time proves that it was never actually as excellent as it seemed. For a romantic, however, there exist people, places, and times whose excellence can only be apprehended retrospectively or prospectively, from the vantage point of someone who is no longer or who is not yet there. It is for that reason that Arthur always has to be—to quote the Alliterative *Morte Arthure* (ca. 1400)—"the once and future king."[53]

52. Antonia Grandsen, *Historical Writing in England*, 202.

53. "rex quondam rexque futurus," *King Arthur's Death: The Middle English Stanzaic "Morte Arthur" and Alliterative "Morte Arthure,"* ed. Larry D. Benson, rev. ed., Edward E. Foster (Kalama-

The Sword in the Stone

As some learned men questioned whether the historical Arthur mentioned in scattered early Latin chronicles could ever have been the fantastical king depicted in Geoffrey's *Historia regum Britanniae*, the barons of the Kingdom of Logres in Robert de Boron's *Merlin* question whether the young Arthur could ever be the king for whom they yearn. As Robert tells the tale, when King Uther dies, apparently without an heir, his kingdom descends into an interregnum. That Christmas Eve, all of the lords of the land gather in the kingdom's major town and attend midnight Mass, where they pray that God will designate for them their rightful ruler. Among those present is a vavasor of low rank by the name of Antor, who has brought with him his two sons, Kay and Arthur. The next morning, when the people emerge from Mass, they find in the square outside the church an enormous stone and, in the middle of the stone, an anvil with a sword thrust into it. On the stone is an inscription in gold letters: "He who can draw out [this sword] would be king of the land by the election of Jesus Christ."[54] To everyone's surprise, the individual who succeeds in removing the sword from the stone turns out to be not a powerful and prestigious baron, but the insignificant youth Arthur. For a long time, the lords refuse to accept that their true king should be such a lad. Yet as the work unfolds, it becomes clear that because human beings can grasp only who someone appears to be, as seen in his outer, actualized traits, and not who someone truly is, as seen in his inner, potential attributes, they cannot see the king who lies latent in this boy. The sword in the stone functions as a marker of human beings' failure to ascertain who someone truly is.

If it is disconcerting to the barons that Arthur should be chosen to be a king, it is because they are proud and they assume that their king will be proud as well. When the sword in the stone first appears in the church square, the text relates, "The high-born, rich, and powerful

zoo: Published for TEAMS in association with the University of Rochester by Medieval Institute Publications, Western Michigan University, 1994), 131–261, at v. 4347. This phrase, which is said to be on Arthur's tomb, is repeated in *The Works of Sir Thomas Malory*, ed. Vinaver, vol. 3, bk. XXI, p. 1242. The familiar rendering of this phrase in English comes from the title of T. H. White's *The Once and Future King* (London: Collins, 1958).

54. "tel qui la pouïst d'iqui traire seroit rois de la terre par l'election Jhesu Crist," Robert de Boron, *Merlin*, ed. Micha, 83, 269.

men who had the strength to do so said that they would try it first."[55] With their distinguished birth and their great property, they take for granted that one of them will be chosen to become the rightful king of Britain and that they should therefore enjoy the first opportunity to pull the sword from the stone. Two hundred and fifty of these men struggle to draw out this weapon, though to no avail. In contrast to the barons, Arthur does not intend to try to remove the sword from the stone. On the Feast of the Circumcision, a bohort has broken out, and Kay, who has recently been knighted, wishes to join in the fray. He tells Arthur, who is serving as his squire, to fetch him a sword from the hostel where they are staying. Spurring his horse, Arthur rides back quickly to their lodgings, but he cannot find his brother's sword, or any sword at all, because their landlady has hidden the weapons in her room and has gone out to watch the bohort with everyone else. As Arthur is riding back to Kay, he passes through the church square, where he sees the sword in the stone. The text continues: "Then [Arthur] thought that, if he could, he would carry [the sword] to his brother. So he came straight back on horseback, took the sword by the hilt, [and] drew it out."[56] He aims to take the sword from the stone, not out of any ambition to rule of his own, but out of a desire to be of service to someone else, and, when he succeeds in doing so, he thinks little of what he has accomplished. When the barons learn that Arthur has succeeded at the feat at which they have failed, it is said, "The barons were very anguished."[57] They protest, "It is a very great marvel to us if such a young man, and one of such low rank, should be our overlord."[58] As they see it, the rightful king should be a mature man of high status who is confident in his claim to the throne, and not a boy of low rank who does not even dream of this position.

As the barons assume that their king will be proud, they assume that he will be assertive. Of the two brothers, it might seem that Kay would be the more appropriate ruler. Kay is a knight who wants to join in combat with other knights in the bohort. He gives orders, bidding his brother to fetch his sword. So proper does it seem to Kay that he, and

55. "li haut home et li riche et li puissant et chascuns qui la force avoit, dit qu'il essaieroit avant" ibid., 84, 270.

56. "Lors se pensa que, se il povoit, il la porteroit a son frere, si vint par iqui a cheval, si la prant par le poingnal, si l'en porte," ibid., 274–75.

57. "Li baron furent molt angoisseus," ibid., 87, 279.

58. "ce nos est molt grant merveille de si jone home et de si bas afaire qui einsis sera sires de nos," ibid., 89, 283.

not his younger brother, should become king that he initially claims that it was he who withdrew the sword from the stone. Seeking out Antor, he announces to him, "Sire, I will be king. See here the sword from the stone,"[59] and he admits that Arthur gave this sword to him only under questioning. In contrast to Kay, Arthur is still an attendant who assists his brother in combat. Told to retrieve Kay's sword, he replies, "Very willingly,"[60] because, we are informed, "He was very worthy and very eager to be of service."[61] While Kay remains in the public, martial space, near the bohort, where the other knights are fighting, Arthur withdraws to the private, domestic space of the hostel, which has been deserted even by its female proprietor. Failing at first to find a sword for his brother, it is said, "He wept and was very distressed and anguished."[62] As Arthur obeys Kay, he obeys Antor and the archbishop. In response to their demands, he explains how he obtained the sword, and he shows them how he removed it from the stone. In all of these episodes, those who wield authority over Arthur—whether as his elder brother, his father, or his prelate—give orders to him, and he obeys their orders without hesitation. The text attributes direct speech to Kay, Antor, and the archbishop as they utter their series of imperatives ("Go seek a sword for me";[63] "Tell me how you got this sword";[64] and "Give me this sword"[65]), and it attributes only indirect speech to Arthur as he complies with these commands, if it attributes any speech to him at all. Because of Arthur's subservient manner, the barons protest that they do not know who this lad is. They tell the archbishop, "Sire, . . . we have not seen or known him, nor do we know anything about his ways."[66] Soon thereafter, they beseech Arthur "that he speak to them"[67] and that he do so "according to [his] will, without any counsel."[68] In order for them to accept someone as king, the barons indicate, they need to know that he is capable of acting on his own, without just relying upon others, and they need to know how he will act when he does so. As they see it, the rightful king should be a masterful figure, capable

59. "Sire, je serai rois, vez ci l'espee dou perron," ibid., 86, 275.
60. "molt volentiers," ibid., 85, 274.
61. "Cil fu molt preuz et molt serviables," ibid.
62. "si plora et fu molt destroiz et angoisseus," ibid.
63. "Va moi querre une espee," ibid., 85, 274.
64. "me dites coment vos avez ceste espee eue," ibid., 86, 276.
65. "si me bailliez ceste espee," ibid., 88, 280.
66. "Sire, . . . nos ne l'avons ne veu ne coneu, ne ne savons gaires de son aistre," ibid., 89, 284.
67. "que il parlast a els," ibid., 89, 285.
68. "vostre volanté tout sanz consoil," ibid., 89, 285.

of giving commands to others, and not someone who just follows the will of others.

The barons proclaim that they wish to accept whomever God chooses as their king, but they are puzzled that he should choose Arthur. Though the sword in the stone recalls traditions more pagan than Christian,[69] the inscription on the stone makes clear that this test will identify the king chosen "by the election of Jesus Christ." From the ninth century on, people throughout Latin Christendom had relied upon the "judgment of God" (*iudicium Dei*) to reveal the truth in difficult matters,[70] but, at the turn of the twelfth and thirteenth centuries, when this text was being composed, this custom was being subject to criticism. The Parisian theologian Peter the Chanter argued influentially, citing the Gospel of Matthew, "'Do not tempt your Lord God' when you have something you can do in accordance with human reason."[71] It is one thing to supplicate God, by praying to him, Peter suggests, but it is another thing to attempt to manipulate him, by asking him to pass judgment in a trial. In 1215, influenced by Peter's and other theologians' writings, the Fourth Lateran Council forbade clerics from blessing the water or the hot iron used in ordeals, and other prohibitions of this practice soon spread throughout western Europe. In 1231, the rationalist Emperor Frederick II condemned the judgment of God in his *Liber Augustialis*: "We, who scrutinize and inspect the true science of laws and reject errors from our courts, prohibit those laws that are called by simple people 'apparent,' which neither consider the Nature of things nor attend to the truth."[72] Frederick mocks those foolish enough to think that a hot iron will grow cool or that a body will float in water for supernatural, rather than natural, reasons. In the context of this shift in judicial practice, some of the barons of the King-

69. See, for example, the *Völsunga saga*, where Sigmund is the only man who can withdraw a sword that Odin has driven into a tree. In the *Queste del Saint Graal*, Galahad is the only knight who can withdraw a sword from a floating stone. Odysseus is the only man who can bend his bow in Homer's *Odyssey*.

70. On the trial by God, see Robert Bartlett, *Trial by Fire and Water: The Medieval Judicial Order* (Oxford: Clarendon Press, 1986); Peter Brown, "Society and the Supernatural: A Medieval Change," *Daedalus* 104 (1975): 133–51; and John W. Baldwin, "The Intellectual Preparation for the Canon of 1215 against Ordeals," *Speculum* 36, no. 4 (1961): 613–36.

71. "'Non tentabis Dominum Deum tuum,' dum scilicet habes quid agas secundum humanam rationem," Peter the Chanter, *Verbum abbreviatium*, ed. Boutry, I, 76, p. 512. Cf. Matt. 4:7.

72. "Leges quae a quibusdam simplicibus sunt dictae paribiles quae nec rerum naturam respiciunt, nec veritatem attendunt, nos qui veram legum scientiam perscrutamus, et inspicimus, errores a nostris judicibus separamus," *Die Konstitutionen Friedrichs II. für sein Königreich Sizilen*, ed. Wolfgang Stürner, MGH, Leges 5 (Hannover: Hahnsche Buchhandlung, 1996), II, 31, p. 337.

dom of Logres oppose appealing to God to identify their rightful ruler. It is said that "there were many men who said that they were mad to believe that Our Lord intended to choose their king."[73] Other barons, while accepting God's right to decide upon their king, still resist recognizing Arthur as their divinely appointed lord: "We do not at all go against the will of Jesus Christ, but it is a very strange thing for us that a boy should be our overlord."[74] Even when the barons wish to accept God's judgment, they are reluctant to put aside their own judgment, which deems Arthur to be an improper choice for a monarch.

Yet while the barons are proud and assume that their king will be proud, Arthur is humble, and that humility is ultimately recognized to be desirable in a ruler. The barons are right, Robert suggests, to think that their king should be of high rank. A king must be of high and, ideally, royal birth because he must have the nature befitting a king, which, it was thought, is normally transmitted from father to son. If Arthur should be king, it is in part because he is not, in fact, the son of the lowly vavasor Antor, but the son of King Uther, who begot him on Ygerna, the wife of his vassal Gorlois, when he had taken on Gorlois's appearance, thanks to Merlin's magic, and who was obliged to forsake him to Merlin immediately after his birth as repayment for this favor. While the significance of his parentage is implicit throughout Robert's *Merlin*, it becomes explicit in the Post-Vulgate *Merlin*, when Merlin finally informs Arthur that he is Uther's son. Arthur exclaims, "In the name of God, . . . if he of whom you speak to me was my father, I cannot fail to be worthy."[75] If he were, in fact, of such noble birth, he continues, "I would never stop or take rest until I had put into subjection the greater part of the world."[76] If one knows that one's father was a worthy man, as Arthur now does, one must hold oneself responsible to measure up to the standard this sire has set. At the same time, the barons are wrong, Robert also indicates, to assume that their king should have always been aware of his high rank. If Merlin removes Arthur from his parents as a newborn, it is because he knows that, though the king must be of royal birth, it would be better for him to grow up

73. "si i ot mainz homes qui distrent que molt estoient fol dont il cuidoient et creoient que Nostres Sires meist entention de lor roi eslire," Robert de Boron, *Merlin*, ed. Micha, 82, p. 266.

74. "nos n'alons mie contre la volanté Jhesu Crist, mais il nos est molt estrange chose que uns garçons soit sires de nos," ibid., 87, p. 280.

75. "En non Dieu . . . se chis dont tu m'aparoles fu mes peres, je ne puis faillir a estre preudom," *La Suite du Roman de Merlin*, ed. Roussineau, vol. 1, I, 13, p. 9.

76. "je ne fineroie jamais ne averoie gramment de repos devant que je avroie mis en ma subjection la gregnour partie dou monde," ibid.

ignorant of that origin, so that he will not become proud of his status, like the barons themselves. Indeed, when Arthur learns that he is the son of the king, he does not glory in the acquisition of this new identity, but, rather, mourns the loss of his old identity, lowly as it may have been. He tells Antor, "Sire, . . . I beg you not to disown me as your son, for I would not know where to go."[77] In the Post-Vulgate *Merlin*, when he learns that Uther was his father, he is at first confused. If he were this man's son, he says, "I would not be as unknown as I am."[78] As someone unknown to himself as well as to others, he looks upon the kingship of Logres, not as position to which he feels entitled, given his high birth, but merely as a role he is now assigned to play. It is his recognition of the gap between his self and this role that makes him occupy this role better than anyone else. While all of the most important Arthurian heroes—Lancelot, Perceval, Galahad, Tristan, and Gawain—are brought up in ignorance of their origins, Arthur's ignorance of his distinguished parentage is more charged than that of these other knights, as it is the combination of the worthiness he has inherited from his father and the humility he has acquired from his upbringing that makes him qualified to rule the kingdom. As Robert and succeeding authors see it, the rightful king should be a man of high, indeed, royal status, but one who does not feel a priori entitled to wear the crown.

While the barons are assertive and assume that their king will be assertive, Arthur is meek, and it is this meekness, too, that is ultimately recognized to be beneficial in a king. Not only is Arthur the son of the worthy King Uther, but, thanks to Merlin's arrangements, he is also the suckling of Antor's wife, who is said to be "the worthiest woman, the most loyal, and the most endowed with good traits that there be in this kingdom."[79] As he benefits from the "nature" (*nature*) he has inherited from his father, he benefits from the "nurture" (*norriture*) he absorbs from his foster mother. While Arthur was nursed by Antor's wife, Kay was handed over to a peasant girl to be fed, and he drank in her evil qualities. As Antor informs Arthur, "If [Kay] is foolish, villainous, and wicked, . . . he obtained these bad traits for you, and he took them from the peasant girl he suckled. He was denatured [*desnaturez*]

77. "Sire, . . . je vos pri que vos ne me desavouoiz de fil, que donc ne savroie je ou aler," Robert de Boron, *Merlin*, ed. Micha, 87, p. 278.

78. "ne fuisse pas si mesconneus comme je sui," *La Suite du Roman de Merlin*, ed. Roussineau, vol. 1, 13, p. 10.

79. "la plus prodefemme et la plus loial et la mielz entechiees de toutes teches qui soit en cest regne," Robert de Boron, *Merlin*, ed. Micha, 73, p. 248.

in order to nourish [*norrir*] you."[80] In this context, it is clear, Kay's tendency to order Arthur about, without any apparent recognition of his merits, and his mendacious claim to have drawn the sword from the stone, without any apparent appreciation of his brother's rightful allegation to have done so, reflect his vicious character. What he seeks, he seeks for himself, not for anyone else. In contrast, Arthur's behavior toward others shows that he aims, not to empower and enrich himself, but to empower and enrich others. When Antor requests that Arthur grant him a reward for supporting his claim to the throne, Arthur protests, "Sire, you are my lord, as my father."[81] Because Antor is (he still thinks) his father, he is, by definition, his lord, and all that he has is his. When the archbishop instructs him to select his counselors and courtiers, Arthur asks him to assist him in this matter. Because the archbishop is his religious superior, he too is his lord, and he too can therefore advise him. If Arthur submits himself to others, obeying his brother's, his father's, and the archbishop's orders, it is because he recognizes and respects their authority, and this recognition and respect for authority bodes well for his own kingship. Around the same time, the barons give him many beautiful possessions, "in order to test whether his heart was covetous or grasping."[82] Instead of keeping these goods for himself, he inquires as to the value of each of these items, and he gives each of them to an appropriate recipient, which helps him win the skeptical barons to his side. It is not through pride, ambition, and covetousness (that is, qualities that seek to accrue benefits for the self), but through humility, obedience, and generosity (that is, qualities that accrue benefits for others) that he becomes the greatest of kings. As Robert sees it, the rightful king should be a masterful figure, but one who uses that mastery to recognize and reward others instead of to aggrandize the self.

If God chooses Arthur as king, it is because he alone knows who the best king would be. Even as Latin Christendom was making the transition from the judgment of God to the judgment of man in judicial cases, many people still remembered the old ethos, which taught that in accordance with Scripture, God alone knows the hearts of men. The Carolingian Capitularies had decreed that while human beings may pass judgment on clear cases, they should leave it to God to decide am-

80. "Et se il est fols et vilains et fel . . . ces mauvaises tesches a il eues por vos et prises en la garce que il alaita, et por vos norrir est il desnaturez," ibid., 87, p. 278.

81. "Sire, . . . vos . . . soiez sires comme mon pere," ibid., 86, p. 277.

82. "por essaier se son cuer seroit convoiteus ne enfrun," ibid., 90, p. 286.

biguous ones: "We must not judge uncertain things until God comes, who will draw hidden things out into the light, who will 'illumine those things hidden in darkness, and who will make manifest the secrets of hearts.'"[83] In the mid-ninth century, Hincmar, the archbishop of Reims, points to examples from Scripture, such as the waters of the Flood, the fires of Sodom, and the fire and water of the Apocalypse, as evidence that God punishes the wicked and saves the innocent. In trials by oath and ordeal, he similarly sees God as "bringing into sight those doubtful and obscure matters that cannot be proven or settled by law through judicial processes."[84] Even Ivo of Chartres, writing in the early twelfth century, who was generally opposed to reliance upon the judgment of God, notes of trials by ordeal, "We do not deny that there should be recourse to divine testimony when the preceding accusation is in order and human testimony is altogether lacking."[85] There are matters that can be determined by human reason, these clerics agree, but there are also matters that can be resolved only through divine revelation. For this reason, judges in France continued to resort to trials by ordeal sporadically through at least the 1230s. It is in the context of this lingering judicial tradition that the archbishop in Robert's *Merlin* appeals to God to identify the rightful king of Logres. He informs his flock, "Our Lord knows better than you who each person is."[86] As human beings cannot ascertain the truth about another human being through their own perceptions, he asserts, the people of Logres cannot ascertain the identity of their rightful king without assistance. As the archbishop reminds the barons that they must accept whomever God designates as their king, he reminds Arthur that he has been selected by God for this position. During the coronation ceremony, he asks if he is willing to swear to be a just ruler and, if so, to come forth and take the sword "by which Our Lord has made his choice know to them."[87] Arthur answers, weeping, "As truly as God is Lord of all things, may he give me the strength and

83. "Incerta . . . non debemus judicare quoadusque veniat Dominus, qui latentia producet in lucem, et 'inluminabit abscondita tenebrarum, et manifestabit consilia cordium,'" *Capitularia regum Francorum*, ed. Alfredus Boretiuu, 2 vols. (Hannover: Impensis Bibliopolii Hahn, 1883–97), in MGH, Leges 2, bk. VII, chap. 259, at vol. XX, p. 118. Cf. 1 Cor. 4:5.

84. "visui praesentanda quae dubia vel obscura, quae ex lege iudiciario ordine comprobari vel convinci non possunt," Hincmar of Reims, *De divortio Lotharii regis et Theutberga reginae*, PL, vol. 125, cols. 619–760, at col. 660.

85. "Non negamus tamen quin ad divina aliquando recurrendum sit testimonia quando, praecedente ordinaria accusatione, omnino desunt humana testimonia," Ivo of Chartres, *Epistola* 252, PL 162, cols. 257–58, at col. 258.

86. "Nostre Sires set mielz qui chascuns est que vos," Robert de Boron, *Merlin*, ed. Micha, 87, p. 279.

87. "dont Nostre Sires a lor esciant lor avoit fait election," ibid.

the power to uphold what you have said and what I have heard."[88] With these words, the young king makes clear that he recognizes that, well born and virtuous as he may be, his election is contingent upon his willingness to do God's will and upon God's willingness to help him do so. At this point in the ceremony, Arthur removes the sword from the stone one final time, raises it aloft, and brings it to the altar, where he sets it down. With this gesture, he makes clear that he recognizes that he has become king, not thanks to human beings, who never would have recognized the virtues that lay latent within him, but thanks to God, who alone is capable of this insight and who has used the marvel of the sword in the stone to make it manifest to the people of Logres. If Arthur becomes an excellent king, it is because, humble and meek as he is, he never fails to recognize God's sovereignty over him and to pray to God for his guidance. In the Post-Vulgate *Merlin*, Merlin interprets a dream that Arthur has had by predicting that he will ultimately be destroyed. When Arthur suggests that he should not have informed him of this sad fate, Merlin replies, "I do it . . . so that, in all your great joys, you will remember this sorrowful day; so that you will be more humble toward your Creator, who has placed you in the high position where you are; and so that you will doubt yourself and therefore sin less than you would otherwise do."[89] Arthur must never glory in his power, as a tyrant does, but, on the contrary, must always remember that he owes this power, not to himself, but to God, and that, as it was given to him, it will also, one day, be taken away. Far from being arrogant, he must doubt himself, and this self-doubt will be the source of his justice as a ruler. It is only insofar as the barons put aside their own judgment and accept God's judgment in its stead that they, too, are able to recognize Arthur as the proper choice as king.

In the end, as Arthur's existence had been called into question by historians both medieval and modern, it was called into question by the early literature about this king. From the very beginning, Arthur was known more as an idea in the mind than as a reality in the flesh. He is someone whom his parents know to exist but whom they do not see. Because his father begot him upon his mother Ygerna illicitly, with

88. "Einsi voirement comme Dieux est sires de toutes les choses me doinst il force et pooir de ce maintenir que vos avez dit et que j'ai entendu," ibid., 289–90.

89. "Je le fais . . . pour chou que se en toutes tes grans joies te souvenoit de cele dolereuse jornee, tu en seroies plus humelians vers ton Creatour qui en ceste hauteche te mist ou tu ies et plus t'en douteroies, si em pecheroies mains que tu ne feras," *La Suite du Roman de Merlin*, ed. Roussineau, vol. 1, XI, 248, p. 203.

the assistance of Merlin's magic, his parents have no right to him. After Ygerna gives birth to Arthur, she asks her maidservant to learn the identity of the mysterious man who comes to her door to take away her newborn son, but he will not disclose who he is. It is said, "The queen wept like a mother who has great sorrow."[90] She dies without ever seeing her child again and without ever learning what has become of him. Years later, when Uther is ailing, he asks Merlin about his son, but Merlin answers only that he is tall, handsome, and well brought up. Still later, when the king is on his deathbed, so weak that he is not expected to speak again, Merlin comes to him and tells him that Arthur will succeed him as ruler and that he will complete the Round Table. Drawing Merlin to him, Uther utters his final words: "By God, beseech him to pray Jesus Christ for me."[91] As Arthur's mother loved him, wanting to know who was taking him away and weeping when he was separated from her, his father loved him, wondering what has happened to him, thinking of him as he is dying, and longing for his prayers. As Arthur's parents suffered, never knowing the son who would have loved them, Arthur suffers, never knowing his parents, who would have loved him in return. While Arthur's parents know him but do not see him as he grows up, Antor and Uther's other subjects see him but do not know him. In the Post-Vulgate *Merlin*, Merlin tells his lord, "King Arthur the Adventurous, who were conceived by a marvel and were brought up by adventure, so that that he who brought you up did not know who you were, when you came as a young man among your liegemen, who did not know you, Our Lord knew you well, raised you over them all through his grace, and made you their lord, as you should be."[92] Cut off from his origins, Arthur depends upon divine intervention to become what he is meant to be. Yet as tragic as the severance of the natural bond between parents and child may have been, it is this loss of origins and the consequent loss of identity that enables him to become the best of kings.

90. "La reine plore comme mere qui grant dolor a," Robert de Boron, *Merlin*, ed. Micha, 76, p. 253.

91. "Por Dieu, prie li que il prie Jhesu Crist por moi," ibid., 79, p. 261.

92. "Rois Artus aventureus, ki fus concheus par miervelles et fus norris par aventure tel que chis qui te norrissoit ne savoit qui tu estoies, et quant tu venis jovenes enfes entre tes houmes liges qui ne te connissoient Nostres Sires te connut bien et t'esleva par sa grasce dessus eus tous et t'en fist signeur ensi coume tu le devoies estre," *La Suite du Roman de Merlin*, ed. Roussineau, vol. 1, XII, 278, p. 234.

The Court at Camelot

Just as Arthurian texts of the twelfth and thirteenth centuries respond to questions about Arthur's identity, they respond to questions about the nature of his court. In representing Arthur as the most glorious of kings and his realm as the most glorious of empires, these works might seem to have succumbed to what has been called, since the nineteenth century, "nostalgia." For modern scholars like Fredric Jameson[93] and Linda Hutcheon,[94] nostalgia leads us to look back upon the past, not as the reality it was, but as the ideal we imagine it to have been. As Hutcheon puts it, through nostalgia, "The ideal . . . is 'memorialized' as past, crystallized into precious moments selected by memory, but also by forgetting, and by desire's distortions and reorganizations."[95] Like Arthur himself, it would seem, Arthur's court never existed, at least as the magnificent political and cultural entity it is represented as having been, and any claim to the contrary reflects more the desire of people in the present than any experience of people in the past. On one level, these texts anticipate such charges by affirming that this court did, in fact, take place, whether at Caerleon, a town in South Wales that had once been an important Roman military base, or at Camelot, an unidentified town somewhere in the Kingdom of Logres. For as long as it was held, these texts allege, this court embodied a political ideal of peace and unity and a cultural ideal of courtliness and chivalry. Geoffrey relates, "Britain was at that time of such worthiness that, in the abundance of its wealth, the luxury of its decorations, and the courtliness of its inhabitants, it excelled all other kingdoms."[96] The knights of this court are said to have gathered around the Round Table, where they unanimously recognized Arthur as their sovereign and each other as their peers. On another level, however, these texts also indicate, if Arthur's court was what is said to have been—that is, the incarnation of

93. See Fredric Jameson, "Nostalgia for the Present," *South Atlantic Quarterly* 38, no. 2 (1989): 517–37; rpt. in *The Cultural Logic of Late Capitalism* (Durham, NC: Duke University Press, 1991), 279–96.

94. Linda Hutcheon, "Irony, Nostalgia, and the Postmodern," in *Methods for the Study of Literature as Cultural Memory*, ed. Raymond Vervliet and Annemarie Estor (Atlanta: Rodopi, 2000), 189–207.

95. Ibid., 195.

96. "At tantum eteneim statum dignitatis Britannia tunc reducta erat quod copia divitiarum, luxu ornamentorum, facetia incolarum cetera regna excellebat," Geoffrey of Monmouth, *Historia regum Britanniae*, ed. Reeve, IX, p. 213.

a certain political and cultural ideal—it could never have been experienced as something that exists in the present. Instead, it is remembered as something that existed in the past, or it is anticipated as something that will exist in the future. Insofar as it exists in the present, it does so only briefly, and the joy it brings is mitigated by the awareness that it will not last for long. The court is always in the process of ascending to a perfect state or of declining from that state, but it is never in this perfect state, except for one precious but ephemeral moment. Insofar as cynics deny that an ideal could ever become real, it is because they forget that an ideal, like Arthur's court, is something that can never be perceived straight on, but can only be glimpsed at an angle.

It might seem that Arthur's kingdom reaches its apogee politically when it achieves peace and unity. According to Geoffrey, Arthur fought for many years, first defeating local populations, such as the Saxons, the Picts, the Scots, and the Irish, and then conquering foreign nations, including the Danes, the Norwegians, and the Icelanders. He fought for nine long years in Gaul alone, subduing that land and distributing its fiefdoms among his followers. Finally, in the spring of an unnamed year, Arthur returns to Britain, where he decides to hold court at Pentecost. If this court is as magnificent as it is, we are told, it is because it commemorates the moment when Arthur's realm is finally able to turn from war and conflict to peace and unity. He summons to Caerleon all of the kings and dukes who do homage to him "so that he might celebrate the feast-day venerably,"[97] and all of them come. The unity of those in attendance is represented symbolically by the procession in which they participate. As Arthur advances to the metropolitan cathedral, he is escorted not only by archbishops on each side of him and a choir of clergy ahead of him, but by the kings of Scotland, North Wales, South Wales, and Cornwall, each bearing a golden sword. In a kind of *pax Arthuriana*, these kings, who might be vying with Arthur for power, converge at this court, happy, we are told, to recognize this ruler as their overlord. Guinevere is similarly accompanied by the wives of these kings, each bearing a white dove. All the married women follow the queen "with great rejoicing,"[98] apparently delighted to submit to such a worthy lady. The unity of those assembled is symbolized by the clothing they wear. Geoffrey writes, "The most noble men were stirred to count themselves as nothing unless they were dressed or armed in

97. "ut et illam venerabiliter celebraret," ibid.
98. "cum maximo gaudio," ibid., IX, p. 213.

the manner of Arthur's knights."[99] As the noblemen yearn to wear Arthur's livery, the "women . . . of courtly style"[100] also aspire to wear his colors. If all the distinguished men and women from near and far want to submit to Arthur and to demonstrate that submission by taking part in his procession and wearing his clothing, it is because they feel affection for the man from whose generosity they stand to benefit. Of the court at Caerleon, Geoffrey relates, "Arthur's liberality, made known throughout the world, drew everyone to him out of love."[101] Wace recounts that Arthur bestowed fiefs and dominions upon the high nobility; bishoprics and abbeys upon the clergy; and warhorses, greyhounds, birds, furs, tunics, and cups upon knights. It is not that he pays these men for their service; rather, we are led to believe, he impresses them with his munificence, and for that virtue that they see in him, they flock to his side. Under Arthur's rule, the many have become one, and all rejoice in the harmony that results from his reign.

It might seem that Arthur's kingdom reaches its apogee culturally when it achieves "courtliness" (*facetia*). Geoffrey reports, "[Arthur] began to increase his household, and he developed such a code of courtliness in his household that he inspired peoples living far away to emulate him."[102] Instead of waging wars against enemies, Arthur's men now engage in tournaments with each other. Whereas they once participated in battles, they now participate in jousts, which demonstrate their prowess at arms but without the same risk to life and limb. Instead of striving for victory over fellow warriors, they strive for the admiration of ladies. During the tournaments, we are told, "The ladies, watching from the battlements, fanned the flames in the knights' hearts into furious passion through their flirtatious behavior."[103] Instead of seeking the honor of martial victory, they seek the pleasure of visual and auditory stimulation. Wace enumerates all of the sights and sounds to admire at this court, from the ladies frequenting church services, to the choirs of clerics singing, to the servants rushing about, erecting tents, hanging up tapestries, and tending to horses. "You would see many squires,"[104]

99. "nobilissimus quisque incitatus nichili pendebat se nisi sese sive in induendo sive in arma ferendo ad modum militum Arturi haberet," ibid., IX, p. 205.

100. "Facetae . . . mulieres," ibid., IX, p. 213.

101. "largitas . . . Arturi, per totum mundum divulgata, cunctos in amorem ipsius allexerat" ibid., IX, p. 211.

102. "coepit familiam suam augmentare tantamque faceciam in domo sua habere ita ut aemulationem longe manentibus populis ingereret," ibid., IX, p. 205.

103. "Mulieres in edito murorum aspicientes in furiales amores flammas more ioci irritant," ibid., IX, pp. 213–15.

104. "mult veïssiez as esquiers," Wace, *Roman de Brut*, ed. Weiss, v. 10358.

he writes. "You would see servants and chamberlains in several directions."[105] Of the knights who pass their time milling about and absorbing these sights and sounds, he observes, "They could not have enough of either seeing or hearing. If the whole day had passed this way, I believe they would never have gotten bored."[106] With so much occurring, the court functions as a spectacle, where everyone is watching everyone else and displaying themselves to be watched. Living together in harmony, Arthur and his men turn from the brutality of war, on the battlefield with other knights, to the refinement of culture, in a town with ladies, clerics, and other civilians.

If there is any one moment in its history when Arthur's kingdom achieves its greatest perfection, at least in the vernacular texts, it is that day when the Round Table is brought to completion. Once, knights had prided themselves on their superiority to others around them, and they had expected to sit at the highest seats at a table as a result. Now, with the invention of the Round Table, they recognize each other, not as inferiors or superiors, but as peers. Wace, who is the first to mention this circular table, reports, "The vassals . . . were placed equally around the table and were equally served."[107] Once, knights had been recognized on the basis of their wealth or high rank. Now, those knights who are valiant, but poor, are included in the Round Table, while those who are not chivalric are excluded, even if they are rich.[108] Once, knights had clashed with each other over their competing claims to preeminence. Now, they join in the "fellowship" (*compaignie*) of the Round Table, where they experience only concord. Like the Apostles joined in the fellowship of the Last Supper, upon whom they are modeled, the knights wish to leave their domains with their wives and children and to spend their youth here at court, cleaving to each other as if they are, not strangers, but kinsmen. In the *Queste del Saint Graal*, the last vacant seat of the Round Table, which is known as "the Seat Perilous" (*le Siege Perillos*), is finally occupied. On Pentecost, Galahad, the Good Knight, comes to the court and takes this place at the table. Like a medieval image of Paradise, all of the worthiest knights of Arthur's realm have been identified and brought together in a circle. Individuals still, each of them has allowed himself to be subsumed into an orderly and harmonious group, where everyone occupies his destined seat. Years before,

105. "mult veïssiez en plusurs sens / errer vaslez e chamberlens," ibid., vv. 10353–54.

106. "ne se poeient saüler / ne de veeir ne d'esculter; / se tuz li jurs issi durast, / ja, ço qui, ne lur ennuiast," ibid., vv. 10432–36.

107. "li vassal / . . . / A la table egalment seeient / e egalment servi esteient," ibid., vv. 9753–56.

108. Cf. *La Suite du Roman de Merlin*, ed. Roussineau, vol. 1, XI, 247, p. 201.

according to the Post-Vulgate *Merlin*, Merlin had said of this table, "For my part, I would count myself fortunate if I could see the day when it will be achieved, for in this land there will come a joy so great that neither before nor after will there be like."[109] The Holy Grail descends among the knights in recognition of the blessedness of that moment. Now that table is perfected; that joy is felt by all.

Yet even as Arthur's kingdom attains its apogee politically, one can see evidence of the political conflicts that had surfaced in the past and that would resurface in the future. As laudable as peace and unity may seem to be, these values were achieved in the kingdom through war and conquest. The Saxons, Scots, Picts, and Irish all submit to his suzerainty, not because they choose to do so, but because they are forced to do so. Other peoples submit to him willingly, but only after they had seen how he had defeated other nations. Once Arthur had defeated the Irish and the Icelanders, Geoffrey reports, "A rumor spread through all the other islands that no country could resist [him]."[110] If people submit to Arthur, it is not just out of love, but also out of fear. Geoffrey states, "As his reputation for liberality and probity spread to the farthest corners of the world, kings of nations overseas, oppressed by worry, feared that he would invade and that they would lose the nations subject to them."[111] Knights ally themselves with Arthur, not only out of recognition of his liberality, but out of recognition of their lack of other good options. Wace attests that the French went over to his side, "partly for his generous gifts,"[112] but also "partly for fear, partly for refuge."[113] The court at Caerleon is not only a celebration of Arthur's power but also a demonstration of that power, meant to test the loyalty of his subjects by seeing whether they will respond to his summons and to reinforce that loyalty by obliging them to stand in attendance to him. If Arthur holds this court, Geoffrey makes clear, it is not only so that he might observe Pentecost suitably, but also "so that . . . he might renew among his chieftains the most firm peace."[114]

109. "Je endroit de moi me tenisse a boin euré se je peusse chelui jour veoir que che sera acompli, car en cest païs avra adont joie si grant que devant ni aprés n'avera autretel," *La Suite du Roman de Merlin*, ed. Roussineau, vol. 1, XI, 248, p. 203.

110. "Exin, divulgato per ceteras insulas rumore quod ei nulla provintia resistere poterat," Geoffrey of Monmouth, *Historia regum Britanniae*, ed. Reeve, IX, p. 205.

111. "Denique, fama largitatis atque probitatis illius per extremos mundi cardines divulgata, reges transmarinorum regnorum nimius invadebat timor ne inquietatione eius oppressi nationes sibi subditas amitterent," ibid., IX, p. 205.

112. "tant pur sun largement duner," Wace, *Roman de Brut*, ed. Weiss, v. 9950.

113. "tant pur poür, tant pur refui," ibid., v. 9952.

114. "ut . . . inter proceres suos firmissimam pacem renovaret," Geoffrey of Monmouth, *Historia regum Britanniae*, ed. Reeve, , IX, p. 209.

As Wace sees it, people come to this court for a variety of motives: "some for Arthur, some for his gifts, some to know his barons, some to see his wealth, some to hear his courtly speech, some out of love, some because they were commanded, some for honor, some for power."[115] Given that some kings, dukes, and knights join Arthur because they are forced to do so, others because they are afraid not to do so, and others because they hope to benefit from doing so, it is not surprising that after another man comes to power in Logres, a certain contingent should shift their allegiance to this new ruler. When Mordred usurps Arthur's throne during his temporary absence from the kingdom, the kings of the Danes and the Norwegians remain loyal to him, even dying by his side at Camlann, but other subjects rise up against him. The king of Ireland, though he had been present at the plenary court at Caerleon, rebels against him. According to Geoffrey, "[Mordred] had brought the Scots, the Picts, and the Irish into his alliance, along with anyone else he knew to have hatred for his uncle."[116] Even at the height of the reign of the most glorious of kings, some of his subjects recall the past, when he conquered them, and look forward to the future, when they hope to be independent of him. While under Arthur's rule, the many have become one, some resist his dominion, experiencing it not as harmony, but as oppression.

Even as Arthur's court attains its apogee culturally, its members are already remembering it as something that existed in the past, which they are now attempting to recuperate. In the midst of the celebrations at Pentecost, Geoffrey relates, twelve venerable old men arrive with a letter from Lucius, the procurator of the Roman Republic, which demands that Arthur either travel to Rome to be tried for his refusal to pay tribule and for his conquest of their tributaries or prepare for war. As members of Arthur's council are climbing up the tower stairs to the room where they will deliberate upon how to respond, Cador, the duke of Cornwall, begins to laugh and speak "in a happy tone."[117] As he sees it, the five years of peace they have enjoyed have not necessarily been to the Britons' benefit. He states, "Until now I was in fear lest the idleness which the Britons have enjoyed in this long period of peace might make them slack and efface their renown for fighting, through which

115. "tant pur Artur, tant pur ses duns, / tant pur cunustre ses baruns. / tant pur veeir ses mananties, / tant pur oïr ses curteisies, / tant pur amur, tant pur banie, / tant pur enur, tant pur baillie," Wace, *Roman de Brut*, ed. Weiss, vv. 10331–37.

116. "Associaverat . . . sibi Scotos, Pictos, Hibernenses, et quoscumque callebat habuisse suum avunculum odio," Geoffrey of Monmouth, *Historia regum Britanniae*, ed. Reeve, XI, p. 251.

117. "laeti animi," ibid., IX, p. 217.

they are more famous than other nations."[118] By the same token, he suggests, the years of war, which now seem to be returning, may not be to their detriment. God has inspired the Romans to confront the Britons in this manner, he asserts, "so that they may lead our virtue back to its earlier state."[119] With these words, the duke makes clear that the greatest moment for Arthur's realm lies not in the present, during the plenary court at Caerleon, when his men can enjoy the peace and unity that resulted from their many conquests, but in the past, during the years of battle that led up to this court, when they were achieving these conquests. Even though, when they were struggling against opponents in far-off lands, Arthur and his men had looked forward with anticipation to a future time when they would enjoy a well-earned reward for their efforts, once they have conquered their opponents and returned home, they look back with nostalgia to that past time when they were still struggling, and they hope that this past time will return in the future. Arthur appears to share Cador's views. When he addresses his men before their battle with the Romans, he too praises them for not having lost their virtue during this time of peace. He states, "Although you have not campaigned for five years and were devoted to the pleasures of rest rather than to military service, you have by no means lost your natural prowess."[120] He proposes that the greatest moment for his realm will lie in the future, when his men will have defeated the Romans in battle and made him emperor. Living together in harmony, Arthur and his men realize that the best moment is not when one has attained what one was striving for, but when one is still striving for it and still unsure that one will attain it.

Arthur's court may achieve perfection on the day when the Round Table is brought to completion, but that perfection only lasts one day, during which its imminent loss is already being mourned. For all the years of its existence, the Round Table was only rarely occupied, at the great feast days of Advent, Easter, and Pentecost, if that. As knights errant, the companions of the Round Table spend their time, not relaxing in the safety of court, but exposing themselves to the dangers of the world, where they seek adventure. Even when all of the knights do happen to be at court, the Seat Perilous remains for years ominously vacant. In Robert's *Merlin*, we are told, "Many others saw it, but they

118. "Hucusque in timore fueram ne Britones longa pace quietos ocium quod ducunt ignavos faceret famamque militiae, qua ceteris gentibus clariores censentur, in eis omnino deleret," ibid.

119. "ut in pristinum statum nostram probitatem reducerent," ibid.

120. "Quamquam quinque annis inexercitati oblectamentis ocii potius quam usui miliciae dediti sitis, nequaquam tamen ab innata bonitate degeneravistis," ibid., IX, p. 237.

did not know what it signified, nor why it was empty."[121] Merlin explains that this seat is called the Seat Perilous because any knight who attempts to sit in it will die or be wounded until Galahad, the Good Knight, comes to take his place. Until then, he informs Arthur in the Post-Vulgate *Merlin,* "Your table will never be . . . wholly perfect or complete."[122] Over the years, many knights dare to sit in the Seat Perilous, and all are killed or maimed, including one who is immediately incinerated into ashes. As a result, the unfilled seat casts a pall over the table, reminding its occupants that its number is not yet perfect or complete and that the best among them has yet to arrive. Even at that great Pentecost when Galahad finally appears and takes his place, it is foreknown that, as Merlin had warned, "He will sit there and rest, but it will not be for long."[123] The day that the Round Table is completed is also the day that the Round Table is disbanded, never to achieve completion again. The moment of Arthur's joy is also, therefore, the moment of his sorrow. He laments, "Never has a Christian king had as many good knights or worthy men at his table as I have had here today, nor will one ever do so when they depart from here."[124] With the Round Table now complete, the Holy Grail descends to bedazzle the knights with its grace, inspiring them to embark on the Quest of the Holy Grail. At the very moment when the court has achieved its fullest realization—when the greatest number of admirable knights ever to assemble have assembled around its table—he realizes that this court will decline from this moment, forever after. For that reason, Arthur informs his knights, "Fair lords, . . . because I know well that I will never see you all together again, as I see you know, I want there be a tournament in the field outside Camelot so marvelous and so spirited that, after our deaths, our descendants who come after us will make mention of this day."[125] The tournament is magnificent, many great feats of arms are performed, and Galahad takes the day, but the pleasure that Arthur and the others take at this event is overshadowed

121. "maint autre le virent, mais il ne savoient que il senefioit ne por quoi il estoit voiz," Robert de Boron, *Merlin,* ed. Micha, 49, p. 188.

122. "vostre table ne sera . . . dou tout parfaite ne assoumee," *La Suite du Roman de Merlin,* ed. Roussineau, vol. 1, XI, 248, p. 202.

123. "Cil s'i asserra et reposera, mais che ne sera mie lonc tans," ibid., vol. 1, XI, 248, p. 203.

124. "onques rois crestians n'ot autant de bons chevaliers ne de proudomes a sa table comme j'ai hui eü en cest jor, ne jamais n'avra, quant il de ci se partiront," *Queste del Saint Graal,* ed. Gros, 19, p. 831.

125. "Biaus signours, . . . pour ce que je sai bien que je ne vous verrai jamais ausi tous ensamble conme je vous voi orendroit, revoel je que en la praerie de Kamaalot soit orendroit conmenciés uns tournoiemens si merveillous et si envoisiés que aprés nos mors en facent nostre oir mencion, qui aprés nous venront," ibid., 14, p. 825.

by the knowledge that it marks not only the highest point the Round Table would ever achieve, but its conclusion. As Arthur's words indicate, the pleasure they take in the Round Table's perfection is not from the perspective of the present, but from the perspective of the future, when, they know, people will look back upon this past moment and will treasure what was lost.

In the end, as the existence of Arthur's court had been called into question by historians both medieval and modern, it was called into question by this early literature. This court was, again, known more as an idea in the mind than as a reality in the flesh. The adventures that distinguished this court and provided the context within which its knights proved their worth existed for a time, it is said, but this was in the past. In the Post-Vulgate *Merlin*, Merlin speaks of "so many and such marvelous adventures"[126] that have happened and will continue to happen in his lands. He adds, "Therefore, I say that you should be called the Adventurous King and your kingdom the Adventurous Kingdom."[127] Yet over the course of the Quest of the Holy Grail, the Grail knights put an end to these adventures. It is said of Perceval and Galahad that "they had so achieved the adventures of the Kingdom of Logres that there are not many anymore, if it is not a demonstration of Our Lord."[128] As a Christian, the author of this text believes that events contrary to the laws of Nature still occur, but these are miracles, which occur as a result of God's intervention, and not marvels, of the kind that once defined Arthur's reign. Yet disappointing as the passing of these adventures may have been, the texts suggest, they may possibly resume. One day, after the Quest has come to an end, the knights of the Round Table see a magnificent bark drift down the river to Camelot with a dead damsel on board. Gawain exclaims, "By faith, . . . I would almost say that the adventures were beginning again."[129] The enchantments happened in the past, but they may also, just possibly, occur in the future as well.

126. "tantes aventures et si mervilleuses," *La Suite du Roman de Merlin*, ed. Roussineau, vol. 2, p. 97.

127. "Et pour chou di jou que tu dois estre apielés rois aventureus et tes roiaumes aventureus," ibid.

128. "orent il si achievees les aventures del roialme de Logres, que poi i avoit mais, se ce n'ert demoustrance de Dieu," *Queste del Saint Graal*, ed. Gros, 354, p. 1159.

129. "Par foi . . . a poi que je ne di que les aventures recommencent," *La Mort du roi Arthur*, ed. Speer, 113, p. 1277.

The Isle of Avalon

It was in Glastonbury, in the final years of the twelfth century, that the history and fiction of Arthur converged.[130] On the one hand, the Isle of Avalon became identified with the ancient, rich, and powerful abbey of this town, a place that, due to its surrounding marshes, could have the appearance of an island. King Henry II told the abbot Henry of Sully that he had heard from "an aged British bard"[131] that Arthur had been buried in his abbey, between two ancient pyramids, or standard crosses, adjacent to the monastery cemetery dedicated to Saint Dunstan. One day in 1191, shortly after the king had died, the abbot ordered the excavations to begin which resulted, we are told, in the discovery of a heavy slab inscribed with the words, "Here lies buried the famous King Arthur, on the Isle of Avalon, with Guinevere, his second wife"[132] and, underneath, an oaken casket with the bones of a man and a woman.[133] A skeptic may question whether these bodies were really those of Arthur and Guinevere and even whether their purported

130. Arthur had long been associated with Glastonbury. In his *Vita Gildae*, Caradoc of Llancarfan recounts how King Melwas of Somerset (Meleagant in Chrétien de Troyes' *Le Chevalier de la charrette*) had abducted Guinevere and brought her to Glastonia, counting upon the inaccessibility of this city, due to its reeds, river, and marshes, to protect them from attack, how Arthur had besieged Glastonia, and how Gildas and the abbot of Glastonbury reconciled Melwas and Arthur. See Edward Donald Kennedy, "Glastonbury," in *The Arthur of Medieval Latin Literature*, ed. Echard, 108–31; *Glastonbury Abbey and the Arthurian Tradition*, ed. James P. Carley (Cambridge: D. S. Brewer, 2001), including Aelred Watkin, "The Glastonbury Legends," 13–27; Valerie M. Lagorio, "The Evolving Legend of St. Joseph of Glastonbury," *Speculum* 46 (1971): 209–31; and J. Armitage Robinson, *Two Glastonbury Legends: King Arthur and St. Joseph of Arimathea* (Cambridge: University Press, 1926).

131. "cantore Britone . . . antiquo," Gerald of Wales, *Liber de Principis Instructione*, ed. Warner, I, 9, p. 128, and *Speculum ecclesiae*, ed. Brewer, II, 9, p. 49.

132. "Hic iacet sepultus inclytus rex Arthurius, in insula Avallonia, cum Wennevereia uxore sua secunda," Gerald of Wales, *Speculum Ecclesiae*, ed. Brewer, II, 9, p. 50, and *Liber de Principis Instructione*, ed. Warner, I, 20, p. 127. There are four other different versions of the inscription.

133. Other accounts of this exhumation are provided by Ralph of Coggeshall, in his *Chronicon Anglicanum* (ca. 1223), ed. Joseph Stevenson, Rolls Series (London: Longman, 1875); the chronicler of Margam Abbey in Glamorgan, in his *Annales Monastici* (1234), ed. H. R. Luard, Rolls Series (London: Longman, 1864–69), vol. 1, 21–22; and Adam of Domerham, in his late thirteenth-century *Historia de rebus gestis Glastoniensibus*, ed. Thomas Hearne, 2 vols. (Oxford: E Theatro Sheldoniano, 1727). For discussion of this exhumation, see James P. Carley, "A Grave Event: Henry V, Glastonbury Abbey, and Joseph of Arimathea's Bones," in *Culture and the King: The Social Implications of the Arthurian Legend; Essays in Honor of Valerie M. Lagorio*, ed. Martin B. Shichtman and James P. Carley (Albany: State University of New York Press, 1994), 129–48; Antonia Grandsen, "The Growth of the Glastonbury Traditions and Legends in the Twelfth Century," in *Legends, Traditions, and History in Medieval England* (London: Hambledon Press, 1992), 153–74; rpt., *Glastonbury Abbey and the Arthurian Tradition*, ed. James P. Carley (Cambridge: D. S. Brewer, 2001), 337–58; and W. A. Nitze, "The Exhumation of King Arthur at Glastonbury," *Speculum* 9 (1934): 360–61.

discovery was not just a ruse concocted by the monks in order to increase the number of visitors to their abbey and the amount of their donations. Indeed, Glastonbury had suffered a disastrous fire in 1184 and was badly in need of new streams of revenue at this point. Yet Gerald of Wales, who seems to have been present at this occasion, insists upon the legitimacy of this discovery by emphasizing the precise details of the inscription and the bones, which he inspected thoroughly.[134] He reports (in accordance with accounts of Arthur's prowess) that the man's skull showed evidence of ten or more wounds, each of which had healed into scars, except the last and deepest one, which had apparently brought about his death. On the other hand, even as the Isle of Avalon was identified with Glastonbury, it continued to be identified with a mysterious otherworld across the western sea, where crops grow in abundance without any human toil and where heroes live forever, in youth, beauty, and good health. From Geoffrey's *Vita Merlini* on, this island was associated in a somewhat confused fashion with the classical "Fortunate Isles" (*Fortunatarum insulae*), the residence of departed heroes; with the Irish "Isle of Apple Trees" (*Emhain Abhlach*), the residence of Manannán mac Lir, the god of the sea; and with the Welsh "Isle of Apples" (*Ynys Avallach*), the home of a certain Afallach and his daughters, including Modron (otherwise known, in Breton, as Morgen). Even as Avalon was believed to be Glastonbury, Morgan Arthur's distinguished kinswoman, and Arthur the dead king she had buried in the abbey's holy precincts, Avalon was also believed to be a distant island across the sea, Morgan a "fantastical sorceress"[135] who heals her kinsman's wounds through her magical art,[136] and Arthur someone whose body, "as if fantastical in its end, was transferred, as if by a spirit, to a distant place and was not subject to death."[137] It is in the context of these two competing interpretations of Avalon that the author of the Vulgate Cycle's *La Mort le Roi Artu* situates the last

134. See Gerald of Wales, *Speculum ecclesiae*, ed. Brewer, II, 9, p. 50, and *Liber de Principis Instructione*, ed. Warner, I, 20, p. 127.

135. "dea phantastica," Gerald of Wales, *Speculum ecclesiae*, ed. Brewer, II, 9, p. 49.

136. There are many accounts of a king who who resides in a mountain and who will return to aid his people in their hour of need. Typically, these kings sleep in remote places, including caves, mountains, or islands, and are stumbled upon by herdsmen who are looking for a lost animal. These kings include Fionn mac Cumhaill; the Mahdi, or Twelfth Imam in Shi'ite Islam; and Constantine XI, the last Byzantine emperor. This motif is included as number 766 in the Aarne-Thompson classification system for folkloric motifs.

137. "quod quasi phantasticum in fine, et tanquam per spiritus ad loninqua translatum, neque morti obnoxium," Gerald of Wales, *Liber de Principis Instructione*, ed. Warner, I, 20, p. 127.

section of his work.[138] While this author composed the preceding narrative from an omniscient perspective, emphasizing the political and personal conflicts that lead to the Kingdom of Logres' destruction, here he shifts to the point of view of Girflet, Arthur's one surviving retainer, and the marvelous events he may—or may not—behold. Like Gerald, who stressed his own firsthand observation of Arthur's exhumation, this author stresses Girflet's firsthand observation of Arthur's last two days. While the dominant judicial and scholarly thought of this time depended upon eyewitnesses' testimony and upon writings based upon this testimony, this author draws out the problems with these two sources of knowledge. As a result, *La Mort le Roi Artu* refuses to provide one clear answer to the question, "Is Arthur dead or not?," yet its refusal to do so itself constitutes a kind of answer.

From what Girflet sees in *La Mort le Roi Artu*, Arthur dies as other men die. Not long beforehand, Gawain had insisted upon fighting Lancelot in single combat, and he had suffered a serious blow to the head during this encounter. He had not died immediately, but the wound would prove fatal. In the days that followed, Gawain had acted as medieval people were expected to act as they were dying.[139] He had a presentiment of his death. He announced, "I know well that I will not live for two more weeks."[140] He repented of his sins, especially of the unwarranted anger he had shown Lancelot, which had led him to challenge him. When he died, it was with his hands crossed on his

138. Norris J. Lacy, "The Sense of an Ending: *La Mort le Roi Artu*," in *A Companion to the Lancelot-Grail Cycle*, ed. Carol Dover (Cambridge: D. S. Brewer, 2003), 115–24; Norris J. Lacy, "The *Mort Artu* and Cyclic Closure," in *The Lancelot-Grail Cycle: Text and Transformations*, ed. William W. Kibler (Austin: University of Texas Press, 1994), 85–97; and Fanni Bogdanow, "La Chute du royaume d'Arthur: Evolution du thème," *Romania* 107 (1986): 504–19, read this work as a tragedy. R. Howard Bloch, "From Grail Quest to Inquest: The Death of King Arthur and the Birth of France," *Modern Language Review* 69, no. 1 (1974): 40–55, interprets the destruction of the Kingdom of Logres as reflecting the failure of feudalism during the increasingly centralized reign of Philip Augustus or Saint Louis. See also R. Howard Bloch, "The Death of King Arthur and the Waning of the Feudal Age," *Orbis Litterarum* 29 (1974): 291–305, and *Medieval French Literature and Law* (Berkeley: University of California Press, 1977), as well as R. Howard Bloch and L. R. Micha, "Further Thoughts on the *Mort Artu*," *Modern Language Review* 71 (1976): 26–30. For other readings of this work, see Karen Pratt, *La Mort le roi Artu* (London: Grant and Culter, 2004); Virginie Greene, *Le Sujet et la mort dans la "Mort Artu"* (Saint-Genouph: Nizet, 2002); the essays in *La Mort du Roi Arthur ou le Crépescule de la chevalerie*, ed. Jean Dufournet (Paris: Honoré Champion, 1994), and Christopher *Passing of Arthur: New Essays in Arthurian Tradition*, ed. Baswell (New York: Garland, 1988), 5–15; and Jean Frappier, *Etude sur "La Mort le roi Artu"* (Geneva: Droz, 1968); 3rd rev. ed. (Geneva: Droz, 1972).

139. On the heroic death in the Middle Ages, see Philippe Ariès, *L'Homme devant la mort* (Paris: Editions du Seuil, 1977), 13–36.

140. "je sai bien que je ne vivrai pas .XV. jours," *La Mort du roi Arthur*, ed. Speer, 279, p. 1420.

chest and the words "Jesus Christ, Father, do not judge me according to my misdeeds"[141] on his lips. Now, during the battle at Salisbury Plain, Arthur is fighting Mordred, and he suffers a blow to his head so savage that a piece of his skull is dislodged.[142] The text relates, "Thus . . . did the son give his father a mortal wound,"[143] just as the father kills his son. He does not die immediately, but the wound is, we are told, lethal. Like Gawain, Arthur has a presentiment of his death. He informs Girflet and Lucan, his two remaining companions, "I see well that my end is approaching."[144] The men leave the battlefield and ride to what is called the Black Chapel. There, like Gawain, Arthur turns to God. He kneels down before the altar and remains there, in prayer and meditation, throughout the night. The text reports, "He did not cease praying that our Lord would have mercy on the souls of his men who had been killed that day."[145] As Girflet and Lucan heard Arthur predict his end, they now hear him grieve. We are told, "While he was making this prayer, he was weeping so bitterly that those who were with him heard well that he was weeping with great anguish."[146] He embraces Lucan at this time, but so altered is his state that he unintentionally crushes him to death. In accordance with the custom of dying medieval heroes, Arthur is wounded in battle, he foresees his death, and he turns to God, weeping and praying for his mercy. If Arthur seems to be dying, it appears to be because he is, in fact, dying. On the first page of this work, it is said that "Master Walter Map . . . called it *The Death of King Arthur,* because in the end it is written how King Arthur was wounded at the Battle of Salisbury and how he departed from Girflet, who had long kept him company, so that, after him, there was no man who saw him alive."[147] The title of the work itself seems to indicate that Arthur died in the aftermath of this battle, just as this passage indicates that Girflet was the one who attended him during these last moments.

From what Girflet observes, Arthur rids himself of Excalibur, and he

141. "Jhesu Cris, Peres, ne me juge mie selonc mes mesfais," ibid., 293, p. 1431.

142. Jean Frappier, "La Bataille de Salesbieres," in *Mélanges offerts à Rita Lejeune* (Gembloux: Duculot, 1969), 1007–23; rpt. in *La Mort le Roi Artu*, ed. Emmanuèle Baumgartner (Paris: Klincksieck, 1994), 27–58.

143. "Ensi . . . li fiels navra le pere a mort," *La Mort du roi Arthur*, ed. Speer, 328, p. 1463.

144. "je voi bien que ma fins aproce," ibid., 330, p. 1465.

145. "sa proïere ne fina vers Nostre Signour qu'il eust merci des ames a ses homes qui le jour avoient este ocis," ibid., 330, p. 1465.

146. "Et en ce qu'il faisoit ceste proiere, il plouroit si durement que cil qui avoc lui estoient entendirent bien qu'il plouroit angoissousement," ibid.

147. "maistres Gautiers Map . . . l'apela *La Mort au roi Artu*, pour ce que vers la fin est escrit conment li rois Artus fu navrés en la bataille de Salesbieres et conment il s'en parti de Gyrflet, qui tant fist compaignie, que aprés lui ne fu nus hom qui le veïst vivant," ibid., 1, p. 1181.

then departs across the sea on a ship. Now, after the night in the Black Chapel, we are told, Arthur and Girflet ride off toward the sea. When they reach the shore, they stop, and Arthur ungirds his sword, draws it from its scabbard, and addresses it. "Ah, Excalibur, good sword, . . . now you will lose your master and your lord!"[148] he exclaims. Like Roland in the *Chanson de Roland* (1090s),[149] he decides to rid himself of his sword so that no unworthy warrior may gain possession of it. For that purpose, he asks Girflet to climb a nearby hill and to throw the sword into the lake he will find on the other side. Though Girflet agrees to do as Arthur has bidden, he cannot bear to dispose of the sword because he admires this weapon too much. Twice, he flings another object—first, his own sword and, then, the scabbard—into the lake in its place. Twice, when Arthur asks him what he saw when he threw the sword, he says that he saw nothing unusual. Twice, Arthur sees through this deception. "Go, and throw it," he tells him. "Thus you will know what will happen to it, for it will not be lost without some great marvel."[150] Finally, Girflet climbs the hill a third time and hurls the sword into the deepest part of the lake. When he returns to Arthur and informs him what he saw when he did so, the king sighs and says, "By faith, . . . I was right to think that my end was fast approaching."[151] Despite Girflet's protests, Arthur then insists that he leave him alone on this shore. As the retainer rides off, the text at first recounts entirely ordinary and everyday events. We are told, "A rain began to fall, very great and very marvelous, which lasted until he reached a hill which was a half league from the king. When he had come to the hill, he stopped underneath a tree until the rain had passed. And when it had passed, he began to look at that place where he had left the king."[152] The knight rides his horse. When it begins to rain heavily, he takes shelter underneath a

148. "Ha! Escalibor, bone espee, . . . ore perdras tu ton maistre et ton signour!" *La Mort du roi Arthur,* ed. Speer, 332, pp. 1466–67.

149. *La Chanson de Roland,* ed. Ian Short (Paris: Librairie générale française, 1990), 173, vv. 2344–51. In the *Völsunga saga,* a thirteenth-century prose version of a story in existence by the tenth or eleventh century, the hero Sigmund knows that his end has come when his sword breaks. In Alexandre Micha, "Deux Sources de la *Mort Artu,*" *Zeitschrift für romanische Philologie* 60 (1950): 369–372; rpt., *La Mort de Roi Artu,* ed. Emmanuèle Baumgartner (Paris: Klincksieck, 1994), 39–42, Micha connects the necessary disappearance of Excalibur to that of Roland's Durendal in the *Karlamagnussaga* (late 1200s) and to that of the Grail in the *Queste del Saint Graal.* See also Joël H. Grisward, "Le Motif de l'épée jetée au lac: La mort d'Arthur et la mort de Batradz," *Romania* 9 (1969): 289–340.

150. "Va tost, se li jete, si savras qu'il en avendra, car sans grant merveille ne sera ele pas perdue," *La Mort du roi Arthur,* ed. Speer, 333, p. 1468.

151. "Par foi . . . ce pensoie je bien, car ma fins aproce durement," ibid., 334, p. 1469.

152. "conmencha une pluie a cheoir grant et merveillouse, qui li dura jusqu'a un tertre qui estoit bien loing del roi demie lieue; et quant il fu venus au tertre, il s'arresta desous un arbre tant

tree. He looks back to the king he has left behind. At that point, however, the text shifts. It is said of Girflet, "He saw come across the sea a ship which was filled with ladies. When they came to the shore, their lady, who was holding Morgan, King Arthur's sister, by the hand, began to call the king to enter the ship."[153] From the amount of detail the text devotes to this passage, it is evident that Girflet is interested in these ladies on the ship and their interaction with his king, yet he does not see or hear all that he would like. He recognizes Morgan as one of these ladies because he has seen her many times before, but he does not recognize the dominant lady who holds Morgan by the hand and who calls out to Arthur, nor does he hear the words they exchange. Though Girflet sees all of these actions, his perception seems to be impeded by the distance that separates him from the shore. Finally, his desire to see and hear more than is possible from half a league away gets the better of him. The text reports, "When Girflet, who was on the hill, had seen all of this, how King Arthur had entered the ship with the ladies, he returned back as fast as his horse could go, until he had come back to the shore."[154] So fast does Girflet have his horse gallop and so jumbled is his sight during this ride that he seems to have no clear view of the ship and its passengers again until he reaches his destination. Once there, he realizes that he has come too late. We are told, "The ship had distanced itself from the shore in little more time than the shot from a crossbow."[155] Whereas, before, he was too far away from the shore to grasp properly what was happening, now that he is on the shore, the ship is too far away. Yet he knows, from what he has seen, that Arthur has gone off with his kinswoman.

From what Girflet perceives, just as Arthur dies as other men die, he is buried as other men are buried. Three days after Arthur's departure on the ship, Girflet returns to the Black Chapel, and he finds before the altar a rich and beautiful tomb, with an inscription that reads, "Here lies King Arthur, who through his valor subjected twelve kingdoms."[156]

---

que la pluie fu passee. Et quant ele fu passee, il conmencha a regarder cele part ou il avoit le roi laissié," ibid., 336, p. 1470.

153. "si vit venir parmi la mer une nef qui toute estoit plaine de dames; et quant eles vindrent a la rive, la dame d'eles, qui tenoit Morgain, la serour le roi Artu, par la main, conmencha a apeler le roi Artu qu'il entrast en la nef," ibid.

154. "Quant Gyrflés, qui estoit el tertre, ot tout ce veü, conment li rois Artus entra en la nef avoc les dames, il retourna ariere quan qu'il pot del cheval traire, tant qu'il est ariere revenus a la rive," ibid., 337, p. 1470.

155. "la nef se fu eslongie em poi d'ore plus d'une arbalestree," ibid.

156. "ci gist li rois artus qui par sa valour mist en sa subjection .xii. roiaumes," ibid., 338, p. 1471.

Upon reading this inscription and realizing that his king is dead and buried here, he faints. When he revives, he kisses the tomb and weeps bitterly. Though he laments as if he is fully persuaded of the truthfulness of this inscription, he nevertheless seeks confirmation of its words. He asks the hermit who lives nearby the chapel, "Sire, is it true that King Arthur lies here?"[157] The hermit replies, "Yes, fair friend, . . . he lies here, know it truly. And know that some ladies or damsels—I know not who—brought him here three days ago."[158] Reflecting upon the hermit's words, it is said, "Girflet then thought that they were the ones who put him on the ship."[159] Girflet did not see Arthur die, and he does not now see his dead body, but he recognizes the hermit to be a credible witness, and he therefore accepts his claim to have seen this corpse. The hermit acknowledges that he does not know who the ladies were who brought Arthur's body to the chapel, but Girflet connects his description of these ladies with his memory of the ladies who took Arthur away on the ship, and he infers that they must be the same women. Given the inscription on this tomb, the hermit's testimony, and the conformity of his testimony to what he himself observed, he does not doubt that Arthur is, in fact, buried in this chapel.

At the same time, however, it seems that, in *La Mort le Roi Artu*, Arthur does not die as other men die, but, rather, continues to live. At the end of the text he is physically failing, yet he is not as weak as someone who has lost part of his skull might be expected to be. He is strong enough to mount his horse, to ride from the battlefield with Girflet and Lucan, and to spend the night on his knees in the Black Chapel, praying and weeping. Even more remarkably, he is strong enough to crush Lucan to death in his embrace, without even being aware of the force he is exerting. Though Arthur has a presentiment that his end is near, in several respects, he does not act as medieval heroes were expected to act as they were dying. At the Black Chapel, he prays for the souls of his men, but it is not said that he prays for his own soul or that he repents of his sins. He weeps, but it is not said that he weeps for his misdeeds. It was customary for the dying to want to be with those who love them and who will therefore mourn their departure. When Gawain dies, for example, it is at Dover Castle, where he is surrounded by Arthur's men. Yet Arthur, it seems, chooses to meet his

157. "Sire, est ce voirs que ci gist li rois Artus?" ibid., 338, pp. 1471–72.

158. "Oïl, biaus amis, . . . il i gist, vraiement le saciés; et saciés que ci l'aporterent ne sai quels dames ou damoiseles tiers jour a," ibid., 338, p. 1472.

159. "Et Gyrflés s'apensa maintenant que ce furent celes qui le misent en la nef," ibid.

end, not in the company of his last remaining retainer, but alone on a beach. He tells Girflet, "It is necessary for you to go from here and to leave me."[160] It was customary for the dying to arrange for the place where their body was to be buried and for the inscription that was to be carved on their tomb. Gawain makes such plans before he expires, as do numerous other knights and damsels in this work. Yet Arthur makes no such arrangements. Finally, it was customary for the dead to appear in a vision to those who survive them. After Gawain passed away, Arthur saw his nephew coming to him, "more handsome than he had ever seen him,"[161] along with a crowd of poor people who inform him that he, Arthur, has ensured his nephew's salvation through the great generosity he has shown them. Yet after Arthur departs, neither Girflet nor anyone else has a vision of him ascending to heaven, though it seems impossible that such a noble king, whose charity has already brought about his nephew's salvation, should not be saved as well. Though the title of this work is *The Death of King Arthur,* the passage on the first page indicates that it may not be about Arthur's death after all. The text says it will relate how "King Arthur was wounded at the Battle of Salisbury,"[162] but it makes no reference to how he died. On the contrary, it reports merely that after this battle, "there was never a man who saw him alive,"[163] and it thus leaves open the possibility that he continued to live, unseen by other people. Indeed, all along Arthur has spoken of the end toward which he is headed, not as death, but as a state where he will not be seen. He informs Girflet, "From now on, as long as you live, you will never see me,"[164] and he makes clear that his companion will not see him, not because he is dying, but because he is going away. When the passage from the first page announces that it will relate "how King Arthur . . . departed from Girflet,"[165] it refers, again, not to Arthur's death, but to such a departure. Intuiting Arthur's fate, Girflet asks him, "In what region do you believe yourself to go, fair sir?"[166] but Arthur answers, "That I will not tell you at all."[167] Though Girflet infers from what he has seen that Arthur dies, the fact

160. "Il vous covient aler de ci et partir de moi," ibid., 334, p. 1469.
161. "plus biaus qu'il ne l'avoit onques mais veü a nul jour," ibid., 301, p. 1437.
162. "li rois Artus fu navrés en la bataille de Salesbieres," ibid., 1, p. 1181.
163. "ne fu nus hom qui le veïst vivant," ibid.
164. "a tel ore que jamais, tant conme vous vivrés, ne me verrés," ibid., 334, p. 1469.
165. "conment li rois Artus s'en parti de Gyrflet," ibid., 1, p. 1181.
166. "En quel part quidiés vous aler, biaus sire?" ibid., 336, p. 1470.
167. "Ce ne vous dirai je mie," ibid.

that his observation is incomplete—that he does not see Arthur die—undermines the value of his testimony.

As Arthur may not die as other men die, he does not rid himself of Excalibur as other men rid themselves of their swords. When Girflet finally hurls the sword into the lake, he sees something he does not expect. The text reports, "As it approached the water, he saw a hand emerge from the lake and appear up to the elbow, but he did not see the body whose hand it was. And the hand took the sword by the hilt and began to brandish it three times in the air. When Girflet saw this clearly, the hand withdrew into the water with the sword."[168] In mentioning how "he saw" the hand and how "he saw . . . clearly" the way in which the hand brandished the sword, the text emphasizes what Girflet beholds. At the same time, the text also notes that he does not see the body of whoever it was who seized the sword; that he does not, therefore, know who that person was, whether man or woman; and that he does not, therefore, know who can live in a lake, ready to reach up and catch a falling weapon. Though he sees clearly, he does not comprehend what he sees. The marvel happened so quickly that he lingers by the lake to see more, but to no avail: "He waited for a long time to know if [the hand] would show itself again. When he saw that he was wasting his time for nothing, he left the lake and came to the king."[169] Girflet is the only person to see the hand reach up, grab the sword, and sink into the water with it. He therefore has no one to confirm his observation of this marvelous event and to reassure him that he was not suffering from a psychic delusion or an optical illusion. While law in the twelfth and thirteenth centuries affirmed the value of two or more eyewitnesses who saw and heard that of which they spoke, it rejected the value of a single witness, whose testimony could not be verified. According to the Theodosian Code, which was incorporated into medieval civil law, "No judge should ever allow the testimony of one person to be admitted in any case whatsoever."[170] As the saying went, "one witness, no witness" (*testis unus, testis nullus*). It

168. "et maintenant qu'ele aprocha de l'aigue, il vit une main qui issi del lac et apparut jusques au coute, mais del cors dont la main estoit ne vit il point; et la mains prist l'espee parmie le heut et le conmencha a branller .III. fois contremont. Et quant Gyrflés ot ce veü apertement, la main se rebouta en l'aigue a toute l'espee," ibid., 334, pp. 1468–69.

169. "et il attendi illoc grant piece pour savoir s'ele se mousterroit plus. Et quant il voit qu'il i musoit pour noient, si s'en parti del lac et vint au roi," ibid., 334, p. 1469.

170. "unius testimonium nemo iudicum in quacumque causa facile patiatur admitti," *Codex Theodosianus*, in *Theodosiani Libri XVI*, ed. Theodor Mommsen and Paulus M. Meyer, 2 vols. in 3 (Berlin: apud Weidmannos, 1954), XI, 39, 3.1 = brev. XI, 14, 2.1, at p. 657.

is true that the Post-Vulgate *Merlin* explains ex post facto what Girflet observed when he threw the sword into the lake.[171] Yet the beauty of *La Mort le Roi Artu* lies in the fact that it provides no such explanation. Instead of making the marvel understandable and, hence, not a marvel at all, the text preserves the wonderousness of this wonder. Though Girflet clearly witnesses the hand catch the sword, the fact that he cannot fathom what he has witnessed, again, undermines the value of what he believes he has seen.

As Girflet cannot make sense of what he sees when he throws the sword into the lake, he cannot make sense of what he sees when Arthur departs with the ladies in the ship. Arthur seems to expect that these ladies will arrive and take him away, yet, as far as Girflet can tell, he has not been in communication with them and therefore cannot have made arrangements to meet them at this time and place. Among the ladies on the ship, Girflet notices, is Morgan, which is curious, given that, along with Agravain, she was one of the two people who informed Arthur about Lancelot's love for Guinevere and, hence, conspired to bring about the war that brought about the destruction of the kingdom. As malicious a character as she has often been in the Vulgate Cycle, she appears entirely benign here in her concern for her wounded brother, and Arthur appears entirely trusting of her. When the ladies call out to him to board the ship, the text reports, "The king, as soon as he saw Morgan, his sister, immediately rose from the ground where he was, and he entered onto the ship, and he drew his horse after him, and he took his arms."[172] Arthur departs not like a Christian believer, whose soul would be borne by angels up to heaven, but like a pagan warrior, whose body, with his horse and arms, is taken by his kinswoman across the sea. When the ship arrives, Girflet notices that it is "filled with ladies," but there is no indication that it includes sailors directing its path. When it leaves, it is said that it crosses the water more quickly than an arrow. Whether the sudden placement of the ship out to sea is due to a distortion of Girflet's vision or to the marvelous speed of this

171. Geoffrey of Monmouth writes, in *Historia regum Britanniae*, ed. Reeve, "He girded himself with Caliburn, the best sword and one forged on the Isle of Avalon [*Accinctus etiam Caliburno gladio optimo et in insula Avallonis fabricato*]" (IX, p. 199). In the Post-Vulgate *Merlin*, Merlin brings Arthur to this lake and explains that it is inhabited by fairies, whose palaces are enchanted so that no one can see them. While they are talking on the banks of the lake, an arm clothed in white samite emerges from the water, wielding this sword, and a damsel arrives, walks across the water to retrieve the weapon, and then offers it to the young king.

172. "Et si tost conme li rois vit Morgain sa serour, il se leva isnelement de la terre ou il se seoit et entre en la nef, et traist son cheval aprés lui et prist ses armes," *La Mort du roi Arthur*, ed. Speer, 336, p. 1470.

ship is left unclear. (Fairies, who did not have to traverse intermediary space, were known to travel far more easily and rapidly than ordinary mortals.[173]) Other passages, from the earlier, omniscient sections of *La Mort le Roi Artu,* could provide some explanation for the mysterious details Girflet observes here. At one point, Arthur happened to meet Morgan at her manor and attempted to persuade her to return to his court with him, but she refused, saying, "When I leave here, I shall go to the Isle of Avalon, where are the ladies who know all the enchantments of the world."[174] The ladies in the ship are not identified, but they are joined with Morgan, here explicitly named "Morgan Le Fay"; they travel by water, perhaps to and from the Isle of Avalon; and they thus recall for us this earlier reference to "ladies . . . who know all the enchantments of the world." Though the text never states that the ladies are bringing Arthur to Avalon to be healed of his wounds, all of these details might seem to point in this direction. Again, however, the beauty of this work lies in the fact that it provides no such explanation of what Girflet sees. Though he observes the arrival of the ship, the interaction of its ladies and his lord, and their departure together, his failure to make sense of what he sees once more draws into question the value of his testimony.

If Arthur has, in fact, journeyed to Avalon, then he is not buried in the tomb at the Black Chapel. While Girflet knows from his own sight that ladies took the living Arthur across the sea, he knows only from hearsay and inference that these ladies brought the dead Arthur to the Black Chapel and had him buried there. As credible a witness as the hermit may seem to be, it is possible that he was lying, intentionally deceiving Girflet as to the identity of the dead knight who was brought to be buried in the chapel (if a knight was, in fact, brought there) or ignorant, unintentionally mistaking the dead knight for the living king. As reasonable as it might seem to be for Girflet to identify the ladies he saw in the ship with the ladies who are said to have brought Arthur's body to the chapel, it is possible that they were not the same. In medieval jurisprudence, hearsay and inference were both weaker forms of proof than direct observation. Ultimately, Girflet decides that his and the hermit's accounts of Arthur's end can be reconciled—that the dead king was indeed brought to the Black Chapel by the ladies who

173. On Morgan's speed, and her skill at healing, see Geoffrey of Monmouth, *Vita Merlini*, ed. Clarke, vv. 908–28, which itself recalls the first-century geographer Pomponius Mela's *De situ orbis*, III, 6.

174. "quant je me partirai de ci, je m'en irai en l'ille d'Avalon, ou les dames sont qui sevent tous les enchantemens del monde," *La Mort du roi Arthur*, ed. Speer, 71, p. 1245.

had taken away the living king—but the text leaves these accounts suspended as alternate versions of the tale. Given this ambiguous conclusion to the Vulgate Cycle's *La Mort le Roi Artu*, it is not surprising that the Post-Vulgate Cycle's version of this text makes the uncertainty of this ending manifest. In this later text, Girflet again seeks Arthur's tomb and again learns from the hermit that some ladies, whom the hermit did not know, brought the body of a knight to the chapel and told him that this was the body of King Arthur. Yet in this version, Girflet is not convinced by the sight of the tomb and by the words he hears that Arthur is, in fact, dead. The text relates, "He said to himself that, all the same, he would like to know for certain if it were King Arthur who was lying inside the tomb."[175] Raising its lid, he sees nothing inside except the helmet that Arthur had worn on the day of the battle. He asks the hermit, "Did you see the body of King Arthur placed here?"[176] The hermit answers, "By faith, . . . I saw a body placed here, and I was made to understand that it was the body of King Arthur. Another truth I cannot tell you."[177] Girflet concludes, "In vain do I exert myself to inquire into the passing of my lord King Arthur. Truly, he is the Adventurous King, about whose end no mortal man will ever know. For just as he came to the Kingdom of Logres by adventure, by adventure did he depart from it."[178] Though the Girflet of the Vulgate version decides that Arthur has died and has been buried at the Black Chapel, he suggests implicitly what the Post-Vulgate version states explicitly: Arthur's end remains doubtful.

In the end, *La Mort le Roi Artu*, like much of the early vernacular tradition about Arthur, does not assert that Arthur is dead and buried or that he is alive and destined to return, but, instead, emphasizes the uncertainty of his fate. In his *Historia regum Britanniae*, Geoffrey writes that after the Battle of Camlann, "The illustrious King Arthur was mortally wounded. He was taken away to the Isle of Avalon to have his wounds tended."[179] By representing Arthur at once as mortally wounded and as

175. "si dist a soi mesmes que toutes voies voudra il savoir por voir se cil ert li rois Artus qui çaiens gisoit," *La Version Post-Vulgate de la "Queste del Saint Graal" et de la "Mort Artu,"* ed. Bogdanow, vol. 3, chap. 58, p. 474.

176. "Ve[i]stes vous mectre icy le corps du roy Artus?" ibid., vol. 3, chap. 58, p. 474.

177. "Par foy . . . je vy que on y mist ung corps et me fist on entendant que ce estoit le corps du roy Artus. Autre verité je ne vous en sçay dire," ibid., vol. 3, chap. 58, p. 475.

178. "pour nient me travailleray je de enquerir le trespassement de monseigneur le roy Artus. Vraiement, c'est le Roy Aventureux dont nul home mortel ne savra la fin. Et tout ainsi qu'il vint au royaume de Logres par aventure, par aventure s'en est il allé," ibid.

179. "inclitus rex Arturus letaliter vulneratus est; qui illinc ad sananda vulnera sua in insulam Avallonis evectus Constantino cognato suo et filio Cadoris ducis Cornubiae diadema Britanniae concessit anno ab incarnatione Domini .dxlii.," ibid., p. 253.

taken away to have his wounds healed, Geoffrey indicates at once that he is dying and that he may be cured (though he never states that he was, in fact, cured). He thus confirms the doubtful nature of the fate Merlin had ascribed him. *La Mort le Roi Artu,* as we have seen, likewise leaves us with two accounts of Arthur's end, one of which suggests that he is dead and buried in a religious house and the other of which suggests that he was carried away by mysterious ladies, and it refuses to subordinate one of these accounts to the other. In doing so, it shows that, as much as one may rely upon the perceptions of eyewitnesses and the testimony of reliable sources, one must always interpret, and that that interpretation always remains provisional. By refusing to declare either "Arthur is dead" or "Arthur is alive and will return" and by thus refusing to label the legends about Arthur either history or fable, truth or lie, *La Mort le Roi Artu* invites us to resist the desire for certitude. In the Post-Vulgate *La Mort le Roi Artu,* Arthur tells Girflet to leave, "for my end is approaching, and it is not right that anyone should know the truth of my end. Just as I became king here by adventure, so shall I pass from this kingdom by adventure, for no one will be able to boast after this that he knows for certain what has become of me."[180] The life that began with uncertainty, at its very conception, will end (if one even considers it to end) with uncertainty. It is in this doubtful ontological state—between existence and nonexistence, between truth and fiction, between history and fable—that the text invites us to linger.

180. "Ca mia fin se achega, e nom é cousa posta que nẽhuũ sayba verdade de mia fin, ca bem como eu aqui per ventura fuy rey, assi passarey deste reyno per ventura, ca nenguũ nom se podera louvar, des aqui adiante, que certamente sayba que seera de mim," *La Version Post-Vulgate de la "Queste del Saint Graal" et de la "Mort Artu,"* ed. Bogdanow, vol. 3, chap. 58, p. 469.

FOUR

Lancelot of the Lake: The Reality of the Ideal

If Lancelot of the Lake was troubling to learned authors of the Middle Ages, as he was, it was not because he threatened accepted views of science, as Merlin did, nor because he threatened accepted views of history, as King Arthur did, but because he threatened accepted views of morality, particularly as regards love and marriage. It was only gradually that Lancelot emerged in Arthurian literature and only gradually that his character took on this subversive orientation. The early Latin chronicles and Welsh triads represent Arthur, Gawain, and Kay, among other ancient warriors, but they make no mention of Lancelot. Geoffrey of Monmouth depicts Guinevere as unfaithful to Arthur, but he identifies her lover as Mordred. Caradoc of Llancarfan portrays King Melwas as abducting Guinevere in his *Vita sancti Gildae* (ca. 1130), but he identifies her rescuer as Arthur. When Lancelot does emerge in the second half of the twelfth century, he seems to be a relatively undistinguished knight in Arthur's court. A lost French text may have provided the foundation for Ulrich von Zatzikhoven's Middle High German *Lanzelet* (ca. 1194), which depicts Lancelot as saving the queen from her abductor without imputing any amorous connection between them. Chrétien de Troyes mentions "Lanceloz del Lac" in passing in *Erec et Enide* (ca. 1170) and *Cligés* (ca. 1176) as one of the members of Arthur's Round Table, apparently assuming that we are already familiar with him. But it is only with Chrétien's *Le Chevalier de la charrette* (ca. 1177–81) that Lancelot becomes the best knight of Arthur's court and Guinevere's lover and champion. In the Vulgate Cycle, the lengthy *Prose Lancelot,* which subsumes the plot of Chrétien's romance within it, provides the most extensive and most influential treatment of this figure in medieval literature. It is thus that Lancelot becomes at once the greatest knight of the Round Table and the adulterous lover of his lord's wife, combining laudable and blameworthy qualities in his paradoxical persona.[1]

If Lancelot threatened accepted views of morality, according to Dante Alighieri's *Inferno* (1314), it was not only because he pursued a love affair with a married woman, but because he and the love affair were what we now call "idealized." As the Dante pilgrim and Virgil make their way through the Circle of the Lustful, they encounter a lady, identified here as Francesca, and her onetime lover, identified elsewhere as Paolo. The pilgrim asks Francesca, "At the time of the sweet sighs, how and by what did Love grant that you know your uncertain desires?"[2] In her response to this question, Francesca recounts how she and Paolo had been reading the *Prose Lancelot,* which seems to have been known in Italy as the *Book of Galehaut,*[3] after the Lord of the Distant Isles and Lancelot's companion, and, in particular, the passage in this book where Galehaut arranges for Lancelot and Guinevere to pledge their love to each other and to seal that love with a kiss.[4]

1. For an overview of depictions of Lancelot across time and place, see *Lancelot and Guinevere: A Casebook,* ed. Lori J. Walters (New York: Garland, 1996); *Lancelot-Lanzelet hier et aujourd'hui: Recueil d'articles assemblées par Danielle Buschinger et Michel Zink pour fêter les 90 ans de Alexandre Micha* (Greifswald: Reineke-Verlag, 1995); and *Lancelot: Actes du Colloque d'Amiens des 14 et 15 janvier, 1984, Université de Picardie,* ed. Danielle Buschinger (Göppingen: Kümmerle, 1984). For readings of Lancelot in the *Prose Lancelot* in particular, see Elspeth Kennedy, "Le Personnage de Lancelot dans le *Lancelot en prose,*" in *Lancelot,* ed. Buschinger, 99–106, and Fanni Bogdanow, "The Treatment of the Lancelot-Guinevere Theme in the *Prose Lancelot,*" *Medium Aevum* 41 (1972): 110–20.

2. "al tempo d'i dolci sospiri, / a che e come concedette amore / che conosceste i dubbiosi disiri?" Dante Alighieri, *The Divine Comedy: Inferno,* ed. and trans. Charles S. Singleton (Princeton, NJ: Princeton University Press, 1970), Canto V, vv. 118–20. Singleton writes, "*Dubbioso,* referring to the desire of lovers, can mean 'hesitant,' 'not yet manifested,' i.e., desire of which neither lover is wholly conscious. . . . But *dubbioso* can also mean 'dangerous,' 'that which is to be feared,'" *Inferno,* V, n. 120, pp. 92–93.

3. Paolo and Francesca appear to have been reading the noncyclic version of the *Prose Lancelot,* which ended with the death of Galehaut and was thus referred to as *The Book of Galehaut.* In MS Brit. Mus., Harl., 6341, for example, the colophon to the section of the *Prose Lancelot* to which Francesca alludes states, "Cy fine Gallehoz." One thinks also, of course, of the subtitle to Giovanni Boccaccio's *Decameron*: *Il libro chiamato "Decameron" cognominato "Principe Galeotto."* See Paget Toynbee, "Dante and the Lancelot Romance," *Dante Studies and Researches* (London: Methuen, 1902; rpt., Port Washington, NY: Kennikat Press, 1971), 1–37, at 6n3.

4. Critical treatments of Francesca's speech have been abundant. For just a few, see Teodolinda Barolini, "Dante and Francesca da Rimini: Realpolitik, Romance, Gender," *Speculum* 75,

She relates, "We read one day, as a pastime, of Lancelot, how Love had constrained him. We were alone, without any suspicion. Several times that reading led our eyes to meet, and made our faces pale, and yet one point alone vanquished us: when we read how the desired smile was kissed by so great a lover, this one, who never shall be parted from me, all trembling, kissed my mouth. A Galehaut was that book and he who wrote it. That day we read in it no further."[5] As Lancelot had not intended to enter into a love affair with Guinevere but had been "constrained" by Love into doing so, Francesca suggests, she and her companion had not intended to kiss but had been "vanquished" by this reading. Like Galehaut, who encourages Lancelot and Guinevere to acknowledge their attraction toward each other and to act upon that attraction, the *Prose Lancelot* encouraged Paolo and Francesca to kiss by providing them with an irresistible model of infidelity. As Renato Poggioli observes in an influential 1957 article on these verses, Dante is showing not only how Francesca blames this romance for her misdeed, but how she recognizes, too late, the gap between its idealized depiction of its lovers and her own experience. Though Lancelot kissed Guinevere's "desired smile," Poggioli points out, Paolo kissed Francesca's "mouth." With this shift from the fleshless, spiritual kiss of a smile

no. 1 (2000): 1–28; Daniela Delcorno Branca, "Dante and the *Roman de Lancelot,*" in *Text and Intertext in Medieval Arthurian Literature,* ed. Norris J. Lacy (New York: Garland, 1996), 133–45; Donald Maddox, "The Arthurian Intertexts of *Inferno* V," *Dante Studies* 114 (1996): 113–27, and "Le Motif de la lecture interrompue: L'*Inferno* V de Dante et le *Lancelot en Prose,*" in *Lancelot-Lanzelet hier et aujourd'hui,* ed. Buschinger and Zink, 253–62; Christopher Kleinhenz, "Dante as Reader and Critic of Courtly Literature," in *Courtly Literature: Culture and Context; Selected Papers from the 5th Triennial Congress of the International Courtly Literature Society, Dalfsen, Netherlands (9–16 August, 1986),* ed. Keith Busby and Eric Kooper (Amsterdam: Benjamins, 1990), 379–93; René Girard, "The Mimetic Desire of Paolo and Francesca," in *"To Double Business Bound": Essays on Literature, Mimesis, and Anthropology* (Baltimore: Johns Hopkins University Press, 1978), 1–8; Anna Hatcher and Mark Musa, "The Kiss: *Inferno* V and the Old French *Prose Lancelot,*" *Comparative Literature* 20 (1968): 97–109; Renato Poggioli, "Tragedy or Romance? A Reading of the Paolo and Francesca Episode in Dante's *Inferno,*" *PMLA* 72, no. 3 (1957): 313–58; rpt. and abridged as "Paolo and Francesca," in *Dante: A Collection of Critical Essays,* ed. John Freccero (Englewood Cliffs, NJ: Prentice-Hall, 1965), 61–77.

5. "Noi leggiavamo un giorno per diletto / di Lancialotto come amor lo strinse; / soli eravamo e sanza alcun sospetto. / Per più fiate li occhi ci sospinse / quella lettura, e scolorocci il viso; / ma solo un punto fu quel che ci vinse. / Quando leggemmo il disïato riso / esser basciato da cotanto amante, / questi, che mai da me non fia diviso, / la bocca mi basciò tutto tremante. / Galeotto fu 'l libro e chi lo scrisse: / quel giorno più non vi leggemmo avante," Dante, *The Divine Comedy,* ed. Charles S. Singleton, 3 vols. (Princeton, NJ: Princeton University Press, 1970–75), vol. 1, pt. 1, *Inferno,* V, vv. 115–38. Singleton comments on the words "sanza alcun sospetto," "It is possible to understand this to mean 'without reason to fear that anyone might surprise us,' thus reinforcing the *soli,* but it seems better, given the context, to understand 'knowing nothing,' i.e., 'unaware of the love we already felt for one another,'" *Inferno,* vol. 1, pt. 2, 94n129.

to the fleshly, physical kiss of a mouth, there occurs a shift, as he puts it, "from literature to life, from fiction to reality, from romanticism to realism, or, more simply, from sentimental fantasy to moral truth."[6] As Francesca realizes that Guinevere's kiss with Lancelot was unlike her kiss with Paolo, he adds, "She . . . realizes that she was no Guinevere, and that Paolo was no Lancelot."[7] She learns, in other words, that she has confused literary characters, who can only exist within the realm of fiction, with Paolo and herself, who exist within the realm of reality, and, in doing so, has confused the exalted passion that is beautiful only in the pages of romance with the sordid adultery that is experienced in real life.

Dante is not the only learned vernacular author of his time to criticize the *Prose Lancelot* for "idealizing" Lancelot and his love affair with Guinevere. In his *Corbaccio* (ca. 1355), Giovanni Boccaccio mentions a widow for whom "her prayers and her Pater are French romances and Italian songs, in which she reads about Lancelot and Guinevere, Tristan and Iseut. . . . She suffers when she reads that Lancelot, Tristan, or someone else unites with their ladies in a chamber, secretly and alone. It seems to her that she sees what is going on; she would willingly do that which she imagines they do."[8] So intense are women's attachments to the loves of Lancelot and Guinevere and Tristan and Iseut, Boccaccio suggests, that they imaginatively partake in these liaisons when they read about them, and they seek to imitate these liaisons in their own lives. In the *Songe du vieil Pelerin* (1389), Philippe de Mézières likewise cautions his readers, "You must keep yourself from taking too much pleasure from . . . romances which are filled with deceptions and which often attract the reader to impossibility, folly, vanity, and sin, like the books of the deceptions of Lancelot and those like him. . . . Though the said histories and deceptions attract their readers to the valor of chivalry, they also attract them to courtly love [*amer par amours*], which is worse, and which can hardly happen without great sin, by attracting them to the sin of lechery."[9] Like Boccaccio, Philippe worries that the

6. Poggioli, "Paolo and Francesca," 65.

7. Ibid., 63.

8. "le sue orazioni e paternostri sono i romanzi Franceschi, e le canzoni latine: ne' quali ella legge di Lancelotto, e di Ginevra, e di Tristano, e d'Isotta. . . . Ella tutta si stritola quando legge, Lancelotto, o Tristano, o alcuno altro con le loro donne nelle camere segretamente e soli raunarsi: siccome colei, alla quale par vedere ciò che fanno, e che volentieri, come di loro immagina, così farebbe," Giovanni Boccaccio, *Corbaccio*, in *Opera*, ed. Segre, 1236–37.

9. "tu (te) doyes garder de toy trop delicter es . . . des romans qui sont rempliz de bourdes et qui attrayent le lysant souvent a impossibilite, a folie, vanite et pechie, comme les livres des

Prose Lancelot will persuade readers to pursue illicit love affairs themselves, under the impression that what is impossible is possible, that sin is virtue, and that "lechery" is "courtly love." In the *Canterbury Tales* (1387–1400), Geoffrey Chaucer has his Nun's Priest allude to "the book of Launcelot de Lake, / that wommen holde in ful greet reverence."[10] These commentators make clear that the *Prose Lancelot* appealed to women readers more than it did to their male counterparts and that it appealed to them because they saw Lancelot as attractive and wished to partake in a love affair with someone like him. While women readers confuse the ideal, fictional Lancelot with their real, factual lovers, these critics propose that they would do well to recognize and respect the boundary between literature and life.[11]

Yet as natural as it may seem to us to regard Lancelot and his love affair with Guinevere as "idealized" and to assume that medieval critics of romance did so as well, this knight was always seen, not as the "ideal" knight, but as the "best" knight, and his love affair as the best of love affairs. The word "ideal" did not exist in Old French, and the tendency to define the "ideal" in opposition to the "real" would not emerge in Western thought until the eighteenth century. Instead of the binary opposition between the "ideal" and the "real," medieval literature and philosophy erect a gradation of the good, the better, and the best. In Boethius's *De consolatione Philosophiae* (523), for example, Lady Philosophy maintains, "It cannot be denied that [the perfect good] exists, and that it is, so to say, the font of all good things. All that is said to be imperfect is said to be imperfect through the diminishment of this perfection. If, in any category, something is said to be imperfect, it is necessary that there also be something in this category that is perfect. If this perfection is removed, it cannot be conceived how that which is said to be imperfect can have come to exist."[12] Insofar as one

---

bourdes de Lancelot et semblables. . . . Et combien que les dictes ystoires et bourdes attraient les lisans a vaillance de chevalerie, toutefois elles attrayent, qui pis est, a amer par amours, qui mal se puet faire sans grant pechie en attrayant au pechie de luxure," Philippe de Mezieres, *Le Songe du vieil pelerin*, ed. G. W. Coopland, 2 vols. (Cambridge: University Press, 1969), vol. 2, 221.

10. Geoffrey Chaucer, *The Canterbury Tales*, in *The Riverside Chaucer*, ed. Benson, "The Nun's Priest's Tale," vv. 4402–3.

11. Jacob van Maerlant dismisses Lancelot as a purely invented character, in contrast to Arthur, Gawain, and Kay, in *Spiegel Historiael*, ed. Matthias De Vries and Eelco Verwijs, 4 vols. (Leiden: Brill, 1863–79), vol. 2, Part III, Book 5, chap. 54, vv. 51–57. A final medieval text that mentions the *Prose Lancelot* is *Les Quatres Ages de l'Homme: Traité moral de Philippe de Navarre*, ed. Marcel de Fréville (Paris: Librairie de Firmin Didot, 1888), where mention is made of the "livre Lancelot, ou il i a mout de biaus diz et de soutis" (23).

12. "quin exsistat sitque hoc veluti quidam omnium fons bonorum, negari nequit; omne enim quod imperfectum esse dicitur id imminutione perfecti imperfectum esse perhibetur. Quo

apprehends that which is imperfect, such as an imperfect knight, Lady Philosophy argues, one necessarily also apprehends, implicitly, that which is perfect, such as the perfect knight. It is only through the standard established by that which is perfect that one is able to measure that which is imperfect and, indeed, that that which is imperfect is able to exist at all. Anselm of Canterbury makes a similar argument in the course of his ontological proof of the existence of God. He writes, "Everything that is less good, insofar as it is good, is similar to that which is more good. It is therefore evident to any rational mind that, by ascending from lesser goods to greater goods, regarding those things by which something greater can be conceived, we can conjecture that than which nothing greater can be conceived."[13] If there is a good, there must be a better, and if there is a better, there must be a best. Like God, who is the summit of all beings, the best knight may seem not to exist, but the logic of the universe demands that he exist, as his existence underwrites that of all other knights. And that best knight, the Vulgate Cycle makes clear, is Lancelot. According to these volumes, he is "the best knight in the world,"[14] "the best . . . knight who ever was,"[15] and "a knight, the best who now exists."[16] He is "the flower of all knights"[17] and "the most valiant,"[18] to the point where "there cannot be another of his valor."[19] Outstanding in feats of arms, Lancelot is no less outstanding as a lover. He is "the most beautiful knight in the world"[20] and "the most loyal of all lovers."[21] In sum, he is "the worthi-

fit ut, si in quolibet genere imperfectum quid esse videatur, in eo perfectum quoque aliquid esse necesse sit; etenim perfectione sublata unde illud quod imperfectum perhibetur exstiterit ne fingi quidem potest," Boethius, *Consolatio Philosophiae*, ed. Bieler, III, 10, p. 53.

13. "omne minus bonum in tantum est simile maiori bono inquantum est bonum; patet cuilibet rationali menti, quia de bonis minoribus ad maiora conscendendo ex iis quibus aliquid maius cogitari potest, multum possumus coniicere illud quo nihil potest maius cogitari," Anselm of Canterbury, *Responsio editoris*, in *Opera omnia*, ed. Schmitt, vol. 1, pp. 130–39, at VIII, p. 137. In *Logical Fictions in Medieval Literature and Philosophy*, Greene proposes that medieval philosophers, like Anselm, "with their investigations on the border between the real and the non-real, the true, the false, and the fictional" (85), may have laid the foundation for modern fictionality.

14. "li mieudres chevaliers del monde," *Lancelot*, ed. Micha, vol. 8, 121. Cf. also ibid., vol. 4, 157, 162, 216, 231, 391, and ibid., vol. 8, 36 and 462.

15. "li millor chevalier . . . qui or fust," ibid., vol. 4, 209. Cf. also ibid., vol. 4, 187 and vol. 8, 58–59.

16. "uns chevaliers, li mieudres qui orendroit soit," ibid., vol. 8, 207. Cf. also ibid., vol. 8, 74.

17. "la flors de tous les chevaliers," ibid., vol. 8, 461–62. Cf. also ibid., vol. 5, 29; vol. 8, 461–62.

18. "li plus vaillanz," *La Mort le Roi Artu*, ed. Frappier, 71, p. 90.

19. "de sa valor ne porroit uns autres estre," *Lancelot*, ed. Micha, vol. 4, 187.

20. "li plus biaux chevaliers dou monde," ibid., vol. 4, 187. Cf. also ibid., vol. 1, 353, and vol. 4, 209.

21. "de tos les amis le plus loial," ibid., vol. 1, 357.

est man in the world."[22] "the non-pareil of the good,"[23] and "the best of all the good."[24] Insofar as Lancelot differs from other knights, it is not absolutely, as the "ideal" differs from the "real," but relatively, as the "best" differs from the "good" and the "better." He stands on the highest step of the ladder of excellence, but this is a ladder on whose rungs all noble men can be found. As the best of knights, Lancelot is unique and therefore hard to find, but he nonetheless exists and, indeed, must exist. For that reason, he is not ideal, but real, as God is real; he is not fictional, in the sense that a frivolous literary character is fictional, but true, as God is true. He is in literature, but he is also, necessarily, in life as well.

Because Lancelot is the "best" knight, as the Vulgate Cycle represents him, he threatens accepted notions of morality, not in that he falls short of them, but in that he surpasses them. At one point, King Bademagu asserts of Lancelot, "God did not make him except to be a mirror for other knights."[25] Among its various meanings at this time, a "mirror" was a text, like Scripture or the lives of the saints, in which one finds represented exemplars of the virtues.[26] Gazing upon these reflections, one sees paragons of behavior one should attempt to imitate, as well as the differences between oneself and these paragons, which reveal how one is falling short of these models. Augustine refers to Scripture as "a faithful mirror, which indicates not only the beauties and wholeness, but the deformities and defects, of those persons who approach it."[27] In reading this text, he advises, "See if you are what it says. If you are not this, sigh that you may be it."[28] Bernard of Clairvaux recommends similarly, "Consider all that is shining in the mirror. If you apprehend in yourself something crooked, correct it; something right, hold to it; something deformed, put it in order; something beau-

22. "li plus prodome dou monde," ibid., vol. 6, 179. Cf. also ibid., vol, 4, 216, and 391; ibid., vol. 8, 36, 60, and 462; and *La Mort le roi Artu*, ed. Frappier, 32, p. 32.

23. "li nompers des buens," *Lancelot*, ed. Micha, vol. 4, 23. Cf. also ibid., vol. 5, 29.

24. "el meilleur de touz les bons," *La Mort le roi Artu*, ed. Frappier, 32, p. 32. Cf. *Lancelot*, ed. Micha, vol. 1, 353, and vol. 7, 338.

25. "onques Diex nel fist fors por estre mireor as autres chevaliers," ibid., vol. 4, 187.

26. See Ritamary Bradley, "Backgrouds of the Title *Speculum* in Mediaeval Literature," *Speculum* 29, no. 1 (1954): 100–115, at 105.

27. "speculi fidelis . . . admotarum sibi personarum non solum, quae pulchra atque integra, verum etiam quae deformia vitiosaque sint, indicat," Augustine, *Contra Faustum*, in *Sancti Aureliu Augustini "De utilitate credendi,"* ed. Joseph Zycha, CSEL, vol. 25 (sect. 6, par. 1) (Prague: F. Temsky, 1991), 249–797, at XXII, 60, p. 655.

28. "vide si hoc es quod dixit; si nondum es, geme ut sis," Augustine, *Enarrationes in Psalmum*, ed. E. Dekkers and J. Fraipont, CIII, sermo 1, 4, p. 1476. Gregory the Great likewise writes in his *Moralia in Job*, ed. Marcus Adriaen, CCSL, vol. 143, "Scriptura sacra mentis oculis quasi quoddam speculum opponitur, ut interna nostra facies in ipsa videatur" (II, 1, p. 59).

tiful, polish it."[29] As a mirror, Lancelot serves as an image epitomizing what a knight should be and, in doing so, instructs the knights who contemplate him as to how they should best act and how they fall short of this goal. Like other men, he is at times uncertain as to how he should act, but, unlike them, he consistently chooses the better path, in ways that the reader often cannot anticipate. Even as his hesitation reflects his human fallibility, his wise judgment reflects his human excellence. In all of these ways, the text allows the reader to see, not just Lancelot, in his perfection, but the reader himself, in his imperfection, and, in doing so, inspires him to want to imitate this exemplary character. While an "ideal" knight would be opposed to a "real" knight, like, potentially, the reader of this text or that reader's lover, the "best" knight is also a "real" knight and, hence, a model for these lesser figures.

In defending itself against the Dantes, the Boccaccios, the Philippes, and the Chaucers of the world, the *Prose Lancelot* illustrates what excellence would look like in the world and the challenges this excellence presents to the rest of us. It shows, first, that Lancelot's love of Guinevere is not emotional but, rather, rational, philosophical, and, therefore, virtuous, grounded as it is in his perception of the good in her and in his cultivation of the good in himself for her benefit. It shows, second, that, while some knights and ladies in this work, like "realist" critics of this genre, may doubt that Lancelot is as great a knight and lover as he is alleged to be, their skepticism is grounded, not in an objective evaluation of his character, but in their own subjective biases against him, as a result of their pride, envy, and wrath. It shows, third, that, while other knights and ladies in this work, like "romantic" enthusiasts of this genre, may affirm that Lancelot is, indeed, as great a knight and lover as he is said to be, their openness to his excellence often leads to their own destruction. As intolerable as it may be for Lancelot's opponents to acknowledge his superiority to themselves or to their lovers, it is no less difficult for his supporters to acknowledge that excellence, as they can neither be nor possess the man who stands above all others. The problem, it turns out, is not that Lancelot is not as excellent as he is reputed to be, but that he is even more excellent, and people are unsure as to how to respond to his superlative status. In

29. "ibi totum in speculo quodam refulgente considera: si quid in te pravum deprehenderis, corrige; quod rectum, tene; quod deforme, compone; quod pulchrum, excole," Bernard of Clairvaux, *Instructio sacerdotis seu tractatus de praecipuis mysteriis nostrae religionis*, PL, vol. 184, cols. 771–90, at II, 11, col. 788.

the end, the only way to approach Lancelot is neither with the aim of surpassing him, as his rivals do, nor with the aim of possessing him, as his admirers do, but with the goal of contemplating his excellence, as the audience does in reading this romance.

The Lovers

The threat that Lancelot represents to traditional views of morality, especially as regards love and marriage, is evident in the trajectory of his life. When he was a baby, Claudas, the king of the Terre Deserte, conquered the lands of his father, Ban, the king of Benoic, causing Ban to die of despair and his wife Elaine to withdraw into a convent. Orphaned, Lancelot was brought up by the Lady of the Lake, together with his cousins Bors and Lionel, who had also been disinherited by Claudas. When he came of age, he set off for Arthur's court to become a knight and, before long, the finest warrior of his age. Years pass, and he returns to his ancestral kingdom, defeats Claudas, and retakes his and his cousins' lands. At this point, one might expect Lancelot to retire to Benoic, marry a suitable woman, and have children with her, including a son who could one day inherit his territory. In Ulrich von Zatzikhoven's *Lanzelet*, Lanzelet retires to the kingdom his father had left to him, marries his beloved Iblis, and has three sons and a daughter with her. Ulrich writes, "Iblis and Lanzelet were blessed with lovely children, such as people always wish for,"[30] children, he notes, who "inherited from them their lands and their possessions, their virtues and their noble spirits."[31] Yet despite the precedent of Lanzelet, Lancelot does not settle down on his lands. After he reconquers Benoic, he offers its crown to his half brother Hector. He does not marry. His love for Guinevere prevents him from uniting with any of the many beautiful, noble damsels who come his way, nor does he have any interest in wedding the queen when she becomes free at the end of *La Mort le Roi Artu*. Never marrying, Lancelot never has legitimate children. Seduced, through trickery, by the Daughter of King Pelles, he sires Galahad, but he plays no role in his upbringing, nor does he arrange for him to in-

30. "Iblis und Lanzelet / gewunnen lussamiu kint, / als die liute algernde sint," Ulrich von Zatzikhoven, *Lanzelet*, ed. K. A. Hahn (Berlin: Walter de Gruyter, 1965), vv. 9368–70. I am citing Ulrich von Zatzikhoven, *Lanzelet*, trans. Thomas Kerth (New York: Columbia University Press, 2005).

31. "an ir habe und an ir guote, / an tugenden und an muote," ibid., vv. 9377–78.

herit his lands. Instead of progressing from a knight to a ruler, from a lover to a husband, and from a childless youth to a father, as a man of his birth would be expected to do in the course of his life, Lancelot serves Arthur as knight for almost all of his adult existence. If Lancelot rejects the conventional life stages of someone of his class, it is because the love that he bears for Guinevere constitutes, not a personal affection that makes him want to be with her, let alone marry, settle down, and raise a family with her, but an impersonal recognition and appreciation of the queen's excellence that makes him want to achieve great feats of arms, in order that he may be worthy of her. Where critics of Lancelot might see a life driven by irrational desire, the romance itself depicts a life driven by a desire that is entirely rational and even philosophical.

Lancelot loves Guinevere, it is clear, because he perceives excellence in her. When he is a youth of eighteen, he arrives for the first time at Camelot. Guinevere sits down next to him, takes his hand, and looks at him "very tenderly."[32] She asks him what his name is and where he is from. During this initial encounter, he is struck by her beauty, which seems to gush forth within her, ever fresh and ever renewed, and which he judges to be superior to that of any other lady or damsel. The text relates, "Neither the beauty of his Lady of the Lake nor that of any other woman he had ever seen did he esteem compared to this."[33] If Lancelot judges the Guinevere's beauty to be superior that of any other woman, the text observes, it is because it is, in fact, superior. So supreme is her beauty, the text itself affirms, that "never during her lifetime in the Kingdom of Logres was there a woman who could approach her in her great beauty, except only two,"[34] the Daughter of King Pelles and Elaine the Peerless (who are the same women in the Vulgate *Merlin* and the Post-Vulgate Cycle). Struck by the queen's beauty, Lancelot is also struck by her worthiness. Her decision to sit beside him, to take his hand, and to speak gently to him on his arrival at court reflects what he will later refer to as "the courtesies she showed to foreign knights,"[35] courtesies for which he will remain forever grate-

32. "moult doucement," *Lancelot*, ed. Micha, vol. 7, 274.

33. "ne de la biauté sa dame del Lac ne de nule qu'il on ques veist mais ne prise il rien envers chestui," ibid.

34. "onques a son tans el roialme de Logres n'en ot une qui s'aparellast a lui de grant biauté fors que .II. seulement, fors que .II. seulement," ibid., vol. 7, 59.

35. "les courtoisies qu'ele a fait as chevaliers estranges," *La Mort du roi Arthur*, ed. Speer, 124, p. 1284.

ful. Beautiful as Guinevere is, we are informed, "This beauty was nothing compared to the merit she had."[36] If Lancelot eventually judges not only the queen's beauty, but her merit to be superior to that of any other woman, it is, again, because it is, in fact, superior. "There was no woman, either poor or rich, of her merit,"[37] the text states. "She was the worthiest of all ladies and the most meritorious."[38] Lancelot's love of Guinevere is thus the result, not just of his objective evaluation of her as an individual, but of his objective comparison of her to a hierarchy of ladies and damsels and his determination that she is at its summit. Beholding her beauty and her merit, Lancelot decides, not emotionally and impulsively, but rationally and deliberately, to "place" his heart in her. He loves the queen as absolutely as he does because she is, absolutely speaking, the most excellent of all ladies, and he never wavers in his love of her because her excellence never wavers.

Because of the excellence Lancelot perceives in Guinevere, he determines to achieve an equivalent excellence in himself so that he may merit her. In this text, a "high" (*hauz*) man is someone who belongs to the high estate of the nobility. Lancelot is "high" because he is the son of King Ban and Elaine and because, as the Lady of the Lake states, "No one who is from such a lineage could have a heart of cowardice."[39] At the same time, a "high" man is also someone who aspires to belong to "so high an order as chivalry."[40] Lancelot is "high" because he possesses what he refers to as "quality of heart" (*corage*), namely, valor, boldness, courtesy, wisdom, and loyalty, which make him "aspire" (*bae*) to become ever better. Excellent as Lancelot may be, it is not because this excellence comes naturally to him (as it does to his son Galahad), but because he struggles to achieve it, often through great physical and mental exertion. He can become flushed in battle, and he is often wounded, at times seriously. In the course of his instruction by the Lady of the Lake, Lancelot affirms, "Each person should always aspire [*baer*] to strengthen and improve his good traits."[41] In contrast, the man who does not have "quality of heart" does not aspire to become better. Lancelot informs the Lady of the Lake, "He who fails to take up

36. "riens ne monta la biauté a la valour que ele avoit," *Lancelot*, ed. Micha, vol. 7, 60.

37. "nule n'estoit, ne povre ne riche, de sa valor," ibid., vol. 7, 274.

38. "che fu de toutes les dames la plus preus et la plus vaillans," ibid., vol. 7, 60.

39. "nus qui de teil lignage fust ne devroit pas avoir corage de malvaistié," ibid., vol. 7, 257–58.

40. "si haute ordre comme de chevalerie," ibid., vol. 7, 257. Cf. also ibid., vol. 7, 257.

41. "chascuns doit baer tous jours a enforchier et a amender de boines teches," ibid., vol. 7, 247.

chivalry on account of fear . . . should feel himself to be very cowardly and very devoid of good traits. . . . He should hate himself if, through his laziness, he loses something that everyone can have."[42] "Highness" (*hautesce*), in this sense, is opposed, not to "baseness" (*basseur*), as one would expect it to be if it depended exclusively on social class, but to "cowardice," "contemptibleness," or "wickedness" (*malvaistié*) and "laziness" (*perece*), which depend upon quality of heart. After Lancelot has departed for Arthur's court, the Lady of the Lake sends him a message reminding him that "a heart . . . that aspires every day to improve itself can attain all the high things that it dares to undertake."[43] While a man becomes "high" through aspiring to deeds of chivalry, he also becomes "high" through aspiring to the love of a high woman, who will motivate him to achieve such deeds. For that reason, the Lady of the Lake advises Lancelot "that you place your heart, not in a love that will make you lazy, but in one that will improve you, for a heart which becomes lazy through love cannot attain high things."[44] It is because Lancelot places his heart in Guinevere, the highest of ladies, that he aspires to become the highest of knights and, thus, to achieve the highest of things. As he explains to the queen, "The fact that I aspired to you and your great beauty made my heart so proud that I could not find an adventure that I was not able to bring to an end. For I knew well that, if I could not achieve adventures through prowess, I could not win you, and it was necessary for that to befall me or for me to die."[45] While pride can be a vice in romance, insofar as it leads a knight to refuse to acknowledge another knight to be superior to himself, it can also be a virtue, as it is here, insofar as it leads a knight to improve himself over what he has been before. As Lancelot tells Guinevere, "My lady, . . . know that I would never have come to the great height where I am were it not for you."[46] Because Lancelot

42. "se doit chil sentir a moult malvais et a moult vuis de boines teches qui por ceste paor laisse a prendre chevalerie . . . et moult se doit haïr qui par sa pareche pert che que chascuns poroit avoir," ibid., vol. 7, 247.

43. "cuers . . . qui a tous jors bee a amender puet ataindre a toutes hautes choses autresi come il l'ose emprendre," ibid., vol. 7, 349–50.

44. "que vous ne metés vo cuer en amor qui vous fache aparechier, mais amender, car cuers qui por amors devient perecheus ne puet a haute chose ataindre," ibid., vol. 7, 349–50.

45. "ce que je baoie a vos et a vostre grant biauté mist mon cuer en l'orgueil ou j'estoie si que je ne poïsse trouver aventure que je ne menasse a chief; car je savoie bien, se je ne pooie les aventures passer par prouesce, que a vos ne vandroie je ja, et il m'i couvenoit avenir ou morir," ibid., vol. 5, 3.

46. "Dame, . . . [s]achiez que je ja ne fusse venuz a si grant hautesce com je sui, se vos ne fussiez," ibid., vol. 5, 3.

judges Guinevere to possess an excellence beyond that of all other ladies, in order to win her he must achieve an excellence beyond that of all other knights.

By the same token, it is because of the excellence Guinevere perceives in Lancelot that she loves him. During their first encounter at Camelot, she is struck by his beauty, as is everyone else at court. When she asks who the youg man is who has just arrived, Yvain replies, "the handsomest youth you ever saw with your eyes."[47] With his emerald-green eyes, his curly golden (or, later in his life, auburn) hair, and his red lips, it is said, "No one could have found anything to reproach in him."[48] Impressed by Lancelot's beauty, the queen is also impressed by his worthiness after he leaves the court. News arrives of various unnamed knights who have performed great feats—rescuing the Lady of Nohaut, championing the Wounded Knight, and releasing the prisoners of the Dolorous Guard—and she comes to realize that these are all the same knight. If Guinevere eventually judges Lancelot's beauty and worthiness to be superior to those of every other man, it is because they are, in fact, superior. Gawain tells her, gesturing toward Lancelot, "My lady, my lady, behold the knight than whom there is no better in the world, for I have never seen a knight bear arms as well as this one bears them."[49] Yet whereas Lancelot simply admires Guinevere for her excellence, in and of itself, Guinevere glories in her affiliation with a knight as excellent as Lancelot. In Chrétien's *Chevalier de la charrette,* she presides over a tournament where the damsels in attendance hope to identify the best knights and, in doing so, to determine whom they would like to wed. It is one of the queen's duties to arrange such marriages, but, after Lancelot appears and defeats all the other knights, she delights in the fact that the damsels resolve to marry no one but him this year: "The queen, who heard that of which they were boasting, laughed to herself and made fun of them."[50] The *Prose Lancelot* similarly represents the queen as rejoicing to think that what other women want, she possesses. The Lady of the Lake informs Guinevere, "You can boast that never has a lady been able to do what you can do, for you are the companion of the worthiest man and the lady of the best knight

47. "li plus biaus vallés que vous onques veissiés de vos iex," ibid., vol. 7, 272.

48. "ne en lui ne trovast ja nus hom plus que reprendre," ibid., vol. 7, 73.

49. "Dame, dame, veés le chevalier ou en tot le monde n'a nule millor, que onques mais a chevalier ne vi si bien et si bel porter armes comme chil les porte," ibid., vols. 58–59.

50. "Et la reïne qui antant / ce dom eles se vont vantant, / a soi meïsmes an rit et gabe," Chrétien de Troyes, *Le Chevalier de la charrette,* ed. Méla, vv. 6007–9.

in the world."[51] The queen takes pride not only in Lancelot's superiority to other knights, but in her superiority to other ladies and damsels, who must either settle for lesser knights than Lancelot or go without a knight. If she loves this knight as absolutely as she does, it is because he is, absolutely speaking, the most excellent of all knights, and, in his love of her alone, he confirms her own excellence.

Because of the excellence Guinevere perceives in Lancelot, she determines that he deserves her. At one point, when Arthur, Guinevere, Gawain, and Galehaut are discussing Lancelot's excellence, Galehaut asks, hypothetically, how much they would give in order to have his company forever.[52] Gawain answers, "I would straightaway wish to be the most beautiful damsel in the world, happy and healthy, on condition that he would love me above everything, for all his life and mine."[53] When asked for her opinion in the matter, Guinevere replies, "By God, . . . Sir Gawain has put forward all that a lady can put forward, and a lady can offer no more."[54] So compelling is Lancelot that both men and women seek his love, and they conceive of that love as epitomized most fully in the exclusive and lifelong attachment a knight might feel for a damsel. While Lancelot's overall excellence makes him merit the love of anyone who knows him, his services to the Kingdom of Logres make him merit the affection of its rulers in particular. When Arthur's kingdom is about to be conquered by Galehaut, it is Lancelot who holds this opponent back and who brings about his reconciliation with Arthur. So grateful is Guinevere to the knight who saved her husband's kingdom that (to his great embarrassment) she embraces and kisses him before Arthur and his men. In doing so, she announces publicly, "Sir knight, . . . for the love of my lord and for my own honor, which you have upheld today, I grant you my love and myself, as a

51. "Si vous poés de ce vanter que onques mais dame ne pot faire ce que vos poés, car vous estes compaigne au plus preudome et dame au millor chevalier du monde," *Lancelot*, ed. Micha, vol. 8, 461–62.

52. On Galehaut's complex character, see Simon Gaunt, *Love and Death in Medieval French and Occitan Courtly Literature: Martyrs to Love* (Oxford: Oxford University Press, 2006), 191–203; Carol Dover, "Galehot and Lancelot: Matters of the Heart," in *The World and Its Rival: Essays on the Literary Imagination in Honor of Per Nykrog*, ed. Kathryn Karczewska and Tom Conley (Amsterdam: Rodopi, 1999), 119–35; and Philippe Ménard, "Galehaut, prince conquérant dans le *Lancelot en prose*," in *Lancelot-Lanzelot: Hier et aujourd'hui; Recueil d'articles pour fêter les 90 ans de Alexandre Micha*, ed. Danielle Buschinger and Michel Zink (Griefswald: Reineke-Verlag, 1995), 263–73.

53. "je voldroie orendroit estre la plus bele damoisele del mont saine et haitie, par covent que il m'amast sor toute rien toute sa vie et la moie," *Lancelot*, ed. Micha, vol. 8, 94.

54. "Par Dieu, . . . mesire Gauvain i a mis quanque dame i puet metre, ne dame ne puet plus offrir," ibid.

loyal lady must give it to a loyal knight."[55] The king and his men esteem the queen all the more for having displayed such affection for her husband and her defender, not recognizing the adulterous implications of what she has said. Ironically, it is because Guinevere is such a good wife—supportive of her husband and of the knight who has preserved her husband's kingdom—that she becomes an adulterous one. Whenever other knights reproach a married woman for sleeping with a man who is not her husband, it is never simply because she is sleeping with another man, but always because she is sleeping with a man who does not deserve her as well as her husband or another suitor may do. At one point, Meleagant, a wicked knight who has abducted Guinevere, is under the impression that she has been sleeping with Kay, and he reproaches her for having chosen such an unworthy man as her lover over himself and, even more, Lancelot: "My lady, . . . I am worth more than him, for I won you from him through force of arms. And indeed Lancelot is worth still more, who has suffered such misfortunes for you."[56] A loyal lady, he makes clear, is not one who sleeps only with the man to whom she is married, but one who sleeps with the man who has served her well through force of arms. Because Guinevere judges Lancelot to possess an excellence beyond that of other knights, and because he has served her husband and herself better than anyone else, she is right to grant herself to him.

As rational and philosophical as Lancelot's love for Guinevere may be, it is not easy for everyone in the Vulgate Cycle to comprehend. In his *Nicomachean Ethics*, which was translated into Latin by Robert Grosseteste in the 1240s, Aristotle writes that one may love a person because one finds him or her to be "pleasurable" (*delectabilis*, in the medieval Latin translation), in accordance with the judgment of one's senses; if one does so, one loves that person out of "concupiscence" (*concupiscentia*), that is, out of a desire to obtain some benefit for oneself.[57] In his gloss of this passage, Thomas Aquinas notes, "That which is loved with the love of concupiscence is loved, not simply and for itself, but for something else. . . . That is called 'concupiscence' which we wish for

55. "Sire chevaliers, . . . pour l'amour mon seignor, et por la moie honnor que vos avés hui maintenue vous otroi jou m'amor et moi si com loial dame le doit donner a loial chevalier," ibid., vol. 8, 484.

56. "Dame, . . . al mains vail je miels de lui, kar je vos conquis vers lui par force d'armes. Et certes miels valt encore Lancelos qui por vos a tans mals eus," ibid., vol. 2, 76–77.

57. See Aristotle, *Ethica Nicomachea*, trans. Robert Grosseteste, ed. René Antoine Gauthier (Leiden: E. J. Brill, 1972), in *Aristoteles Latinus*, ed. Verbeke, vol. 26, VIII, 3.

ourselves."[58] Those who object to Lancelot's love of Guinevere assume that because he sleeps with her, he loves her for his own sexual gratification and, hence, out of concupiscence. Hermits reproach Lancelot with a Christian vocabulary, accusing him of having succumbed to "sin" (*pechié*) and "lust" (*luxure*) in speaking of his misdeed. One such holy man informs him, "You are vile, filthy, and lustful, and you have squandered your youth in wretchedness and filth."[59] It is predicted that on account of the great sin he has committed with the queen, which he has never confessed or atoned for, he will be unable to complete the Quest of the Holy Grail, and, indeed, he is never able to do so. Knights repudiate Lancelot with a feudal terminology, charging him with having incurred "shame" (*honte*) and "dishonor" (*desenneur*) through his "treason" (*traïson*). When Agravain informs Arthur, "My lord, . . . [Lancelot] is is so disloyal to you that he has caused you dishonor through your wife, for he has known her carnally,"[60] the king is baffled by this news. He conceives of such a liaison as an act of violence by Lancelot against himself, and he protests, "Lancelot could not degrade me more than by shaming me through my wife."[61] The bond he understands is a feudal one, between a vassal and a lord; the breaking of that bond, through the vassal's affair with the lord's wife, would constitute an act of treason; and the queen is merely the means by which that treason would occur. Whether they speak of sin or of shame, all of these men assume that in loving Guinevere, Lancelot seeks to enjoy her carnally, for his own benefit. It is because Lancelot's opponents presuppose any love he bears toward Guinevere to be carnal and self-interested that they condemn it.

The confusion of many of Lancelot's contemporaries, when faced with his love of Guinevere, signals what is distinctive and, indeed, noble about this passion. In his *Nicomachean Ethics*, Aristotle maintains that it is possible to love a person, not because one finds him or her to be pleasurable, but because one finds him to be "good" (*honestus* or *bonus*), in accordance with "the judgment of reason";[62] if one does so, one loves that person not out of "concupiscence" but out of "friend-

58. "id quod amatur . . . amore concupiscentiae, non simpliciter et secundum se amatur, sed amatur alteri. . . . [I]llud . . . dicimur concupiscere, quod volumus nobis," Aquinas, *Summa theologiae*, ed. Blackfriars, I^{a}–II^{ae}, qu. 26, art. 4 ad 1.

59. "vos estes vilz et orz et luxurieux et avez usé vostre jouvente en chetivité et en ordure," *Lancelot*, ed. Micha, vol. 5, 127.

60. "Sire, . . . il vos est si desloiaus qu'il vous a fait deshounour de vostre feme, car il l'a coneüe charnelment," *La Mort le Roi Artu*, ed, Speer, 141, p. 1298.

61. "plus ne pooit Lanselos avillier que de moi honir de ma fame," ibid., 73, p. 1246.

62. "iudicium rationis," Aristotle, *Ethica Nicomachea*, trans. Grosseteste, VIII, 3.

ship" (*amicitia*), that is, out of a desire to do him some benefit. In his commentary of this work, Aquinas writes, "That which is loved with the love of friendship is loved," not "for something else," but, rather, "simply and for itself."[63] He adds, "He is called a 'friend' [*amicus*], properly speaking, for whom we wish good."[64] Despite what Lancelot's opponents assume, this knight loves the queen for her honor not for his own sexual gratification. He conceives of his liaison with Guinevere not as an act of violence against the king, but as an act of love toward the queen, in which her husband plays no part. He is loyal, but loyal to the queen, whose knight he is, and not to the king, to whom he became affiliated only through the queen. For that reason, when Guinevere is, at one point, staying with him, he decides not to retain her, for which she would be blamed, but to return her to her husband, the king of Britain and the worthiest man in the world, for which she will be honored. He explains, "My lady, . . . if we did what my heart desires and what it would like better, you would stay. . . . Nevertheless, because I prefer that this business be resolved more to your honor than to what I would like, I wish you to return to my lord, King Arthur."[65] In considering the moral value of Lancelot's love for Guinevere, the work suggests, it is necessary to consider, again, for whose benefit he acts in loving her. The fact that he seeks to serve her, far more than he seeks to sleep with her, shows that he loves her for her own advantage rather than his own and, hence, that his love for her is praiseworthy.

The Realists

There are knights, ladies, and damsels—"realists," one might call them—who deny that Lancelot is, in fact, as superlative a knight and lover as he is reputed to be. If these skeptics doubt that Lancelot is as excellent as he seems, it is because they doubt that anyone can be that excellent. How could any knight be so valiant at arms that he defeats all other knights, even when they are assembled against him? How could any lover be so faithful to his lady that he is indifferent to all other

63. "id quod amatur amore amicitiae, simpliciter et per se amatur," Aquinas, *Summa theologiae*, Blackfriars, I^a^–II^ae^, qu. 26, art. 4.

64. "ille proprie dicitur amicus, cui aliquod bonum volumus," ibid., I^a^–II^ae^ qu. 26 art. 4 ad 1.

65. "Dame, . . . se on faisoit ce que mes cuers desire et que il voldroit mils, vous i remanrié. . . . Et nonpourquant, pour ce que j'aim miels que cis affaires soit fais selonc vostre honour que selonc ce que je mils ameroie, vous lo je que vous railliés a mon signour le roi Artu," *La Mort le Roi Artu*, ed. Speer, 201, p. 1352.

women, even when the most beautiful among them attempt to seduce him? When one knows how imperfect knights and lovers are, as a general rule, it is difficult to believe that there is one knight, one lover, who alone exceeds that norm. Yet as the work develops, Lancelot demonstrates that he is, in fact, not only just as excellent a knight and lover as people say, but even more excellent, and, in doing so, he exposes the bad faith of those who had doubted him. These "realists" may think that they are relying upon objective perception when they deny that the actual Lancelot can be identified with the "Lancelot" of popular repute, yet in doing so, they are actually influenced by subjective bias against him, due to their pride, envy, or anger. Whatever the reason, these knights, ladies, and damsels reject Lancelot's supremacy over other men of his kind, not because of a failure of their perception, but because of a refusal of their will, and it is for this that they are blamed. If some of us fail to see the superlative among us, the work suggests, the problem is not that the superlative does not exist (for it does), but that we cannot bring ourselves to acknowledge it.

Yder, the king of Cornwall, and many of his fellow knights of the Round Table doubt that Lancelot is as excellent a knight as he is said to be. One day, as these knights are preparing for a tournament, Arthur expresses regret that Lancelot is not among them. With him present, the king declares, his knights would defeat all of its opponents at the tournament, but, with him absent, they will all be dead and vanquished. Yder takes exception to Arthur's remarks because he feels that he is overestimating Lancelot's worth. Were Lancelot to fight on the same side as the knights of the Round Table at the tournament, he complains, no matter who fought the most valiantly, he would be credited with having done so. He alleges, "If we were to vanquish everyone . . . and Lancelot were with us, without striking a blow, still people would say he had vanquished everyone and had carried off the prize."[66] If people perceive Lancelot as the single best knight in the world, Yder maintains, it is not because he is, in fact, superior to others around him, but because people are predisposed to perceive him as superior. He suspects that spectators at tournaments and battles say to themselves, "That is Lancelot. Therefore, he will be the best knight," and that they thus allow Lancelot's (inflated) reputation to influence their interpretation of what they see happening on the field. Guinevere warns, "King Yder, . . . do not put Lancelot on the same level as our

66. "se nous vainquions tout . . . et Lanceloz fust avec nos sanz cop ferir, si diroit l'an qu'il avroit tout vaincu et emporteroit tout le pris," *Lancelot*, ed. Micha, vol. 4, 350.

other knights,"[67] but he insists that Lancelet is, indeed, on that level. As Yder feels that Arthur overestimates Lancelot's worth, he feels that the king underestimates the worth of the other members of the Round Table. Were Lancelot to fight against these knights, he continues, "He would not go away except defeated."[68] Despite objections raised by Arthur, Guinevere, and Gawain, 114 knights agree with Yder that they would be able to best Lancelot, and they resolve to oppose him at the next tournament in order to prove this point. As these knights see it, Lancelot is not adequate to "Lancelot" because many other knights—including themselves—are as excellent as he is held to be.

In response to Yder and his allies, however, Lancelot demonstrates that he is not only as excellent a knight as he is said to be but even more excellent. At the tournament where Yder and the other members of the Round Table intend to oppose him, Lancelot does not appear, but a new knight arrives in his stead. Unrecognized, he ends up defeating sixty-four knights; not one combatant can unseat him. So extraordinary is this mysterious victor's performance in battle that Yder feels that his doubts about Lancelot have been vindicated. "In the name of God," he proclaims, "never did Lancelot demonstrate so much prowess, nor could he do so, for he was never of his prowess."[69] Yet it turns out, to Yder and the other knights' discomfiture, that the new knight was, in fact, Lancelot, forewarned by Guinevere to don new armor and a new shield before his arrival. Indeed, though Yder claims that Lancelot is said to triumph at tournaments because people expect him to do so, he customarily enters such sites of combat incognito, as he does here. When his fellow combatants ask who he is, he answers only, "I am a knight";[70] "I am a knight errant";[71] or "I am a knight, . . . of King Arthur."[72] By preventing other knights from knowing him for who he is, Lancelot forces them to know him for what he does. If people perceive Lancelot as the single best knight in the world, it is not because they are predisposed to perceive him as superior to others around him, but, on the contrary, because he is, in fact, superior. Far from saying to themselves, "This is Lancelot. Therefore, he will be the best knight," onlookers at tournaments and battles say to themselves, "That is the

67. "Rois Ydiers, . . . ne metez ja Lancelot el ranc de noz autres chevaliers," ibid., vol. 4, 349.

68. "il ne s'en iroit ja se desconfit non," ibid.

69. "En non Deu, . . . onques Lanceloz ne fist tant de prouesce ne il ne les porroit pas faire, car onques ne fu de la proesce cestui," ibid., vol. 4, 372.

70. "Je sui . . . uns chevaliers," ibid., vol. 7, 362. ibid., vol. 7, 370.

71. "Je sui .I. chevaliers errans," ibid., vol. 2, 7.

72. ".I. chevaliers sui, . . . au roi Artu," ibid., vol. 7, 430. ibid., vol. 7, 389.

best knight," and then discover that it is Lancelot. As Yder and his allies thus learn, Lancelot is, indeed, adequate to "Lancelot," despite their efforts to establish otherwise.

Yder and his allies doubt that Lancelot is as excellent a knight as he is said to be, not because they have failed to see his excellence, but because they do not want to see it. When Lancelot proves that he is, indeed, the extraordinary knight they had resisted recognizing him as being, these knights could humbly acknowledge his superiority and beg his pardon for having refused to acknowledge it thus far. Gawain provides a model of such behavior. At the end of a tournament, he tells Lancelot, "I keep company with you as with the best and worthiest knight in the world and the one I love most. . . . You have proven it in such a manner that there will never be a day that I do not remember it, and those of the Round Table."[73] Though Gawain is himself a knight (and, indeed, the best of the Round Table after Lancelot), he recognizes that Lancelot is a better knight than himself and, indeed, than anyone else, and he loves him all the more for this excellence. Yet far from following Gawain's example, Yder and his companions persist in their antipathy toward Lancelot. They are blinded by pride, that is, by a love of one's own excellence that leads one to want to see one's neighbor's excellence diminished.[74] Arthur rebukes the "pride"[75] of these knights, and Gawain censures "their pride . . . and the wickedness . . . that they, in their pride, had undertaken against [Lancelot]."[76] When Lancelot triumphed over these knights at the tournament, uncle and nephew agree, "their pride was cast down"[77] and "their wickedness was turned to to nothing."[78] In addition to pride, these knights are blinded by envy, that is, by the hatred of one's neighbor's excellence, which comes out of the fear of seeing one's own excellence diminished.[79] In speak-

73. "vos feisse compaingnie conme au millor chevalier del monde et au plus prodom et que je plus aim; si . . . l'avez vos monstré en tel manniere qu'il ne sera jamais jor qu'il ne m'en doie membrer et a cels de la Table Reonde," ibid., vol. 4, 391.

74. On pride, see Augustine, *De civitate Dei* XIV, 13, p. 434; Prosper of Aquitaine, *Sententiarum ex operibis Augustini liber unus*, sentence 294, in PL, vol. 51, col. 471; Isidore of Seville, *Etymologiae*, ed. Lindsay, X, 248; and Gregory the Great, *Moralia in Job*, ed. Adriaen, XXIV, 8, p. 1203.

75. "orgueil," *Lancelot*, ed. Micha, vol. 4, 398.

76. "lor orgueil . . . et lor felonnie . . . qu'il avoient par lor orgueil comancié contre vos," ibid., vol. 4, 391.

77. "est lor orgueil abatuz," ibid., vol. 4, 391.

78. "est . . . lor felonnie tornee a noiant," ibid., vol. 4, 391.

79. On envy, see John of Damascus, *De fide orthodoxa: Versions of Burgundio and Cerbanus*, ed. Eligius M. Buytaert (Saint Bonaventure, NY: Franciscan Institute; Louvain: E. Nauwelaerts, 1955), Burgundio, 28, p. 121, and John of Salisbury, *Policraticus*, ed. Webb, vol. 2, bk. 7, chap. 24, p. 702b.

ing of their decision to oppose Lancelot in the tournament, Guinevere remarks, "I know that they have done this all out of envy,"[80] and the narrator confirms that "They hated him out of great envy for his prowess."[81] In their pride and envy, Yder and his fellow knights illustrate the challenge of responding to the excellence of another person, especially when that person occupies the same category as oneself. To acknowledge Lancelot's superiority would be to acknowledge their own inferiority, and that is something they cannot bring themselves to do. When Arthur asserts again that Lancelot has once again earned far more glory for the Round Table than the rest of the knights combined, it is said, "From these words that King Arthur spoke, those of the Round Table were so affected that ever afterwards they hated Lancelot with a mortal hatred."[82] Though they say nothing now, the work predicts that these knights will bide their time until that moment when Agravain will expose his love affair with Guinevere and when they will thus be able to accuse him of treason and disloyalty.

As Yder and his allies doubt that Lancelot is as excellent a knight as he is said to be, Morgan doubts that he is as excellent a lover as he is reported as being. Seventeen years earlier, she discovered her lover in a beautiful valley with another damsel. If her lover was false to her, she decided, it was because all knights are false to their ladies. The only way to keep her lover and all other unfaithful lovers from straying, she decides, will be to prevent them from ever leaving this spot. She casts an enchantment over the valley, so that any knight may enter it, but none may leave if he has ever been false to his lady. By the time Lancelot arrives in "the Valley of False Lovers,"[83] 250 such false lovers have been taken prisoner with their beloveds. It is said that should there ever arrive even one faithful lover—"a knight . . . who had never committed a fault toward his beloved in any way, neither in thought, nor in desire, nor in deed"[84]—the logic upon which the spell is based will be broken, and all of these unfaithful lovers will be freed, but Morgan is confident that this will never happen. She states, "I never thought to see a knight who had not committed, in some way, a fault

80. "tout ce ont il fait par envie," *Lancelot*, ed. Micha, vol. 4, 350.

81. "cels qui par sa grant prouesce le haoient par envie," ibid., vol. 5, 150.

82. "De cele parole que li rois Artus dist furent si atorné cil de la Table Reonde que il en haïrent puis touz dis Lancelot de mortel haine," ibid., vol. 4, 399.

83. "li Vals as Faus Amans," ibid., vol. 1, 275.

84. "uns chevaliers . . . qui de nule chose n'avroit onques mespris envers s'amie ne de pensé, ne de talent, ne de fet," ibid., vol. 1, 276.

in love."[85] As she sees it, though knights commonly pledge their undying fealty to ladies and damsels, it is impossible that their affection will not, at some point, stray. Because all knights are faulty in love, in desire, if not in deed, it necessarily follows that Lancelot, who is one such knight, must be faulty as well. For Yder and his companions, Lancelot is not adequate to "Lancelot" because many knights are as excellent as he alone is held to be, but, for Morgan, Lancelot is not adequate to "Lancelot" because no knight is that excellent.

In response to Morgan, however, Lancelot proves that he is, in fact, as excellent a lover as he is said to be, if not more excellent. While Morgan assumes that there is no knight who is not, in some way, faulty in love, he is faithful to Guinevere in deed, desire, and thought. Throughout the romance, a long series of ladies and damsels (including Morgan herself) attempt to seduce him, but Lancelot repulses all of them, as gently as he can. He tells one damsel of his beloved, "My heart is there in sleeping and in waking, my thoughts are with her night and day, and my mind is intent on nothing except her."[86] He tells another, "My heart is not my own,"[87] and, as a result, he is one who "cannot act with himself or with his heart at his command."[88] With both of these damsels, Lancelot distinguishes his heart (and his thoughts and his mind) from his self, and he locates his heart, not in his self, but in his lady. Dispossessed of his heart, he could not give his love to any other woman, even if he wished to do so, and he does not wish to do so. He states, "It is exactly where I wish it to be. I would not wish it to be anywhere else, for it could not be provided for as well in any other place as it is in the place where I have set it."[89] Devoted as he is to his beloved, Lancelot rides into the Valley of False Lovers, and, as he does so, the walls that imprison the captives crumble, and all of the knights kept there are set free. Far from proving that Lancelot is not adequate to "Lancelot," Morgan is confronted with the fact that he, again, exceeds his reputation.

Morgan doubts that Lancelot is as excellent a lover as he is said to

85. "je ne cuidai ja veoir chevalier a nul jor ki n'eust aucune chose mespris en amor," ibid., vol. 1, 300.

86. "mes cors i est en veillant et an dormant et mes pensers i est nuit et jour et mes esperiz n'antant fors a lui," ibid., vol. 4, 156.

87. "mes cuers n'estoit mie a moi," *La Mort du roi Arthur*, ed. Speer, 81, p. 1253.

88. "ne peüst faire de soi ne de son cuer son commandement," ibid., 48, p. 1224.

89. "il est del tout la ou je voel, ne en nul autre lieu ne voel je qu'il soit; car il ne porroit estre en nul lieu si bien assenées com il est el lieu ou je l'ai assis," ibid., 49, p. 1225.

be, not because she does not want to see his excellence, as Yder and his allies did not want to see it, but because she does not want to celebrate that excellence. In contrast to these men, she recognizes Lancelot's virtues, but such is her hatred of Guinevere that she cannot bring herself to honor them, given that her enemy is the one who benefits from their presence. Many years before, when Morgan was still living at court with Arthur and Guinevere and serving as lady-in-waiting to the queen, she fell in love with a knight. Concerned that the king might be shamed by his sister's lubriciousness, Guinevere appealed to the knight to abandon her, and, given the tepidness of his affection for his mistress, she easily persuaded him to do so. Filled with sorrow at the unfaithfulness of her lover, Morgan was filled with anger at the queen who had convinced him to leave her. We are told, "This was the reason for the hatred that she felt for Queen Guinevere all the days of her life."[90] When Morgan hears that a knight has succeeded in breaking the enchantment upon the Valley of False Lovers through his fidelity toward his lady, she at first rejoices in the knight and in the lady who can claim this knight as her own. She exclaims, "The knight deserves to be honored and esteemed in every land for the great loyalty he has in him,"[91] and "his lover, whoever she may be, can well boast that she is the best loved of all."[92] Yet like Yder, who ceased to praise the knight who triumphed at the tournament once he learned that it was Lancelot, Morgan ceases to praise this knight and this lady once she learns that they are Lancelot and Guinevere. She knows that he is the most loyal of all lovers, but, it is said, "It troubled her that the queen had the most loyal of all lovers."[93] If Morgan resists appreciating Lancelot's excellence, it is not out of pride and envy toward Lancelot, as was the case with Yder, but, rather, out of anger toward Guinevere. A personal grievance overshadows her impersonal recognition of excellence, so that she is incapable of celebrating it as she otherwise might have done. For that reason, when the rumors begin to circulate again about Lancelot's affair with the queen, Bors hypothesizes, "If a knight spoke about it, it was Agravain, and if it was a woman, it was Morgan, King Arthur's sister."[94]

90. "Por ce fu la haine qu'ele ot envers la roine Genievre tos les jors de sa vie," *Lancelot*, ed. Micha, vol. 1, 301.

91. "li chevaliers a bien deservi k'il soit honorés et prisiés en totes terres por la grant loialté qui est en lui," ibid., vol. 1, 299–300.

92. "s'amie, ki qu'ele soit, se puet vanter qu'ele est la miels amee de totes les autres," ibid.

93. "si l'en poise de ce qu'ele a de tos les amis le plus loial," ibid., vol. 1, 357.

94. "se chevaliers le dist, ce fust Agravains, et se ce fu fame, ce fu Morgue, la suer le roi Artu," *La Mort le Roi Artu*, ed. Frappier, 89, p. 114.

Not only Morgan, but Guinevere herself occasionally doubts that Lancelot is as excellent a lover as she had thought. A series of misunderstandings leads her three times to think that he has been unfaithful to her. She sees an unnamed damsel at a tournament wear a belt that she had given him. She sees him wear a sleeve of the Damsel of Escalot at another tournament.[95] She finds Lancelot in a bed in her own chamber with the Daughter of King Pelles. On the last occasion, convinced that he has betrayed her, she cries out in sorrow and anger, "Ah, God, who will ever prove loyalty again in any knight or in any man, when disloyalty has lodged itself in the best of all the good ones?"[96] If Guinevere is distressed to think that Lancelot has been consorting with these damsels, it is in part because she thinks that her lover has been unfaithful to her, but it is also in part because, if the most loyal of all men has acted disloyally, he has demonstrated that all men will, at some point, act in such a manner. While all men's faithlessness makes Morgan think that Lancelot, too, must be unfaithful, Lancelot's apparent faithlessness makes Guinevere think, despairingly, that all men must be unfaithful.

In response to Guinevere, Lancelot demonstrates, again, that he is as excellent a knight as he is said to be, if not more excellent. As the queen learns, if the damsel wore his belt and if he wore the Damsel of Escalot's sleeve, it was not because he had any particular affection for either of them, but only because they demanded these boons of him in a way he could not refuse. If he slept with the Daughter of King Pelles, it was, not because he desired to do so, but only because she deceived him into thinking she was Guinevere. Even when the queen exiles him from court as a result of these perceived infractions, he remains true to her. At a certain point in *La Mort le Roi Artu,* during his absence, Guinevere is accused of having murdered a knight of the Round Table, and none of the other knights will defend her in a trial by combat. Yet when Lancelot hears this news, he does not hesitate to come to her aid. The personal injury he has suffered from her unjustified accusations and expulsion from her presence does not interfere with his impersonal recognition and appreciation of her excellence. As he explains to Bors, "Even if she should hate me for all days in such a manner that I never found my peace with her, I should not wish her to be dishon-

95. On the Damsel of Escalot, see Amy L. Ingram, "Death of a Maiden: *La Demoiselle d'Escalot* in *La Mort Artu,*" *Vox Romanica* 62 (2003): 127–35, and Virginie Greene, "How the Demoiselle d'Escalot Became a Picture," *Arthuriana* 12, no. 3 (2002): 31–48.

96. "Ha! Dex, qui esprovera mes loiauté en nul chevalier ne en nul home, quant desloiauté s'est herbergiee el meilleur de touz les bons?" *La Mort le Roi Artu*, ed. Frappier, 32, p. 32.

ored while I lived, for she is the lady in the world who has paid me the greatest honor since I have been bearing arms."[97] In a similar manner, when Gawain turns against him later on, Lancelot continues to bear affection toward him. Bors remarks, "It is certainly marvelous that you love him with great heart and he hates you mortally,"[98] to which Lancelot replies, "You can see this as marvelous if you wish. He will never be able to hate me so much that I do not love him."[99] Far from being disloyal, "the best of all the good ones" shows himself to be loyal beyond end, so that nothing his lady or anyone else he loves does to him can prevent him from remaining true to them. Even if all men are unfaithful, Lancelot, it turns out, remains true.

Guinevere occasionally doubts that Lancelot is as excellent a lover as he is said to be, not because she is disinclined to see his excellence, as Yder and his allies are, or to celebrate that excellence, as Morgan is, but because, when all evidence points against this knight, she lacks sufficient confidence in him to put this evidence to the side. At the beginning of their love, the Lady of the Lake had warned Guinevere, "I beseech you . . . to cast off all pride toward him, for he neither wants nor esteems anything but you."[100] As pride made Yder deny Lancelot's superiority as a knight, pride makes Guinevere periodically forget Lancelot's superiority as a lover, suspecting that he desires someone aside from herself and taking offense at that possibility. Bors attempts to correct Guinevere on these occasions. When rumors spread that Lancelot loves the Damsel of Escalot, he assures her, "I know that my lord Lancelot is of such a high heart that he would not deign to do this. . . . Know well that he has loved you more loyally than any knight has ever loved a lady, without falsity."[101] When she has caught Lancelot with the Daughter of King Pelles, Bors reproaches her for having cast away "my lord Lancelot, who was the worthiest man in the world and who most

97. "s'ele me devoit haïr a touz jorz en tel maniere que ge ne trouvasse jamés pes a li, si ne voudroie ge pas qu'ele fust deshonoree a mon vivant; car c'est la dame del monde qui plus m'a fet d'enneur puis que ge portai arms," ibid., 75, p. 97.

98. "moult estes ore merveillous qui si l'amés de grant cuer, et il vous het mortelment," *La Mort du roi Arthur*, ed. Speer, 244, 1390.

99. "Par foi . . . ceste merveille poés veoir; il ne me savra ja tant haïr que je ne l'aim," ibid.

100. "Et si vos pri que vous . . . metés jus tot orguel vers lui, car il ne veut riens ne nule riens ne prise envers vous," *Lancelot*, ed. Micha, vol. 8, 461–62.

101. "je sai bien que mé sire Lanselos est de si haut cuer qu'il nel daingneroit faire. . . . Et bien savés qu'il vous a plus loialment amee que onques chevaliers ama nule dame sans fauseté," *La Mort du roi Arthur*, ed. Speer, 43–44, p. 1220.

loved you."[102] He addresses, not what Lancelot is alleged to have done or even has done, but, rather, who he is. Because he knows that Lancelot has a "high heart" and that he is "the worthiest man in the world," he knows that he has loved Guinevere loyally and will continue to love her loyally, whatever evidence there may be to the contrary. Because Bors knows that Lancelot is the best lover, he knows that he will always act as the best lover would do, even if he has (accidentally) slept with another woman. In contrast to Yder, Guinevere doubts Lancelot only for a brief time, when she is in the heat of emotion, and she then repents of her hesitation. She says to herself, "You unhappy woman, how did you dare believe that a man as worthy as Lancelot would be inconstant and would love another lady than you? Why have you so betrayed and deceived yourself? . . . No man has ever loved a lady as much or as loyally as he has loved me."[103] She realizes that it is not Lancelot who has betrayed and deceived her, but she who, in doubting Lancelot, has betrayed and deceived herself. She realizes that what Bors said was right—that Lancelot *is* the best of lovers, even when appearances suggest otherwise, that he will therefore always act as loyally as the best of lovers would do, and that the universal, abstract quality of loyalty can, in fact, be found embodied in this particular, concrete individual.

The problem, as the authors of the Vulgate Cycle see it, is not that the perfect knight does not exist in the world, but that, as fallen human beings, we have difficulty recognizing his existence. At the end of *La Mort le Roi Artu*, Arthur has exiled Lancelot from Logres and has then pursued him to Gaul to wage war against him there, but he is forced to return to his own kingdom because Mordred has usurped his throne in his absence. As Arthur is preparing to march on Mordred, the dying Gawain urges him to request Lancelot's assistance in this war, because it is only by doing so that he will achieve victory, but Arthur refuses. He explains, "I have acted so badly toward him that I do not believe my appeal to him would be of any use. For that reason, I shall not request it of him."[104] Yet Gawain knows, with a clear-sightedness that Arthur,

102. "mon signor Lancelot qui ert li plus prodome dou monde et qui plus vos amoit," *Lancelot*, ed. Micha, vol. 6, 179.

103. "Maleürouse feme, conment osas tu quidier que si prodom com est Lanselos fust noveliers et amast autre que toi? Por coi t'es tu si traïe et deceüe? . . . [O]nques hom n'ama autretant dame, ne si tres loialment, com il a fait moi," *La Mort du roi Arthur*, ed. Speer, 118–19, pp. 1280–81.

104. "je me sui tant meffais vers lui que je ne quit mie que proiere i puist avoir mestier, et por ce nel requerrai je pas," ibid., 281, p. 1422.

tragically, cannot share, that despite the harm Arthur has done him, Lancelot would indeed come to his aid. He tells his king, "He is by far the worthiest man I have ever seen and the most courtly. . . . And he loves you with such great love that I know truly that he will come to you, if you send for him."[105] Because Gawain knows who Lancelot is, namely, the worthiest and most gallant of knights, he knows how he will act, namely, by rescuing Arthur in his hour of need, despite everything Arthur has done against him. His words prove correct when, too late, Lancelot learns that Arthur has been mortally wounded in battle with Mordred on Salisbury Plain, and he crosses the Channel to defeat the last remnants of this usurper's followers. Now, however, Gawain tells Arthur, "My lord, . . . he loves you much more than you believe."[106] Though Arthur has interacted with Lancelot for many years by this point, Gawain suggests, he still does not grasp the extent of Lancelot's love for him because he still does not grasp the possibility of such a superlative individual, who loves those who hate him. Of course, medieval audiences would have been familiar with a man who was more excellent than all other men, who was hated, arrested, and killed by those who would not recognize that excellence, and who continued to love those who hated, arrested, and killed him. They would have known that given our tendency to rely upon observation of the world as a way of determining what is possible in the world, it is difficult for us to believe that someone can be excellent to a degree we have never observed in other men. They would have known that this reliance upon what we have beheld thus needs to be supplemented by a faith in the substance of things hoped for and the evidence of things not seen. It is not that Lancelot is Jesus Christ or represents Jesus Christ. (Galahad will later play that role.) But Lancelot represents a certain excellence, beyond what is normally seen in the world, which people have difficulty believing exists. Even those who are closest to Lancelot—Guinevere, Gawain, Arthur—cannot always believe that he is as excellent as he is. If these figures err, it is because they need to function more like readers of romance, who know that that which is not probable is, nonetheless, possible; that someone we ourselves have never observed may, nonetheless, exist; and that true excellence can indeed walk among us.

105. "c'est outreement li plus prodom que je onques trovaisse, et li plus cortois . . . et si vous aime de si grant amour que je sai vraiement qu'il venra se vous le mandés," ibid.

106. "Sire, . . . il vous aime assés plus que vous ne quidiés," ibid.

The Romantics

In contrast to the "realists," there are knights, ladies, and damsels—"romantics," if one will—who recognize that Lancelot is as superlative a knight and lover as he is said to be. If these believers accept that Lancelot is as excellent as he seems, it is because they accept that one individual can, indeed, surpass all others of his class. Given that some knights are valiant in arms and some are more valiant, does it not stand to reason that one knight must be the most valiant of them all? Given that some lovers are loyal and some more loyal, does it not stand to reason that one lover must be the most loyal? Even if one knows how imperfect knights and lovers are, as a general rule, one can still hold out hope that there may be one knight, one lover, who stands as an exception. Yet while the knights, ladies, and damsels who recognize Lancelot's excellence are shown to be justified in their beliefs about him, they err insofar as they aspire to possess him. They think, "Because Lancelot is excellent, I must have him," and this logic leads inexorably to their suffering and, in the most extreme cases, to their death. Whether men or women, they want to love Lancelot and be loved by him, exclusively and permanently, yet they can never attain a companionship with him as absolute as they would wish. Ultimately, in loving Lancelot, they love Lancelot's excellence, and, in loving Lancelot's excellence, they love something that exceeds even himself and that he therefore cannot grant them. If some of us acknowledge the superlative among us, but suffer from this acknowledgment, the problem is that we mistake the superlative for something we can own.

Galehaut recognizes that Lancelot is as excellent a knight as he is said to be. At the time when he first meets this knight, he is a young man of twenty-five years of age, noble, gracious, and generous, and he is better loved by his people than any lord in the world. During a battle with Arthur's troops, one of his men informs him that an unknown knight on the other side is defeating their side all by himself. Intrigued, he goes to watch the knight attack his men, and he is amazed by the extraordinary feats at arms he beholds: "When Galehaut saw the marvels that he was performing, he marveled at how the person of one knight could do this."[107] Insofar as Galehaut is attracted to this knight

107. "Quant Galahos vit ces merveilles que il faisoit, si se merveilla comment le cors d'un chevalier pooit ce faire," *Lancelot*, ed. Micha, vol. 8, 70.

at this point, it is not because of a personal interest he has taken in him, but because of an impersonal interest he has taken in his prowess. He does not know what this knight's name is, he does not know what he looks like underneath his armor, and he has not heard him speak. He knows only the ability with which he fights, which exceeds that of any other knight. When this unknown knight's horse falls dead beneath him and he seems to be in danger of being killed or taken captive, Galehaut makes his way to him, dismounts, and offers him his own charger. He reasons, we are told, "It would not be worth it to have conquered all the lands that exist under the heavens on the condition that such a worthy man died through his fault."[108] Though this one knight is preventing him from conquering the Kingdom of Logres, he values less the conquest of this kingdom than the continued existence of a man of such quality. He informs the knight that should he continue to bear arms as he has been doing, he will give him his protection, serve him as his squire, and provide him with horses all day. Should he cease fighting out of cowardice, however, he warns him, he will not prevent him from being taken prisoner. By making clear that he will aid and protect him only if he fights well, he makes clear that he loves, not this knight, but the excellence he finds in this knight. Like Lancelot's love for Guinevere, Galehaut's love for Lancelot is objective, impersonal, and rational, the result of his recognition that he is the worthiest of men.

As a result of his apprehension of Lancelot's excellence as a knight, Galehaut forsakes his desire to conquer the world. At the time when he meets this knight, he has already overtaken twenty-eight kingdoms, and, as he later discloses to Lancelot, "He aspired to conquer the whole world."[109] To that purpose, he is waging war against Arthur, and he is just about to achieve victory over him. The text indicates, "If Galehaut had been able to live out a full life with all the courage that he had when he began to wage war against King Arthur, he would have surpassed all those who had surpassed all others."[110] It seems that it will be he, and not Arthur, who will establish himself as the preeminent sovereign of his time. Yet because Galehaut wants Lancelot to be his companion, he ends up abandoning these temporal ambitions. At the end of the battle where he first sees Lancelot fight, he approaches him and invites him

108. "il ne vaudroit avoir conquis toutes les terres qui sont desous le trosne par covent que .I. si preudom fust mors par ses coupes," ibid.

109. "baoit il, a tot le monde conquerre," ibid., vol. 1, 2.

110. "se Galahout puist vivre son droit aage al point et al corage qu'il avoit quant il comença a guerroier le roi Artu, il passast tos cels qui les autres avoient passés," ibid., vol. 1, 1.

to spend that night with him. Lancelot is understandably taken aback to be addressed so courteously by the head of the opposing army, and he hesitates to consent. In order to reassure him of his good intentions, Galehaut therefore offers to grant him a boon, and, the following day, he fulfills it. Having defeated Arthur decisively in battle, he rides up to the despairing king, dismounts, and kneels down before him with his hands joined. He tells him, "My lord, I come to you to make reparation for the wrongs I have done you. I repent and place myself entirely at your mercy for everything."[111] He comports himself, not like the victor in the war, as he has the right to do, but like the vanquished party. As Galehaut humbles himself by asking Arthur's mercy, in order to fulfill his boon to Lancelot, he humbles himself further by becoming Arthur's vassal, in order to remain in this knight's company. He declares, "Riches lie, not in land or possessions, but in worthy men, for lands do not make worthy men, but worthy men make lands."[112] If he is right that riches lie not in lands but in worthy men, it is reasonable for him to abandon claims to the Kingdom of Logres in order to have Lancelot. The same ambition that leads him to want to possess lands leads him, even more, to want to possess this knight, who, in his worthiness, is better than any territory. Far from begrudging the loss of his temporal ambitions, he boasts of having forsaken them for love of Lancelot. "As God is truly my witness," he announces to Lancelot at one point, "I would not want to have power over all the lands that are under heaven if I were to lose your companionship and your love."[113] His kinsmen are appalled at Galehaut's submission to Arthur and, by extension, "the shameful peace he has made for the sake of a single man,"[114] yet he announces that if this peace will bring him Lancelot's companionship, "I would wish to have my great honor turned to shame."[115] When Galehaut speaks of his willingness to renounce not only the Kingdom of Logres but all the lands in the world and, in doing so, to turn his honor into shame in order to possess Lancelot's companionship, he measures his love for Lancelot by that which he is willing to sacrifice for him, and he demonstrates how surpassing that love is.

111. "Sire, je vous vieng faire droit de ce que vous ai mesfait, si m'en repent et me met en vostre merci del tout outreement," ibid., vol. 8, 85.

112. "il n'est pas . . . richece de terre ne d'avoir mais de preudome, ne les terres ne font mie les predomes, mais li predome font les terres," ibid., vol. 1, 2.

113. "si voirement m'aït Dieux . . . ne je ne voldroie pas avoir en baillie totes les terres qui sont sos ciel par covent que je perdisse vostre compaignie et vostre amor," ibid., vol. 1, 36.

114. "la honteuse pes que il avoit fete por un sol home," ibid., vol. 1, 2.

115. "j'en vaudroie avoir tournee ma grant honor a honte," ibid., vol. 8, 94.

Forsaking his desire to conquer the world for Lancelot, Galehaut ultimately forsakes his desire to live as well. Though he becomes Lancelot's companion, he never ceases to worry that he will lose him, whether because of his attachment to Guinevere, because of his attachment to Arthur, or because of some altercation between them. He tells him, "I fear very much that I will lose you soon and that we will be parted by death or by some other separation."[116] What troubles him, ultimately, is not Lancelot's separation from him or his death—for Lancelot is never separated from him for long, nor does he die before him—but Lancelot's separability and his mortality. He cannot bear the thought that the person he loves most in the world could leave him or be taken from him. So much does he dread Lancelot dying that he fantasies that he himself will die before him, preferably by Lancelot's hand. At one point, when Lancelot has gone mad and has started attacking people arbitrarily, Galehaut insists upon remaining with him, explaining, "It would be better that he killed me than that he be parted from me."[117] If he cannot be bound to Lancelot in his presence, he would like to be bound to him in his absence, through the intimacy of a death his companion has brought about. At one point, Galehaut returns to his native land of Sorelois, where he learns that Lancelot stayed there not long ago but disappeared during the night, leaving behind bloody sheets. Lancelot is, in fact, alive—he had incurred a nosebleed and had fled from the house—yet Galehaut's people suspect that he is dead, and they share this suspicion with their lord. Persuaded that Lancelot is dead, Galehaut ceases to eat or drink. When his clerics warn him that he is threatening to damn his soul by killing his body, he begins to take nourishment again, but the damage to his body has been done. He dies, at the age of thirty-nine. Having striven so long to possess Lancelot, he is buried at the fortress of the Joyous Guard, where the inscription on his tomb reads, "Here lies Galehaut, the son of the Giantess, the Lord of the Distant Isles, who died for the love of Lancelot."[118] Many years later, after Lancelot has participated in the Quest of the Holy Grail, after he has fought in the wars against Arthur and against Mordred's heirs, and after he has become a hermit, Lancelot lies dying, and he asks that he be buried at the Joyous Guard, in Galehaut's tomb.

116. "Et criem molt que je vos perde par tens et que nos soions departi par mort or par autre desevrement," ibid., vol. 1, 13.

117. "miex voldroie que il m'ocheist qu'il se departesist de moi," ibid., vol. 8, 452.

118. "Ci gist Galehout li fiz a la Jaiande, li sires des Lointaignes Iles, qui por l'amor de Lancelot morut," ibid., vol. 2, 212.

In the end, it is only in death that Galehaut is united with Lancelot as exclusively and as permanently as he had always wished.

Like Galehaut, two damsels recognize that Lancelot is as excellent as he seems. On one the feast day of Saint John, Lancelot is riding through a meadow in the company of an old woman when he finds a knight and two damsels who are reclining on a white cloth on the bank of a spring and are having a picnic. Upon their invitation, he dismounts, removes his helmet, and joins them. One of these damsels—the sister of the knight—sees that though his face is flushed from his exertions, his hair curls in golden waves and his eyes sparkle like emeralds. "Never, to her knowledge, had she seen a lady or a damsel so beautiful,"[119] the text states. "He . . . was so endowed with beauty that no one could be more beautiful."[120] The old woman later identifies this knight to this company as "my lord Lancelot of the Lake, the best knight in the world, as far as one knows."[121] While the damsel does not observe Lancelot fight in battle, as Galehaut does, she too understands that he occupies the highest rank in the category to which he belongs, both because of his beauty and because of his prowess, and she too loves him as a result. At another point, Lancelot is journeying to a tournament in Winchester when he lodges at the house of a vavasor and his three children—two knights and a damsel—in Escalot. The Damsel of Escalot asks Lancelot's squire who this knight is, but he refuses to answer except to say, "He is the best knight in the world."[122] Later, when Gawain stops by the vavasor's house and recognizes the shield the unknown knight left on the wall, he concurs with the squire's description of this knight. "He . . . is the best knight in the world,"[123] he tells the damsel, including "a better knight than I am, more beautiful and more charming."[124] As a result, it is said, "The damsel . . . loved him greatly for of all the good things that were said of him and for the beauty she saw in him."[125] Again, while the damsel does not observe Lancelot fight in battle, she understands that he is supreme in his category, and she loves him for that reason. From the beauty these damsels see in this

119. "onques mais a son esciant dame ne damoisele ne vit si bel," ibid., vol. 4, 134.

120. "il . . . fu de toutes biautez si garniz que nus ne poïst estre si biaux," ibid.

121. "mes sires Lanceloz del Lac, li mieldres chevaliers del monde que l'an saiche," ibid., vol. 4, 135.

122. "c'est li miudres chevaliers del monde," *La Mort du roi Arthur*, ed. Speer, 11, p. 1190.

123. "cil . . . est li miudres chevaliers del monde," ibid., 29, p. 1208.

124. "il est miudres chevaliers que je ne sui, et plus biaus, et plus avenans," ibid.

125. "la damoisele . . . l'enama tant, pour les biens que on en disoit et pour la biauté qu'ele en lui veoit," ibid., 48, p. 1224.

knight and from the valor they hear attributed to him, they know that he ranks above all of his peers. Like Galehaut's love for Lancelot, these damsels' love of this knight is objective, impersonal, and rational.

In recognition of Lancelot's excellence as a knight, these damsels forsake their desire to marry. Just as Galehaut is a valiant lord who could have become the greatest ruler of his day, they are beautiful virgins who could have become the wives of well-born knights. Of the first damsel, it is said, "She was so beautiful of body and of manner that there was not one so beautiful in all the country, nor a knight so powerful that he would not willingly take her for her beauty."[126] Of the Damsel of Escalot, Gawain states that "if the highest man in the world placed his heart there, he could not rightly be blamed for it."[127] Yet like Galehaut, who has no interest in conquering lands or becoming king if he cannot have Lancelot, these damsels have no interest in wedding a man if they cannot have him. In the past, the first damsel tells Lancelot, many men have courted her, but now that she has met him, she realizes, "I could not deprive myself of as valiant a man as you are."[128] When the brother of the Damsel of Escalot learns of her love for Lancelot, he warns her, "Fair sister, . . . if you wish to love, it is necessary that you set your heart lower, for you will not be able to pluck the fruit from such a high tree,"[129] but this she refuses to do. The very fact that any other knight would necessarily be "less valiant" or on a lower branch than Lancelot would make this knight less loveable in these damsels' eyes and, hence, not loveable at all. As was well known in the Middle Ages, the courtesan Aspasia is said to have declared to a man's wife, "Unless you come to believe there is no better man . . . on earth, you will always be looking for what you judge best of all: to be . . . the wife of the best of husbands."[130] The very fact that in accepting any other knight, these damsels would be accepting someone inferior to Lancelot would make them feel inferior in their own eyes. If the first damsel were the beloved of Lancelot, she tells him, "I would hold myself

126. "estoit si bele de cors et de façon que an tout le païs n'avoit si bele ne chevalier si puissant que volentiers ne la preist por sa biauté," *Lancelot*, ed. Micha, vol. 4, 134.

127. "se li plus haus hom del monde i avoit mis son cuer, ne l'en porroit on a droit blasmer," *La Mort du roi Arthur*, ed. Speer, 31, p. 1209.

128. "je ne m'en porroie consirrer por nul si vaillant home com vos estes," *Lancelot*, ed. Micha, vol. 4, 158.

129. "Bele suer, . . . se vous volés amer, que vous metés vostre cuer plus bas, car de si haut arbre ne porriés vous mie le fruit cueillir," *La Mort du roi Arthur*, ed. Speer, 51, p. 1226.

130. "Quare, nisi hoc peregeritis, ut neque vir melior . . . in terris letior sit, profecto semper id, quod optimum putamus esse, multo maxime requiretis, ut . . . quam optimo viro nupta sit," *The Letter Collection of Peter Abelard and Heloise*, ed. David Luscombe, trans. Betty Radice, Oxford Medieval Texts (Oxford: Oxford University Press, 2013), Heloise, *Epistola* II, 11, p. 134.

in better esteem."[131] If the Damsel of Escalot were the beloved of this knight, Gawain informs her, "It is my view that you should hold yourself in better esteem."[132] These damsels love Lancelot and only Lancelot because they both understand him to be the best of knights, because that which is best is, by definition, that which is most loveable, and because they can only bear loving that which is most loveable.

Forsaking the desire to marry anyone but Lancelot, these damsels ultimately risk forsaking, or even do forsake, their lives. Spurned by this knight, the first damsel languishes. As her health declines, she explains, "Nothing hurts me except my heart, which does not have what it would like."[133] Because she does not obtain what she wants, she is dying from her unsatisfied desire. As Lancelot sleeps, she says to him, "I love you so deeply that I cannot remove my heart from you. Rather, I would like better to die than to remove it."[134] She cannot cease loving him, even if this love is not reciprocated, nor does she wish to cease loving him, even if it is at the cost of her life. In the end, she accepts that Lancelot will continue to love his lady, as his lady, but she persuades him to love her as well, as his maiden, because those loves are not in conflict with each other. She tells him, "I will pledge to you that, as long as I live, I will never love another than you and that no man will ever touch me carnally."[135] Despite her beauty and her charm, this damsel renounces the pleasures of love and marriage, and she does so out of a sense that in preserving her virginity for Lancelot, she binds herself to him. Spurned by the same knight, the Damsel of Escalot also languishes. She loves him so much that she ceases to eat, drink, or sleep. Like the first damsel, she feels that, because she does not have what she wants, she will die, and she does die. She tells her brother, "It is destined that I die for him, and you will see this happen soon."[136] Instead of dying a natural death, she dies a heroic death, arranging for herself to lie dead on a richly adorned bed, on a richly adorned barge, and to float down a river toward Camelot. From her belt, she carries a

131. "je m'en priserai mielz," *Lancelot*, ed. Micha, vol. 4, 158.

132. "si m'en est avis que vous vous en poés miels proisier," *La Mort du roi Arthur*, ed. Speer, 30, pp. 12080–89.

133. "nus ne me fait mal fors mes cuers qui n'a pas quanqu'il voudroit," *Lancelot*, ed. Micha, vol. 4, 141.

134. "Et or vos aing si durement que ge n'am puis mon cuer oster, ainz me voil mielz morir que oster l'an," ibid., vol. 4, 140.

135. "je vos creanterai que jamais jor que je vive n'amerai autre de vos ne a home n'atoucherai charnelment," ibid., vol. 4, 157.

136. "il m'est ensi destiné que je morrai pour lui, et ce verrés vous avenir prochainement," *La Mort du roi Arthur*, ed. Speer, 51, p. 1226.

purse with a letter addressed to the knights of the Round Table, informing them that "through loving loyally, I came to my end."[137] She prides herself on the persistence with which she loved the man who never loved her back. In a manner similar to Galehaut, she is buried with an inscription on her tomb that reads, "Here lies the Damsel of Escalot, who died for love of Lancelot."[138] Lancelot's exclusive love of the queen leads other women to remain celibate or to die because they cannot possess him, yet these women clearly feel empowered by making these vows, whether to remain a virgin or to die for love of him, and to have their status thus marked by the man they love.

The problem, as the authors of the Vulgate Cycle see it, is that while the perfect knight does exist in the world, we cannot all hope to attain him. For as long as Galehaut and the damsels are sustained in their love of Lancelot, it is because they hope that he will one day be with them. As the first damsel says of Lancelot, "Looking at him brings such a great sweetness and such a good hope into my heart that I would be rich from the hope alone."[139] When she begins to languish for him because of her unrequited desire, Lionel revives her by giving her hope that this love might, one day, be reciprocated. She relates, "I would have died without fail if there had not been a cousin of his who assured me of his love. From this, I was restored to health."[140] In a like manner, the Damsel of Escalot tells Lancelot that if he had rejected her less bluntly, "You would have put my heart in a languor filled with all good hopes, so that the hope would have made me live in all the joy in which a loving heart can dwell."[141] If hope sustains these lovers, it is, as Aquinas argues, because hope makes that which one does not have seem to be in one's possession: "That which is desired, though really in the future, is, nevertheless, in a way, present, inasmuch as it is hoped for. . . . Desire gives pleasure, so long as there remains hope of obtaining that which is desired."[142] Though the damsels do not have Lancelot as their lover, they hope that they will one day do so, and this

137. "pour loialment amer sui je a ma fin venue," ibid., 115, p. 1278.

138. "ci gist la damoisele d'escalot, qui pour l'amour de lanselot morut," ibid., 120, p. 1281.

139. "li resgarz am porte a mon cuer une si grant douçor et une si bonne esperance que de l'espoir seulement fusse je riche," *Lancelot*, ed. Micha, vol. 4, 139.

140. "morte fusse je sans faille, s'uns suens cousins ne fust qui m'aseura de s'amor. De ceste novele fui je toute asouagie," ibid., vol. 4, 369.

141. "vous eüssés mis mon cuer en une langour raplenie de toute bone esperance, si que l'esperance me feïst vivre en toute la joie ou cuers amourous peüst demourer," *La Mort du roi Arthur*, ed. Speer, 49, p. 1225.

142. "illud quod concupiscitur, etsi realiter sit futurum, est tamen quodammodo praesens, inquantum speratur . . . concupiscentia est delectabilis, quandiu manet spes adipiscendi quod concupiscitur," Aquinas, *Summa theologiae*, Blackfriars, vol. 20, I^{a}–II^{ae}, qu. 36, art. 2, ad 2 and ad 3.

hope allows them to enjoy their desire for him. Yet though Galehaut and the damsels are sustained by the hope that they will one day have Lancelot, they are destroyed when they lose that hope. As Galehaut approaches his death, it is said, "He would have been greatly comforted if he did not believe for certain that [Lancelot] was dead."[143] If he dies, it is because he succumbs to "despairing,"[144] that is, literally, to the loss of hope that his companion is still alive. The damsels likewise come close to dying or even die when Lancelot makes clear that he will never be their lover. Galehaut and these damsels err, again, because they cannot entertain the mental image of a beloved figure and take pleasure in that mental image without hoping that they will one day possess what it represents.

The Readers

Confronted with Lancelot's excellence, the "realists" are unhappy because they cannot be him, and the "romantics" are unhappy because they cannot have him, yet the knights, ladies, and damsels whom we might call "readers" are content because they can contemplate him. When the first damsel gazes upon the sleeping Lancelot, she chides herself for considering his appearance: "What good is his beauty to me, when he is not for me?"[145] It is said, "She had such desire for him that she did not know what she could do."[146] The perception of Lancelot's excellence makes her desire the man who possesses it, but, if she cannot have him, she does not know how to act upon that desire. The *Prose Lancelot* suggests that if the damsel could learn simply to admire Lancelot—if she could seek, not the egotistic delight of possessing such a person, but the aesthetic delight of beholding him—she could be satisfied. The damsel might object that she yearns, not to be an extraneous third party to the love affair between Lancelot and Guinevere, but to be central to that love affair. Yet the text shows time and again that far from extraneous, the third party is central to and even constitutive of that love. When Lancelot and Guinevere consider their attachment to each other, it is always already mediated by an awareness of the third party, who, by observing and registering their bond, ends

143. "il s'en confortast durement, s'il ne cuidast certainement que il fust mors," *Lancelot*, ed. Micha, vol. 1, 388.

144. "desesperer," ibid.

145. "Et la biautez que me vaut, quant il ne m'en est de mielz?" ibid., vol. 4, 139.

146. "si en a tel anvie qu'ele ne set qu'ele poïst faire," ibid., vol. 4, 134.

up confirming its existence. The pleasure the lovers themselves take in their love is thus always based, not in the experience of the love, but in their reflection upon that experience, where they too are situated, like a third party, in relation to it.

While Galehaut worries that he will lose Lancelot, as a result of Lancelot's attachment to Guinevere, it is he who ultimately enables their love affair to take place.[147] He observes Lancelot's distress in speaking of the queen, and he deduces from this distress the passion he feels for her. It is Galehaut who sets up a meeting between the queen and this knight. One evening, after dinner, a seneschal escorts Lancelot to a meadow where Galehaut and Guinevere are waiting for him, in the company of the Lady of Malehaut, Lady Lore of Carduel, and an unnamed maiden. As he approaches the queen, Lancelot sinks to his knees, lowers his eyes, and trembles so violently that he can barely greet her. So paralyzed is he by the power of his love that it is Galehaut, not Lancelot, who informs Guinevere that Lancelot loves her more than himself and who persuades her to grant him her love. He says to her, "My lady, . . . I beseech that you give him your love, that you take him as your knight for all days, and that you become his loyal lady for all the days of your life."[148] And it is Galehaut, not Lancelot, who persuades her to confirm that love with a kiss, as a "preliminary pledge."[149] In order to prevent the ladies nearby from suspecting what is going on, he proposes that the three of them withdraw, "as if we were conferring together,"[150] for this kiss. At this supremely intimate moment, when Lancelot and Guinevere are sharing their first kiss, the lovers are acting at the behest of Galehaut, who initiates, supervises, and shields this physical encounter and who joins his head to theirs. The kiss of Lancelot and Guinevere is not a lascivious act, engaged in by the two lovers, but, rather, a legal act, instigated and presided over by Galehaut.[151] In contracts of this time, a third party, like Galehaut, would need to be

147. See Philippe Ménard, "La Déclaration amoureuse dans la littérature arthurienne du XIIe siècle," *Cahiers de civilisation médiévale* 13 (1970): 33–42.

148. "Dame, . . . je vous pri que vous li donés vostre amor et que vous le prenés a vostre chevalier a tous jours et devenés sa loiax dame a tous les jors de vostre vie," *Lancelot*, ed. Micha, vol. 8, 115.

149. "commencement de seurté," ibid.

150. "ausi comme se nous conseillisiens," ibid.

151. On the kiss of vassalage, see Jacques Le Goff, "Le rituel symbolique de la vassalité," in *Pour un autre Moyen Age: Temps, travail et culture en Occident; 18 essays* (Paris: Gallimard, 1977), 349–420. See also J. Russell Major, "'Bastard Feudalism' and the Kiss: Changing Social Mores in Late Medieval and Early Modern France," *Journal of Interdisciplinary History* 17, no. 3 (1987): 509–35, which addresses the resemblance between the kiss between the lord and his vassal and that between the courtly lady and her lover.

present in order to witness the alliance that was being made and in order to rectify this alliance, should its terms be violated.[152] Though a contract brings together two parties, it cannot function legally as a contract without this third party serving as witness and guarantor of this union. While this third party may seem extraneous to this contract, he is integral to it, as it is his presence that makes the contract legally valid. In the words with which Guinevere establishes the bond between Lancelot and herself, she addresses Galehaut, not Lancelot, and she makes him into an essential component of this bond: "I grant that [Lancelot] should be all mine and I all his, and that any breach or violation of our covenant should be repaired by you."[153] However supplementary Galehaut may seem to be to Lancelot and Guinevere's love affair, it is he who brings about its realization.

While the Lady of Malehaut mourns the fact that she will never possess Lancelot, as a result of his attachment to Guinevere, it is she, too, who ultimately defines the shape that this love affair will take. Early in the *Prose Lancelot*, when Lancelot is fighting outside the town of Malehaut Bluff, which the Lady of Malehaut has ruled since the death of her husband, she takes him prisoner, and she thus has opportunity to apprise herself of his great valor. If he performs great feats of alms, she reasons, it must be because he has placed his heart "in a very high place."[154] Though she would have liked to be the lady for whom he enacts such deeds, she understands that she is not sufficiently high to occupy this position. If she cannot be the object of Lancelot's love, she resolves, she will know who the object of that love is because that knowledge will, in some way, compensate her for the fact that it is not she. To that purpose, she joins Arthur's court and attaches herself to Guinevere, as if she is thinking that the queen might be the "high place" where this knight has set his heart. During the meeting in the meadow, she is present, and she keeps her eyes open. When Lancelot finally brings

152. Kiril Petkov, in *The Kiss of Peace: Ritual, Self, and Society in the High and Late Medieval West* (Leiden: Brill, 2003), discusses circumstances in which feuding parties would kiss in order to symbolize their agreement to abide by a court's or an arbiter's decision (69). He also describes "guarantors" (*fideiussores*) of this pact, that is, noblemen who assumed the responsibility of ensuring that the two parties would fulfill their oaths (63).

153. "Ensi . . . l'otroi je que il soit tous miens et je soie toute sieue, et par vous soient amendé li mesfait et li trespas des covenenches," *Lancelot*, ed. Micha, vol. 8, 115. In the noncyclic *Lancelot*, which Dante seems to have been familiar with, Guinevere states, "Ansi . . . l'otroi ge que il soit toz miens, et ge tote soe, et que par vos soient amandé li meffait et li trepas de covenanz," *Lancelot do Lac*, ed. Kennedy, vol. 1, 348.

154. "en moult haut lieu," *Lancelot*, ed. Micha, vol. 8, 118.

himself to speak of his love to Guinevere, he is distracted by the presence of this lady, whom he had not yet recognized. At a certain point while he is talking with the queen, we are told, "The Lady of Malehaut Bluff cleared her throat deliberately, and she raised her head, which she had lowered. And he heard her now, who had heard her many times in the past, and was so overcome with fear and anguish in his heart that he could not respond to what the queen was saying."[155] At this supremely intimate moment, when Lancelot and Guinevere are first revealing their love to each other, Lancelot is worried that the Lady of Malehaut is nearby, and he is so distressed at her presence that he cannot attend to what the queen is saying to him. Noticing his distraction, Guinevere teases him, suggesting that he loves not her but one of the ladies in the nearby group: "I see well that your heart is over there, even though your body is here."[156] When Galehaut proposes that Guinevere and Lancelot kiss, the queen confesses that she is willing, but she, like Lancelot, is distracted by the presence of the nearby ladies. She tells Galehaut, "There are ladies over there who are marveling greatly at what we have done so far. It could not happen that they would not see it."[157] It is in order to avoid such observation that Galehaut arranges for the three of them to withdraw a few yards apart and to bend their heads together, as if speaking to one another. When the text finally describes this first kiss, it emphasizes not so much what is happening between Lancelot and Guinevere as what is happening between the two lovers and the Lady of Malehaut. It reports, "The queen . . . took him by the chin and kissed him in front of Galehaut long enough that the Lady of Malehaut knew that she was kissing him."[158] At this supremely intimate moment, when Lancelot and Guinevere are sharing their first kiss, the queen is worrying that the ladies nearby are watching them; she is arranging matters with Galehaut so that these ladies will not be able to watch; and she is, in fact, being watched. Distracted as they are by the Lady of Malehaut and her companions, these lovers do not experience their initial amorous encounter directly and immediately, as

155. "la dame del Pui de Malohaut s'estousi tout a essient et drecha la teste que ele avoit enbroncie. Et chil l'entendi maintenant, qui maintes fois l'avoit oïe. Et il l'esgarde, si la connut, si en ot teil paor et teile angoisse en son cuer que il ne pot respondre a che que la roine li disoit," ibid., vol. 8, 110.

156. "je voi bien que vostre cuer est la, comment que li cors est ci," ibid., vol. 8, 112.

157. "ches dames sont iluec qui moult se merveillent que nous avons tant fait: si ne porroit estre que eles ne le veïssent," ibid., vol. 8, 115.

158. "Et la roine . . . le prent par le menton et le baise devant Galahot assés longuement si que la dame de Malohaut seit qu'ele le baise," ibid., vol. 8, 115–16. Cf. *Lancelot do Lac*, ed. Kennedy, vol. 1, 348.

something that they perceive with their own senses; rather, they observe it indirectly and mediately, as something that is refracted through these other ladies' perspective. However supplementary the Lady of Malehaut may seem to be to Lancelot and Guinevere's love, it is she whom both lovers are thinking of when they first embrace.

So central are Galehaut and the Lady of Malehaut to Lancelot and Guinevere's love affair that this knight and this queen at times seem less interested in their relationship, in and of itself, than in the discussion of their relationship with their companions. After nighttime falls on the meadow, the different members of this gathering retire to their separate camps. Once Lancelot and Galehaut are back in Galehaut's tent, the text relates, "They lay down together in one bed and spoke all night about that from which their hearts were greatly gratified."[159] Once Guinevere and the Lady of Malehaut are back in their lodgings, they too begin to confer. Seeing the queen standing alone by the window, "think[ing] about what pleased her most,"[160] the Lady of Malehaut approaches her and says, "Ah, my lady, how good a company is four people!"[161] She tells Guinevere that she knows what has happened between Lancelot and her and that Lancelot and Galehaut will be discussing this development in their relationship. With such conversations, she predicts, "They will delight in each other from now on in whatever land where they may be."[162] As Lancelot and Galehaut will take comfort from each other by unburdening their thoughts to each other, she proposes that Guinevere and she take comfort from each other by acting likewise. She explains, "If it pleased you that I were fourth in the company, the two of us could offer each other solace, just as the two of them are doing, and then you would be more gratified."[163] Guinevere agrees to this suggestion, and she invites the Lady of Malehaut to join her in bed that night. The text relates, "When they were in bed together, they began to speak of this new love. . . . Then they spoke for a long time between the two of them. They had great joy in their new intimacy."[164] In the aftermath of their initial amorous encounter, Lancelot and Guinevere thus both spend the night in bed,

159. "se couchent ambedoi en .I. lit et parolent toute nuit de ce dont lor cuer sont moult a aise," ibid., vol. 8, 118.

160. "penser a che que plus li plaisoit," ibid.

161. "Ha, dame, come est boine compaignie de .IIII.," ibid.

162. "des ors mais s'en deporteront li uns a l'autre en quel que terre qu'il soient," ibid., vol. 8, 120.

163. "s'il vous pleust que je fuisse quarte en la compaignie, si nous solaseriemes entre nous .II. autresi comme entr'ax .II. feroient, si en fuissiés plus aise," ibid.

164. "Et quant eles furent couchies, si commenchierent a parler de ches noveles amors. . . .

not with each other, but with their same-sex companions. They experience "great joy," but this joy consists not in physical intercourse with their lovers but in verbal intercourse with their friends. On the day following this initial amorous encounter, Guinevere and the Lady of Malehaut revisit what had happened the previous evening in body and mind. At the meadow, the queen tells her new companion about what had happened with Lancelot, and she does so so completely, we are told, that "she did not fail to say anything she could remember."[165] Already Guinevere is taking pleasure, not in seeing Lancelot and kissing him again, but in recalling having seen and kissed him the evening before, and she is doing so for the Lady of Malehaut's benefit. Already she is transforming what should have been an experience, perceived in the present and shared with her lover (though it never was that), into a memory, recollected from the past and shared with her friend, and she is cherishing that process. Given the brevity and awkwardness of Lancelot and Guinevere's first encounter, it seems that the pleasure of love lies not in interacting with one's lover but in reminiscing about that interaction with a companion and, hence, not in the experience in and of itself but in the reflection upon that experience with someone else.

So central are observers to Lancelot and Guinevere's love affair that the lovers can at times seem less interested in their relationship than in the representation of that relationship in an artwork. Toward the beginning of Lancelot and Guinevere's liaison, a damsel from the Lady of the Lake comes to the queen and gives her a shield that depicts, on one side, a knight, and on the other, a lady.[166] The knight has his arms around the lady and would have been kissing her, were it not for the fact that the shield was split from the base to the top, with a gap the width of one's hand between the two halves; only the cross-piece keeps the shield together. The damsel explains that the shield represents the best knight presently alive and a lady who, recognizing this knight's merit, has granted him her love. If the shield is cracked, she continues, it is because, so far, the knight and the lady have exchanged only kisses and embraces. As the knight and the lady in the image are separated by the crack in the shield, which prevents them from kissing, so too, the damsel intimates, are Lancelot and Guinevere separated by their fail-

---

Ensi parolent moult longement entr'eles .II., si font moult grant joie de lor novel acointement," ibid., vol. 8, 121.

165. "Riens n'en laisa a dire dont il peust ramenbrer," ibid., vol. 8, 122.

166. On shields in this work, see Carol Dover, "The Split-Shield Motif in the Old French *Prose Lancelot*," *Arthurian Yearbook* 1 (1991): 43–61.

ure thus far to make "complete"[167] their love. That night, Lancelot and Guinevere do consummate their relationship, yet the work is less interested in this act itself—about which it says virtually nothing—than in the effect of this act upon the shield. Around midnight, Guinevere rises and goes to find the shield. The text relates, "She touched it without putting on a light, and she found it all whole, with no crack. She was very happy about this, for now she knew well that she was better loved than any other beloved."[168] Guinevere feels that she is loved, not because of anything that Lancelot has said or done during their night together, but because of what the shield represents. The physical union that is stressed is, not that of the two lovers, but that of the two sides of the shield; the physical contact in the darkness that is emphasized is, not Guinevere's touch of her lover, but her touch of the painting. In the morning, a little before daybreak, the Lady of Malehaut also goes to the shield, examines it by candlelight, and perceives it to be repaired. She says to the queen, "Lady, we see well that the love is complete."[169] Galehaut soon joins them before the shield. The text states, "They inspected it, marveling, for a long time."[170] Once again, the pleasure that Lancelot and Guinevere take in each other lies not in their experience of each other, but in their (now aesthetic) reflection upon that experience and in their friends' reflection upon that experience with them.

In the end, the Lady of Malehaut represents the proper response to someone as exemplary as Lancelot, whether in literature or in life. Like the reader of the *Prose Lancelot*, she observes Lancelot's excellence, and she is attracted to it. Like the reader, she recognizes that, however much Lancelot may be the object of her longing, she will never be the object of his desire. Instead of succumbing to despair at this fact, however, like the reader, she considers it upon herself to observe the love affair between Lancelot and Guinevere, and she savors what she observes. If she understands what the knight and the queen experience, it is not only because she considers this affair but because she herself experiences something parallel to it. As Guinevere embarks on her affair with Lancelot, she arranges for the Lady of Malehaut to enter into a similar liaison with Galehaut. On the night when Guinevere and Lancelot first sleep together, it is said, "She embraced Lancelot in his suit of armor,

167. "enterines," *Lancelot*, ed. Micha, vol. 8, 207.

168. "si taste sans alumer, si le trueve tout entier sans fendure, si en est moult lie, car or seit ele bien que c'est la miex amee de nule autre amie," ibid., vol. 8, 444.

169. "Dame, or veons nos bien que l'amor est enterine," ibid.

170. "Si l'ont a merveilles esgardé et longuement," ibid., vol. 8. 445.

and the Lady of Malehaut embraced Galehaut."[171] Because both knights and both ladies are involved in these relationships, the queen reasons, both partners in the same-sex pairs will be able to share their sorrows and their joys with each other. Even if one is not Lancelot, even if one is not Guinevere, one can have access to what they experienced in love by hearing about it, from one's friend or from this text, and by imitating it, in one's own behavior.

If we turn back to Dante's depiction of Paolo and Francesca in the *Inferno*, we can see that, far from condemning an idealized love affair in contrast to realistic adultery, the learned poet is regretting the fate of sinners who died too soon. One might expect Dante to keep his blessed Beatrice as far as possible from the Lady of Malehaut, abettor of Guinevere's sin. Yet in *Paradiso*, when he depicts Beatrice attempting gently to correct the Dante pilgrim, he has her cough like "the one who had coughed at the first fault ascribed to Guinevere."[172] One might expect Dante to keep Beatrice as far as possible from the sinful Francesca. Yet as Francesca claims that "love . . . seized me,"[173] in regard to Paolo, Beatrice informs Virgil that "love moved me,"[174] in regard to the Dante pilgrim. At the climactic moment of *Purgatorio*, when Beatrice reveals her "holy smile [*santo riso*]"[175] to the Dante pilgrim, she does so only after having been urged by her maidens to unveil her "mouth [*bocca*]"[176] to her lover. If Beatrice, the Lady of Malehaut, and Francesca can all share behavior, it may well be because the difference between a saint and a sinner is never absolute during their lifetimes. Paolo and Francesca are condemned to Hell because they were killed by Francesca's husband before they had a chance to repent. Tristan is said to end up in the same circle, presumably because he too dies before he has had a chance to atone for his sin. In contrast, Lancelot and Guinevere are not mentioned among the damned lovers of the Second Circle, presumably because they did repent and end their lives in religious orders. In his *Convivio* (1304–7), Dante compares Lancelot to Guido of Montefeltro, the thirteenth-century Ghibelline lord of Urbino, given that both men turned their back on the world at the conclusion of their lives in order to gain admission to heaven: "The knight Lancelot did not wish to en-

171. "et ele embrace Lancelot tot armé et la dame de Malahot Galahot," ibid., vol. 8, 441.

172. "quella che tossio / al primo fallo scritto di Ginevra," Dante Alighieri, *The Divine Comedy*, ed. Singleton, vol. 3, pt. 1, *Paradiso*, XVI, vv. 14–15.

173. "Amor . . . / mi prese," Dante, *Inferno*, V, vv. 103–4.

174. "Amor mi mosse," ibid., II, v. 72.

175. Dante, *The Divine Comedy*, ed. Singleton, vol. 2, pt. 1, *Purgatorio*, XXXII, v. 5.

176. Ibid., XXXI, v. 137.

ter the port with his sails raised high, nor did the most noble of our Italians, Guido of Montefeltro. These noble men lowered the sails of their worldly preoccupations so that, in their advanced age, they gave themselves to religious orders, abandoning all worldly delights and affairs."[177] It may be in part because of the spiritual turn at the end of the Vulgate Cycle that, in *De vulgari eloquentia* (1302–5), when Dante is praising the literary accomplishments of the Old French language, he alludes to "the most beautiful meanderings about King Arthur."[178] As it is not a medieval but a modern thinker who would oppose the "ideal" and the "real," it is not a medieval but a modern thinker who would imagine Arthurian sinners, like Arthurian romance, to be incapable of redemption.

As Dante is not condemning an idealized love affair, in contrast to realistic adultery, in the *Inferno,* he is also not condemning romance, like the *Book of Galehaut,* in contrast to his own Christian comedy. Francesca, it is clear, rewrites the scene of Lancelot and Guinevere's kiss. Though she alludes to Galehaut, she edits both Lancelot's companion and the Lady of Malehaut out of the scene, focusing exclusively upon the two lovers. And though she must have known that it was Guinevere who kissed Lancelot, in her version of the encounter, it is Lancelot who kisses Guinevere and, by extension, Paolo who kisses her. It is Francesca—or Dante through Francesca—who thus "idealizes" the encounter between the knight and the queen, making their kiss more private than it had been and making the man and the woman conform to more traditional gender roles. Just as Francesca rewrites the *Prose Lancelot,* Dante, it is also clear, rewrites this lady. There was a real Francesca. According to the fourteenth-century commentators of Dante's great work,[179] her full name was Francesca da Rimini, and she was the daughter of Guido Minore da Polenta, the lord of Ravenna, and the wife of Giovanni Malatesta, the deformed elder son of the lord of Rimini. There was a real Paolo (also known as "il Bello"), who was Giovanni's

177. "Certo lo cavaliere Lanzalotto non volse [in porto] intrare colle vele alte, né lo nobilissimo nostro latino Guido montefeltrano. Bene questi nobili calaro le vele delle mondane operazioni, che nella loro lunga etade a religione si rendero, ogni mondano diletto ed opera disponendo," Dante, *Convivio,* ed. Franca Brambilla Ageno, 2 vols. (Florence: Casa editrice le letter, 1995; rpt., 2003), IV, 28, 7–9, vol. 2, p. 445.

178. "Arturi regis ambages pulcerrime," Dante Alighieri, *De vulgari eloquentia,* in *Opera,* ed. Marco Santagata, 2 vols. (Milan: Arnoldo Mondadori, 2011–), vol. 1, 1124–1547, at I, 10, 2, p. 1234.

179. The fourteenth-century commentators of Dante's great work, Jacopo Alighieri (ca. 1322), Jacopo della Lana (1324–28), the author of the *Ottimo Commento* (1330–40), and Giovanni Boccaccio (1373–74) all discuss the historical Paolo and Francesca. Two fourteenth-century historians, Marco Battagli and the author of the *Cronaca malatestiana,* also make brief reference to them.

younger brother. The two of them were said to have been killed in the region of Ravenna about three decades before Dante himself began to live in this city, where he received hospitality from Francesca's nephew. Yet this "real" Francesca was not the "ideal" Francesca of the *Inferno.* From records we possess about this pair, we know that at the time of their death, Francesca was not a tender courtly lady, but a matron of ten years standing with a nine-year-old daughter, and Paolo not a tremulous youth, but a married man of some forty years of age. Boccaccio attests in his *Esposizioni sopra la "Comedia" di Dante* (1373–75), "How she joined with him, I have never heard tell, if it is not what the author wrote. It is possible that it occurred in that way, but I believe this to be rather a fiction constructed out of what could have happened."[180] There is a romance being written here, as Poggioli himself acknowledges,[181] but it is Dante himself who is writing it.

If there is something else that the author of the *Prose Lancelot* and, indeed, the authors of much medieval vernacular literature knew, it is that romance (as a literary genre) is always at the heart of romance (as love). For a certain type of "romantic" reader, a man and a woman meet, fall passionately in love, and join in physical union. The companions with whom they discuss the love affair, the memories and hopes they share with these companions about their love affair, and the artworks they create as an aid to these memories and hopes are all supplementary to the love affair itself. For the author of the *Prose Lancelot,* however, a man and a woman fall in love because they judge their beloved to exceed all members of his or her sex. In his treatise *De Amore* (1180s), Andreas Capellanus famously defines love as "a certain inborn suffering which proceeds from the sight of and immoderate thinking [*cogitatione*] about the beauty of the other sex."[182] In this romance, the pleasure of love continues to reside not so much in the experience of an affair as in the reflection upon that experience. It thus resides in talking about that experience with others, in representing it verbally and visually, and in inspecting these representations. Because the representation of love is constitutive of that love, romance—the

180. "Col quale come ella poi si giugnesse, mai non udi' dire se non quello che l'autore ne scrive; il che possibile è che così fosse: ma io credo quello essere più tosto fizione formata sopra quello che era possibile ad essere avvenuto," Giovanni Boccaccio, *Esposizioni sopra la Comedia di Dante,* ed. Giorgio Padoan, in *Tutte le opere di Giovanni Boccaccio,* ed. Vittore Branca (Milan: Mondadori, 1965), Canto V, 516.

181. Poggioli, "Paolo and Francesca," 76.

182. "passio quaedam innata procedens ex visione et immoderata cogitatione formae alterius sexus," *Andreas Capellanus on Love,* ed. and trans. P. G. Walsh (London: Gerald Duckworth, 1982), I, 1, p. 32.

genre in which the love affair is most abundantly recounted—is constitutive of that bond. Even as the romance sets up Lancelot as the best of knights, Guinevere as the best of ladies, and their love, by extension, as the best of loves, it makes clear that these lovers' experience of their love is always mediated by the observers of their love—the original readers of this romance—through whose eyes they themselves perceive their beloved.

FIVE

The Quest of the Holy Grail: The Sacredness of the Secular

If the story of the Grail differs from the stories of Merlin, King Arthur, and Lancelot, it is largely because of the sacredness that permeates this narrative.[1] The story starts as a chivalric tale. In the *Conte du Graal*, Chrétien de Troyes recounts how Perceval the Welshman, the son of the widow of the Waste Forest, is growing up entirely ignorant of chivalry when an encounter with some passing knights of the Round Table inspires him to leave his rustic home and travel to King Arthur's court so that he can become a knight as well. After Perceval is dubbed, he meets the beautiful damsel Blancheflor, who is being besieged in her castle, and rescues her from her aggressors. It is after Perceval departs from this love interest that the story becomes not just chivalric but spiritual. Riding alongside a river, he encounters a man fishing in a boat—later identified as the Fisher King—who offers him hospitality for the night. Over dinner in this king's manor, he beholds a procession of damsels and squires who repeatedly carry

1. For the best general treatment of this topic, see Barber, *Holy Grail*. For useful collections of articles, see *The Grail, the Quest, and the World of Arthur*, ed. Norris J. Lacy (Rochester, NY: D. S. Brewer, 2008); *The Grail: A Casebook*, ed. Dhira B. Mahoney (New York: Garland, 2000); and *Les Romans du Graal aux XIIe et XIIIe siècles. Strasbourg (29 mars–3 avril 1954)* (Paris: Editions du Centre National de la Recherche Scientifique, 1956). See also Ramm, *A Discourse for the Holy Grail in Old French Romance*.

before him a series of mysterious objects, including the Holy Grail and the Bleeding Lance, but he refrains from inquiring about them. For the rest of the romance, various damsels and hermits reproach him for having failed to ask about these objects, and he wanders about, attempting to return to the castle and to make amends. It is clear that the Grail and the Lance are not just marvelous phenomena, like those we have run across before, but sacred objects, and that the failure to respond to them properly constitutes, not just a fault of decorum, but a sin.[2] As the account of his adventures is taken over by Chrétien's Continuators, Perceval becomes a saintly and even ascetical figure. He may return to the Grail Castle, ask the questions he was supposed to ask, and succeed the Fisher King as his rightful heir, but, according to Manassier, after a seven-year reign, he retires to the woods to become a hermit and dies shortly thereafter. He may wed Blancheflor, but, according to Gerbert of Montreuil, he never consummates his marriage. While the *Conte du Graal*, the Continuations,[3] the *Didot-Perceval*, and *Perlesvaus* represent Perceval as the primary Grail knight, the later Vulgate and Post-Vulgate Cycles focus instead upon "the Good Knight" Galahad and, in doing so, take an even more explicitly religious turn. In the *Queste del Saint Graal*,[4] the Grail knights must defeat not simply other knights but their own sinful inclinations, an endeavor in which only the most

2. The literature on Chrétien de Troyes' *Conte du Graal* is enormous. For some standard readings, see Alexandre Micha, "Deux Etudes sur le Graal," in *De la Chanson de geste au roman: Etudes de littérature médiévale offertes par ses amis, élèves et collègues* (Geneva: Droz, 1976), 462–79, and Jean Frappier, *Chrétien de Troyes et le Mythe du Graal: Etude sur "Perceval" ou le "Conte du Graal"* (Paris: Société d'Edition d'Enseignement Supérieur, 1972). Jeff Rider, in "The Perpetual Enigma of Chrétien's Grail Episode," *Arthuriana* 8, no. 1 (1998): 6–21, argues that Chrétien both encourages and frustrates an allegorical interpretation of his *Conte du Graal*.

3. On the Grail Continations, see Thomas Hinton, *The "Conte du Graal" Cycle: Chrétien de Troyes's "Perceval," the Continuations, and French Arthurian Romance* (Rochester, NY: D. S. Brewer, 2012); Leah Tether, *The Continuations of Chrétien's "Perceval": Content and Construction, Extension and Ending* (Cambridge: D. S. Brewer, 2012); Matilda Tomaryn Bruckner, *Chrétien Continued: A Study of the "Conte du Graal" and Its Verse Continuations* (Oxford: Oxford University Press, 2009), and "Authorial Relays: Continuing Chrétien's *Conte du* Graal," in *The Medieval Author in Medieval French Literature*, ed. Virginie Green (New York: Palgrave Macmillan, 2006), 13–28.

4. On the *Queste del Saint Graal*, see Alexandre Leupin, *Le Graal et la littérature: Etude sur la Vulgate arthurienne en prose* (Lausanne: L'Age d'Homme, 1982); Emmanuèle Baumgartner, "The *Queste del Saint Graal*: From *Semblance* to *Veraie Semblance*," in *A Companion to the Lancelot-Grail Cycle*, ed. Dover, pp. 107–14, and *L'Arbre et le Pain: Essai sur la "Queste del Saint Graal"* (Paris: SEDES, 1981); Fanni Bogdanow, *The Romance of the Grail: A Study of the Structure and Genesis of a Thirteenth-Century Arthurian Prose Romance* (Manchester: Manchester University Press, 1966); and Frederick W. Locke, *The Quest for the Holy Grail: A Literary Study of a Thirteenth-Century French Romance* (Stanford, CA: Stanford University Press, 1960). On the interpretative questions that arise with this romance, see Michel Stanesco, "Parole autoritaire et 'accord des semblances' dans *La Queste del saint Graal*," in *Miscellanea Mediaevalia: Mélanges offerts à Philippe Menard*, ed. J. Claude Faucon, Alain Labbé, and Danielle Quéruel, 2 vols. (Paris: Honoré Champion, 1998), vol. 2, 1267–79; Robert S. Sturges, *Medieval Interpretation: Models of Reading in Literary Narrative, 1100–1550*

holy among them—Galahad, Perceval, and Bors—ultimately succeed. In the sacred objects he seeks and the spiritual purity he must attain in order to find them, the Grail knight pursues what Bors calls "the highest quest that was ever undertaken,"[5] yet one whose precise nature has always been a source of contestation.

It is true that the story of the Grail derives in large part from Scripture and Church tradition. According to the Gospels, during the Last Supper, Christ shared bread with his disciples and predicted that he would be betrayed by one among them who put his hand "into the dish."[6] He then took a "chalice"[7] of wine, offered thanks, and shared it with his companions. It was during that same evening that he is said to have poured water into a "basin"[8] and, with it, to have washed the feet of his disciples. Later, after Christ had been crucified, the rich decurion Joseph of Arimathea took his body down from the Cross and interred it in a tomb with the help of the Pharisee Nicodemus. There is no mention in the Gospels of Joseph catching Christ's blood in a basin during the Crucifixion or the Deposition, yet a series of images from manuscripts and decorated objects from the ninth century onward represent such a vessel (occasionally suspended in midair) receiving Christ's blood at this time.[9] In the hours preceding, during, and after his Passion, Christ is thus associated with four vessels—the dish containing the bread of the Last Supper, the chalice containing the wine of this meal, the basin containing the water with which the disciples' feet were cleansed, and the basin containing the blood that Christ shed as he died—each of which becomes identified, in different romances, with the Grail. In addition to the French literary texts, two Latin historical sources trace the Grail to Christ's Passion. In 1211 or 1223, the Flemish monk Helinand of Froidmont records in his *Chronicon* that in the year 718, in Britain, "A hermit was shown by an angel a marvelous

(Carbondale: Southern Illinois University Press, 1991), 32–74; and, especially, Tzvetan Todorov, "La Quête du récit," in *Poétique de la prose* (Paris: Editions du Seuil, 1971), 129–50.

5. "la plus haute queste qui onques fust conmencie," *Queste del Saint Graal*, ed. Gros, 222, p. 1028.

6. "paropside," Matt. 26:23 or "catino," Mark 14:20.

7. "calix," Matt. 14:23; Luke 22:17 and 22:20.

8. "pelvis," John 13:5.

9. See, for example, the miniature from the Utrecht Psalter, Utrecht, University Library MS 32, psalm 115, f.67r, from the mid-ninth century, where an unidentified figure holds up a chalice to receive Christ's blood flows during the Crucifixion; a miniature from the Gospel of the Abbey of Weingarten from the early twelfth century, where an unidentified figure performs this action during the Deposition; and an enamel plaque from Hildesheim, Paris, Musée de Cluny from around 1170, where a figure identified as *Ecclesia* commits this deed. For discussion, see Barber, *Holy Grail*, 121–22.

vision of Saint Joseph the decurion, who deposed the body of the Lord from the Cross, and of the bowl or dish in which the Lord took dinner with his disciples. The history, which is called 'of the Grail,' was written down by this hermit."[10] At the end of the thirteenth century, the Dominican friar and hagiographer Jacobus de Voragine referred in his *Chronica civitatis Januensis* to "the Holy Grail [*Sangreal*],"[11] from which Christ and his disciples ate and with which Nicodemus collected Christ's blood, and he identifies this vessel with the "Holy Bowl" (*sacro catino*) that King Alfonso VII of Castile gave to the Genoese in recompense for their assistance with a military campaign. At a time when the True Cross, the Crown of Thorns, and the Blood of Christ were being venerated as Christian relics and when pilgrims were traveling en masse to the cathedrals that were being built to house such items, the Grail could be regarded as another Christian relic and the Quest of the Grail knights to find this vessel as another Christian pilgrimage.

Given their apparent basis in Scripture and Church tradition, it may seem that the Grail romances should be read as Christian allegories.[12] The story of the Grail obviously departs from the story of Christ's Passion as we are given it in the Gospels, but apocryphal accounts of these events were respected as serious and even holy works in the Middle Ages. In a letter appended to one such apocryphal gospel sometime between the sixth to eighth centuries, an author said to have been Saint Jerome writes, "Whether these stories be true or invented from something, . . . they can be believed and read without danger to the soul by those who believe that God can do these things."[13] What matters,

10. "cuidam eremitae monstrata est mirabilis quaedam visio per angelum de sancto Joseph decurione, qui corpus Domini deposuit de cruce; et de catino illo sive paropside, in quo Dominus coenavit cum discipulis suis; de quo ab eodem eremita descripta est historia, quae dicitur de gradali," Helinand of Froidmont, *Chronicon*, in PL, vol. 212, cols. 771–82, at XLV, cols. 814–15.

11. "Sangraal," Iacopo da Varagine, *Cronaca di Genova dalle origini al MCCXCII*, ed. Giovanni Monleone, 2 vols. (Rome: Tipografia del Senato, 1941), vol. 2, 312.

12. On Christianity and the Grail, see, for some of the more recent treatments, Stephen Knight, "Celticity and Christianity in Medieval Romance," in *Christianity and Romance in Medieval England*, ed. Field, Hardman, and Sweeney, 26–44; Richard W. Barber, "Chivalry, Cistercianism, and the Grail," in *A Companion to the Lancelot-Grail Cycle*, ed. Dover, 3–12; Kathryn Marie Talarico, "Romancing the Grail: Fiction and Theology in the *Queste del Saint Graal*," in *Arthurian Literature and Christianity: Notes from the Twentieth Century*, ed. Peter Meister (New York: Garland, 1999), 29–59. Among the classic older studies, see Jean Frappier, "Le *Conte du Graal* est-il une allégorie judéo-chrétienne?" in *Autour du Graal* (Geneva: Droz, 1977), 225–305; Daniel Poirion, "L'Ombre mythique de Perceval dans le *Conte du Graal*," *Cahiers de civilisation médiévale* 16 (1973): 191–98; and Paul Imbs, "L'Elément Religieux dans *Le Conte del Graal* de Chrétien de Troyes," in *Les Romans du Graal aux XII*^e^ *et XIII*^e^ *siècles. Strasbourg (29 mars--3 avril 1954)* (Paris: Editions du Centre National de la Recherche Scientifique, 1956), 31–58.

13. "sive haec vera sint, sive ab aliquo conficta, . . . ab his qui ista deum facere potuisse credunt, sine periculo animae suae et credi et legi posse," *Libri de Nativitate Mariae: Pseudo-Matthaei*

Pseudo-Jerome suggests, is not whether a text's claim to evangelical authority is true, but whether the text is useful or at least not harmful to the spiritual lives of its readers. Robert de Boron suggests that the story of the Grail constitutes this kind of extracanonical gospel. Like the Apostles, Merlin indicates, his amanuensis Blaise will write a book that will prove beneficial to those who read it: "Many people who hear this book will be better as a result of it and will keep themselves from sinning again."[14] If the story of the Grail was influenced by the apocryphal gospels, it was also influenced by discussions of the sacraments of the Eucharist and penance that were occurring at the time when these romances were being composed. Throughout these works, the Christian knight learns to see through the literal, physical level of reality in order to apprehend the figurative, spiritual level of reality. In their efforts to perceive the transcendent through the immanent, the intelligible through the sensible, and the abstract through the concrete, these romances reflect theological and pastoral shifts that were taking place as they were being written.

Yet whatever claims the French romances made about the Grail, with the support of a few Latin texts, there is no evidence that this vessel was ever generally believed to be grounded in Scripture or Church tradition. Neither the canonical Gospels, nor the apocryphal gospels, nor the countless commentaries on such texts attribute any special significance to the dish, the chalice, or the basin of the Last Supper. Helinand of Froidmont (who had been a minstrel before entering religious life) acknowledges, "I have not been able to find this history written down in Latin, but it has been written down by some noblemen in French."[15] Jacobus de Voragine observes, not that this vessel was used to collect Christ's Blood, but that "it is reported in English books"[16] to have been used for this purpose, and, not that it *is* the Holy Grail, but that "the English call this vessel the Holy Grail in their books."[17] While he devotes a chapter of his famous *Legenda aurea* to Joseph of

Evangelium, textus et commentarius; Libellus de Nativitate Sanctae Mariae, textus et commentarius, ed. Jan Gijsel and Rita Beyers, Corpus Christianorum Series Apocryphorum 10, 2 vols. (Turnhout: Brepols, 1997), vol. 2, 275.

14. "maintes genz qui ce livre orront en seront meillor et se garderont plus de pechier," Robert de Boron, *Merlin*, ed. Micha, 16, 72.

15. "Hanc historiam Latine scriptam invenire non potui, sed tantum Gallice scripta habetur a quibusdam proceribus, nec facile, ut aiunt, tota inveniri potest," Helinand of Froidmont, *Chronicon*, cols. 815.

16. "in quibusdam libris Anglorum reperitur," Iacopo da Varagine, *Cronaca di Genova dalle origini al MCCXCII*, ed. Giovanni Monleone, 2 vols. (Rome: Tipografia del Senato, 1941), vol. 2, 312.

17. "illud vas dicti Anglici in libris suis 'Sangraal' appelant," ibid.

Arimathea, he makes no mention of the Grail in its pages. As the only two Latin authors to make any reference to the Grail, Helinand and Jacobus both wrote after the Grail romances had entered into circulation, and both refer to the Grail not as something that exists but as something that French or English books claim to exist. It seems that learned clerics could believe that a vessel that had been used at the Last Supper or the Deposition had survived as a relic to their day, but they could not believe that this vessel had been brought to England; that it had been placed in the manor of a Fisher King; or that it had been the object of a quest by knights of the Round Table. Jacob van Maerlant, for example, writes, "The liars about the Grail compose their fables about this Joseph of Arimathea, which I consider to be complete nonsense,"[18] and he condemns "the silly fictions about the Grail, the lies about Perceval, and the other very false stories."[19] As Jacob's tone reflects, serious authors of the Middle Ages tended not so much to criticize the stories of the Grail as to ignore them altogether, as something beneath their contempt. At a time when relics and the holy figures identified with them were widely venerated, there was never a vessel recognized as the Grail that became the object of such a cult, and Perceval, Bors, and Galahad were never regarded as saints. Though enormous numbers of pages were devoted to the Grail in vernacular literature between the late twelfth and mid-thirteenth centuries, this vessel never crossed the boundary from romance into hagiography.[20]

Given their lack of an actual basis in Scripture and in Church tradition, while the Grail romances resonate with Christian allegories, they cannot, ultimately, be categorized in this manner. For many readers, the Grail legend derives not from Christian but from Celtic sources.[21]

18. "Van desen Joseph van Arimathien / maken hare favelien / die logenaren vanden Grale, / dat ic vor niet houde altemale," Jacob van Maerlant, *Spiegel historiael*, ed. De Vries and Verwijs, vol. 1, pt. I, bk. VII, 39, vv. 61–64.

19. "Dien dan die boerde vandem Grale, / die loghene van Perchevale, / ende andere vele valscher saghen," ibid., vol. 1, pt. I, bk. I, prologue, vv. 55–57. Maerlant refers also to the "trifles about the Grail [*truffen vanden Grale*]," ibid., vol. 2, pt. III, bk. 2, 42, v. 15.

20. John of Glastonbury, in his *Cronica sive antiquitates Glastoniensis ecclesie* (ca. 1350), ed. James P. Carley, 2 vols. (Oxford: British Archaeological Reports, 1978), XIV, 30, wrote that Joseph, when he came to Britain, brought with him vessels containing the blood and sweat of Christ (without using the word Grail).

21. Alfred Nutt was the first to identify the Grail with the Celtic cauldron of plenty in his *Studies on the Legends of the Holy Grail, with Especial Reference to the Theory of Its Celtic Origin* (London: D. Nutt, 1888); *Celtic and Mediaeval Romance* (London: D. Nutt, 1899); and *The Legend of the Holy Grail* (London: D. Nutt, 1902). Arthur C. L. Brown identified the Grail with Irish legends in *Origin of the Grail Legend* (Cambridge, MA: Harvard University Press, 1943). See also Roger Sherman Loomis, *Celtic Myth and Arthurian Romance* (New York: Columbia University Press, 1927); "The Origin of the Grail Legends," in *Arthurian Literature of the Middle Ages*, ed. Loomis, 274–94;

The Grail itself has often seemed to recall not so much a container of the Eucharist as a pagan Welsh vessel, such as the Cauldron of Annwn (a Welsh otherworld), which identified a coward by refusing to boil his food; the Horn of Brân Galed, which provided whatever drink one wished; or the Hamper of Gwyddno Long Shank, which furnished whatever food one desired. By the same token, the Quest of the Holy Grail is often seen to evoke not so much the pilgrimages of Christian penitents as the heroic journeys of Celtic warriors to obtain these vessels, such as those recounted in *Preiddeu Annwn* (ca. 900) and *Culhwch ac Olwen* (ca. 1000s). These legends survive in Middle Welsh, and not in French, but we know that Breton, Cornish, and Welsh minstrels frequented French courts, where they may have sung of them.[22] Yet if the Grail romances have appeared to many readers to evoke Celtic rather than Christian prototypes, it is not because the romances make any explicit reference to these pagan legends—they never mention them at all, whereas they cite Christian tales constantly—but, rather, as we shall see, because they are so clearly not reducible to Christianity, or perhaps one should say, to a particular type of Christianity. If these romances were allegories, then the Grail would be a container of the Eucharist and the Quest would be an act of penance, yet there is much in these motifs that exceeds and even contradicts the practice of these Christian sacraments. If these romances were allegories, *X* would equal *Y*, with no remainder left over, yet there exists such a remainder. Throughout these works, the Grail knight learns not just to see *through* the literal, physical level of reality in order to apprehend the figurative, spiritual level, as happens in allegory, but to see *in* the literal, physical level, and to savor it. In their insistence upon valorizing the immanent, and not just the transcendent; the sensible, and not just the intelligible; and the concrete image, and not just the abstract concept, these romances resist, even as they recall, the theological and pastoral developments of their time.

---

and *The Grail: From Celtic Myth to Christian Symbol* (New York: Columbia University Press, 1963). Jean Marx provides an exhaustive discussion of this Celtic thesis in his *La Légende Arthurienne et le Graal* (Paris: Presses Universitaires de France, 1952).

22. On Bledhri, one such Welsh minstrel, see Second Continuation, British Library Add. 36614; Thomas of Britain, *Tristran*, vv. 2120–24; and Gerald of Wales, *Descriptio Kambriae*, ed. Dimock, bk. 1, chap. 17, p. 202.

The Eucharist and the Grail

In the course of his wanderings, a knight—Perceval, Gawain, Lancelot, or Bors—arrives at a mysterious manor, where he receives hospitality in accordance with medieval customs. After he dismounts, his horse is taken away, fed, brushed, and stabled. He is escorted into an antechamber where his armor is removed and he is given a beautiful garment to wear. He is then led into a magnificent hall, where he meets the lord of the manor, who is sitting by the fire. The lord welcomes him, apologizes for not being able to stand to greet him, and converses with him courteously for several minutes. When the lord finally asks for dinner, the servants place the table on the trestles; they set the table with tablecloths, knives, and salt cellars; and they bring the lord and his guest a basin of water, with which they wash their hands. Other members of the household join them at the table, but the lord honors the knight by having him sit next to him and share his dish. It is while they are seated at table that the knight beholds a series of damsels and youths proceed, one after the other, across the hall, each carrying an object into an adjacent room.[23] According to Chrétien's *Conte du Graal*, the first text to describe this procession, after some youths had passed, "A damsel, fair, noble, and well attired, who came with the youths was holding a grail between her two hands."[24] In addition to the damsel who carries the Grail, another damsel or a squire transports a lance from whose tip a stream of blood runs down its shaft. Other items may be borne in the procession, such as a broken sword, a silver serving platter, and a bier with a dead body, sometimes with the broken sword lying on top of it. These objects may be preceded by candelabra filled with lit candles, by censers, or by doves or angels bearing censers. The knight marvels at this procession, but the lord (if he is present) provides no explanation to his guest of what they are beholding.

Repeated throughout all of the Grail romances,[25] often multiple

23. See Jean Frappier, "Le Cortège du Graal," in *Lumière du Graal*, ed. René Nelli (Paris: Cahiers du Sud, 1951), 175–22.

24. "Un graal entre ses .II. meins / une damoisele tenoit, / qui aviau les vallez venoit, / et bele et gente et bien senee," Chrétien de Troyes, *Conte du Graal*, ed. Méla, vv. 3158–61.

25. This scene features in the First (ed. Roach, vol. 1, vv. 1327–68), Second (ed. Roach, v. 32396), and Manassier's Third Continuation (ed. Roach, vv. 32616–22 and vv. 42488–522), as well as in Gerbert de Montreuil's Continuation (ed. Oswald, vol. 3, vv. 17021–38), the *Didot-Perceval*, ed. Roach (245), *Lancelot*, ed. Micha (vol. 2,377), and *Perlesvaus*, ed. Nitze and Jenkins (Branch VI, 119). The *Didot-Perceval*, ed. Roach, is the one text that identifies the bearer of the

times in a single romance, the scene of the Grail procession seems at once profoundly meaningful and profoundly ambiguous. What is the Grail? Who is the damsel carrying this vessel? Where is she taking it, and for what purpose? On one level, the answer to these questions is that the Grail is a relic of Christ's Passion, now being used as a container of the Eucharist.[26] In the seventy years between the 1180s and the 1240s, when all the major Grail romances were being composed, a Eucharistic fervor spread throughout western Europe unlike anything that Christendom had witnessed before.[27] Whether in the cathedral schools or the universities, virtually every important theologian of this time wrote a treatise about the Eucharist, contributing to a total of what Gary Macy has estimated to be 250 works on this subject.[28] At the Fourth Lateran Council of 1215, the Church required for the first time that all Christians receive Holy Communion at least once a year. It was not only the clergy who expressed enthusiasm for this sacrament. In towns and villages as well as in monasteries, people longed to behold the Eucharist, and, when they did so, they occasionally witnessed miracles related to this sacrament,[29] miracles that were

---

Grail as a youth rather than a damsel (245). The *Queste del Saint Graal* does not include this series of damsels and youths, but it begins and ends with meals where the Grail is present.

26. On the Eucharist and the Grail, see Patrick J. Geary, "Liturgical Perspective in *La Queste del Saint Graal,*" *Historical Reflections / Réflexions historiques* 12 (1985): 205–17; Richard O'Gorman, "Ecclesiastical Tradition and the Holy Grail," *Australian Journal of French Studies* 6 (1969): 3–8; Jean Frappier, "Le Graal et l'Hostie (*Conte del Graal*, v. 6413–6431)," in *Les Romans du Graal aux XIIe et XIIIe siècles. Strasbourg (29 mars–3 avril 1954)* (Paris: Editions du Centre National de la Recherche Scientifique, 1956), 63–81; Eugene Anitchkof, "Le Saint Graal et les rites eucharistiques," *Romania* 55 (1927): 174–94. See also Alexandre Leupin, *Fiction et incarnation: Littérature et théologie au Moyen Age* (Paris: Flammarion, 1993).

27. On the Eucharist at this time, see Thomas M. Izbicki, *The Eucharist in Medieval Canon Law* (Cambridge: Cambridge University Press, 2015); J. G. Snoek, *Medieval Piety from Relics to the Eucharist: A Process of Mutual Interaction* (Leiden: Brill, 1995); Gary Macy, *The Theologies of the Eucharist in the Early Scholastic Period: A Study of the Salvific Function of the Sacrament According to the Theologians c. 1080–c. 1220* (Oxford: Clarendon Press, 1984), and "The Theology of the Eucharist in the High Middle Ages," in *A Companion to the Eucharist in the Middle Ages*, ed. Ian Christopher Levy, Gary Macy, and Kristen Van Ausdall (Leiden: Brill, 2012), 365–98; David N. Bell, *Many Mansions: An Introduction to the Development and Diversity of Medieval Theology, West and East* (Collegeville, MN: Cistercian Publications, 1996), chap. 15, "The Mystery of the Eucharist," 285–302; Brian Stock, *The Implications of Literarcy: Written Language and Models of Interpretation in the Eleventh and Twelfth Centuries* (Princeton, NJ: Princeton University Press, 1987), esp. chap. 3, "The Eucharist and Nature," 241–314; and Peter Browe, *Die Verehrung der Eucharistie im Mittelalter* (Munich: M. Hueber, 1933), and *Die eucharisten Wunder des Mittelalters* (Breslau: Verlag Müller and Seiffert, 1938).

28. See Macy, "Theology of the Eucharist in the High Middle Ages," 373.

29. See Miri Rubin, "Popular Attitudes to the Eucharist," in *A Companion to the Eucharist in the Middle Ages*, ed. Levy, Macy, and Van Ausdall, 447–68, and *Corpus Christi: The Eucharist in Late Medieval Culture* (Cambridge: Cambridge University Press, 1991).

taken seriously and addressed by the theologians in their works.[30] In this context, it is no surprise that the sanctity of the Grail is explicitly linked to the sanctity of the Host. In Chrétien's *Conte du Graal* and its Continuations, the Grail is said to contain the Eucharist, which the damsel (who is often identified as the Fisher King's daughter) is bringing to the Fisher King's father, who waits unseen in the nearby room. On another level, however, the answer to these questions about the Grail is that the vessel is a kind of splendid cornucopia. During these same years, the practice of knighthood—which originally had no connection to Christianity—was increasingly being sanctified: the process by which youths ascended to knightly status was being ritualized as dubbing, and the standard of behavior to which knights were expected to adhere was being formalized as the code of chivalry.[31] In this context, it is no surprise that the sanctity of the Grail is explicitly linked not always to the Host but always to knights and noble maidens. In the Vulgate Cycle, the Grail that is borne in the procession does not contain the Eucharist, and the damsel who carries it (who is identified as King Pelles's daughter) does so to no evident purpose. If the "Holy Grail" continues to signify in our cultural vocabulary today an ultimate object of desire which can only be attained with great difficulty, it is because, though its meaning derives from the Eucharistic theology and spirituality of the Middle Ages, that meaning was never, even during that time, limited to a Christian register. The question of what the Grail is, in the end, is the question of how to interpret what we see, with its surface and hidden levels of meaning.

At the turn of the twelfth and thirteenth centuries, both clerics and laypeople were becoming increasingly aware that the literal, physical appearance of the Eucharist concealed a figurative, spiritual reality. According to the synoptic Gospels, at the Last Supper, Christ took bread, blessed it, broke it, and gave it to his disciples, telling them, "Take it and eat. This is my body."[32] He then took the cup, offered thanks, and gave

30. See Ian Christopher Levy, "The Eucharist and Canon Law in the High Middle Ages," in *A Companion to the Eucharist in the Middle Ages*, ed. Levy, Macy, and Van Ausdall, 399–45.

31. On the connection between stories of the Grail and chivalry, see Raluca L. Radulescu, "How Christian Is Chivalry?" in *Christianity and Romance in Medieval England*, ed. Field, Hardman, and Sweeney, 69–83; Ad Putter, "Knights and Clerics at the Court of Champagne: Chrétien de Troyes' *Conte du Graal*," in *Pulp Fictions of Medieval England: Essays in Popular Romance*, ed. Nicola McDonald (Manchester: Manchester University Press, 2004), 171–96; Pauline Matarasso, *The Redemption of Chivalry: A Study of the "Queste del Saint Graal"* (Geneva: Droz, 1979); Jean Frappier, "Le Graal et la chevalerie," *Romania* 75 (1954): 165–210.

32. "Accipite, et comedite: hoc est corpus meum," Matt. 26:26. Cf. Mark 14:22; Luke 22:19; and 1 Cor. 11:24.

it to the followers, saying, "Drink, all of you. This is my blood."[33] From these words, clerics had always known that the bread of the Eucharist was Christ's Body and the wine of this sacrament his Blood, but they were not always sure what this identification meant, given that the food and drink continues to appear to one's senses just as it did before the moment of consecration. Some medieval theologians lamented the way in which our sensory perception of the Eucharist prevents us from apprehending its true nature. Borrowing the language of Aristotle's categories, they explained that, while the accidents (that is, the external, sensory appearance) of the Eucharist may remain those of the bread and wine, the essence or substance of this sacrament (that is, its internal, intelligible reality) is transformed—or, as they would ultimately put it, "transubstantiated"[34]—during this process. Peter Lombard dwells upon "the accidents, . . . namely, appearance, taste, and weight, . . . by which the body of Christ . . . is hidden,"[35] which ensure that "one thing is seen, and another is understood."[36] While some theologians stressed the failure of the senses to apprehend the true nature of the Eucharist, others stressed the success of these faculties in giving us some access to God. Anselm of Laon, for example, argues that because God knows human beings to be incapable of uniting with God spiritually, as angels do, on account of their bodies, he has provided us with the Eucharist, which enables us to unite with him physically.[37] Hugh of Saint-Victor maintains that Christ uses the appearance of the bread and wine on the altar, which can be perceived through our senses, to enable us to apprehend the reality of the Body and Blood of Christ, which can only be believed through grace.[38] Even as these latter theologians were affirm-

33. "Bibite ex hoc omnes. Hic est enim sanguis meus," Matt. 26:28. Cf. Mark 14:24; Luke 22:17 and 22:20; and 1 Cor. 11:25.

34. Hildebert of Lavardin, the archbishop of Tours, may have been the first to use the word "transubstantiation" to describe the transformation of the bread and wine into the Body and Blood of Christ in this sacrament around 1079. See Joseph Goering, "The Invention of Transubstantiation," *Traditio* 46 (1991): 147–70. The Fourth Lateran Council famously employed this term in its first canon. See *Decrees of the Ecumenical Councils*, ed. Tanner, vol. 1, "Lateran IV," 229.

35. "de accidentibus, . . . scilicet de speciebus et sapore et pondere, . . . quibus corpus Christi . . . tegitur," Peter Lombard, *Sententiae*, vol. 2, IV, 12, 1, p. 304.

36. "aliud videtur, aliud intelligitur," ibid., vol. 2, IV, 11, 2, p. 299. Cf. Augustine, Sermo 272, *Ad infantes, de sacramento*, PL, vol. 38. col. 1247.

37. Anselm of Laon, *Sententie Anselmi*, in *Systematische Sentenzen*, ed. Franz Pl. Bliemetzrieder, 2 vols. (Münster: Verlag der Aschendorffschen Verlagsbuchhandlung, 1919), vol. 1, 47–153, at 116–18.

38. Hugh of Saint-Victor's two main treatments of the Eucharist appear in his *Commentariorum in "Hierarchiam Coelestem" S Dionysii Areopagitae*, PL, vol. 175, cols. 923–1154, bk. II, chap. 1, at cols. 940–49, and in *De sacramentis christianae fidei*, PL, vol. 176, cols. 173–608, esp. bk. II, pt. 8, chap. 7, cols. 389–91.

ing the usefulness of sense perception in apprehending the true nature of the Eucharist, ordinary people were confirming their arguments by claiming to have miraculously seen the Body and Blood of Christ in the bread and the wine. Alger of Liège,[39] Alan of Lille,[40] Gerald of Wales,[41] Caesarius of Heisterbach,[42] and Matthew Paris,[43] among others, tell stories of Hosts that appeared to their beholders to be lumps of flesh or to bleed,[44] whether in order to correct those who denied the Real Presence of Christ in the Eucharist (such as the Cathar heretics) or in order to reward those who did believe in it. In one of his hymns, Thomas Aquinas asks, "Jesus, whom I now behold veiled, when will I be granted what I so desire, to behold you openly, with your face unveiled, and be truly blessed, seeing your glory?,"[45] but visionaries of this time were regularly said to have been accorded that grace.

At the same time as people were becoming increasingly conscious of the Eucharist, authors of the Grail romances were representing the Grail as a container of the Eucharist, which sometimes enables spectators to apprehend with their senses, not just the literal, physical appearance of the Host, but its figurative, spiritual reality. According to these romances, the Grail is a kind of ciborium, that is, the liturgical vessel, which, during the Mass, holds within it the Body of Christ. In Chrétien's *Conte du Graal,* long after Perceval has left the Fisher King's manor, he meets a hermit who informs him, "The rich Fisher King, I believe, is the son of the king who has himself served from the Grail. . . . A single host . . . is brought to him in that Grail."[46] In Gerbert de Montreuil's Continuation, it is said of Perceval's aunt that "she often

39. Alger of Liège, *De sacramentis corporis et sanguinis Dominici,* PL, vol. 180, cols. 727–856.

40. Alan of Lille, *De fide Catholica contra haereticos,* PL, vol. 210, cols. 303–430, esp. bk. 1, chap. 57–62, cols. 359–66.

41. See Gerald of Wales, *Gemma ecclesiastica,* ed. Brewer, in *Opera,* ed. Brewer, vol. 2, at distinctio 1, chap. 11, 40–42. Browe, *Wunder,* 19, gives references to the many other witnesses to the Arras miracle.

42. Caesarius of Heisterbach includes more than fifty such accounts in his *Dialogus miraculorum,* ed. Strange, vol. 2, IX, pp. 164–217, and in his unfinished *Libri octo miraculorum,* in *Die Fragmente der "Libri VIII miraculorum" des Caesarius von Heisterbach,* ed. Aloys Meister (Rome: Spithöver, 1901), I, 1–3, pp. 1–9 passim.

43. Matthew Paris (attributed), *La Estoire de Seint Aedward le Rei,* ed. Kathryn Young Wallace (London: Anglo-Norman Text Society, 1983), XLI, vv. 4927–32.

44. See the *Verba seniorum,* PL 73, cols. 851–1066, at cols. 978–79, and Peter Damian, *Opuscula,* PL 145, XXXIV, cols. 571–90, at col. 573.

45. "Iesu, quem velatum nunc aspicio, / quando fiet illud quod tam cupio, / ut te revelata cernens facie / visu sim beatus tuae gloriae?" Thomas Aquinas, "Adore devote, latens veritas," in *One Hundred Latin Hymns: Ambrose to Aquinas,* ed. and trans. Peter G. Walsh with Christopher Husch, Dumbarton Oaks Medieval Library (Cambridge, MA: Harvard University Press, 2012), 366–69, at 368.

46. "Et del Riche Pescheor croi / que il est filz a celui roi / qui del graal servir se fet / . . . / . . .

saw many legions of angels who go gently to the house of the Fisher King and hold among them the Holy Grail and the Host inside."[47] Even more often than the Grail romances depict the Grail as a kind of ciborium, they portray it as a kind of chalice, that is, the liturgical vessel, which, during the Mass, holds within it the Blood of Christ. In the Second Continuation, the Third Continuation, the *Didot-Perceval*, and *Perlesvaus*, the Grail is identified, following Robert de Boron's *Joseph d'Arimathie*, as the basin in which Joseph of Arimathea had collected Christ's blood after his Deposition from the Cross. A damsel who is speaking with Perceval in the Second Continuation, for example, refers to "the Grail, which is so beautiful and precious, in which the bright and glorious blood of the King of Kings was received when he was hung upon the Cross."[48] From the First Continuation onward, the Lance is identified as the lance the Roman centurion Longinus used to pierce Christ's side during the Crucifixion,[49] which continues to drip his blood even now; at the end of the *Queste del Saint Graal*, the Grail collects the blood trickling from this Lance. While in all of the Grail romances, the Grail is identified as a container of the Eucharist, in some of them, it is a liturgical vessel that enables one to behold openly the presence of Christ in this sacrament. In the *Queste del Saint Graal*, Galahad, Bors, Perceval, and nine other knights see a bishop remove from the Grail a Host that is "made in the semblance of bread"[50] but that, when it is raised aloft, receives into it "a figure in the form of a child."[51] In *Perlesvaus*, when Gawain looks above the Grail, we are told, "He saw . . . a man crucified on a Cross, and the Lance was plunged into his side."[52] While the Grail contains the Eucharist, like any ciborium or chalice, it contains it in such a way that the accidental qualities of the bread disappear and the essential nature of Christ's body appears in its place.

As both clerics and laypeople became increasingly conscious of the

---

une seule hoiste / . . . l'an en cel graal li porte," Chrétien de Troyes, *Conte du Graal*, ed. Méla, vv. 6343–49.

47. "Sovent voit mainte legion, / des angles qui vont sanz desroi / a l'ostel le Pescheor Roi / et entr'aus le saint Graal tienent, / et l'oist ens," Gerbert de Montreuil, Continuation, ed. Williams, vol. 2, vv. 8792–96.

48. "li Graaux, / qui tant est biaux et precïeux, / an quoi li clers sens glorïeux / dou roi des rois fu receüz / qant il an la croiz fu panduz," Second Continuation, ed. Roach, vv. 25792–96.

49. See Konrad Burdach, *Der Gral: Forschungen über seinen Ursprung und seinen Zusammenhang mit der Longinuslegende* (Darmstadt: Wisseneschaftliche Buchgesellschaft, 1938; rpt., 1974).

50. "en samblance de pain," *Queste del Saint Graal*, ed. Gros, 360, p. 1164.

51. "une figure en fourme d'enfant," ibid.

52. "Et voit . . . un home cloufichié en une croiz, et li estoit le glaive fichié eu costé," *Perlesvaus*, ed. Nitze and Jenkins, Branch VI, 119–20.

figurative, spiritual reality that lies underneath the Eucharist's literal, physical appearance, they became increasingly reverent toward this sacrament. The clerics who displayed the Eucharist to the people drew attention to the Real Presence of Christ within it. In the past, ecclesiastics had occasionally authorized processions with the Blessed Sacrament, especially during Palm Sunday and other days during Holy Week. Now, at the turn of the twelfth and thirteenth centuries, such processions became more frequent and more elaborate. In 1209, Saint Juliana of Cornillon, a member of a circle of Flemish women with special devotion to the Eucharist, had a vision inspiring her to promote a feast day dedicated to the Body of Christ. A regular part of the Feast of Corpus Christi would be the procession of the Blessed Sacrament, which would be carried through the streets, brought to the church, and displayed to the congregation during the Mass. As ecclesiastics carried the Eucharist through the streets in order to honor it during feast days, they also carried it through the streets in order to bring it to invalids who needed to receive Holy Communion, especially as they approached death. In 1219, Pope Honorius III writes of the priest bearing the Host, "Let him bear it before his breast with all reverence and trepidation, with lights always preceding him."[53] While priests were expected to transport the Host to ailing parishioners, we know that in some circumstances, women—who were typically responsible for tending to the sick—sought out the sacrament from priests and brought it back with them.[54] In the past, when the priest had celebrated the Eucharist in minsters and cathedrals, he had performed this rite in the choir, separated from the rest of the church by an iron grille, with his back toward the congregation.[55] Now, at the turn of the twelfth and thirteenth centuries, during the consecration, the choir doors would be flung open and the priest would elevate the Host, so that the transformation of the species could be beheld by all.[56] In 1210, Odo of Sully, the bishop of Paris, prescribes how the priest should first hold the Host

53. "referat . . . ante pectus cum omni reverentia et timore, semper tamen lumine praecedente," Honorius III, in *Corpus Corpus iuris canonici*: *Decretum Magister Gratiani*, ed. Richter and Friedberg, vol. 2, lib. III, tit. XLI, cap. 10, col. 642.

54. See Herbert of Clairvaux, *De miraculis*, in PL, vol. 185, cols. 1271–381, at III, 20, col. 1370, and Gerald of Wales, *Gemma ecclesiastica*, ed. Brewer, distinctio 1, chap. 11, 40.

55. See Patrick J. Geary, "Liturgical Perspective in *La Queste del Saint Graal*," *Historical Reflections / Réflexions historiques* 12 (1985): 205–17.

56. On the elevation of the Host, see M. Camile Hontoir, "La Dévotion au saint Sacrement chez les premiers cisterciens (XIIe–XIIIe siècles)," *Studia eucharistica DCC anni a condito festo sanctissimi Corporis Christi* (Antwerp: De Nederlandsche Boekhandel, 1946), 132–56, and V. L. Kennedy, "The Moment of Consecration and the Elevation of the Host," *Mediaeval Studies* 6 (1944): 121–50.

before his breast and then, once it has been consecrated, raise it high enough so as to be seen by all.[57] He should turn to the right and the left, so that congregants on both sides could be sure to behold it.[58] In order to highlight the solemnity of this moment of consecration, clerics began to light additional candles at the altar; to swing thuribles, so that incense filled the sanctuary; and to ring the church bells, so that all people, near and far, could know that the bread and wine had just become the Body and Blood of Christ. As clerics drew attention to the Real Presence in the Eucharist, the people recognized the holiness of this sacrament. In the beginning of the thirteenth century, whether they were watching the Eucharist be displayed during a procession or watching it be elevated during the Mass, they began to bow or kneel down before it[59] and to pray, at first silently and then aloud.[60] So intense was the visual apprehension of the Host that it was believed to constitute a kind of "communion with the eyes," which, to some degree, took the place of the communion with the mouth.[61] As the people knew the literal, physical appearance of the Eucharist, as bread, to be accompanied by its figurative, spiritual essence, as the Body of Christ, they knew to revere what they saw.

At the same time as people were becoming increasingly reverent toward the Eucharist, the authors of the Grail romances were representing people as reverent toward the Grail on account of the figurative, spiritual reality they knew to lie underneath its literal, physical appearance. The damsel who displays the Grail to the knight and the other guests draws attention to the Real Presence within it. Like the ecclesiastics who bear the Blessed Sacrament, she takes part in a procession with her companions, and she does so not once but multiple times. Like the ecclesiastics who bear the Blessed Sacrament, she is ac-

57. See Kennedy, "Moment of Consecration," 122n4.

58. See William of Auxerre, *Summa de officiis ecclesiasticiis*, ed. Franz Fischer (Cologne: http://guillelmus.uni-koeln.de/tcrit/tcrit_prologu, 2007–13), bk. II, tractate 1, chap. 9, no. 17.

59. See the 1219 regulation of Honorius III and Gregory IX, *Corpus iuris canonici*: *Decretum Magister Gratiani*, ed. Richter and Friedberg, vol. 2, bk. III, tit. 41, chap. 10, p. 642. From the twelfth century, and even more the thirteenth century, the rules of the orders and the synodal decrees insisted on people kneeling in the street when the procession passed by with the viaticum.

60. Peter Lombard, *In Totum Psalterium Commentarii*, in PL, vol. 191, cols. 31–1296, at col. 1648, and Hervaeus of Bourg-Dieu, *Commentariorum In Isaiam Libri Octo*, in PL, vol. 181, cols. 591–1692, at cols. 937–38, write about the proper attitude of communicants toward this sacrament.

61. While one risked eternal damnation if one ate the Host in a state of sin, one exposed oneself to no such danger if one merely gazed upon the Host. See William of Auxerre, *Summa aurea*, ed. Jean Ribaillier, 4 vols. (Paris: Centre National de la Recherche Scientifique, 1980–85), esp. vol. 4, Liber IV, Tractatus 7, qu. 3, pp. 170–71.

companied by attendants who carry candles and swing censers. Like the ecclesiastics who elevate the Host, she carries the Grail high above her head. In the First Continuation, for example, it is said, "Between her hands and high up she carried the Holy Grail uncovered."[62] Honoring the Grail through her solemn and repeated movements, the damsel honors it through her very person. She is, and must be, a virgin in order to perform this sacred function. In the Third Continuation, the lord states, "She who carries the Grail is . . . a virginal maiden, for otherwise, . . . she would never hold it in her hands."[63] The damsel is beautiful, but with a virginal beauty, like that of the most holy of women. In the *Prose Lancelot,* it is said, "She was so beautiful . . . that a more beautiful woman has never been seen, save only for the Virgin Mother who carried Jesus Christ in her womb."[64] As the damsel draws attention to the Real Presence in the Grail, the knights in the hall recognize the holiness of this sacrament. Like people beholding the Eucharist, they bow down or kneel, and they pray or sing. In the *Prose Lancelot,* we are told, "As the damsel passed in front of the table, each [knight] knelt down before the holy vessel."[65] In the *Didot-Perceval,* we are informed, "When the lord saw it, he bowed, . . . and all those of the household did likewise."[66] All of these texts accentuate not just what happens during the procession, but what the Grail knight and the other guests see happen. In Chrétien's *Conte du Graal,* it is said of the damsel and her companions, "The youth saw them pass";[67] with each course that was served, "He saw the Grail pass by completely uncovered before them."[68] As the members of the procession pass through the house three times, the First Continuation observes, "Those who were in the hall saw them openly. And Gawain, together with all of them, saw them with the others."[69] The Third Continuation relates of Perceval, "The Welshman gazed at them intently, so that he left off eating. Three times the Grail

62. "Entre ses mains en haut aporte / le saint Graal a descovert," First Continuation, ed. Roach, vol. 1, vv. 1362–63.

63. "celle qui porte lou Graal / si est . . . / pucelle virge, n'autremant, / . . . / ja antre ses mains nou tenist," Manassier, Third Continuation, ed. Roach, vv. 32793–97.

64. "si estoit si bele . . . que onques plus bele feme ne fu veue fors solement la Virge Mere qui porta Jhesu Crist dedens son ventre," *Lancelot,* ed. Micha, vol. 2, 376–77.

65. "Et ensi come la damoisele passe par devant le dois, si s'agenoille chescuns devant le saint vaissel," ibid., vol. 2, 377.

66. "Et quant li sire le vit, si l'enclina, . . . et tot cil de l'ostel autresi," *Didot-Perceval,* ed. Roach, 245.

67. "Et li vallez les vit passer," Chrétien de Troyes, *Conte du Graal,* ed. Méla, v. 3180.

68. "par devant els trespaser voit / lo graal trestot descovert," ibid., vv. 3237–38.

69. "cil qui en la sale erent / les virent tot apertement. / Et Gavains trestot ensement / avec les autres les veoit," First Continuation, ed. Roach, vol. 1, vv. 1412–15.

passed among the tables, so that Perceval saw it well and all those who were there."[70] Even when the knights dining in the hall are not specifically described as marveling at the Grail and the Lance, they are described as gazing at these objects in a manner that implies such wonderment. As the Grail knight knows the literal, physical appearance of the Grail, as a vessel, to be accompanied by its figurative, spiritual essence, as a ciborium or chalice, he knows to worship what he sees.

Recognizing and revering the Eucharist, both clerics and laypeople appreciated that the nourishment it provided was figurative and spiritual. The Eucharist is said to be unusually delicious to those who know how to taste it. Jacques de Vitry writes of the holy woman Marie d'Oignies, "She felt all delight and all sweetness of taste in her perceptions, not only inwardly, in her soul, but even in her mouth, where it was like honey."[71] Caesarius of Heisterbach writes of a certain Cistercian nun, "Whenever she makes her communion, she tastes from the sacred body as much sweetness as if she had received honey."[72] So delicious is the Eucharist that it was thought to accommodate itself to each communicant's dietary preferences. Bernard of Clairvaux attests, "For the various desires of the soul, it is essential that the taste of the divine presence be varied too, and that the infused flavor of supernal sweetness should titillate in different ways the palate of the desiring soul."[73] If the Eucharist tastes delightful, however, it is not because it is literal, physical food, like honey or another dish which appeals to one's senses, but, rather, because it is figurative, spiritual food, like the "bread of angels,"[74] which appeals to one's soul. Peter Lombard writes, "Just as bread refreshes and sustains the body more than other foods and wine gladdens and inebriates a man, so the flesh of Christ spiritually refreshes and nourishes the interior man more than other

70. "Molt les regarda li Galois, / tant que le mengier en laissa. / Par trois foiees trespa[ssa] / parmi les tables li Graax, / si que bien le vit Percevaux / et tuit cil qui laienz estoient," Manassier, Third Continuation, ed. Roach, vv. 41962–67.

71. "omnem delactionenem et omnem saporis suavitatem in eius perceptione non solum interius in animo, sed etiam in ore eius mellifluo sentiebat," Jacques de Vitry, *Vita Marie de Oegnies*, ed. R. B. C. Huyegens, CCCM (Turnhout: Brepols 2012), 43–164, 8, 145.

72. "quando communicat tantam ex ipso sacro corpore dulcedinem sentiat, ac si mel receperit," Caesarius of Heisterbach, *Dialogus miraculorum*, ed. Strange, vol. 2, IX, 39, p. 195.

73. "Oportet namque pro variis animae desideriis divinae gustum praesentiae variari, et infusum saporem supernae dulcedinis diversa appetentis animi aliter atque aliter oblectare palatum," Bernard of Clairvaux, *Sermones super Cantica canticorum*, in *Opera*, ed. Jean Leclercq, Charles H. Talbot, and Henri Rochais, 8 vols. (Rome: Editiones Cistercienses, 1957–77), vol. 1, XXXI, 7, p. 223. Cf. Wisd. of Sol. 16:20–21.

74. "panem angelorum," Ps. 78:25.

graces."[75] Because the Eucharist is such figurative, spiritual food, the virtuous were believed to be able to live on it alone. In the late twelfth century, a young girl from the village of Cudot, near Sens, was said to have survived on the Host alone for forty years. At the same time, another young girl from Vernon, on the border of France and Normandy, was said to have eaten nothing but this sacrament for decades. Both of these incidents happened in the region of northern France and Flanders, where Chrétien and the other authors of the first Grail romances lived, and both were well publicized. Because the Eucharist is figurative, spiritual food, the sinful were believed to be incapable of truly consuming it. William of Auxerre maintains that while all Christians who take communion receive the Body and Blood "sacramentally,"[76] that is, under the species of bread and wine, only those in a state of grace receive it "spiritually,"[77] that is, in such a manner that they are incorporated into Christ. Peter Lombard reiterates this distinction, claiming that while all receive "the flesh of Christ assumed from the Virgin,"[78] only the good receive "the mystical flesh."[79] If the Christian is nourished by the Eucharist, it is, not insofar as it is literal, physical food, which preserves the body, but insofar as it is figurative, spiritual sustenance, which preserves the soul.[80]

Recognizing and revering the Grail, the people in the Grail romances appreciate that the nourishment it provides is, likewise, not just literal and physical but figurative and spiritual. While the food offered by the Grail is literal, physical food, which the knights take into their mouths, eat, and digest, it is, like the Eucharist, unusually delicious to those who know how to taste it. In the *Queste del Saint Graal*, when Perceval, Bors, and Galahad consume the food at the table of the Grail, it is said, "It seemed to them so sweet and marvelous that it was their opinion that all of the delights that one could think of in one's heart could not compare to it."[81] So delectable is the food provided by the Grail that it accommodates itself to each communicant's tastes.

75. "sicut panis prae ceteris cibis corpus reficit et sustentat, et vinum hominem laetificat atque inebriat, sic caro Christi interiorem hominem plus ceteris gratiis spiritualiter reficit et saginat," Peter Lombard, *Sententiae*, IV, 8, 7, p. 285. Cf. Luke 15:4–5.

76. "sacramentaliter," William of Auxerre, *Summa de officiis ecclesiasticiis*, ed. Fischer, Liber Primus, Pars Prima, II, 14, 1.

77. "spiritualiter," ibid.

78. "carnem Christi de Virgine sumptam," Peter Lombard, *Sententiae*, IV, 9, 2, p. 288.

79. "mystica . . . caro," ibid.

80. See Caroline Walker Bynum, *Holy Feast and Holy Fast: The Religious Significance of Food to Medieval Women* (Berkeley: University of California Press, 1987), 31–69.

81. "tant lor sembloit douce et merveilleuse qu'il lor ert avis que toutes les soatumes que l'em porroit penser de cuer ne s'i poïssent acomparagier," *Queste del Saint Graal*, ed. Sommer, 344, 270.

When Arthur expresses gratitude that God has fed the knights of the Round Table through the Grail, Gawain points out, "Sire, . . . there is another thing that you do not know, for there is no man here who was not served with whatever he asked and thought of."[82] Yet if the food provided by the Grail tastes delicious, it is not just because it is literal, physical food, which appeals to our senses, but because it is figurative, spiritual food, which appeals to one's soul. For that reason, the virtuous can live on it alone. In Chrétien's *Conte du Graal,* we recall, the Fisher King's father is said to survive only on the Host, which the damsel brings to him in the Grail. The hermit states, "With a single Host, which is brought to him in this Grail, the holy man sustains and strengthens his life. . . . He needs nothing more than the host that comes in the Grail."[83] In the Third Continuation, when Perceval becomes a hermit at the end of the romance, he too is kept alive by the Grail's contents alone. It is said, "He ate and drank nothing but what God sent him by the Holy Grail."[84] Because the Grail furnishes figurative, spiritual food, the sinful cannot consume it. In the *Prose Lancelot,* when Gawain is in the presence of the Grail, he receives nothing for dinner. As he beholds his empty plate, the text relates, "He knew well that he had done something wrong because he had nothing to eat like the others did."[85] If the Grail provides extraordinarily delicious food, but only to those who are graced to receive it, it is because, like the Eucharist, it is designed to satisfy human beings' most essential hunger.

Yet even as the authors of the Grail romances stress the figurative, spiritual meaning of the Grail, as a container of the Eucharist, they also stress its literal, physical value, as a rich and ornate vessel. To state the obvious, the Grail is described throughout the romances not as a ciborium or a chalice, but as a "grail" (*graal* in Old French). Though the Grail legend is of northern origin, the word *graal* derives from *greala* in Catalan or *grazala* in Occitan, in which languages it indicated a rich and expensive platter, large enough to contain a substantial piece of meat or fish. In Chrétien's *Conte du Graal,* the hermit informs Perceval

82. "Sire, . . . encor i a il autre chose que vos ne savés, car il n'a chaiens home qui n'ait esté servis de quanqu'il demandoit et pensoit," *Queste del Saint Graal,* ed. Gros, 17, p. 829.

83. "D'une sole hoiste li sainz hom, / que l'an en cel graal li porte, / sa vie sostient et conforte / . . . / . . . autre chose ne li covient / que l'oiste qui el graal vient," Chrétien de Troyes, *Conte du Graal,* ed. Méla, vv. 6348–54.

84. "ne onques n'i menja ne but / fors ce que Diex li anveoit / par le Saint Graal," Manassier, Third Continuation, ed. Roach, vv. 42586–88.

85. "bien set qu'il a mespris en aucune chose, por quoi il n'a eu a mengier ausi come li autres," *Lancelot,* ed. Micha, vol. 2, 378.

that the Grail does not contain "pike, lamprey, or salmon,"[86] as if it might be assumed to serve one of these types of fish. In the First Continuation, it is said of Gawain that at a dinner, "He saw more than one hundred boars' heads on silver grails."[87] Because of the rich matter it was made out of, because of the distinguished people who owned it, and because of the choice foods it contained, a grail seems to have been a luxury item, common to aristocratic households at this time. As grails in general were secular rather than ecclesiastical vessels, it is not surprising that the romances commonly represent the Grail in such a manner. In the *Conte du Graal*, Chrétien writes, "The Grail . . . was of pure gold. The Grail had precious stones of many kinds, the richest and the costliest that were in the sea or on the earth. The Grail's stones surpassed all others, without doubt."[88] In the *Prose Lancelot*, Lancelot says to himself that "the vessel . . . was to his mind the richest ever seen by mortal man";[89] Gawain perceives it as "the richest vessel that had ever been seen by an earthly man."[90] These knights perceive the Grail as a material object, albeit the best of all material objects. Never described as a ciborium or a chalice, the Grail is, all the more remarkably, never subordinated to the Host it is said to contain. When the hermit in Chrétien's *Conte du Graal* informs Perceval that the Grail contains the Eucharist, he refers to the Host as "the Host which comes in the Grail,"[91] as if, in some strange way, it is not the Grail that receives its power from the Host, but the Host that receives its power from this container. After the hermit explains that a single Host sustains and comforts the Fisher King's father, one might expect him to exclaim, "Such a holy thing is the Host!" or "Such a holy person is the man!" but, instead, he declares, "Such a holy thing is the Grail!"[92] as if, again in some strange way, it is the Grail that imparts its holiness upon the sacrament.

86. "luz ne lamproies ne salmon," Chrétien de Troyes, *Conte du Graal*, ed. Méla, v. 6347.

87. "Vit sor graals d'argent ester / plus de cent testes de sangler," First Continuation, ed. Roach, vol. 1, vv. 9648–49. See also *Girart de Roussillon*, ed. W. Mary Hackett, 3 vols. (Paris: A. and J. Picard, 1953–55), vol. 1, v. 1622, and Helinand de Froidmont, *Chronicon*, col. 815. For discussion, see Barber, *Holy Grail*, 95–96.

88. "Li graaus . . . / de fin or esmeré estoit, / pierres precïeuses avoit / el graal de maintes menieres, / des plus riches et des plus chieres / qui an mer ne an terre soient. / Totes autres pierres passoientt / celes do graal sanz dotance," Chrétien de Troyes, *Conte du Graal*, ed. Méla, vv. 3170–77.

89. "le vessel . . . est li plus riches a son esciant qui onques fust veuz par home mortel," *Lancelot*, ed. Micha, vol. 4, 206.

90. "le plus riche vaissel qui onques par home terrien fust veus, et fu fes en samblance de calice, et le tint plus haut de son chief si que totes voies l'enclinoit," ibid., vol. 2, 377.

91. "l'oiste qui el graal vient," Chrétien de Troyes, *Conte du Graal*, ed. Méla, v. 6354.

92. "Tante sainte chose est li Graals," ibid., v. 6351.

Indeed, the title of Chrétien's romance is not "The Story of the Eucharist," but "The Story of the Grail,"[93] a story that is described as "the best story that has ever been recounted in a royal court."[94] Though medieval people knew to move beyond the literal, physical level of the Eucharist and to apprehend the figurative, spiritual level as well, the authors of these romances insist upon the Grail's materiality and luxuriousness.

Even as the authors of the Grail romances represent the Grail as revered on account of its figurative, spiritual meaning, they represent it as acquiring this meaning only because it is revered, especially by such a beautiful and high-born company. The damsel who carries the Grail does so in a manner that establishes its holiness to all who watch her. She does not leave the Grail lying on the table in the hall, holding a boar's head for the guests to consume, like the grails Gawain sees in the First Continuation, but, rather, carries it aloft across the hall three times, as part of a formal procession, and, in doing so, identifies it to the spectators as something to be worshiped rather than used. If the Grail knights treat the Grail as a sacred object, it is not because they perceive in it any special sacredness, but because they are imitating their fellow guests in doing so. In the *Prose Lancelot*, Gawain and Lancelot see the other knights in the hall sit down silently at the table and pray in the presence of the Grail. It is said of Gawain, "Without anyone saying a word, . . . he sat down with the others and saw that they were all at their prayers and orisons."[95] It is said of Lancelot, "He acted like the others and sat down before the king. He saw that they were at prayer and orisons, and he acted as the others did."[96] When the damsel passes by with the Grail, "Everyone knelt before of the holy vessel, and he did as well."[97] By introducing the Grail from these knights' point of view, the text makes this vessel seem holy, not because of itself, but because of the procession that frames it and because of the audience that responds to this procession. If the knights do not initially perceive the Grail as a relic or a liturgical vessel, it is, in part, because it is borne not by ecclesiastics, as one would expect in a Eucharistic procession, but by a damsel, who obviously has not been ordained and who thus occupies no such institutional role. Even if some unseen priest in the

93. "li contes do greal," ibid., v. 64.

94. "lo meillor conte, / qui soit contez en cort reial," ibid., vv. 62–63.

95. "sans ce que nus i deist mot, . . . si s'asiet avec les autres et voit qu'il soit tuit en proieres et en oroisons," *Lancelot*, ed. Micha, vol. 2, 376.

96. "si fait autel come li autre et s'asiet devant le roi et voit qu'il sont tuit em prieres et en oroison et il fait autel comme li autre font," ibid., vol. 4. 205.

97. "s'agenoille chascuns devant le saint vessel et il si fait ausi," ibid., vol. 4, 206.

manor has consecrated the Host, the damsel should not be carrying it. However frequently women may have borne the Host to invalids, this practice was regularly condemned by canonists,[98] such as Regino of Prüm,[99] Burchard of Worms,[100] Ivo of Chartres,[101] and Gratian.[102] In the *Prose Lancelot*, the damsel stands out in the secular, and not merely sacred, nature of her attractions: she has braided hair, a marker of female adornment; despite her seemingly virginal beauty, she becomes an object of desire for Gawain; and she will eventually trick Lancelot into sleeping with her and will bear his child Galahad. In the Third Continuation, she is praised as much for her royal birth as for her chastity. Even as medieval people knew to move beyond the literal, physical level of the procession and to apprehend its figurative, spiritual level as well, the authors of these romances emphasize the Grail's association with a beautiful and noble young lady.

As much as the authors of the Grail romances represent the Grail as providing figurative, spiritual sustenance, they also depict it as furnishing literal, physical nourishment, marvelous in its deliciousness and in the manner in which it is served. They describe the food offered by the Grail with such precision that it seems to be genuine, material food. In the *Conte du Graal*, Chrétien writes, "They were not stingy in bringing to the table food or wine, which was pleasant and delightful."[103] He lists among the courses a haunch of venison cooked in hot pepper; baskets of dates, figs, nutmeg, cloves, and pomegranates; and, for dessert, Alexandrian gingerbread, electuaries, and pliris. In the Third Continuation, it is said, "The tables . . . were all laden with delectable dishes and were replenished so elegantly that a man could not name a dish but that he would find it there, along with wines of every kind."[104]

98. See Gary Macy, *The Hidden History of Women's Ordination: Female Clergy in the Medieval West* (Oxford: Oxford University Press, 2007), 60–63, and Michel Lauwers, "Les Femmes et l'eucharistie dans l'Occident médiéval: Interdits, transgressions, dévotions," in *Practiques de l'eucharistie dans les Eglises d'Orient et d'Occient (Antiquité et Moyen Age)*, ed. Nicole Bériou et al. (Paris: Institut d'études augustiniennes, 2009), 445–76.

99. Regino of Prüm, *Libri duo de synodalibus causis et Disciplinis Ecclesiasticis*, ed. F. G. A. Wasserschleben (Lipsiae: Sumtibus G. Engelmann, 1840; rpt., Graz: Akademische Druck- u. Verlagsanstalt, 1964), L. 1, c. 121, pp. 77–78.

100. Burchard of Worms, *Decretorum libri XX*, in PL, vol. 140, cols. 557–1058, at V, 40, col. 758.

101. Ivo of Chartres, *Decretum*, cols. 47–1036, at Pars II, cap. 39, col. 169.

102. *Corpus iuris canonici*: *Decretum Magister Gratiani*, ed. Richter and Friedberg, vol. 1, Distinctio II, *De consecratione*, c. 29, col. 1323.

103. "C'an n'aporte mie a dangier / les mes ne lo vin a la table, / tant sont plaissant et delitable," Chrétien de Troyes, *Conte du Graal*, ed. Méla, vv. 3251–52.

104. "devant les tables / . . . furent de mes delitables / trestotes les tables garnies / et si gentement replenies / que honme nonmer ne seüst / nul mes que trouver ne peüst, / et vin de toutes les manieres," Manassier, Third Contination, ed. Roach, vv. 42501–7.

The emphasis is not upon the spiritual gratification felt by those who consume this food but upon the physical pleasure of diners who feast on such delicious, abundant, and varied fare. The authors of the texts describe the food not as a miracle, provided by God, like the manna given to the Israelites, but as a marvel, provided by the Grail itself, like a horn of plenty. The fact that the Grail can move of its own accord, to the puzzlement of the Grail knights, accentuates its marvelousness. While Chrétien hints at the ability of the Grail to zoom about on its own,[105] the First Continuation makes this trait explicit: "The rich Grail, which served without anyone carrying it, served them very honorably. It came and went swiftly before all the knights,"[106] so that "the good knight . . . wondered intently about what was thus serving him."[107] In the First, Second, and Third Continuations and in the *Prose Lancelot*, and the *Queste del Saint Graal*, the Grail continues to furnish the diners with one course after another quickly, efficiently, and, for the Grail knights, delightfully. There is nothing in these romances to support the claims of Roger Sherman Loomis or Jean Marx that the Grail derives from Celtic cauldrons, horns, or hampers. Still, the inclination of these scholars to look for the origin of the Grail outside Christian sources reflects the fact that in the marvelous food it provides and in the marvelous manner in which it provides that food, the Grail cannot be accounted for in exclusively Christian terms.

In the end, while the Grail romances build upon contemporary Eucharistic theology and ritual, the Grail they represent cannot be limited to this thought and this practice. Among those who interpret these texts objectively, as a Christian allegory, there is little consensus as to what exactly this vessel means. For Albert Pauphilet, writing about *Queste del Saint Graal*, "The Quest of the Grail . . . is nothing . . . but the search for God, the effort of men of good will toward the knowledge of God."[108] For Etienne Gilson, in contrast, "The Grail . . . is manifestly nothing but the grace of the Holy Spirit, in which the Christian soul

105. See Chrétien de Troyes, *Conte du Graal*, ed. Méla, v. 3170 and vv. 3238–40.

106. "Le riche Graal, qui servoit / qui que nus ne le soztenoit, / molt par les sert honestement, / et va et vient isnelement / par devant toz les chevaliers," First Continuation, ed. Roach, vol. 1, vv. 13281–85.

107. "li buens chevaliers. / . . . / trop durement se merveilla / de ce que il servoit ensi," ibid., vv. 13291–301.

108. Albert Pauphilet, *Etudes sur la "Queste del Saint Graal" attribuée à Gautier Map* (Paris: Honoré Champion, 1921; rev. ed., 1980), at 25. Pauphilet modified his views in *Les Legs du Moyen Age: Etudes de la littérature médiévale* (Melun: Librairie d'Argences, 1950), where he too comes to write, "Le Graal est une manifestation de la grâce de Dieu" (191).

delights."[109] While Pauphilet sees the Grail as representing the Godhead and Gilson sees it as representing the grace bestowed by this deity, the fact that both critics are able to use passages from the text to support their arguments reflects the challenge inherent in reading the Grail as any one Christian signified.[110] In the Vulgate Cycle, those passages in the text that come closest to defining what the Grail is speak of it, not objectively, as a Christian allegory, but subjectively, as a universal sensation. In Robert de Boron's *Joseph d'Arimathie,* when Joseph of Arimathea's followers ask their leader Petrus what to call the vessel, he replies, "Those who wish to call it rightly and give it a name, in our view, will call it the Grail [*Graal*], which . . . agrees with [*agree*] and pleases those who can stay in its company."[111] In the *Queste del Saint Graal,* when Galahad gazes inside the Grail as he alone is permitted to do, he thanks God for having granted his wish "to see what I have always desired."[112] At the point in which this most Christian of all the Grail romances defines the Grail, it defines it not as the repository of the Eucharist but as the repository of that which one most longs for, and, in doing so, it allows it to acquire a meaning that extends beyond adherents to the Catholic faith. Ultimately, the Grail is not an idea that must be understood with the intellect, like the hypostatic union, but an image that must be seen with the eyes, namely, that of a rich and splendid vessel. It is not transcendent, something seen *through* matter, but immanent, something seen *in* matter. By demonstrating that the Grail possesses a literary meaning that can never be rendered in philosophical or theological terms,[113] the authors of these romances demonstrate the essential untranslatability of this object.

109. Etienne Gilson, "La Mystique de la grace dans la *Queste del Saint Graal,*" *Romania* 51 (1925): 321–47; rpt. in *Les Idées et les lettres,* 2nd ed. (Paris: J. Vrin, 1955), 56–91, at 62.

110. Pauline Matarasso, *The Redemption of Chivalry: A Study of the "Queste del Saint Graal"* (Geneva: Droz, 1979), and A. M. L. Williams, in *The Adventures of the Holy Grail: A Study of "La Queste del Saint Graal"* (Oxford: Peter Lang, 2001), emphasize this point.

111. "Cil qui bien le vodront clamer et metre non, a nos esïent, le clameront le Graal, qu'il agree . . . et anbelit a cez qui tel sont qu'i en sa conpaignie peuent durer," Robert de Boron, *Joseph d'Arimathie,* ed. O'Gorman, 263.

112. "veoir ce que j'ai touz jors desirré," *Queste del Saint Graal,* ed. Pauphilet, 278.

113. On the connection between the Grail and apophatic theology, see Leupin, *Le Graal et la littérature,* 134–35.

Penance, Pilgrimage, and the Quest

Having seen or heard of the Grail, the knight embarks on a "quest" (*queste*). He is determined that, through his own actions, he will locate that which he seeks. He may seek the Grail or the Lance[114] or the Fisher King's manor, where these objects are housed,[115] or he may seek the knowledge of who is served from the Grail and why the Lance bleeds.[116] At the same time, he does not know where that which he seeks is located. In the *Queste del Saint Graal,* when a damsel asks Lancelot where he is going, he replies, "In truth, damsel . . . I do not know, except there where adventure leads me, for I do not know in what region I can find that which I go seeking."[117] Because the knight does not know where to look for the Grail, the Lance, or the Fisher King's manor, he does not travel in a straight line, but, rather, "wanders" (*erre*) with a goal but no route toward that goal. As eager as he may be to find the object of his desire, he expects some other power to decide whether or not he shall succeed in this endeavor and, if he shall succeed, when he will do so. It is this combination of the knight's determination to find what he seeks and his recognition that it is not, in the end, his determination that will matter that makes his journey a quest.[118]

A constant theme in all of the Grail romances, the Quest, like the Grail itself, seems at once profoundly meaningful and profoundly ambiguous. What is the connection between the Grail knight's search for the Grail and his wanderings? Given that he does not know where the Grail is to be found, why does he assume that he will track it down by erring? On one level, the answer to these questions is that the Quest is a penitential voyage, like a pilgrimage. Since the earliest years of the Church, Christians had undergone penance for their sins, but this sacrament had been infrequent, often undertaken only on one's deathbed, and standardized, with set penances assigned for sins. Now, at the turn

114. See Chrétien de Troyes, *Conte du Graal,* ed. Méla, vv. 4665–69.

115. See the *Didot-Perceval,* ed. Roach, p. 151.

116. See Chrétien de Troyes, *Conte du Graal,* ed. Méla, vv. 4657–59.

117. "Certes . . . damoisele, je ne sai, fors la ou aventure me menra. Car je ne sai mie bien quel part je puisse trover ce que je vois querant," *Queste del Saint Graal,* ed. Gros, 176, p. 983.

118. On questing, see Richard W. Kauper, *Chivalry and Violence in Medieval Europe* (Oxford: Oxford University Press, 2001), 253–72; E. Jane Burns, "Quest and Questioning in the *Conte du Graal,*" *Romance Philology* 41 (1988): 251–66; Richard Hartman, La *Quête et la croisade: Villehardouin, Clari et le "Lancelot en prose"* (New York: Postillion Press, 1977); and *Voyage, quête, pèlerinage dans la littérature et la civilisation médiévales* (Aix-en-Provence: CUERMA, 1976).

of the twelfth and thirteenth centuries, masters and former students of the University of Paris, including Alan of Lille, Jacques de Vitry, Peter the Chanter, Peter Lombard, Robert of Courson, Robert of Flamborough, and Thomas of Chobham, were spearheading the shift to a more frequent and individualized approach to the sacrament.[119] The Fourth Lateran Council, which reflected these clerics' work, demanded for the first time in Church history that all Christians confess their sins at least once a year. Since at least the fourth century, Christians had undertaken pilgrimages to holy sites, perhaps to see famous relics and to be cured by their miraculous powers, perhaps to walk on the earth where a saint or Christ himself had trod, or perhaps merely to divert themselves with new sights and experiences. Now, at the turn of the twelfth and thirteenth centuries, Christians were trekking in massive numbers, not only to local shrines, but to the cathedrals of Canterbury, Compostela, and Rome and even to Jerusalem. The Crusades were considered to be one particular type of pilgrimage, and the knights who embarked on them were termed "pilgrims" (*peregrini*).[120] On another level, however, the Quest is not a penitential journey but what we might call a psychological voyage. The Grail knight progresses not just from sin to salvation, like the hero of a Christian allegory, but from youth to maturity; from lack of self-consciousness to awareness of an unknown failing; and from being at home in the world to alienation from his environment. If a "quest" continues to signify in our cultural vocabulary today the errant pursuit of an object of desire, it is because, again, though its meaning derives from the penitential theology and spirituality of the Middle Ages, that meaning was never, even at this time, limited to a Christian context. The question of how to complete the Quest is, in the end, the question of how to act, given the simultaneous control and lack of control we possess over what happens to us.

At this time period, Christians undertook penance for their sins with a renewed vigor. In part, they relied upon their own efforts in doing so. As students of this sacrament understood it, the penitent must begin with the first step in this process, which was "contrition of the heart" (*cordis contritio*). Alan of Lille writes, "Contrition is the bitterness of mind with which someone grieves about sins he has perpetrated, with

119. See John W. Baldwin, *Masters, Princes, and Merchants: The Social Views of Peter the Chanter and His Circle*, 2 vols. (Princeton, NJ: Princeton University Press, 1970).

120. See Antonio L. Furtado, "The Crusader's Grail," in *The Grail, the Quest, and the World of Arthur*, ed. Norris J. Lacy (Rochester, NY: D. S. Brewer, 2008), 28–47.

the intention of not relapsing into them."[121] The penitent recalls the sins he has committed and, repenting, resolves never to commit them again. It is a commonplace in these theologians' writings that, if the penitent is truly contrite, he will sigh from the depths of his heart, weep as he recalls his sins, and blush as he speaks of them. Thomas of Chobham advises the confessor to consider "if he sighs, if he weeps, [and] if he blushes"[122] as evidence of the penitent's change of heart. In the course of his ruminations, he gains a new perspective upon his earlier actions, seeing in them a depravity he had not perceived earlier. Contrite, the penitent proceeds to the second step of penance, which is "confession of the mouth" (*oris confessio*). He visits his priest, who welcomes him and urges him to make a full confession, despite whatever shame he may feel in acknowledging his sins. He listens to the confessor warn him about the eternal damnation he risks if he refrains from making a full confession, but he also listens to him reassure him about the eternal salvation he will enjoy if he does reject his misdeeds. Robert of Flamborough cites the confessor as praying, "May he receive you, he who, in an embrace of all, spread out his arms on the Cross."[123] After having confessed his sins, the penitent undergoes the final step of the sacrament, "the satisfaction of work" (*operis satisfactio*). He receives from his confessor a task to perform in order to atone for his sins, most commonly, fasts, prayers, and almsgiving, but also, for serious sins, pilgrimage. He is then blessed and absolved. As in confession, blushing is a sign of interior contrition, Thomas writes, "In satisfaction, devotion is a sign of remission."[124] If the penitent can learn to step back from his own life and to look critically upon what he has done; if he can develop what was called a "narration"[125] of his sins, with all of the circumstantial details that can give definition to this account; and if he can then willingly undergo suffering for these sins, he will have made progress toward wiping away these misdeeds. Yet even as the penitent relied upon his own efforts in rejecting sin, he also relied upon God's

121. "Contritio est mentis amaritudo qua aliquis dolet de perpetratis peccatis cum intentione non relabendi," Alan of Lille, *Liber poentitentialis*, ed. Jean Longère, 2 vols. (Louvain: Editions Nauwelaerts, 1965), vol. 2, vol. 4, chap. 4, p. 164.

122. "si gemat, si ploret, si erubescat," Thomas of Chobham, *Summa confessorum*, ed. F. Broomfield (Louvain: Editions Nauwelaerts, 1968), art. 6, dist. 1, qu. I[a], p. 241.

123. "Suscipiat te ille qui in omnium amplexus brachia sua expandit in cruce," Robert of Flamborough, *Liber poentitentialis*, ed. J. J. Francis Firth (Toronto: Pontifical Institute of Mediaeval Studies, 1971), bk. 1, chap. 1, p. 56.

124. "in satisfactione ipsa devotio signum est remissionis," Thomas of Chobham, *Summa confessorum*, ed. Broomfield, art. 1, qu. II[a], p. 8.

125. "narratio," "Robert Grosseteste's Treatise on Confession, *Deus est*," ed. Siegfried Wenzel, *Franciscan Studies* 30 (1970): 218–93, at II, 1.

assistance in this process. Peter Lombard writes, commenting upon Augustine, "The will of man, which he has naturally, is not able to raise itself efficaciously to will the good or to execute it in deed unless it is freed and aided by grace: freed so that he may will, and aided so that he may carry out what he wills."[126] If a Christian rejects his sins, it is because "operating grace" (*gratia operans*) has already enabled his will to incline toward this direction and because "cooperating grace" (*gratia cooperans*) has then helped him to carry out this intention. So essential is grace to the process of penance, writes this master, that contrition, confession, and satisfaction are insufficient without this "infusion of grace"[127] as well. When the penitent humbly prays, "Have mercy on me, God,"[128] as Peter the Chanter puts it, or "I will abstain henceforth from sins . . . if the Lord helps me through grace,"[129] as Robert of Courson puts it, he acknowledges God's necessary role in helping him turn from sin and persevere in his good intentions. In the development of a penitential consciousness, Christians do what they can to turn away from sin, but they also recognize that they will only be able to succeed in this endeavor with God's assistance.

As a form of penance for their sins, Christians undertook pilgrimages. Again, they relied upon their own efforts in doing so. Ordinary pilgrims made solemn vows, typically on their knees, before relics, to make this trip.[130] Crusaders also made such vows, often after a preacher had given a stirring sermon in favor of such military campaigns to an assembly of knights. When Pope Urban II preached at Clermont in 1095, when Bernard of Clairvaux preached at Vézelay in 1146, or when Foulques of Neuilly preached in Champagne in 1199, large number of knights announced their intention to head overseas to fight the Saracens, affixing crosses to their clothing as an outward sign of their inward intentions. Jacques de Vitry commends those "who, accepting the Sign of the Cross out of the devotion of a contrite heart, pledged

126. "voluntas hominis, quam naturaliter habet, non valet erigi ad bonum efficaciter volendum vel opere implendum, nisi per gratiam liberetur et adjuvetur: liberetur quidem ut velit, et adjuvetur ut perficiat," Peter Lombard, *Sententiae*, II, 25, 9, p. 469.

127. "gratie infusio," Peter the Chanter, *Verbum adbreviatum*, II, 49, p. 787.

128. "Miserere mei, Deus," ibid., II, 49, p. 788.

129. "Abstinebo amodo a peccatis . . . si dominus per gratiam me adiuvet," V. L. Kennedy, "Robert Courson on Penance," *Mediaeval Studies* 7 (1945): 291–336 or (1939): 325.

130. For discussion of such vows, see James A. Brundage, *Medieval Canon Law and the Crusader* (Madison: University of Wisconsin Press, 1969), 30–65; James A. Brundage, "*Cruce signari*: The Rite for Taking the Cross in England," *Traditio* 22 (1966): 289–310; Kenneth Pennington, "The Rite for Taking the Cross in the Twelfth Century," *Traditio* 30 (1974): 429–35; and M. Cecilia Gaposchkin, "From Pilgrimage to Crusade: The Liturgy of Departure, 1095–1300," *Speculum* 88, no. 1 (2013): 44–91.

themselves to the Lord in a solemn vow."[131] After having taken these vows, pilgrims were expected to travel as "strangers [*peregrini*] and exiles . . . on earth."[132] Church Fathers like Augustine,[133] Columbanus of Iona,[134] and Gregory the Great[135] had compared Christians in general to wayfarers, willing to use the bed, table, or cup in this earthly hostel, but eager to press on to their heavenly destination. Medieval clerics echoed this language when speaking of pilgrims in particular. Jacques de Vitry writes, for example, "The pilgrim . . . should not delight in the sight of beautiful things, nor should he rejoice until he has returned to his homeland."[136] In his haste to attain his destination, Jacques states, the pilgrim should commit himself to being gone for a year and a day and should spend no more than one night at a particular lodging, because "his ultimate destination should be ever in his mind."[137] At a time when those who could afford to do so traveled with servants, packhorses, and luggage, pilgrims were expected to depart with only a staff and a scrip. While crusaders obviously needed to bring with them horses, armor, and weapons, they too were praised if they observed, as much as possible, a penitential frugality.[138] Yet even as Christians strove, with their vows, their continuous travel, and their light baggage, to complete their pilgrimages, they also recognized that they needed God's assistance in doing so. To travel at this time was

131. "multos . . . qui signum crucis accipientes ex cordis contriti devotione se ipsos voto solempni Domino obligaverunt," Jacques de Vitry, *Sermo II*, in *Crusade Propaganda and Ideology: Model Sermons for the Preaching of the Cross*, ed. Christoph T. Maier (Cambridge: Cambridge University Press, 2000), 100–127, at 116–17.

132. "peregrini et hospites . . . super terram," Heb. 11:13. Saint Paul describes Abraham, Sarah, Isaac, and Jacob as agreeing to look upon themselves in this manner because of their willingness to live far from the land that was promised them. He affirms, more generally. "While we are in the body, we have wandered far from God [*dum sumus in corpore, peregrinamur a Domino*]" (2 Cor. 5:6). The Apostle Peter calls upon other Christians to act "like exiles and strangers [*tamquam advenas et peregrinos*]," 1 Pet. 2:11.

133. See Augustine, *De doctrina Christiana*, I, 4 (Cf. Rom. 1:20); *Tractatus in Johannem* XL, 10; and *Sermo* LXXX, 7.

134. See Columbanus, *Opera*, ed. G. S. M. Walker (Dublin: Dublin Institute for Advanced Studies, 1957), Sermon V, 86.

135. Gregory the Great, *Moralia in Job*, ed. Adriaen, VIII, 54, pp. 453–55. See also Gerhart B. Ladner, "*Homo viator*: Mediaeval Ideas on Alienation and Order," *Speculum* 42, no. 2 (1967): 233–59.

136. Jacques de Vitry, Paris BN, MS Latin 3284, fol. 129v. Quoted in Debra J. Birch, "Jacques de Vitry and the Ideology of Pilgrimage," in *Pilgrimage Explored*, ed. J. Stopford (York: University of York Press, 1999), 84. This sermon is unedited.

137. Ibid. Cf. Bernard of Clairvaux, *Sermones de tempore*, PL 183, Sermo 6, 1, cols. 35–360, at col. 183.

138. See Jean de Joinville, *Historiens et chroniqueurs du Moyen Age: Robert de Clari, Villehardouin, Joinville, Froissart, Commynes*, ed. Albert Pauphilet, Bibliothèque de la Pléiade (Paris: Gallimard, 1952), 203–372, at chap. 27, 233.

to risk one's life, whether from shipwreck, robbery, or the attack of foreign soldiers. As Jacques asks, "What greater alms are there but . . . to expose oneself to dangers on land, dangers at sea, the dangers of thieves, the dangers of predators, the dangers of battles for the love of the Crucified?"[139] Given the way in which crusaders necessarily placed themselves in the hands of God, they attributed their success or failure in their campaigns to his will. When the crusaders succeeded in taking Damietta without resistance during the Fifth Crusade, the chronicler Oliver of Paderborn states, it was "so that the victory may be ascribed to the Son of God alone."[140] When the Saracens then dealt the crusaders a serious blow, Oliver also observes, "Gloom seized our men, but not despair. For we know that this suffering was the punishment of sin."[141] In the development of a penitential consciousness, Christians did what they could on pilgrimages, but they also recognized that they would only be able to triumph in this endeavor with God's assistance.

In undertaking pilgrimages, Christians left their homes, their families, and their loved ones. It was their decision to do so. In the Gospels, Christ had promised everlasting life to "every man who has left behind home, or brothers, or sisters, or father, or mother, or wife, or children, or fields for my name's sake."[142] Because pilgrims saw themselves as acting upon Christ's admonition, they saw themselves as justified in quitting those who were closest to them. Though crusaders' property was hypothetically under Church protection while they were gone, their wives, children, and subjects often suffered from the rapacity of their neighbors during this time.[143] As crusaders saw it, the travails their dependents undergo during their absence is evidence, not of their abandonment of their social responsibilities, but of the sacrifices they are willing to make for Christ. Jacques de Vitry writes that there are no

139. "que maior elemosina quam . . . periculis in terra, periculis in mare, periculis latronum, periculis predonum, periculis preliorum pro amore Crucifixi se exponere?" Jacques de Vitry, *Sermo II*, ed. Maier, 112–13.

140. "ut soli filio Dei ascribatur victoria," Oliver of Paderborn, *Historia Damiatina*, in *Die Schriften des Kölner Domscholasters, späteren Bischofs von Paderborn und Kardinal-Bischofs von S. Sabina, Oliverus*, ed. H. Hoogeweg (Tübingen: Litterarischer Verein in Stuttgart, 1894), 159–280, at chap. 32, 225.

141. "Meror nostros occupavit, sed nulla desperatio. Pro certo enim habemus, quod pena peccati fuit hec castigatio," ibid., chap. 29, 217.

142. "Et omnis qui reliquerit domum, vel fratres, aut sorores, aut patrem, aut matrem, aut uxorem, aut filios, aut agros propter nomen meum," Matt. 19:29.

143. Jean de Joinville writes in *Vie de Saint Louis*, ed. Pauphilet, that when King Louis was pressuring him to accompany him on the Eighth Crusade, he refused, citing the sufferings his people had undergone during his absence on the Seventh Crusade (734–35).

greater alms one can offer God than "to leave behind one's wife, children, kinsmen, and birthplace for the service of Christ alone."[144] He recounts the story of a knight who, about to go off on crusade, gazed upon his little children for a time, so that, he explained, "I will leave them behind with greater anguish of mind for Christ and I will merit more to be in the presence of the Lord."[145] Affection for one's wife, children, or subjects, including concern for their material well-being, was considered carnal love, in contrast to the spiritual love one bears toward God. While carnal love was not sinful in and of itself, it could become so if it was allowed to interfere with spiritual love. Gilbert de Tournai writes that by taking up the sign of the Cross, one defeats not only infernal enemies but "carnal feelings":[146] "Fatherland, property, parents, wife, and children are fetters that hold one back."[147] While love for one's children, one's wife, or one's subjects is love for something mundane and immanent in this world, unworthy of the true pilgrim of Christ, love for God, as measured by the rejection of these other beings, is something glorious and transcendent, for which one stands to be honored.

As Christians underwent penance with a renewed vigor at this time, the Grail romances represent the Grail knight as undergoing penance.[148] In part, this knight relies upon his own efforts in doing so. Looking back upon his actions, he recognizes the sinfulness of what he has done, and he feels contrition for these misdeeds. He sighs, weeps, and blushes. In Chrétien's *Conte du Graal*, it is said of Perceval that "He . . . sighed from the depths of his heart because he felt that he had committed misdeeds toward God, of which he repented greatly."[149] Perceval's confessor observes that "the water drips from his eyes, running

144. "uxorem, filios, consanguineos et natale solum pro Christi servitio relinquere, periculis in terra, periculis in mare, periculis latronum, periculis predonum," Jacques de Vitry, *Sermo II*, 112–13.

145. "cum majori angustia mentis pro Christo relinquam illos, et ita magis merear apud Dominum," Jacques de Vitry, *The Exempla or Illustrative Stories from the "Sermones Vulgares,"* ed. Thomas Frederick Crane (London: D. Nutt, 1890; rpt., New York: Burt Franklin, 1971), CXXIV, 188.

146. "affectus carnales," Gilbert of Tournai, *Sermo III*, in *Crusade Propaganda and Ideology*, 198–209, at 202–3.

147. "Patria, propria, parentes, uxor, et filii vincula sunt retinentia," ibid., at 202–3.

148. Much less has been written about penance and the Grail than about the Eucharist and the Grail. See Richard O'Gorman, "Robert de Boron's *Joseph d'Arimathie* and the Sacrament of Penance," in *Conjunctures: Medieval Studies in Honor of Douglas Kelly*, ed. Keith Busby and Norris J. Lacy (Amsterdam: Rodopi, 1994), 375–85.

149. "cil . . . / . . . sospire del cuer del ventre / por ce que mesfaiz se santoit / vers Deu, dont molt se repantoit," Chrétien de Troyes, *Conte du Graal*, ed. Méla, vv. 6259–62.

down to his chin."[150] In the Second Continuation[151] and in Gerbert de Montreuil's Continuation,[152] it is noted likewise that as Perceval recalls his sins, he sighs and weeps. Repenting of his sins, the Grail knight visits a hermit, who welcomes him and urges him to make a full confession, despite whatever shame he may feel on acknowledging his sins. Here, too, the knight listens as the confessor warns him of the dangers he will face if he does not fully admit his sins and of the benefits he will receive if he does do so. In the *Queste del Saint Graal,* he hears the confessor say, echoing Robert of Flamborough, "Know truly . . . that Our Lord spread out his arms to receive every sinner, both you and the others who address themselves to him."[153] Feeling contrition for his sins and confessing them to the hermit, the knight willingly receives a penance through which he can atone for his misdeeds. In Chrétien's *Conte du Graal,* Perceval is told to believe in God and to go to church every day, whenever possible; to honor worthy men, good women, and priests; and (in some manuscripts) to aid maidens, widows, and orphans. In the *Queste del Saint Graal,* Lancelot is instructed to attend Mass whenever possible, to confess his sins every week, to wear a hair shirt, and to fast. The knight finally receives a blessing and absolution. Yet even as the knight strives, through his own efforts, to atone for his sins, he also recognizes that he needs God's assistance in this process as well. In Chrétien's *Conte du Graal,* the hermit instructs Perceval, "Pray God to have mercy upon the soul of his sinner."[154] In Gerbert de Montreuil's Continuation, Perceval laments the fact that he will never expiate his sins "if [God] will not look upon me with pity."[155] In the development of a penitential consciousness, the knight does what he can to turn away from his sins, but he also recognizes that he can do so fully only with God's aid.

As Christians undertook pilgrimages, the Grail knight undertakes the Quest of the Holy Grail. This knight relies upon his own efforts in doing so. As he decides to go on the Quest, he swears a solemn vow. In Chrétien's *Conte du Graal,* Perceval declares that he will establish why the Lance bleeds, and the fifty knights who follow his example

150. "el menton corrant / l'eve des iauz li degotoit," ibid., vv. 6278–79.

151. See Second Continuation, ed. Roach, vv. 23886–88.

152. See Gerbert de Montreuil, Continuation, ed. Oswald, vol. 3, vv. 14200–201.

153. "Or sachiez . . . a Nostre Sires estendus ses bras conme pour recevoir cascun peceour, et vous et les autres qui a lui s'adrecent," *Queste del Saint Graal,* ed. Gros, 84, p. 894.

154. "prie Deu que merci ait / de l'ame de son pecheor," Chrétien de Troyes, *Conte du Graal,* ed. Méla, vv. 6296–97.

155. "s'il ne me regarde em pité," Gerbert de Montreuil, Continuation, ed. Williams, vol. 1, v. 2745.

"swear"[156] an oath to this effect. In the *Queste del Saint Graal*, Gawain formally announces, "I make here and now a vow"[157] to embark on the Quest, and the other knights of the Round Table imitate him in doing so. As part of his vow, the knight swears not to spend more than one night in a particular lodging[158] and not to return to court for a year and a day, or more if necessary.[159] While it is not stated, it is clear that he travels without servants, packhorses, or luggage and, instead, relies upon the hospitality of the castles or the hermitages he passes. Yet even as the knight strives to complete the Quest, he also recognizes that he needs God's assistance in doing so. Time and again, it is affirmed that God and God alone directs the knight errant on his way and that he alone enables him to reach his destination. In Gerbert de Montreuil's Continuation, it is said that "Perceval . . . set off, and he prayed to the Creator to lead him by the right way, the right turn, and the straightest path there where the Fisher King resided."[160] In the *Queste del Saint Graal*, a voice advises Perceval, "In whatever place you go, God will be conducting you."[161] The challenge of the Grail knight is not just to set out on the Quest and to persevere on this endeavor, but to place himself in the hands of God and allow himself to go wherever God wishes. In *Perlesvaus*, when Gawain asks a hermit the way to the Fisher King's manor, he is told, "Sire, . . . no one can teach you the way if the will of God does not lead you there."[162] As much as the knight may strive on the Quest and may hope, as a result of this effort, to attain the Grail, he knows that grace is given, as a reward, and not earned, as a payment. Though he may pray for that grace, he knows that he cannot demand, let alone expect, to receive it. In the development of a penitential consciousness, the knight does what he can in undertaking the Quest, but he also recognizes that he will only be able to succeed in this endeavor with God's help.

In undertaking the Quest of the Holy Grail, the Grail knight also leaves his home, his family, and his loved ones. In Chrétien's *Conte*

156. "jure," Chrétien de Troyes, *Conte du Graal*, ed. Méla, v. 4673.

157. "par coi endroit moi fais orendroit un veu," *Queste del Saint Graal*, ed. Gros, 17, p. 829.

158. See Chrétien de Troyes, *Conte du Graal*, ed. Méla, vv. 4057–58 and *Didot-Perceval*, ed. Roach, 151.

159. See *Queste del Saint Graal*, ed. Gros, 17, p. 829.

160. "Et Perchevax . . . / s'en vait, et prie al Creator / que droite voie, et le droit tor / et droiturier chemin le maint / la ou li Rois Peschiere maint," Gerbert de Montreuil, Continuation, ed. Oswald, vol. 3, vv. 16840–44.

161. "en quel lieu que tu ailles, te conduira Dix," *Queste del Saint Graal*, ed. Gros, 156, p. 962.

162. "Sire, . . . nus ne vos puet enseignier la voie, se la volentez Dieu ne vos i mainne," *Perlesvaus*, ed. Nitze and Jenkins, III, p. 62.

du Graal, when Perceval is first riding away to become a knight, he looks back and sees that his mother has collapsed by the bridge behind him. Instead of returning to tend to her, he whips his hunter, so that they plunge into the forest ahead. He later learns that his mother was so distressed at his departure that she died of grief. When he is leaving Blancheflor, the damsel begs him to remain with her, marry her, and continue to protect her lands, but to no avail. Even when she has her people join their pleas to hers, "Whatever they said to him had no effect."[163] The knight makes clear that it is not a personal preference but an impersonal demand that makes him depart. In the Second Continuation, Perceval explains that he cannot remain with Blancheflor for even one more day: "I have undertaken a journey that, for all the wealth in Friesland, I would not abandon."[164] Later, when Perceval is leaving his sister, the damsel again begs that he stay with her and take care of her, but he informs her, "I cannot put off the work I have undertaken."[165] In Gerbert de Montreuil's Continuation, Perceval installs his sister in the house of a kinswoman, and in the *Queste del Saint Graal*, he allows her to accompany Galahad, Bors, and himself for a time, but elsewhere he merely departs, promising to return to her when he can. It is not only women who are distressed by the departure of the Grail knights. In the *Queste del Saint Graal*, Arthur grieves that the fellowship of the Round Table will be disbanded, that he will no longer have so many great knights with him, and that many of these knights, so dear to him, will never return from this Quest. As these ladies, damsels, and king see it, it is not only that they love the Grail knight and wish he would stay with them; it is also that he has a responsibility toward them, whether familial, amorous, or feudal, and that, by departing or persisting on the Quest, he fails to live up to that responsibility. Like the crusaders, the Grail knight exhibits what Pauphilet terms "the sublime egotism of virtue."[166] In his pursuit of a peregrinatory vocation, he recognizes his duty toward others and he promises to fulfill that duty as soon as he is able, but, at least for now, he insists that he must be allowed to fulfill his duty toward God instead.

Yet if the Grail knight repents of his misdeeds, it is not only because he is a medieval Christian undergoing the sacrament of penance but because he is a young man becoming conscious of himself for the first

163. "n'a mestier quant qu'il li dient," Chrétien de Troyes, *Conte du Graal*, ed. Méla, v. 2866.

164. "j'ai une voie antreprise / que por trestot l'avoir de Frise / ne la lairoie je a fere," Second Continuation, ed. Roach, vv. 22895–97.

165. "je ne puis metre an delai / iceste euvre que j'ai amprise," ibid., vv. 24206–7.

166. Pauphilet, *Etudes sur la "Queste del Saint Graal,"* 45.

time and because that self-consciousness necessarily entails an awareness of his guilt. Throughout the Grail romances, sin is identified not so much with the committing of a misdeed as with a lack of awareness of what one is doing. In Chrétien's *Conte du Graal*, when Perceval is dining at the Fisher King's manor, he does something for which he will be reproached for the rest of the text, but it is not something he recognizes (or that even we recognize), at the time, as an infraction. With each course they were served, it is said, "He saw the Grail pass completely uncovered before him, but he did not know who was served from it. He wanted very much to know."[167] As Perceval fails to react properly to the Grail, remaining silent when he should speak, other Grail knights fail to respond properly to this vessel as well, falling into a sleep or a stupor when they come into contact with it. In the First Continuation, when the Fisher King is telling Gawain about the secrets of the Grail and the Lance, the knight nods off at the table. In the *Queste del Saint Graal*, when Lancelot sees the Grail approach one night outside a chapel, he does not say a word, "like one who was in such a state that he neither slept nor stayed awake, but, rather, dozed."[168] If the Grail knight falls silent, asleep, or into a stupor in the presence of the Grail or during a discussion of the Grail, it is because he has already committed a sin, though he may not have meant to do so or even known that he was doing so. When Perceval left his mother to go to Arthur, he saw her collapse, yet it is only later that he begins to wonder if he left her alive or dead and still later that he learns that he did, in fact, cause her death. If he did not ask about the Grail, the hermit informs him, it was because "a sin about which you do not know anything has greatly harmed you. . . . Sin stopped your tongue."[169] The failure to respond properly to the Grail makes the knight recognize an earlier failure in his behavior, which he had not recognized until then. In Gerbert de Montreuil's Continuation, when the Fisher King refuses to answer Perceval's questions about the Grail and the Lance, it is said, "Perceval sighed and thought about by what sin, by what prohibition,

167. "Par devant els trespaser voit / lo graal trestot descovert, / mais il ne set cui l'en en sert. / Et si lo vodroit molt savoir," Chrétien de Troyes, *Conte du Graal*, ed. Méla, vv. 3238–41. He is similarly silent about the Lance.

168. "conme chil qui estoit en tel point qu'il ne ne dormoit ne ne veilloit mie bien, ains someilloit," *Queste del Saint Graal*, ed. Gros, 74, p. 885.

169. "mout t'a neü / uns pechiez don tu ne sez mot, / . . . / Pechiez la laingue te traincha," Chrétien de Troyes, *Conte du Graal*, ed. Méla, vv. 6318–35.

he would not know the matter of the Grail."[170] In the *Queste del Saint Graal*, similarly, a squire comments about Lancelot's inertia before the Grail, "By faith, . . . this is indeed a knight who committed a sin of which he never had himself confessed."[171] If to sin, in these romances, is not to be conscious of what one is doing, to act well is to become conscious of one's actions. Over the course of the *Conte du Graal* and the Continuations, Perceval, who had once been thoughtless and inconsiderate of others, becomes aware of himself, aware of others, and aware of the Grail, about which he is now prepared to ask questions. He recognizes and repents of his misdeed toward his mother. In the *Queste del Saint Graal*, Lancelot recognizes and repents of his misdeed with Guinevere. Yet to become conscious of oneself, it is clear, is to become conscious of where one has gone wrong, and that is a hard lesson for these knights to acquire.

If the Grail knight goes on a quest, it is not only because he is a medieval Christian undertaking a pilgrimage but also because, having become conscious of himself and of his guilt, he must become a wanderer on the face of the earth. In Chrétien's *Conte du Graal*, when a damsel reproaches Perceval for not having inquired about the Grail or the Lance, he resolves to seek out adventures. For five years, we are told, "He did not cease to seek out knightly deeds. He went about seeking strange, treacherous, and difficult adventures. He found enough of them to prove himself well."[172] Having acted badly, Perceval determines to act well and to establish himself to be someone who acts well. His behavior is common to knights of his sort. In the *Prose Lancelot*, when Bors informs a hermit, "I am . . . a knight errant from the household of King Arthur,"[173] the hermit concludes, "So, . . . you are one of those adventurous knights who go through strange lands to seek marvelous adventures."[174] Yet even as the Grail knight seeks out adventures, he recognizes that adventures are experiences that he will not find but that will "come to" (*aviennent*) him. An anchoress advises Lancelot

170. "Perchevaus sozpire et s'apense / par quel pechié, par quel desfense / que il ne set du Graal l'oevre," Gerbert de Montreuil, Continuation, vol. 1, ed. Williams, vv. 43–45.

171. "Par foi, . . . ja est auquns chevaliers qui maint en auqun pequié, dont il ne se fist onques confés," *Queste del Saint Graal*, ed. Gros, 76, 887.

172. "ne relaissoit il mie / a requerre chevalerie; / que les estranges aventures, / les felonesses et les dures, / aloit querant, et s'an trova / tant que mout bien s'i esprova," Chrétien de Troyes, *Conte du Graal*, ed. Méla, vv. 6151–56.

173. "Je sui . . . . I. chevaliers erranz de la meson le roi Artus," *Lancelot*, ed. Micha, vol. 4, 272.

174. "Ha, . . . vos estes des chevaliers aventureux qui vont par les estranges terres querre les mervilleuses aventures," ibid.

that, because he has been the most marvelous and adventurous man in the world, "Do not marvel that marvelous adventures come to you."[175] Because Gawain, in contrast, has been a sinful man, he is told, "you are not worthy to see them."[176] One seeks out adventure and one finds adventure, but one finds it, not because one has sought it out, but because one has merited it and because one is rewarded for that merit. All that the Grail knight can do is to actively render himself passive, in the hope that adventure will come upon him. It is for this purpose that in the *Queste del Saint Graal*, "Lancelot rode . . . all across the forest, in such a manner that he did not keep to track or path, but he went as adventure led him."[177] It is for this purpose that when Perceval happens upon a mysterious ship with no crew, he follows the command he hears: "Enter this ship and go where adventure will lead you."[178] If the Grail knight is to reach his destination, it will be not because he follows a straight and definable path, but because he errs, without knowing where he is going. In the decentering, disorienting journey that the Quest always is, to err is to recognize that one can never ultimately determine where one is headed.

After the Grail knight leaves his home, his family, and his loved ones, he finds himself returning to this place and these people, but they are or have become unfamiliar to him. The Fisher King turns out to be his uncle (or, in the *Didot-Perceval*, his grandfather), but they do not recognize each other. The hermit to whom he confesses his sins turns out to be another uncle. When Perceval learns who the hermit is, he proposes, "Fair uncle, . . . since my mother was your sister, you should call me 'nephew' and I should call you 'uncle,' to love all the more."[179] Yet though this uncle counsels and prays for him, he bears toward him a spiritual rather than a carnal affection. A damsel he meets turns out to be his cousin, but he does not recognize her. As she points out in Chrétien's *Conte du Graal*, though she was raised with him, "You do not know who I am."[180] Another damsel he encounters turns out to be his sister, but she does not recognize him either. In the Second and

175. "aventures merveillouses vos avienent, ne vos en esmerveilliés pas," *Queste del Saint Graal*, ed. Gros, 194, p. 1002.

176. "vous n'estes pas dingnes del veoir," ibid., 216, p. 1022.

177. "Lancelot cevauce . . . tout la traverse de la forest, en tel maniere qu'il ne tint ne voie ne sentier, ains s'en vait si com aventure l'en maine," ibid., 73, p. 884.

178. "entre en la nef et va ou aventure te menra," ibid., 156, p. 962.

179. "Biaux oncles, . . . / Quant ma mere fu vostre suer, / bien me devez nevou clamer, / et je vos oncle, et mielz amer," Chrétien de Troyes, *Conte du Graal*, ed. Méla, vv. 6360–64.

180. "tu ne sez pas qui je sui," Chrétien de Troyes, *Conte du Graal*, ed. Méla, v. 3536.

the Third Continuations, this damsel laments her brother's absence without realizing that she is speaking to him. As Perceval encounters strangers who turn out to be his kinsmen and kinswomen, but are no less strangers for that, he encounters manors that turn out to be his home, but are no less a foreign place. He ends up at the Fisher King's manor, which he will ultimately inherit, yet the morning after he fails to ask about the Grail and the Lance, the structure itself guides him to depart, its drawbridge rising up mysteriously behind him. He ends up at his mother's manor, where he grew up, but it is also unsettling. In the Second Continuation, as he is approaching this manor, he stops his horse at a beautiful tree, remembering that it was here that a passing knight first told him about King Arthur. When he catches sight of the house itself, he cries out, "I can see what I have so longed to see!"[181] Yet his mother is now dead, and it is said of the boys who help him off with his armor, "They did not look closely at him nor did they recognize him, either from his face or from his appearance, so they did not remember him."[182] With no one welcoming him back, the joy of homecoming quickly fades. In the *Didot-Perceval,* when the hermit asks him why he does not return to "your home,"[183] he answers, "Sire, so help me God, . . . I would have great sorrow if I saw my father's house emptied of my loved ones, for I would not find a soul there that belonged to me."[184] As that which was foreign turns out to be familiar, that which is familiar turns out to be foreign.

In the end, while the Grail romances build upon the penitential theology and ritual, they too cannot be limited to this thought and practice. It has long been remarked that, as twelfth- and thirteenth-century Christians developed the habit of confessing their sins and, indeed, were required to do so, they had to develop a new sense of their selves.[185] They had to learn to review their past actions and to identify those among them that may have seemed innocent at the time but that now, in retrospect, appear blameworthy. In doing so, they had to learn to see themselves as another person might see them. In the

181. "Je voi ce qu'ai tant desirré," Second Continuation, ed. Roach, v. 23579.

182. "ne l'ont mie ravisé / ne couneü ne tant ne quant / a son vis ne a son samblant, / avec ce ne leur an sovint," ibid., vv. 23594–97.

183. "vostre repair," *Didot-Perceval,* ed. Roach, 221.

184. "Sire, si m'aït Dex, . . . trop aroie grant duel se je veoie le maison mon pere si vuidie de mes amis, que je n'i troveroie ame qui m'apartenist," ibid.

185. See Michel Foucault, *Histoire de la sexualité: La volonté de savoir,* 2 vols. (Paris: Gallimard, 1976), vol. 1, 78–84.

Conte du Graal, when Perceval's cousin asks him his name, it is said, "He, who did not know his name, guessed and said that he had the name 'Perceval the Welshman.' He did not know if it was true or not, but he spoke the truth though he did not know it."[186] Perceval's knowledge of his name is intuitive, but it only comes to the fore when another person demands it of him. In Gerbert de Montreuil's Continuation, Perceval meets his mother's cousin, who makes him realize that he does not know his mother's name. As long as he lived with her, he explains, "I was stupid and brutish, so that I called her nothing but 'mother' as long as I was with her. And she called me 'fair son.'"[187] Earlier, Perceval had conceived of both his mother and himself only in relation to each other, so that she was his mother and he was her child. Now, he learns to conceive of each of them in their individuality, and he castigates himself for not having done so earlier. As Perceval leaves his home only to return and quits his family only to find it again, he speaks with others only to learn about himself. Yet this discovery of himself is not reassuring. As his home and his family turned out to be foreign to him, he too is foreign to himself. He is no longer the thoughtless youth, hunting hinds with bows and arrows and kissing chambermaids, that he once was, but, rather, a pensive knight, seeking adventures at arms and loving a noble damsel. In becoming who he now is, he has become an other to himself. As a modern theorist might say, *je est un autre*. Ultimately, the Quest is not an ecclesiastical practice, requiring contrition, confession, and absolution, in which the penitent must balance his pursuit of merit with a recognition of the necessity of grace, but a process of spiritual maturation demanding consciousness of the self, recognition of others as others, and an acceptance of his place in this alien world. By demonstrating that the Quest possesses a literary meaning that, again, can never be rendered in philosophical or theological terms, the authors of these romances show the essential untranslatability of this action.

186. "Et cil qui son non ne savoit / devine et dit que il avoit / Percevaus li Gualois a non, / ne ne set s'il dit voir ou non, / mais il dit voir, et si ne no sot," Chrétien de Troyes, *Conte du Graal*, ed. Méla, vv. 3511–15.

187. "estoie sos et salvages / si ne l'apeloie fors 'mere,' / tandis que je avec li ere. / Et ele m'apeloit 'biaus fieus,'" Gerbert de Montreuil, Continuation, vol. 1, ed. Williams, vv. 3084–87.

Significance and Semblance

In the course of the Quest of the Holy Grail, the knights of the Round Table undergo what are called "the Adventures of the Holy Grail."[188] For many years, these knights had been experiencing what were known as "the Adventures of Britain."[189] While never defined, these adventures seemed to be synonymous with "the Enchantments of the land of Britain,"[190] that is, with what Gawain calls "the great marvels, strange visions, and strange adventures that have arrived so often and for such a long time."[191] Yet now, with the onset of the Quest, the Adventures of Britain are replaced by the Adventures of the Holy Grail, which are even more marvelous and more strange than those that preceded them. In the *Queste del Saint Graal*, the hermit Nascien explains to the knights, "The adventures that exist now and that come now are the significations [*senefiances*] and demonstrations of the Holy Grail."[192] Faced with the adventures, the Grail knights know that what they see is but a literal, physical "semblance" (*semblance*), and they intuit the existence of a figurative, spiritual "signification" or "significance" (*senefiance*) underlying it. They then seek out a holy man (or, occasionally, a holy woman) who can disclose this significance to them. At one point, for example, Gawain proposes, after they have experienced such adventures, "We have seen such things this night, in both sleeping and waking, that the best thing to do in order to bring this business to an end is to go seek some worthy man, some hermit, who will tell us the significance of our dreams."[193] The Quest of the Holy Grail is the quest of a knowledge that can be attained only when the knight's sensory perception is joined with the holy person's spiritual insight. It is the task of human beings, once again, to proceed from apprehending the

188. "du Saint Graal / les aventures," Manassier, Third Continuation, ed. Roach, vv. 42636–37; *Lancelot*, ed. Micha, vol. 1, 52–53; vol. 4, 210–11; vol. 5, 127; vol. 5, 256; *Queste del Saint Graal*, ed. Gros, 8, p. 817.

189. "les aventures de Bretaigne," *Lancelot*, ed. Micha, vol. 1, 52–53; ibid., vol. 5, 130–31; *La Suite du roman de Merlin*, ed. Roussinau, vol. 1, 141.

190. "li encantement de le terre de Bretagne," *Didot-Perceval*, ed. Roach, 243; ibid., 150–51.

191. "des grans merveilles [et des estranges visions] et des estranges aventures qui tant sont avenues si lonc tans a passé," *Queste del Saint Graal*, ed. Gros, 11, p. 822.

192. "les aventures qui ore sont et qui ore avienent si sont les senefiances et les demoustrances del Saint Graal," ibid., 220, p. 1026.

193. "nous avons anuit tant veü en dormant et en veillant que li miels a nostre afaire mener a fin si est que nous aillons querre aucun prodome, aucun hermite qui nous die la senefiance de noz songes," ibid., 206, p. 1013.

semblance of what they experience to apprehending its significance, and it is only when the secular person submits what he has beheld to the sacred person's interpretation that he is able to do so. On another level, however, the meaning of these adventures exceeds the context of Christianity. While the holy people possess an understanding that the knights do not, the texts emphasize not their perspective, as saints' lives would have done, but that of the frequently sinful knights. For that reason, these works necessarily affirm the truth value not just of signification but of semblance; not just of figurative, spiritual reality but of literal, physical reality; and not just of what is perceived with the spirit, but of what is perceived with the senses. By the end of the Quest, there are no more adventures, that is, no more concrete, physical entities that embody abstract, spiritual truths. Yet even as the romances celebrate the conclusion of the adventures, they mourn the disappearance of a world so rich in meaning.

As the Grail knight undergoes the Adventures of the Holy Grail, he struggles to understand that which he experiences. To take one striking example, in the Vulgate and Post-Vulgate Cycles, three sets of Grail figures—Lancelot and an unnamed youth; Galahad, Perceval, and Bors; and Galahad, Yvain the Bastard, and Dodinel the Wildman—are wandering through a forest when they encounter a white stag. The *Prose Lancelot* recounts of Lancelot and the youth, "They saw going before them a stag, whiter than newly fallen snow. It had around its neck a golden chain."[194] Marvelous because of his white coat and golden chain, this stag is all the more marvelous because of the entourage of lions that surround it. One lion walks on each side of the beast, and one or two (depending upon the manuscript) walk in front of it and behind it. It is said, "The four lions were leading and guarding it, in semblance, as dearly as a mother would guard her child,"[195] or, as Lancelot puts it, "as dearly, in semblance, as if it were a reliquary."[196] While most of the knights behold the stag only as a stag and the lions only as lions, Galahad, Perceval, and Bors have the privilege of seeing these beasts assume other forms. They follow them to a chapel, where a hermit is celebrating Mass. At the moment when the hermit is consecrating the

194. "voient par devant aux aler .I. cerf plus blanc que noif negie et avoit entour le col une chaienne d'or," *Lancelot*, ed. Micha, vol. 5, 133, and ibid., vol. 5, 210.

195. "si le conduisoient et gardoient par semblant cil qatre lion ausi chierement come la mere garde son enfant," *L'Estoire del Saint Graal*, ed. Ponceau, 793, p. 502; *Lancelot*, ed. Micha, vol. 5, 133; ibid., vol. 6, 52.

196. "ausi chierement par samblant come se fust uns saintuaire," ibid., vol. 5, 210.

Host, they see the stag become a "celestial man,"[197] seated on a chair on the altar, and the lions become a man, an eagle, a lion, and an ox, all with wings. They then see the four living creatures lift up the chair on which the celestial man is seated and carry it through a small window in the chapel, in a manner that does not shatter the glass. Yet whether the knights see just the beasts or the beasts' transformation, they do not know the meaning of what they see, and they long to know it. When Lancelot espies the stag, he vows, "I will never leave this forest before I know the truth about this stag, if I can learn it from any man or woman."[198] He is perplexed that though lions are savage beasts inclined to attack deer, here they form an orderly bodyguard around the stag, as if they recognize it to be a sacred thing. He states, "I wonder greatly how this can happen for, without the power of God or without enchantment, it is not possible that a lion have so much intelligence, for his nature does not bring this about. And because of this, I know well that they perform this service by the command of Our Lord or by enchantment."[199] Like Lancelot, Galahad resolves that he will not cease seeking the stag "until I know the truth about this marvel."[200] Because the Grail knight remains at the level of semblance, as grasped by sense perception, he cannot apprehend the significance of what he sees, and he yearns to do so.

When the holy figure hears about the thrilling adventures the Grail knight has undergone, he enables him to understand them. Regarding the adventure of the white stag, the hermit reassures Lancelot, "Know truly that this is not enchantment nor dark deviltry. Rather, it is a marvelous miracle which happened formerly by the will of Our Lord."[201] He places "enchantment" on the same plane as "dark deviltry," and he contrasts both of them with "miracles." In doing so, he sets up a common Christian opposition between the wicked supernatural works produced by the devil and the good supernatural works produced by

197. "home celestiel," *Queste del Saint Graal*, ed. Gros, 314, p. 1124.

198. "jamés de ceste forest ne partirai devant que je sache la verité de cest cerf, se par home ou par fame le doi savoir," *Lancelot*, ed. Micha, vol. 5, 133–34.

199. "si me merveil moult durement conmnet ce puet avenir, car sanz vertu de Dieu ou sanz anchantement n'est ce pas que li lions ait plus de san en soi que sa nature ne li aporte. Et por ce sai je bien qu'il font cestui servise par le conmandement Nostre Seingnor ou par anchantement," ibid., vol. 5, 133–34.

200. "devant que je sache la verité de ceste merveille," *La Version post-Vulgate de la "Queste del Saint Graal" et de la "Mort Artu,"* ed. Bogdanow, vol. 2, chap. 9, 108, p. 143.

201. "saichiez vraiement que ce n'est mie anchantement ne oscure dyablie, ainz est miracle mervilleux qui avint jadis par la volenté Nostre Signor," *Lancelot*, ed. Micha, vol. 5, 211.

God. He informs Lancelot that the white stag is to be identified, not with the former, but with the latter. When Galahad, Perceval, and Bors beg the hermit "that he tell them the significance of what they had seen,"[202] he explains that as the stag is white and spotless, Christ was born of the Virgin Mary, who never had any earthly sin. Indeed, when the knights see the celestial man and the four creatures pass through the window, a voice from above announces, with a flash of light and a clap of thunder, "In such a manner did the Son of God descend into the Blessed Virgin Mary, so that she never lost her virginity."[203] As the stag underwent a transformation when he became a man, the hermit continues, Christ underwent a transformation when he assumed as he did mortal flesh. As the stag, like all stags (it was believed), returns to youth by shedding its hair and skin when it is entering into old age, Christ returned to life when he was dying. Finally, as the stag was accompanied by four creatures who became a man, an eagle, a lion, and an ox, he recounts, Christ was accompanied by the four Evangelists—symbolized by the four living creatures in the Book of Revelations—who wrote down his words. Through the image of the stag, God thus shows these knights visual representations of the doctrines of the Immaculate Conception, the Incarnation, the Virgin Birth, the Resurrection, the Eucharist, and the writing of the Gospels. If God displayed himself to knights in this land in the "semblance"[204] of the stag, the hermit informs the knights, it is "so that those who saw him might take an example from it."[205] Just as a preacher knows that in order for worldly people to grasp an abstract concept, it is helpful for them to have it grounded in a concrete image or "example" (*exemplum*), Christ knows that in order for human beings to grasp the mysteries of the faith, it is helpful for them to have these mysteries illustrated by these beasts. Because the hermit ascends to the level of signification, he is able to help the knights apprehend the meaning of what they seek.[206]

202. "qu'il lor die la senefiance de ce qu'ils ont veü," *Queste del Saint Graal,* ed. Gros, 314, p. 1123.

203. "En tel maniere descendi li Fix Dieu en la Virgene Marie, que onques virginité n'en perdit," ibid.

204. "en tel samblance," ibid., 314, p. 1124.

205. "por ce que cil qui le veissent i preissent essample," *Queste del Saint Graal,* ed. Pauphilet, 236. Cf. "pour ce que cil qui le veïssent i preïssent garde," *Queste del Saint Graal,* ed. Gros, 314, p. 1124.

206. In contrast to Pauphilet, who argued that "the Grail is the romance manifestation of God [*Le Graal est la manifestation romanesque de Dieu*]," Todorov asserts in "La Quête du récit," "God does not manifest himself in romances; romances fall under the domain of the Enemy, not that of God [*Dieu ne se manifeste pas dans les romans; les romans relèvent du domaine de l'Ennemi, non de celui de Dieu*]" (148).

At the same time, however, the semblance perceived by the knights is never entirely superseded by the significance perceived by the hermit. While the hermit links the "enchantment" of which Lancelot speaks with "dark deviltry," Lancelot himself does not do so. On the contrary, when he asks the hermit whether the white stag and the lions act "by the command of Our Lord or by enchantment," he opposes not the good supernatural works produced by God and the wicked supernatural works produced by the devil, but the good supernatural works effected by God and the good, or at least morally neutral supernatural works effected by some third party. "Enchantment," as we have already seen, can occupy a space that is neither diabolical nor divine, especially in the context of romance, and it is in this space that Lancelot locates the white stag. As the knights are impressed by the marvelousness of the stag and the lions, they are also impressed by the beauty of this sight. The whiteness of the stag may signify virtue and virginity, but it is also a color, like that of freshly fallen snow, whose brightness is intensified in the moonlight. The golden chain around the stag's neck may signify humility, as the hermit suggests,[207] but it is also a courtly ornament, at odds with the sylvan environment through which the stag proceeds. The ceremonial stateliness of these beasts may recall that of visionary animals, like those of the Book of Revelations, but it also accords these beasts a dignity they would not otherwise possess. Given the beauty of the stag and the lions, Lancelot describes his encounter with these beasts as "the fairest adventure that I have ever seen."[208] Even as the hermit is able to understand the significance of the white stag, he is not able to see it himself. When Lancelot tells the hermit, "Sire, I saw pass before me a stag whiter than snow,"[209] the hermit asks, "Oh, my lord, . . . did you see then the white stag?"[210] He knows that the white stag exists; he knows that this beast is a unique entity ("the white stag"), and not the member of a class ("a stag"); and he knows that it has existed, seemingly immortal and immutable, since antiquity. Yet he himself has not seen it, as Lancelot has done. Similarly, when Galahad and his companions tell the hermit what they witnessed during the Mass, the hermit asks them, "What thing . . . have you seen?"[211] Though he was the celebrant of the Mass, he did not share their vision of what occurred during the ceremony. Hearing about the transformations of the

207. Cf. *Joseph d'Arimathie*, ed. Gros, 539, p. 498 and 544, p. 502.
208. "la plus bele aventure que je onques veisse," *Lancelot*, ed. Micha, vol. 5, 204.
209. "Sire, je vi par devant moi passer .I. cerf plus blans que noiz," ibid., vol. 5, 210.
210. "Ha, sire, . . . veistes vos dont le blanc cerf?," ibid., vol. 5, 210.
211. "Quel chose . . . avez vos donc veue?," *Queste del Saint Graal*, ed. Pauphilet, 235.

stag and the lions that they saw, he exclaims, "Oh! Lords, . . . you are those to whom Our Lord has shown his secrets and his mysteries."[212] It is Galahad and his companions who see the stag and the lions as they transform themselves into Christ and the Evangelists, and not the hermit, who merely interprets what they see. And it is Galahad who ultimately owns this adventure and brings it to its conclusion. As the hermit predicts to Lancelot, "The Good Knight . . . will achieve the adventure of the lions and the stag and will make known in the world in what manner the lions took guard of the stag."[213] Though the holy figure reduces the adventure to a single, totalizing interpretative framework, the marvelous beauty of the adventure, which the Grail knights alone behold, ultimately resists such constraints.

While the romances suggest that the inhabitants of the Kingdom of Logres are glad for the Grail knights to bring the adventures to an end, this is not entirely the case. It is true, in the Vulgate Cycle, that the adventures are depicted as perils from which the kingdom needs to be delivered. "The Adventurous Kingdom," Britain is also "the Perilous Kingdom"[214] on account of "the perilous adventures which happen . . . every day."[215] Given the perilous nature of the adventures, the people of Britain long for a knight who will deliver them from them. It is said that "in Great Britain, all await to be delivered from the marvels and the adventures that happen there."[216] For years, people look forward to the knight who is predicted "to bring to an end" (*venir a chief, mener a chief, mener a fin, metre a fin*) the adventures; "to accomplish" (*acomplir, achever*) the adventures; "to cast down" (*abatre, cheoir*), "to undo" (*defaire*) or "to destroy" (*faillir*) the adventures; and, in doing so, "to deliver" (*delivrer*) the land from adventures. When Galahad arrives, he is celebrated as "he who . . . brought about the end of the adventures of the Perilous and Adventurous Kingdom, which was the Kingdom of Logres."[217] To bring about the end of the adventures is not only to destroy the marvels but also to destroy the "semblances" that convey such

212. "Ha! seignor, . . . vous estes cil a qui Nostre Sires a mostrez ses secrez et ses repostailles," ibid.

213. "li bons chevaliers . . . achevera l'aventure des lyons et dou cerf et fera savoir au monde par quel manniere li lion pristrent en garde le cerf," *Lancelot*, ed. Micha, vol. 5, 211.

214. "del roialme perelleus," ibid., vol. 7, 59.

215. "les aventures perilleuses qui . . . avienent chascun jor," *Queste del Saint Graal*, ed. Pauphilet, 228.

216. "en la Grant Bartaigne atendent tout a estre delivré des merveilles et des aventures qui i avienent," *Lancelot*, ed. Micha, vol. 7, 192.

217. "chelui qui . . . mena a fin les aventures del roialme perelleus et aventureus, che fu li roialmes de Logres," ibid., vol. 7, 59.

mystic "significances." When the hermit in the *Prose Lancelot* informs Lancelot that the stag he has seen is Christ, he adds, "Know that from now forward, there will be none who see him in such a semblance."[218] After the conclusion that Galahad brings to this adventure, people will continue to know about Christ, but they will no longer see him in this guise. In general, they will know the significations of the semblances, thanks to the explanations of clerics, but they will no longer behold the semblances themselves. The immanent will be replaced by the transcendent, the sensible by the intelligible, and the concrete image by the abstract concept. Yet as alarming as the adventures of the Adventurous Kingdom often are, it is not clear that even the knights who seek to destroy them rejoice at their destruction. In the *Estoire del Saint Graal*, where the coming of the adventures to Britain is predicted, they are understood to be tests by which knights will be able to establish their prowess.[219] When the adventures disappear, according to the *Didot-Perceval*, the young men declare that they will leave Arthur and cross the sea in order to seek out knightly deeds.[220] Without adventures, the forest is disenchanted, and the knightly sojourns in its trackless waste are unrelieved by any marvels. Without adventures, it is clear, the Adventurous Kingdom exists no longer. The ambivalence of the kingdom toward the disappearance of the adventures reflects an ambivalence at the heart of the romances: though the knights yearn to bring about an end to the adventures, they want there to be adventures whose end they can bring about, and though they seek an explanation for the marvels they encounter, they are happiest wondering what that explanation may be.

Composed at the time that Holy Communion and penance were being radically rethought, the Grail romances are permeated by the spirituality associated with these two sacraments, but in a way that complicates our understanding of this spirituality. A sacrament is a sign. In a remark that would be echoed by medieval theologians, Augustine writes, "A sacrifice . . . is the visible sacrament, that is, the sacred sign, of an invisible sacrifice."[221] Because human beings apprehend what is invisible only when it is pointed out to them by a visible sign, he maintains, God instituted the sacraments, which can be perceived by

218. "sachiés bien que dés ore en avant ne sera nus qui en tel samblance le voie," *Queste del Saint Graal*, ed. Gros, 314, p. 1124.

219. See *Joseph d'Arimathie*, ed. Gros, 160, p. 119 and 161, pp. 159–60.

220. See *Didot-Perceval*, ed. Roach, 244.

221. "Sacrificium . . . visibile invisibilis sacrificii sacramentum, id est sacrum signum est," Augustine, *De civitate Dei*, ed. Dombart and Kalb, X, 5, p. 277.

the senses but which signify something beyond that which can be perceived by the senses. It is thus that the sacrament functions, as Augustine puts it, as a kind of "visible word."[222] In order to appreciate sacraments as sacraments, one must apprehend both these signs and the things that they signify: "As soon as anyone perceives them, he knows immediately that to which they refer, so that he venerates them, not with carnal servitude, but, rather, with spiritual freedom."[223] As soon as a Christian perceives the bread and wine on the altar, he knows that they refer to (and, indeed, are) the Body and Blood of Christ. As soon as he perceives the pilgrimage that the penitent undertakes in atonement for his sins, he knows that it refers to his genuine repentance. If one were to read the Grail romances sacramentally, one would know that the Grail signifies God, or the grace of the Holy Spirit, or that which one most desires. One would know that the Quest signifies our life on earth, which is properly oriented toward finding such a desideratum. One would know that the stag signifies Christ and the lions the four Evangelists. If one were to fail to read these texts in this manner, one would fail to recognize these signs as signs, and one would thus fail to discern the things they signify: the Grail would be a platter or cup, the Quest a journey, the stag a deer. Yet signs, including those designated as sacraments, are essentially ambiguous. Even if one knows that the Grail, the Quest, and the stag are signs—and it is impossible to miss the fact that they signify *something*—one could potentially interpret them as signifying other things. Even those who wish to see an exclusively Christian significance in the Grail disagree as to what that significance is. To confused readers, Augustine offers advice: while he who does not recognize a sign as a sign is in bondage, "He who does not understand what a sign signifies, and yet understands it to be a sign, is not in bondage."[224] And, in contrast to those who do not recognize a sign as a sign or who interpret it incorrectly, he writes, "It is better to be in bondage to unknown, but still useful signs."[225] If one can apply Augustine's words to the Grail romances, readers feel drawn to the Grail, the Quest, and the stag because they feel them to be signs,

222. "visibile verbum," Augustine, *In evangelium Ioannis tractatus*, ed. Willems, LXXX, 3, p. 529.

223. "Quae unusquisque cum percipit, quo referantur imbutus agnoscit, ut ea non carnali servitute, sed spiritali potius libertate veneretur," Augustine, *De doctrina Christiana*, ed. Martin, III, 9, p. 86.

224. "Qui autem non intellegit quid significet signum, et tamen signum esse intellegit, nec ipse premitur servitute," ibid.

225. "Melius est autem vel premi incognitis, sed utilibus signis," ibid.

but these are "unknown . . . signs." They know the romances to be filled with meaning, but they are uncertain as to what that meaning is. Because the romances typically describe these phenomena from the perspective of someone who does not know what they signify, because they thus dwell, often for a considerable time, on the indeterminacy of their signification, and because they thus cherish their semblance as much as or, indeed, more than their significance, they preserve the significance of that semblance, even as that semblance itself has disappeared from our world.

SIX

Truth and the Imagination: From Romance to Children's Fantasy

If anything has been seen as distinguishing romance, for good or for evil, over the years, it has been its reliance upon "imagination" (*phantasia* or *imaginatio*) in what it represents.[1] In the classical, medieval, and early modern periods, imagination was regarded as the faculty by which human beings, after having perceived things with their senses, register images of what they have perceived, store those images in their memory, and then retrieve them from this repository as necessary. In the eighteenth century, imagination began to be regarded, instead, as the faculty by which, through some mysterious process, human beings create. The Swiss critic Johann Jakob Bodmer writes in 1741, "The imagination . . . not only places that

1. While distinguished at other points in history, *phantasia* and *imaginatio* were used synonymously in the Middle Ages, thanks to Augustine's translation of the Greek *phantasia* as *imaginatio*. See Michelle Karnes, *Imagination, Meditation, and Cognition in the Middle Ages* (Chicago: University of Chicago Press, 2011), 23n1. On the history of imagination, see also Karnes, "Marvels in the Medieval Imagination"; Peter Dronke, *Imagination in the Late Pagan and Early Christian World: The First Nine Centuries A.D.* (Florence: Sismel/Edizioni dei Galluzzo, 2003); J. M. Cocking, *Imagination: A Study in the History of Ideas*, ed. Penelope Murray (London: Routledge, 1991); Eva T. H. Brann, *The World of the Imagination: Sum and Substance* (Savage, MD: Rowman and Littlefield, 1991); Douglas Kelly, *Medieval Imagination: Rhetoric and the Poetry of Courtly Love* (Madison: University of Wisconsin Press, 1978); and Murray Wright Bundy, *The Theory of Imagination in Classical and Medieval Thought* (Urbana: University of Illinois Press, 1927).

which is real before our eyes in a lively image and makes the most distant things present, but also, with a more than magical power, draws that which does not exist out of the state of potentiality, gives it the appearance of reality, and makes us see, hear, and feel these new creations, as it were."[2] Whether understood as a passive storehouse of received ideas or as an active workshop for the production of new concepts, imagination has proven to be a controversial foundation for literature. Can imagination give us access to truth, as reason and the senses do? Can romance, which is so based on imagination, give us access to truth as well? Even as the understanding of imagination has changed over the course of the centuries, the value of a literature grounded in this faculty has never ceased to be contested.

Today, the literature that most explicitly relies upon imagination is termed, not romance, but "fairy-stories," "fairy-tales," or, most often, "fantasy."[3] Though there is little consensus as to how "fantasy" might best be defined,[4] the nineteenth-century Scottish minister George MacDonald, whose novels are among the first and most influential examples of this genre, associates it with the literary creation of "an imagined world."[5] Just as the natural world has its laws, he proposes, "Man may, if he pleases, invent a little world of his own, with its own laws; for there is that in him which delights in calling up new forms—which is the nearest, perhaps, he can come to creation."[6] And just as Nature must adhere to the laws of its world, the author of such a work must adhere to the laws of his "imagined world" in order for it to be believable. In his important essay "On Fairy-Stories" (1939–46), J. R. R. Tolkien rearticulates MacDonald's definition of this genre. While we

2. "der Einbildungskraft . . . stellet uns nicht alleine das Würkliche in einem lebhaften Gemählde vor Augen, und machet die entferntesten Sachen gegenwärtig, sondern sie zieht auch mit einer mehr als zauberischen Kraft das, so nicht ist, aus dem Stande der Möglichkeit hervor, theilet ihm dem Scheine nache eine Würchlichkeit mit, und machet, daß wir diese neuen Geschöpfe gleichsam sehen, hören, und empfinden," Johann Jakob Bodmer, *Critische Betrachtungen über die poetischen Gemälde der Dichter* (Zurich: Orell, 1741), 13.

3. See Stephen Prickett, "On the Evolution of a Word," in *Victorian Fantasy* (Bloomington: Indiana University Press, 1979; rev. ed., Waco, TX: Baylor University Press, 2005), 5–36.

4. On the difficulty of defining "fantasy," see Edward James and Farah Mendlesohn, Introduction to *The Cambridge Companion to Fantasy Literature*, ed. Edward James and Farah Mendlesohn (Cambridge: Cambridge University Press, 2012), 1–4, at 1, and John Clute, "Fantasy," in *The Encyclopedia of Fantasy*, ed. John Clute and John Grant (New York: St. Martin's Press, 1997), 337–40.

5. George MacDonald, "The Fantastic Imagination" (1890), in *Fantastic Literature: A Critical Reader* (Westport, CT: Praeger, 2004), 64–69, at 65. This text was originally a preface to a collection of MacDonald's short fantasy works, *The Light Princess, and Other Fairy Tales* (Glasgow: Blackie and Sons, 1890), iii–xii.

6. MacDonald, "The Fantastic Imagination," 65.

all experience the "Primary World," which we observe around us with our senses, he writes, the author of "fairy-stories" creates a "Secondary World," which he imagines with his mind.[7] While we all observe, for example, "green grass," such an author disjoins that adjective from that noun and then conjoins it with another noun, to create, perhaps, a "green sun."[8] He then fashions an entire Secondary World within which that green sun will command belief. Like God, who functions as the Creator of the Primary World, which must adhere to his laws, Tolkien states, the author functions as the "subcreator"[9] of this Secondary World, which must conform to his laws no less, if it is to seem credible. As fanciful as this "imagined" or "Secondary" world may seem to be, both theorists affirm that it contains within it a truth. Reverend MacDonald argues that in the fairy-tale, "The beauty may be plainer in it than the truth, but without the truth the beauty could not be, and the fairytale would give no delight."[10] Pleasure in literature cannot exist without beauty, and beauty cannot exist without truth. Because fantasy literature gives pleasure, it must be beautiful, and, because it is beautiful, it must be true. Tolkien likewise claims that a fairy-story is true insofar as it functions in accordance with its own internal logic, which must, if it is to be effective, function in accordance with an external logic as well. When the author achieves an "inner consistency of realities,"[11] he argues, "it is difficult to conceive how this can be, if the work does not in some way partake of reality,"[12] or, in other words, if it does not provide "a sudden glimpse of the underlying reality or truth."[13] While it is with imagination that the author of fantasy literature creates an "imagined" or "Secondary" world, for MacDonald and for Tolkien, the internal coherence manifest in this world makes it *seem* true, and the resonance between this internal co-

7. J. R. R. Tolkien first gave "On Fairy-Stories" as the Andrew Lang Lecture at the University Court of Saint Andrews on March 8, 1939. Between 1943 and 1945 or 1946, he edited the talk, publishing it, first, in "On Fairy-Stories," in *Essays Presented to Charles Williams*, ed. C. S. Lewis (Oxford: Oxford University Press, 1947), 38–89, and then in J. R. R. Tolkien, *Tree and Leaf* (London: Allen and Unwin, 1964), 3–83. I am citing J. R. R. Tolkien, *Tolkien on Fairy-Stories*, ed. Verlyn Flieger and Douglas A. Anderson (London: HarperCollins, 2008), 27–84.

8. Tolkien, *Tolkien on Fairy-Stories*, 41.

9. Ibid., 42.

10. Ibid.

11. Tolkien, "On Fairy-Stories," 59. This definition of "imagination" appears in the entry in the *Oxford English Dictionary* for "fancy," definition 4. The editors observe, "Tolkien changes the final word from 'realities' to 'reality,' thus shifting the reference from plural phenomena to a singular concept, an abstraction" (ibid.).

12. Ibid., 77.

13. Ibid.

herence and an external harmony latent in the "Primary" world shows that it *is* true.

But let us back up. If imagination and the fantasy literature that relies so heavily upon imagination give us access to the truth, what is that truth? Both MacDonald and Tolkien were devout Christians. When Tolkien suggests that "fairy-stories" are true insofar as they give "a far-off gleam or echo of *evangelium* in the real world,"[14] he connects the power of this genre with the power of the Gospels, which constitute, as he sees it, the Ur-"fairy-story." In its account of a man who was God, who died and was resurrected, and who, through his willing sacrifice of himself, redeemed others, he maintains, the life of Jesus Christ is a "fairy-story" that was found to be true in reality, "without thereby necessarily losing the mythical or allegorical significance that it had possessed."[15] Yet while this may be all very well and good for readers of this literature who share the authors' religious affiliations, what does it mean for those who do not do so or who do not wish to limit the value of these texts to a specific creed? Arthurian romance had always been about the encounter of the ordinary with the extraordinary, whether that extraordinary be identified with marvels that break the laws of Nature, a king and a court that transcend the laws of history, a knight who surpasses all standards of knighthood, or a vessel that pours forth something like divine grace. Fantasy, too, is about the encounter between the ordinary and the extraordinary, whether that extraordinary be linked with the protagonists' journey from the Primary to the Secondary Worlds, as happens in what Farah Mendelsohn calls "portal-quest" fantasy, or with their experience of the Primary World being invaded by the Secondary World, as happens in what she terms "intrusive" fantasy.[16] By considering, first, the debate about the truth value of the imagination in Western thought and, then, the echo of that debate in the two most influential examples of portal-quest/intrusive fantasy—C. S. Lewis's *The Chronicles of Narnia* and J. K. Rowling's *Harry Potter* books—we can see how fantasy has been believed to give us access, perhaps indirectly to God, but directly to the radical otherness of a latently marvelous world.[17]

14. Ibid.

15. Ibid., 78.

16. On these distinctions, see Farah Mendlesohn, *Rhetorics of Fantasy* (Middletown, CT: Wesleyan University Press, 2008).

17. Despite its unsurpassed importance in the history of fantasy, I am leaving to the side Tolkien's *The Lord of the Rings* (written 1937–49 and published 1954–55) because it falls into the category of "immersive" fantasy, where the protagonists inhabit the Secondary World, indepen-

Castles in Spain

The debate about the truth value of romance, "fairy-stories," fairy-tales, or fantasy derives from the debate about the truth value of the imagination. For some thinkers from the classical period to the present day, reality is fundamentally physical reality. It is one thing to perceive, for example, a castle. One may have seen the castle from afar, approached it, and entered it. One may have created in one's mind an image of that castle, which is then lodged in one's memory to be retrieved as necessary. Yet it is another thing to perceive what was called, from the thirteenth century onward, "a castle in Spain" or "a castle in the air." One never sees such a castle, at least with the eyes of one's body. One never approaches or enters such a castle, at least with the limbs of one's body. One may have created in one's mind an image of that castle, but that image corresponds to no physical reality and is, for that reason, entirely ephemeral. For other thinkers, again from the classical period to the present day, however, reality is not just physical but also—for lack of a better word—spiritual. The "castle in Spain" or "castle in the air" may epitomize the essential castle-ness of a castle in a way in which no existing castle does. In its perfection, it may embody what one loves about castles and may thus provide the inspiration for some future castle, whether in the Loire Valley, southwest Bavaria, or Orlando, Florida. While, for empiricists, it is impossible to attain truth through imagination because the objects of the imagination are immaterial and, hence, unreal, for this other, less classifiable set of thinkers, it is indeed possible to approach truth through this faculty because mental images are no less real for their intangibility.

For many late antique and medieval clerics, unless people are affected by some illness, they do not err in what they perceive with their senses, but they can indeed go astray in what they perceive with their imagination. Augustine asks of products of this faculty, "Who can doubt that these images are far more false than sensible things?"[18] We

---

dent of the Primary World, and because it thus differs from Arthurian romance, which is always about the encounter between these two realms. Tolkien himself claims to have been inspired in writing his trilogy not by Arthurian romance, but by Norse, Anglo-Saxon, and Finnish mythology. See *The Letters of J. R. R. Tolkien*, ed. Humphrey Carpenter and Christopher Tolkien (Boston: Houghton Mifflin, 1981), Letter 131, to Milton Waldman, 143–61, at 144.

18. "at istas imagines quis dubitaverit istis sensibilibus multo esse falsiores?," Augustine, *Epistula* VII, ed. Daur, chap. 5, 17. See also Augustine, *De Genesi ad litteram*, ed. Joseph Zycha, CSEL, vol. 28 (Prague: F. Tempsky, 1894), XII, 6.387, and *Epistulae I–LV*, ed. K. D. Daur, CCSL, vol. 31, 15–19, at 17.

have all seen white swans, but none of us has seen a black swan.[19] Yet through what he calls "a certain power, innate to the mind, of diminution and augmentation,"[20] we can combine the swanishness we have seen in this bird and the blackness we have seen in other creatures to imagine such a creature. In performing such operations, he warns, we produce, not something true, which would exist as a corporeal being, but "something which is called false,"[21] because it has been fashioned "arbitrarily and fancifully."[22] Anselm of Canterbury echoes Augustine when he contrasts God's creation of the world with a craftsman's creation of an object. While the God of Genesis created the animals ex nihilo, so that they existed as new things, Anselm indicates, man creates the image of "some animal . . . that exists nowhere,"[23] out of old parts. Having observed creatures in the world and retained images of them in his memory, he merely rearranges their parts to produce new combinations. If these thinkers find the capacity of the imagination to create to be disturbing, it is because they assume that the truth is something we find in the world, and not something we fabricate in our minds. Thomas Aquinas is uneasy with the fact that, while we cannot perceive phenomena that do not exist in the world with our senses, we can do so with our imagination. Commenting upon Aristotle, he writes of "fantasy [*phantasia*]," "It is in our power to form something, as it were, appearing before our eyes, such as golden mountains, or whatever else we wish."[24] It is imagination that makes human beings succumb to demons, who cannot alter what is, but can alter what it seems to be, in order to deceive us. It is imagination that makes sleepers dream, madmen rave, and lovers mistake an evil for a good. Aquinas remarks, "It . . . happens, from the fact that a passion is aroused, that that which is set before the imagination is judged to be worth being pursued because, to the man who is held by passion, that to which he is inclined through

19. There is, of course, a black swan (*Cygnus atratus*). Its existence was only known in Europe after Willem de Vlamingh discovered it during his exploration of western Australia in 1697.

20. "vim quamdam minuendi et augendi animae insitam," Augustine, *Epistula* VII, ed. Daur, chap. 6, 18.

21. "aliquid quod ideo falsum dicatur," Augustine, *De Trinitate*, ed. W. J. Mountain, CCSL 50–50A, 2 vols., vol. 1, XI, 10, 17.

22. "pro arbitrio vel opinatione cogitamus," Augustine, *De Genesi ad litteram*, ed. Zycha, XII, 23, 415.

23. "tale aliquod animal . . . quale nusquam sit confingere," Anselm of Canterbury, *Monologion*, in *Opera Omnia*, ed. Schmitt, vol. 1, 1–87, at XI, 26.

24. "in potestate nostra est formare aliquid, quasi apparens ante oculos nostros, ut montes aureos, vel quicquid volumus," Thomas Aquinas, *Sentencia libri De anima*, in *Opera omnia*, ed. Roberto Buso, 7 vols. (Stuttgart-Bad Cannstatt: Frommann-Holzboog, 1980), 341–70, at III, 4, no. 19, 360. Cf. Aristotle, *De anima*, III, 3, pt. 3.

passion seems to be good."[25] Imagination can mislead us, these authors maintain, because it enables us to see things that do not and cannot exist, but that we dream may exist and that we desire.

For many early modern philosophers, people may or may not err in what they perceive with their senses, but they do go astray in what they apprehend with their imagination. Thomas Hobbes, in his chapter "Of Imagination" in *Leviathan* (1651; rev. 1668), distinguishes "simple imagination,"[26] by which a man conceives of a man or a horse, "which he hath seen before," and "compounded imagination," by which he conceives of a centaur, which he has never beheld. It is the compounded imagination that it is at play when one reads romance. Hobbes writes, "When a man compoundeth the image of his own person, with the image of the actions of an other man; as when a man images himselfe a *Hercules*, or an *Alexander*, which happeneth often to them that are much taken with reading of Romants, it is a compound imagination, and properly but a Fiction of the mind."[27] John Locke, in his *Essay Concerning Human Understanding* (1690), makes a similar argument. He too distinguishes simple ideas, like those of a man or a horse, which are "the natural and regular production of Things without us,"[28] and compound ideas, like that of a centaur, which are "*fictions* of our Fancies."[29] The statement "*all Centaurs are Animals*" may be as true as the statement "*all Men are Animals*,"[30] in what he calls "the visionary World in our own Imaginations,"[31] but the failure of the idea of a centaur to correspond to anything we perceive with our senses demonstrates its essential vacuity. To speak of centaurs, despite the absence of such creatures "in Nature,"[32] he writes, is to abuse language. "Though our Words signifie nothing but our *Ideas*," he insists,

25. "Contingit . . . ex hoc quod passio est concitata, ut id quod proponitur imaginationi, iudicetur prosequendum, quia ei qui a passione detinetur, videtur esse bonum id ad quod per passionem inclinatur," Aquinas, *Summa theologiae*, Blackfriars, I^{a}–II^{ae}, vol. 25, qu. 80, art. 2. Cf. Aristotle, *De Somno et Virgil. De Insomn.* iii, iv.

26. For discussion, see Rebecca Tierney-Hynes, *Novel Minds: Philosophers and Romance Readers, 1680–1740* (Basingstoke: Palgrave Macmillan, 2012), 3–6.

27. Thomas Hobbes, *Leviathan*, ed. Noel Malcolm, 3 vols. (Oxford: Clarendon Press, 2012), vol. 2, I, 2, 28–30.

28. John Locke, *An Essay Concerning Human Understanding*, ed. Peter H. Nidditch (Oxford: Clarendon Press, 1979), bk. IV, chap. 4, 4, 564.

29. Ibid.

30. Ibid., bk. IV, chap. 5, 7, 577.

31. Ibid.

32. Ibid., bk. IV, chap. 5, 8, 578.

they are "designed . . . to signifie Things,"[33] and the word "centaur" signifies no such thing. While, for empiricists like Hobbes and Locke, the problem with the imagination is that it is insufficiently grounded in sense perception, for rationalists like René Descartes, the problem with it is that it is excessively grounded in this faculty. In his *Discours sur la méthode* (1637), Descartes states, "We can very distinctly imagine the head of a lion grafted onto the body of a goat without it being therefore necessary to conclude from this that there exists in the world a chimaera."[34] However "vivid and absolute"[35] the products of our imagination may be, he warns, they are not "clear and distinct,"[36] like the products of our understanding, and they ought not be trusted for that reason. Whether empiricists or rationalists, these philosophers agree that imagination can mislead us because it enables us to perceive things that do not exist.

For modern thinkers of a realist orientation, people go astray in what they apprehend with the imagination because they should be relying upon observation instead. Samuel Johnson, writing in *The Rambler* (1730), objects to heroic romances, which represent giants abducting ladies and knights then rescuing these ladies from the giants' clutches. In depicting such scenes, he states, the author needs only "to retire to his closet, let loose his invention, and heat his mind with incredibilities,"[37] without fear of being criticized for misrepresenting these events. In contrast, Johnson praises contemporary novels, which represent familiar people in familiar settings. The author of such works relies not upon the "wild strain of imagination" but upon "accurate observation of the living world,"[38] in which he stands to be corrected by those who can compare his writing with the original it is depicting. In *Adam Bede* (1859), George Eliot likewise rejects works that portray creatures that have never existed. She claims, "Falsehood is so easy, truth so difficult. The pencil is conscious of a delightful facility in drawing a

33. Ibid., 577.

34. "nous pouuons bien imaginer distinctement une teste de lion entée sur le cors d'vne cheure, sans qu'il faille conclure, pour cela, qu'il y ait au monde vne Chimere," René Descartes, *Discours sur la méthode*, in *Oeuvres de Descartes*, ed. Charles Adam and Paul Tannery, 11 vols. (Paris: J. Vrin, 1996), vol. 6, 1–78, at IV, 40.

35. "viues et expresses," ibid.

36. "claires et distinctes," ibid., 39.

37. Samuel Johnson, *The Rambler*, no. 4 (March 31, 1730), in *Novel Definitions: An Anthology of Commentary on the Novel, 1688–1815*, ed. Cheryl Nixon (Buffalo, NY: Broadview Press, 2009), 148–52, at 149.

38. Ibid.

griffin—the longer the claws, and the larger the wings, the better; but that marvelous facility which we mistook for genius is apt to forsake us when we want to draw a real unexaggerated lion."[39] It is a facile and, she suggests, worthless endeavor to represent products of one's imagination, which tend to extremes, and a more difficult and more worthwhile task to represent the objects of one's observation, which tend to the middle path. She affirms that her vocation as a novelist is not "to represent things as they never have been and never will be," but, rather, "to give a faithful account of men and things as they have mirrored themselves in my mind."[40] However defective that mirror may be, she feels herself to be duty bound to attest to what she sees in it, much as if she were a witness speaking under oath from a witness box. As a principle of her writing, she declares, she will represent the "common coarse people"[41] she knows from her own experience, "whose faces I know, whose hands I touch,"[42] as opposed to exalted personages whom "I shall never know except by hearsay."[43] While Eliot acknowledges that the representation of the world in her novels is necessarily mediated by her own perception of the world, she asserts that, in works of fiction, just as in a court of law, such testimony provides the best access to truth. It is when art attunes its audiences to the common people—"the small shopkeepers, artisans, and peasantry"[44]—observed in real life, she argues, that it moves us to feel for these people and to act on their behalf. It aids in "the extension of our sympathies,"[45] enabling us to appreciate the plight of victims of poverty and injustice and stirring us to bring about social reform. As such realist thinkers understand the situation, by focusing upon what one can observe in the world, in terms of people's external living conditions, one can help make that world a better place.

For some twentieth-century thinkers as well, one should rely not upon the imagination, but upon observation because one is ethically obliged to do so. Even among the Inklings (the informal literary society at Oxford in the 1930s and 1940s to which Tolkien and Lewis both belonged), there were those who resisted the imaginative demands that *The Lord of the Rings* (written 1937–49) imposed upon its readers. It is

39. George Eliot, *Adam Bede*, bk. II, chap. 17, 193.
40. Ibid.
41. Ibid., 188.
42. Ibid., 197.
43. Ibid., 189.
44. Ibid., 112.
45. Ibid., 110.

said that Hugo Dyson would lie on the couch and shout, "Oh God, no more Elves."[46] Far from entering into the "enchanted state"[47] that Tolkien deems necessary for appreciation of such literature, these critics remain in a rational state that leaves them outside what they are reading. As these critics deny that the Secondary World can ever be true, they deny that this Secondary World can ever make our own Primary World better. First appearing in the 1930s, the word "escapism" was originally used to describe the refusal to face up to political crises, such as the approach of World War II or the Cold War, or to social and economic crises, such as those brought about by the Depression; it was then applied to Hollywood movies, Broadway musicals, and radio soap operas that encouraged audiences to retreat from such challenges.[48] All fiction (and, indeed, much nonfiction) is, in some sense, "escapist" insofar as it takes the reader into an alternate realm, yet, over time, fantasy came to be perceived as particularly dangerous in this regard. In reviews of *The Lord of the Rings*, some critics saw Tolkien's celebration of good over evil as denying the moral complexity of the modern world. Edmund Wilson objects, "What we get is a simple confrontation—in more or less the traditional terms of British melodrama—of the Forces of Evil with the Forces of Good, the remote and alien villain with the plucky little home-grown hero."[49] Other critics saw Tolkien's idealized portrait of traditional rural society as reflecting a nostalgia for a preindustrial way of life. Instead of addressing the political, economic, and social problems of his day, he is seen as distracting his readers from these problems and as lulling them into dreaming about another, better universe, in which they can dwell contented.[50] Instead of challenging his readers, he is seen as comforting them, echoing, in the very cadence of his sentences, children's classics like lullabies, *Winnie-the-Pooh*, and *Watership Down*.[51] The science fiction writer Michael Moorcock com-

46. Derek Bailey (director) and Judi Dench (narrator), *A Film Portrait of J. R. R. Tolkien* (Visual Corporation, 1992).

47. Tolkien, "On Fairy-Stories," 52.

48. On the many problems with the term "escapism," see Robert B. Heilman, "Escape and Escapism: Varieties of Literary Experience," *Sewanee Review* 83, no. 3 (1975): 439–58, and C. S. Lewis, *An Experiment in Criticism* (Cambridge: Cambridge University Press, 1961; rpt., 2013), 68–70.

49. Wilson, "OO, Those Awful Orcs!" *The Nation* (April 14, 1956): 312–14.

50. See David Brin, "*The Lord of the Rings*: J.R.R. Tolkien vs. the Modern Age," in *Through Stranger Eyes: Reviews, Introductions, Tributes, and Iconoclastic Essays*, ed. David Brin (Ann Arbor, MI: Nimble Books, 2008), 27–38, and Rosemary Jackson, *Fantasy: The Literature of Subversion* (London: Routledge, 1981).

51. See Michael Moorcock, "Epic Pooh," in *Wizardry and Wild Romance: A Study of Epic Fantasy* (London: Victor Gollancz, 1989), 121–39; rpt. in *J. R. R. Tolkien's "The Lord of the Rings,"* ed. Harold Bloom, new ed. (New York: Chelsea House, 2008), 3–18. See also Thomas Reed Whis-

plains that *The Lord of the Rings* proposes to its readers, "Let's all be cozy . . . let's forget about our troubles and go to sleep."[52]

For other late antique and medieval thinkers, however, because reality is not only physical but also spiritual, one perceives it not only through one's senses but also through one's imagination. In his *De oratore* (55 BCE), Cicero recalled how the artist Zeuxis of Heraclea, in order to paint a picture of Helen for the people of Crotona, had assembled the loveliest virgins of the town, and he had used their composite beauties as a model for the painting.[53] While Cicero, following Plato, identified "thought . . . and mind"[54] as that which enables the artist to depict, not just a beautiful girl, but Beauty itself, Philostratus, in his *Life of Apollonius of Tyana* (AD 220), becomes the first to identify "imagination" (*phantasia*) as playing that role. Recalling the example of Phidias, who had carved the statues of Jupiter in Olympia and Minerva in Athens, he attributes Greek artists' representations of the gods, not to "imitation" (*mimēsis*), but to "imagination" (*phantasia*): "Imagination . . . created these objects, . . . a more skillful artist than Imitation. Imitation will create what it knows, but Imagination will also create what it does not know, conceiving it with reference to the real."[55] As pagan authors cite imagination as that which enables us to apprehend, not just visible, imperfect human beings but invisible, perfect forms or gods, Christian authors cite this faculty as that which enables us to apprehend the Christian deity. In the twelfth century, William of Saint-Thierry thanks Jesus Christ in his *Meditationes devotissimae* (ca. 1128–35) for living among us, out of recognition that we need to see God in his humanity before we can apprehend him in his divinity. Even now, he tells his Savior, "You will graciously permit my weak soul to exercise its natural abilities [by dwelling] on your lowliness through some imagination [*imaginatione*] of the mind."[56] If William focuses upon Christ as a man, and not as God, it is because, as a man himself, obliged to perceive through his senses, he needs to imagine him as a

---

sen, *Classic Cult Fiction: A Companion to Popular Cult Literature* (Westport, CT: Greenwood Press, 1992), 149.

52. See Moorcock, "Epic Pooh," 9.

53. See Cicero, *De inventione*, ed. Stroebel, II, 1, 77.

54. "cogitatione . . . et mente," *Ciceros Orator ad M. Brutum*, ed. Karl Wilhelm Piderit (Leipzig: B. G. Teubner, 1865), II, 7, 34.

55. Philostratus, *The Life of Apollonius of Tyana*, ed. and trans. Christopher P. Jones, Loeb Classical Library, 3 vols. (Cambridge, MA: Harvard University Press, 2005–6), vol. 2, VI, 19, 155.

56. "permittes et gratum habebis ipsa mentis imaginatione circa humilia tua infirmam adhuc animam meam suam indolem exercere," William of Saint-Thierry, *Meditationes devotissimae*, ed. Paul Verdeyen, CCCM, vol. 89 (Turnhout: Brepols, 2005), *Meditatio* 10:4, 58.

physical being before he can understand him as a metaphysical Being. Like William, Richard of Saint-Victor promotes imagination as a means by which human beings can gain access to God when they are not yet strong enough to do so through reason alone. He writes, "The mind . . . thinks through imagination because it is not yet strong enough to see through the purity of understanding."[57] He praises imagination as that which allows us to ascend in thought from the created world to the Creator, from mixtures of good and evil to pure good and pure evil, and from our earth to Heaven and Hell. Imagination can lead us to the truth, these authors argue, because it enables us to grasp with the mind's eye that which exists but which we cannot see, at least for now, with our bodily vision. Even as imagination was regarded as a potential source of error, it was regarded as a potential source of truth insofar as it gives us access to realities we could not otherwise detect.

For early modern thinkers of a Neoplatonic bent, because reality is not only physical but spiritual, one aspires to attain that spiritual reality through imagination. Sir Philip Sidney points out in his *Defence of Poesy* that while other artists meekly imitate Nature, the poet freely invents his own version of her, which is typically superior to that around him. He writes, "Only the poet, disdaining to be tied to any such subjection, lifted up with the vigor of his own invention, doth grow in effect into another Nature; in making things either better than Nature bringeth forth, or, quite anew, forms such as never were in Nature: as the heroes, demigods, Cyclops, Chimeras, Furies, and such like."[58] If poets can create a world beyond that of Nature, he argues, it is because, as creatures of God, we still conceive and aspire to an excellence which, as sons of Adam, we can no longer attain. In creating such exemplary figures, he observes, poets write things "not wholly imaginative, as we are wont to say by them that build castles in the air, but . . . substantially," insofar as they create people "as Nature might have done."[59] When poets break free from imitating Nature, with its imperfect human beings, and invent a new Nature, with perfect people, he asserts, they do not lie but, rather, represent a higher, divine truth. In his *Advancement of Learning* (1605), Sir Francis Bacon similarly argues that while reason subjugates man, by convincing him that the physi-

57. "mens . . . cogitat per imaginationem, quia necdum videre valet per intelligentiae puritatem," Richard of Saint-Victor, *Praeparatione animi ad contemplationem (Benjamin Minor)*, PL, vol. 196, chap. 14, col. 10.

58. Sir Philip Sidney, *The Defence of Poesy*, in *Sidney's "Defence of Poesy" and Selected Renaissance Literary Criticism*, ed. Alexander Gavin (Harmondsworth: Penguin Classics, 2004), 1–54, at 8–9.

59. Ibid., 9.

cal world is the only true world, imagination frees him, by enabling him to apprehend an alternate mental universe. While "Reason doth buckle and bow the Mind unto the Nature of things,"[60] as he puts it, "POESIE . . . doth truly refer to the Imagination, which [is] not tied to the Laws of Matter."[61] He writes of "poesy" (or literature), "The use of this FEIGNED HISTORY, hath been to give some shadow of satisfaction to the mind of Man in those points, wherein the Nature of things doth deny it, the world being in proportion inferior to the soul: by reason whereof there is agreeable to the spirit of Man, a more ample Greatness, a more exact Goodness; and a more absolute variety then can be found in the Nature of things."[62] If the world imagined inside literature is superior to the world experienced outside its pages, it is because the soul, which gives birth to literature, is superior to that external world and is therefore dissatisfied with what it has to offer. Human beings suffer from the disjunction between the world as it should be and the world as it is, and literature, by offering us the image of the world as it should be, temporarily assuages that suffering.

For modern thinkers of a Romantic orientation as well, people attain truth through the imagination. In his *Brief über den Roman* (1799), Karl Wilhelm Friedrich Schlegel defines Romanticism in terms of this faculty. Identifying that which is "Romantic"[63] with a "spiritual"[64] feeling, rooted in love, he expounds, "Only fantasy can seize the mystery of this love and represent it as a mystery. This mysteriousness is the source of the fantastic in the form of all poetic representation."[65] While observation enables us to apprehend empirical reality, that is, that which exists in the world, imagination enables us to apprehend a spiritual reality, that is, that which we desire in our minds. Friedrich's brother, August Wilhelm Schlegel, writes of those who value, not "possession [*Besitz*],"[66] or an attachment to something in the present time,

60. Francis Bacon, *The Advancement of Learning*, ed. Michael Kiernan (Oxford: Clarendon Press, 2000), 74. I have modernized Bacon's spelling.

61. Ibid., 73.

62. Ibid.

63. "das Romantische," Karl Wilhelm Friedrich Schlegel, *Brief über den Roman*, in *Kritische Friedrich-Schlegel-Ausgabe*, ed. Ernst Behler, 35 vols. (Munich: Paderborn, 1967), vol. 2, 329–39, at 335.

64. "geistige," ibid., 333.

65. "Nur die Fantasie kann das Rätsel dieser Liebe fassen und als Rätsel darstellen, und dieses Rätselhafte ist Quelle von dem Fantastischen in der Form aller poetischen Darstellung" ibid., 334.

66. "Besitzes," August Wilhelm von Schlegel, *Vorlesungen über dramatische Kunst und Literatur*, ed. Lohner, Erste Vorlesgung, vol. 1, 25.

but "yearning [*Sehnsucht*],"[67] or a memory of something in the past and a presentiment of something in the future. We recognize, he states, "that we strive after a bliss that is unattainable here, that no external object will ever be able to entirely satisfy our souls, that all pleasure is a fleeting illusion."[68] Though Eliot believed that it is realist fiction that represents what is, Percy Bysshe Shelley argues in his *Defence of Poetry* (1840) that it is (Romantic) poetry that achieves this aim. He writes famously, "Poetry lifts the veil from the hidden beauty of the world, and makes familiar objects be as if they were not familiar."[69] Through some "secret alchemy," he claims, "It strips the veil of familiarity from the world, and lays bare the naked and sleeping beauty, which is the spirit of its forms. . . . [I]t purges from our inward sight the film of familiarity which obscures from us the wonder of our being."[70] When we behold a thing again and again, he maintains, we cease to appreciate that which is inherently lovely and marvelous about it. Poetry, by removing the "veil" or "film" of that familiarity, enables us to apprehend its beauty and wondrousness once more. Though Eliot believed that it is observation that enables us to appreciate and love our fellow human beings, Shelley asserts that it is imagination that produces this result. He writes, "A man, to be greatly good, must imagine intensely and comprehensively; he must put himself in the place of another and of many others; the pains and pleasure of his species must become his own. The great instrument of moral good is the imagination."[71] While the realist novel may represent the world as it is, in its manifest aspect, Romantic poetry, these authors affirm, represents the world as it can be, once we open ourselves up to its latent possibilities. As such thinkers understand the situation, by focusing, not only upon what one observes but upon what one imagines, one can see the world from a new perspective and, in doing so, improve it.

For twentieth-century thinkers of this kind, because reality is, in part, spiritual, one perceives it through dreaming of an alternative to what one now knows. These critics assert that the "imagined" or "Sec-

67. "Sehnsucht," ibid.

68. "daß wir nach einer hier enerreichbaren Glückseligkeit trachten, daß kein äußerer Gegenstand jemals unsre Seele ganz wird erfüllen können, daß aller Genuß eine flüchtige Täuschung ist," ibid.

69. Percy Bysshe Shelley, *A Defence of Poetry*, in *Shelley's Poetry and Prose*, ed. Donald H. Reiman and Neil Fraistat, Norton Critical Editions, 2nd ed. (New York: W. W. Norton, 2002), 509–35, at 517.

70. Ibid., 533.

71. Ibid., 517.

ondary" world can indeed be true. G. K. Chesterton, in *Charles Dickens* (1906), recalls how Dickens once read the glass plate of a door in London from the wrong side, so that the words "COFFEE ROOM" appeared to him to signify "MOOR EEFFOC."[72] He comments, "That wild word, 'Moor Eeffoc,' is the motto of all effective realism; it is the masterpiece of the good realistic principle—the principle that the most fantastic thing of all is often the precise fact."[73] While Chesterton identifies the "realism" of this novelist with the fantastic, Tolkien uses his reading of this passage to define fantasy, as he envisions it, setting "realism" to the side. He writes, "*Mooreeffoc* is a fantastic word . . . and it was used by Chesterton to denote the queerness of things that have become trite, when they are seen suddenly from a new angle. . . . The word *Mooreeffoc* may cause you suddenly to realize that England is an utterly alien land."[74] Though Tolkien admires such defamiliarization, which makes one's own country seem foreign, he admires even more what he calls "creative fantasy,"[75] which enables one to envision another, alternate world.[76] He claims that "fairy-stories" teach us, if not to "see . . . things as they are," then to "see . . . things as we are (or were) meant to see them."[77] While critics charge fantasy with "escapism," Tolkien affirms the desirability of escape, "not indeed from life, but from our present time and self-made misery."[78] Though the presentism of realist fiction makes his contemporaries resign themselves to modern inventions in all of their ugliness, the archaism of fantasy makes him wonder if we cannot come up with alternatives to them that would be more beautiful. Comparing the bridge at Bletchley Railway Station with the bridge Bifröst in Norse myth, he asks "whether railway-engineers, if they had been brought up on more fantasy, might not have done better with all their abundant means than they commonly do."[79] As Tolkien questions

72. G. K. Chesterton, *Chesterton on Dickens*, in *The Collected Works of G. K. Chesterton*, 37 vols. (San Francisco: Ignatius Press, 1989), vol. 15, 65. Chesterton is quoting from John Forster, *The Life of Charles Dickens*, 2 vols. (London: Cecil Palmer, 1872–74), vol. 1 (1812–1842), 37.

73. Chesterton, *Chesterton on Dickens*, 65.

74. Tolkien, "On Fairy-Stories," 68.

75. Ibid.

76. Tolkien appears to have relied, not upon Chesterton's passage from *Charles Dickens*, but upon Maisie Ward's retelling of this passage in her introduction to his *The Coloured Lands* (London: Sheed and Ward, 1938), 9–16, at 14–15. There, Ward glosses Chesterton's words by writing, "Gloomy fantasy is truth read backwards. Cheerful fantasy is the creation of a new form wherein man, become creator, co-operates with God" (14–15).

77. Tolkien, "On Fairy-Stories," 67.

78. Ibid., 72.

79. Ibid., 71.

the value of "progressive things like factories, or the machine-guns and bombs,"[80] Ursula K. Le Guin questions the value of "the neutron bomb, the terrorist, and the next plague."[81] As Tolkien praises fantasy for offering an alternative to the seemingly "natural and inevitable, dare we say 'inexorable,' products"[82] of our civilization, Le Guin commends it for suggesting "that there is somewhere else, anywhere else, where other people may live another kind of life." She writes, "The literature of imagination, even when tragic, is reassuring, not necessarily in the sense of offering nostalgic comfort, but because it offers a world large enough to contain alternatives and therefore offers hope."[83] By presenting us with another, better world, fantasy presents us with a model to which we can aspire or in which we can at least temporarily reside.

The stakes of this debate over the truth value of the imagination and the literature it inspires are serious. For its critics, those who write about black swans, griffins, or elves are writing about things that do not exist and cannot exist, at the expense of those that do. The problem with such writing is not only epistemological, insofar as it treats unreal creatures as if they were real, but ethical and political, insofar as it disregards actual people and their actual needs, in all of their urgency. For its defenders, those who write about fantastical beings and the worlds they inhabit are writing about things that *do* exist, though as something metaphysical rather than physical, as something desired rather than possessed, or as something remembered in the past or hoped for in the future, rather than experienced in the present. These beings are no more or less true than beauty, or love, or goodness are true. By lifting us above mundane reality and allowing us to glimpse something more transcendent, these literary works enable us to appreciate the abstract virtue present in concrete individuals and, in doing so, to cherish those individuals all the more.

The Chronicles of Narnia

In accordance with the long series of thinkers before him, Lewis argues in *The Chronicles of Narnia* for the truth value of the imagination, but

80. Ibid.

81. Ursula K. Le Guin, "The Critics, the Monsters, and the Fantasists," in *The Secret History of Fantasy*, ed. Peter S. Beagle (San Francisco: Tachyon, 2010), 355–66, at 366.

82. Tolkien, "On Fairy-Stories," 71.

83. Le Guin, "Critics, the Monsters, and the Fantasists," 366.

he does so through the story he tells.[84] In *The Lion, the Witch, and the Wardrobe*, the first and most famous of the chronicles he wrote, the siblings Peter, Susan, Edmund, and Lucy Pevensie have been evacuated to an old Professor's house in the country during World War II in order to escape the air raids in London. One rainy day, the children are exploring the house, and they happen upon a room that is empty except for a large wardrobe. Peter declares, "Nothing there!" (113). We are told, "They all trooped out again—all except Lucy" (113). Slipping into the wardrobe, Lucy pushes her way past fur coats and finds herself entering into another world, which, she learns, is called Narnia, and in which first Edmund and then the rest of her siblings eventually join her. The truth value of this kingdom is understood in various ways. Narnia is like a dream. When Lucy initially cannot reenter this country through the wardrobe, she wonders if she had not dreamed of traveling there. Narnia is like a game. When Lucy first tells her siblings about this land, Peter suggests, "She's just making up a story for fun" (120). Finally, Narnia is like a fairy-tale. As we are told, it is "a place . . . where there are . . . all the sorts of things you have in fairy-tales" (551). The Pevensie children have read a wide variety of imaginative fiction, including classical myths, the *Arabian Nights*, and stories about chivalry, adventures, and shipwrecks, and this literature helps them to make sense of what they find in this land. Yet while one might assume that children dream, play games, and read fairy-tales in a way in which grownups do not because they are less attached to reality than their elders, Lewis suggests that the opposite is the case. If that to which one gains access when one is dreaming, playing, or reading fairy-tales seems unreal, it is because, in some Platonic sense, it is so real that one is only dimly able to apprehend its reality. In the conclusion of the chronicles, when the Pevensie children arrive in the homeland of the great lion Aslan, the Professor tells them, "Our own world, England and all, is only a shadow or copy of something in Aslan's real world. . . . And of course it is different;

84. On Lewis's *The Chronicles of Narnia*, see Alan Jacobs, "The Chronicles of Narnia," in *The Cambridge Companion to C. S. Lewis*, ed. Robert MacSwain and Michael Wood (Cambridge: Cambridge University Press, 2010), 265–80; William Gray, *Fantasy, Myth, and the Measure of Truth: Tales of Pullman, Lewis, Tolkien, MacDonald, and Hoffman* (New York: Palgrave Macmillan, 2009), esp. chap. 4, "C. S. Lewis: Reality and the Radiance of Myth," 104–51; Peter J. Schakel, *Imagination and the Arts in C. S. Lewis: Journeying to Narnia and Other Worlds* (Columbia: University of Missouri Press, 2002); Joe R. Christopher, *C. S. Lewis* (Boston: Twayne, 1974), esp. chap. 9, "The Romancer (II): *The Chronicles of Narnia* (1950–56)," 110–25; and Walter Hooper, *Past Watchful Dragons: The Narnian Chronicles of C. S. Lewis* (London: Collier Macmillan, 1971). Laura Miller, *A Magician's Book: A Skeptic's Adventures in Narnia* (New York: Little, Brown, 2008), is especially interesting. All references in this section are to Lewis, *The Chronicles of Narnia* (New York: HarperCollins, 2004).

as different as a real thing is from a shadow or as waking life is from a dream" (759). The Secondary World of Narnia and, even more, of Aslan's homeland is ultimately more real than our Primary World.

As books about the truth value of the imagination, *The Chronicles of Narnia* are also books about the truth value of works like itself. An author of what he called at various points "romances,"[85] "fairy-tales,"[86] or "fantasy,"[87] Lewis was also a professor of literature at the University of Oxford and, then, Cambridge, and he situates his and others' fantastical writings within the European literary tradition. If he and his fellow fantasists delight in "dwarfs and giants and talking beasts and witches,"[88] he argues, so did the audiences of Greek and Norse myths, Homer's *Odyssey*, *Beowulf*, Sir Thomas Malory's *Le Morte D'Arthur*, Ludovico Ariosto's *Orlando furioso*, and William Shakespeare's *The Tempest*. Why is it, he wonders, that in the classical, medieval, and Renaissance periods, the taste for the fantastical was common to all audiences, yet in the twentieth century, "a period almost pathological in its anti-romanticism,"[89] it is considered appropriate only for children? Why is it that adults who take pleasure in such works are now regarded as suffering from "nostalgia,"[90] "childishness,"[91] or "arrested development"[92]? The problem, he decides, lies not in fantastical literature but in the manner in which certain readers approach this literature today. In *The Chronicles of Narnia* as well as his literary criticism, Lewis indicates how one should not, and should, respond to the otherness one finds in books and in the world. When Edmund first enters Narnia, his self-centeredness prevents him from enjoying the delightful other-

85. Lewis refers to "my romances" in "A Reply to Professor Haldane," in *Of Other Worlds: Essays and Stories* (New York: A Harvest Book / Harcourt, 1966), 74–85.

86. Lewis refers to "fairy-tales for children and romances for adults," as if he sees the two genres as synonymous, aside from the audiences for which they are aimed. See C. S. Lewis, *An Experiment in Criticism* (Cambridge: University Press, 1961; rpt., Cambridge: Cambridge University Press, 2013), 67. He refers to "fantasy (including *Märchen*)" and to "fantasies and fairy-tales" in ibid., 70.

87. Lewis cites "that particular type of children's story which is dearest to my own taste, the fantasy or fairy-tale" in "On Three Ways of Writing for Children," in *Proceedings, Papers, and Summaries of Discussions of the Annual Conference of the Library Association at the Bournemouth Conference* (April 29–May 2, 1952) (London: Library Association, 1952), 22–28; rpt., *Of Other Worlds: Essays and Stories*, 22–34, at 24–25.

88. Ibid., 25.

89. "The Gods Return to Earth," review of J. R. R. Tolkien, *The Fellowship of the Ring* (being the First Part of *The Lord of the Rings*) (London: Allen and Unwin, 1954), *Time and Tide* 35 (August 14, 1954): 1082–83; rpt., *Image and Imagination: Essays and Reviews*, ed. Walter Hooper (Cambridge: Cambridge University Press, 2013), 99–103, at 99.

90. Lewis, "On Three Ways of Writing for Children," 25.

91. Lewis, *An Experiment in Criticism*, 70.

92. Lewis, "On Three Ways of Writing for Children," 25.

ness he finds there, or could find there if he were receptive to it, just as when the "non-literary" reader enters a fairy-tale, his self-centeredness serves as a barrier to similar delights.[93] In contrast, when Lucy enters this other realm, her openness to otherness enables her to take pleasure in what she discovers, just as when the "literary" reader enters a fairy-tale, her openness gives her access to what it has to offer. If one reads well, it is clear, one allows imagination to heighten one's appreciation of the strange and new things one stands to encounter, even on this side of the wardrobe door.

When Edmund first arrives in Narnia, as when the unliterary reader arrives in a fairy-tale, he focuses, not on this other world, but on himself. Lucy had told Peter, Susan, and Edmund that she had entered another world through the wardrobe, but none of them had believed her. If Edmund now steps into the wardrobe, it is not because he wants to see what is inside, let alone because he thinks he might gain access to Lucy's other world, but because he has just seen Lucy slip into the wardrobe again, and he wants to continue to tease her about "her imaginary country" (122). When he emerges into a snowy wood, he is displeased. Looking around himself, he is unsettled by the strangeness, the coldness, and the silence of this forest: "He . . . decided he did not much like this place, and had almost made up his mind to go home" (123). Hostile toward Narnia, Edmund is hostile toward most of the creatures he encounters there. When Lucy discovers him in Narnia, she happily shares with him what her friend, the faun Mr. Tumnus, has told her about this land, but he announces, "You can't always believe what Fauns say," "trying to sound as if he knew far more about them than Lucy" (128). Even as Lucy rejoices at the thought of the good fun they will have in Narnia together, we are informed, "Edmund secretly thought that it would not be as good fun for him as for her. He would have to admit that Lucy had been right, before all the others" (128). For Edmund, the opportunity to explore another world is less appealing than the opportunity to assert that he is right, to demonstrate to others that he is right, and, in doing so, to establish his superiority to those around him, especially to his little sister. Like Edmund, the unliterary reader focuses, not on the world he finds in his books, but on himself. He seeks not to "receive" the work of art, but to "use"[94] it for his own

93. While Lewis uses the masculine pronoun in speaking of "literary" and "non-literary" readers, it is clear from the examples he provides that he imagines both camps to include men and women, or boys and girls.

94. Lewis, *An Experiment in Criticism*, 18.

purposes, and he is frustrated with fairy-tales because they thwart such an aim. Shown a book of fairy-tales, the unliterary reader will protest that there is "no point in reading about 'things that could never really happen,'" and he will put it down. Such a story admits openly to the reader, "I am merely a work of art. . . . There is no question of anything like this happening to you in the real world."[95] It is about others, not about himself, and unliterary readers seek "reading [that] takes them least out of themselves."[96] Invited into another world, Edmund and the unliterary reader are reluctant to enter into it because they are thinking only of their own interest and doubting that they will profit from this excursion.

Because Edmund and the unliterary reader focus, not upon this other world, but upon themselves, they seek, not to appreciate the world in its enchantments, but to use it for their own purposes. Far from longing to see the world become animate, as Lucy does, Edmund longs to see himself become prince or king of this land. During his first visit to Narnia, he meets the White Witch, who is riding through the snowy wood in a sledge drawn by reindeer. When she sees him, she orders him to enter into the sledge, and she magically produces a hot, delicious drink and a box of Turkish Delight for him to consume. As he gorges himself upon this treat, the White Witch praises his cleverness and his handsomeness. She tells him that, as she has no children of her own, she would like to bring him up as prince and, later, after she is gone, have him become king of Narnia. If Edmund ends up allying himself with the White Witch, it is not because of what he sees in her, in and of herself, but because of what he thinks he can gain from her, for himself. Comparing her to his Peter and Susan, who have been critical of him of late because of his treatment of Lucy, he tells himself, "She was jolly nice to me . . . much nicer than they are. I expect she is the rightful Queen really" (152). What interests Edmund is not whether the White Witch is "jolly nice" in and of herself—he has already seen her act cruelly toward her reindeer—but whether she is "jolly nice *to him*," and this perception leads him to conclude, illogically, but self-interestedly, that she has a legitimate claim on the Narnian throne. Because he grasps not who the White Witch is, on absolute terms, but how she acts, relative to him, he blinds himself to her true identity and, as a result, to her true wickedness. Like Edmund, when the unliterary reader reads, he seeks to use the world for his own aims. Seeking litera-

95. Ibid., 55.
96. Ibid., 51.

ture only "as a help to castle-building,"[97] he prefers to read seemingly realistic books about successful men and women in whose triumphs he can vicariously share. As this reader turns the pages, it is he who makes the million dollars or she whom all eyes follow as she crosses a room. Of such books, Lewis writes, "It is all flattery to the ego. The pleasure consists in picturing oneself the object of admiration."[98] Yet the man is not likely to become a millionaire, the woman not likely to marry a duke. While a fairy-tale does not deceive its readers because it does not pretend to represent possible events, the "superficial realism"[99] of such works does mislead them because it claims that that which almost certainly cannot happen can happen. Lewis writes of the unliterary reader, "He wishes to be deceived, at least momentarily, and nothing can deceive unless it bears a plausible resemblance to reality."[100] Instead of the fantasy world, Edmund and the unliterary reader choose a pseudo-realist world that flatters their self-esteem.

Because Edmund does not appreciate that other world, in its enchantments, he at first resists its deeper reality. During Edmund's second visit to Narnia, this time with all of his siblings, the four children are invited to dine with Mr. and Mrs. Beaver in their den. There Edmund hears for the first time the name of Aslan, which provokes in him "a sensation of mysterious horror" (141). By the time he sneaks out of the Beavers' dam and starts making his way to the White Witch's house, he has developed a full-fledged aversion to what he refers to as "that awful Aslan" (152). When he arrives in the courtyard of the White Witch's house, he finds the statue of a lion, which, he deduces (mistakenly) must be Aslan, now turned to stone by the Witch. He jeers at the statue, "Yah! Silly old Aslan! How do you like being a stone? You thought yourself mighty fine, didn't you?" (154). He understands Aslan to be, not someone who *is* "mighty fine," but someone who *thinks* he is "mighty fine." Confronted with the notion of a truly good being, he tells himself that such goodness must be only a claim to goodness, and a false one at that. He enjoys the idea that such a high being should be cast low by being turned into stone, and he contributes to his debasement by drawing a pair of spectacles and a moustache on the lion's face. If Edmund recoils from Aslan, it is because he knows, from the way Mr. and Mrs. Beaver describe him, that this lion will uproot what

97. Ibid., 53.
98. Lewis, "On Three Ways of Writing for Children," 30.
99. Ibid.
100. Ibid., 56.

Lewis elsewhere calls the "self-centeredness"[101] of natural life. At the end of the book, after the Witch has tried to kill Edmund and after Aslan's followers have rescued him from her clutches, Peter, Susan, and Lucy see their brother walking with the lion. Later, when he watches the Witch and Aslan discuss his fate, we are told, "Edmund had got past thinking about himself after all he'd been through and after the talk he'd had that morning. He just went on looking at Aslan" (175). He has finally shifted his focus from himself to this other and from his own (falsely perceived) self-interest to an appreciation of this other.

In contrast, when Lucy enters Narnia and when the literary reader enters a fairy-tale, they focus, not upon themselves, but upon this other world. The Pevensie children are all exploring the house, and they are all seemingly interested in the suit of armor they discover in one room and the harp they find in another. But it is Lucy alone who thinks that an object as ordinary as a wardrobe may be worth investigating, and it is she alone who stays behind to pursue this possibility. As she makes her way through the wardrobe, she starts to feel something crunching under her feet, something that, when she bends down to feel it, feels cold, soft, and powdery to her touch. "This is very queer" (113), she says to herself. Before long, she has emerged outdoors, into the snowy wood. "Lucy felt a little frightened, but she was very inquisitive and excited as well" (113), we are told. She catches sight of a light in the distance and, walking toward it, is interested to learn that it comes from a lamp-post, somehow planted in the middle of this forest. While she is gazing up at the lamp-post, a faun happens upon her, introduces himself as Tumnus, and invites her to tea. Lucy replies, "I am very pleased to meet you, Mr. Tumnus" (115), and she accepts his invitation: "And so Lucy found herself walking through the wood arm in arm with this strange creature as if they had known one another all their lives" (116). As disconcerting as it may be to enter a wardrobe and come out into another world, let alone one populated by intelligent and talking animals, Lucy is eager to look around this new place, to discover what it holds, and to believe what these creatures tell her. Like Lucy, the literary reader concentrates not on herself but on what she finds in the other world of her reading. In doing so, Lewis writes, she "receives" a work of art. He explains, "When we 'receive' it, we exert our senses and imagination and various other powers according to a pattern invented by the artist."[102] As Lucy enters the wardrobe, as she

101. Ibid., 178–79.
102. Lewis, *An Experiment in Criticism*, 88.

reaches down to touch what she hears crunching underfoot, and as she seeks the source of the light in the snowy wood, the literary reader uses her full capacities of perception to absorb what she is reading, and it is in doing so that she experiences delight in this work. "Only when your whole attention and desire are fixed on something else . . . does the 'thrill' arise,"[103] Lewis states. And, as Lucy does not doubt the faun, the reader does not doubt the book she reads. She accepts, as Lewis puts it, that "the first demand any work of art makes upon us is surrender."[104] Eager to explore the world they have discovered, Lucy and this reader have no concern for themselves or for what they stand to gain from it.

Because Lucy and the literary reader focus upon the other world, they are able to perceive that world as enchanted. In *The Lion, the Witch, and the Wardrobe,* Lucy had delighted in the talking animals and trees. In *Prince Caspian,* she and her siblings return to Narnia, but they discover that during their absence, the foreign Telarmines have conquered the country and have driven these marvelous creatures into hiding or into silence. One night, when Lucy is trying to fall asleep in a wood, it is said, "A great longing for the old days when the trees could talk in Narnia came over her" (369). This longing makes her look upon the trees around her differently. Gazing at a beech with its graceful foliage, she sees a slender, dancing girl. Gazing at an oak with its bulbous trunk, she sees a hearty old man with a beard and warts. She calls out to the trees to awaken. The text relates, "Though there was not a breath of wind, they all stirred about her. The rustling noise of the leaves was almost like words. . . . Lucy felt that at any moment she would begin to understand what the trees were trying to say" (369). Finally, she sees the trees become animate, like human beings or, rather, like giants and giantesses or gods and goddesses, though only for a moment in the moonlight: "When they looked like trees, it was like strangely human trees, and when they looked like people, it was like strangely branchy and leafy people" (379). Given her experiences in Narnia, Lucy can imagine the world becoming animate; because she can imagine this, she longs for it to happen; and, because she longs for it to happen, she is able to perceive it as happening. Like Lucy, the literary reader is open to the magic around her. Echoing Shelley, Lewis writes, "The value of the myth is that it takes all the things you know and restores

103. C. S. Lewis, *Surprised by Joy: The Shape of My Early Life* (London: G. Bles, 1955; rpt., Boston: Mariner Books, 2012), 168.

104. Lewis, *An Experiment in Criticism,* 18. Lewis writes that, when we are dealing with works of art or nature, "total surrender is the first step toward the fruition of either" (*Surprised by Joy,* 146).

to them the rich significance which has been hidden by 'the veil of familiarity.'"[105] If a boy who has read cowboy stories pretends that the cold meat he must eat for dinner is from a buffalo he has shot with his bow and arrow, Lewis suggests, his meat becomes tastier than it would have been if he had accepted that it came from the grocer's. Indeed, he adds, "You might say that only then it is the real meat."[106] If a girl who has read *The Chronicles of Narnia* pretends that the beeches and oaks amid which she is walking can move and speak, she appreciates the vitality of these trees more than she would have if she had accepted that they were inert matter.[107] Lewis writes of the literary reader, "He does not despise real woods because he has read of enchanted woods: the reading makes all real woods a little enchanted."[108] Far from making us disregard the natural, Lewis claims, the supernatural makes us apprehend it in its full reality. He writes, "Only Supernaturalists really see Nature. You must go a little away from her, and then turn round, and look back. Then at last the true landscape will become visible."[109] The fairy-tale, in all of its antirealism, does not draw the literary reader, like Lucy, away from reality, but, on the contrary, draws her back to reality, enabling her to see its irreducible mysteriousness in a way in which realistic genres could never do.

Because Lucy and the literary reader are able to perceive the enchantments of this other world, they are able to perceive the deeper reality that lies behind those enchantments. Until the very end of *The Chronicles of Narnia,* Lucy loves Aslan as a great and magnificent lion. After their first meeting, whenever she sees him, she spontaneously embraces him, buries her face in his mane, and kisses him. Aslan exists as an objective lion—"He was solid and real and warm, and he let her kiss him and bury herself in his shining mane" (498)—but he is perceived, at times, as a subjective phenomenon by those willing or able to behold him. Because Lucy loves Aslan more than any of the other children, she sees him more than any of the others. At one point,

105. C. S. Lewis, "The Dethronement of Power," review of J. R. R. Tolkien, *The Two Towers* (being the Second Part of *The Lord of the Rings*) and *The Return of the Ring* (being the Third Part of *The Lord of the Rings*), *Time and Tide* 36 (October 22, 1955): 1373–74; rpt., *Image and Imagination*, ed. Hooper, 104–9, at 108.

106. Ibid.

107. Lewis writes in "Of Stories," in *Of Other Worlds*, 3–21, "I have seen landscapes (notably in the Mourne Mountains) which, under a particular light, made me feel that at any moment a giant might raise his head over the next ridge" (8).

108. Lewis, "On Three Ways of Writing for Children," 29–30.

109. Lewis, *Miracles: A Preliminary Study* (London: G. Bles, 1947; rev. ed., 1960; rpt., New York: HarperCollins, 2000), 104.

when she and her companions run into trouble at sea, she prays to him for help. An albatross arrives and leads the ship in the right direction, "but no one except Lucy knew that as it circled the mast it had whispered to her, 'Courage, dear heart,' and the voice, she felt sure, was Aslan's" (511). In the final volume of *The Chronicles of Narnia,* Aslan tells Lucy that she is now too old to return to Narnia, yet he reassures her that he exists in our world as well, "but there I have another name" (541). Though the chronicles do not mention the name by which he is known in our world, as they come to their conclusion, Aslan speaks to Lucy and those with her, and it is said, "As He spoke, He no longer looked to them like a lion" (767). If Lucy has desired Aslan so much, it turns out, it is because all along he has been not just a literal lion but also the figurative Lion of the Book of Revelations, whom she has not been ready to recognize as such until now. Like Lucy, who entered Narnia as a child, Lewis relates, he entered the world of Norse and Celtic mythology as a boy. At that stage in his life, he had "surrendered" himself to this reading; he had "received" its stories; and, in doing so, he had undergone "something very like adoration, some kind of quite disinterested self-abandonment to an object"[110]—an object "[that] had, in fact, only shone through that system."[111] This object, he now realizes, exists as an objective Being, though it is perceived, at times, only as a subjective phenomenon by those willing or able to perceive it. If the reader of *The Chronicles of Narnia* desires Aslan, it is because human beings are always yearning for something that they perceive with their imagination—something that, though they cannot perceive it with their senses, must necessarily exist. "Creatures are not born with desires unless satisfaction for those desires exists,"[112] Lewis claims. As there exists food, for which the baby hungers, and water, in which the duck wishes to swim, he extrapolates, there must exist a true object, for which we are longing. Struck by what he calls "the resemblance between the Christian and the merely imaginative experience," he explains, "I think that all things, in their way, reflect heavenly truth, the imagination not least."[113] Just as works of fantasy enable the literary reader, like Lucy, to appreciate her own world all the better, they enable her to glimpse another world, beyond this one, as well.

110. Lewis, *Surprised by Joy,* 76–77.

111. Ibid., 168–69.

112. C. S. Lewis, *Mere Christianity* (New York: Macmillan, 1952; rpt., New York: HarperCollins, 2001), 136.

113. Lewis, *Surprised by Joy,* 167.

In the end, Lewis argues that those who immerse themselves in fairy-tales find, not error, but truth. The Pevensie children are ordinary middle-class schoolchildren who play hide-and-seek, who quarrel and make up, and who, as time goes by, go off to boarding school and study for university examinations. It may seem that they are, in fact, just pretending to travel to Narnia, as children will pretend to do things in their games. As Susan grows older and her attention shifts to "nylons and lipstick and invitations" (741)—that is, the conventional attributes of adult femininity—even she assumes this view. When her siblings speak of Narnia, she exclaims, "What wonderful memories you have! Fancy your still thinking about all those funny games we used to play when we were children" (741). If the children had adventures in Narnia, it would seem, it was only in their imaginations, and therefore not, by definition, in reality. Yet as ordinary as the Pevensie children may be, Lewis insists, they are also extraordinary. In Narnia, the girls become ladies and queens. In the invigorating air of this country, the "spirit of adventure" (322) rises up in them, and they become stronger, braver, and more stalwart than they were at home. The boys become knights and kings. Peter leads Aslan's troops against the White Witch and her army in the Battle of Beruna, and Edmund overcomes the witch by breaking her wand during this clash. Even when the children return to England, the "greatness" (399) that Narnia brought to the forefront of their characters, by giving full scope to their actions, remains latent within them. As Lewis suggests in his literary criticism, it is only when we see man in a "phantasmagoric never-never land,"[114] like Narnia, that we see him as he truly is: "The real life of men is of that mythical and heroic quality. . . . And man as a whole, . . . have we seen him at all till we see that he is like a hero in a fairy-tale?"[115]

In a eulogy for Charles Williams, a fellow Inkling, an editor of Oxford University Press, and the author of numerous novels, plays, and poems, many influenced by Arthurian literature, Lewis portrays his friend as such a hero out of a fairy-tale. Often, he recalls, when he was riding on the top of a bus, he would catch sight of Williams below. He states, "The face and hair being then invisible, he might have passed for . . . a boy of some period when swords were worn."[116] Recalling

114. Lewis, "Dethronement of Power," 108.

115. Ibid.

116. Lewis, preface to *Essays Presented to Charles Williams*, ed. C. S. Lewis (Oxford: Oxford University Press, 1947), 90–105; rpt. in *Of Other Worlds: Essays and Stories*, 110–24, at 118.

their time together at a pub, clouded with tobacco smoke, over a pint mug, he reports, "That face . . . comes back to me, . . . eagerly stretched forward in the cut and parry of prolonged, fierce, masculine argument and 'the rigor of the game.'"[117] As the Pevensies are ordinary, middle-class schoolchildren, Williams is an ordinary, middle-class editor and writer. He could be seen not from the battlements of a besieged castle or engaged in swordplay with a mortal enemy but from the upper level of a bus or engaged in a discussion with companions at a pub. Yet as the Pevensies prove extraordinary, Williams proves extraordinary. The same dignity, tenacity, and manliness that would have made him stand out in a chivalric context made him stand out in an academic setting. As Lewis sees it, he does not "romanticize" Williams, that is, take someone real and cast upon him the illusion of romance. Instead, he recognizes that Williams is, in reality, a romantic figure. In his view, the world *is* enchanted, and romance enables us to appreciate this fact.

Harry Potter

Like Lewis, Rowling argues for the truth value of the imagination through the story she tells.[118] When asked in a 2003 interview whether she believed in magic, she replied (to the disappointment of her young audience) that she did not believe in magic in the way that it appears in her novels, but she quickly added, "I could be slightly corny and say I do believe in other kinds of magic: the magic of the imagination, for example, and love."[119] Children's books as they are, the *Harry Potter* novels offer a sustained reflection on the reality of what we see with

117. Ibid.

118. Among the considerable number of studies of the *Harry Potter* novels that have already been produced, I have found Greg Garrett, *One Fine Potion: The Literary Magic of Harry Potter* (Waco, TX: Baylor University Press, 2010); Shira Wolosky, *The Riddles of Harry Potter: Secret Passages and Interpretive Quests* (New York: Palgrave Macmillan, 2010); and Andrew Blake, *The Irresistable Rise of Harry Potter* (London: Verso, 2002) especially helpful. Maria Nikolajeva, "Harry Potter—a Return to the Romantic Hero," in *Critical Perspectives on Harry Potter*, ed. Elizabeth Heilman (New York: Routledge, 2002), 125–40, and Anne Hiebert Alton, "Playing the Genre Game: Generic Fusions of the Harry Potter Series," in *Critical Perspectives on Harry Potter*, ed. Elizabeth Heilman, 2nd ed. (New York: Routledge, 2003), 199–223, at 218–20, examine the Harry Potter series from the perspective of Northrop Frye's theories of romance. See also Jack Zipes, "The Phenomenon of Harry Potter, or Why All the Talk?," in *Sticks and Stones: The Troublesome Success of Children's Literature from Slovenly Peter to Harry Potter* (New York: Routledge, 2000), 170–89.

119. J. K. Rowling, interview by Stephen Fry, Royal Albert Hall (June 26, 2003). http://www.accio-quote.org/articles/2003/0626-alberthall-fry.htm.

the mind's eye. Mental images in these works are often highly dangerous, in a way in which medieval scholastics would have recognized. At the beginning of *Harry Potter and the Philosopher's Stone*,[120] the first book in the series, the wicked wizard Voldemort, who had long oppressed the magical community, has murdered the parents of the one-year-old Harry and has attempted to murder the baby as well, though, for some mysterious reason, the killing curse he uttered ricocheted back upon him, defeating him for a time. For years afterward, the orphaned Harry does not think about Voldemort. He is brought up in his aunt and uncle's house in Little Whinging, Surrey, in ignorance of the magical world. When he is eleven years old, he heads off to Hogwarts School of Witchcraft and Wizardry, which is presided over by the wise headmaster Albus Dumbledore and where he thrives, honing his magical skills, becoming fast friends with Ron Weasley and Hermione Granger, and feeling himself to be at home for the first time in his life. Yet by attempting to kill Harry, Voldemort had created a curious bond between the older and the younger wizard, which gives them access to each other's minds. At one point, he is able to implant the false image of Harry's godfather being tortured in the Ministry of Magic in his mind so that Harry flies to the office building to rescue him, only to discover that he has been led into a trap. As one of Voldemort's followers jeers at that moment, "It's time you learned the difference between life and dreams, Potter" (5: 782). At the same time, mental images in these novels are also often beneficial, in a way in which Romantic poets would have understood. Over the course of the novels, Harry methodically prepares himself to meet his great antagonist by gaining access to memories, whether they are his own, traumatic recollection of his parents' death, or other people's recollections of important incidents in their past, which help him to take action against Voldemort when he returns to power. Ultimately, it is because Harry's imagination is so vivid, especially in its capacity to bring back the dead, that he becomes powerful enough to vanquish this superior wizard. If imagination is "magical" for Rowling, as she claims that it is, it is because it can

120. J. K. Rowling's *Harry Potter and the Philosopher's Stone* (London: Bloomsbury, 1997) was retitled *Harry Potter and the Sorcerer's Stone* (New York: Scholastic, 1997), for the American edition. All references in this section will be to *Harry Potter: Complete Book Series* (New York: Scholastic, 2015):1: *Harry Potter and the Philosopher's Stone* (1997); 2: *Harry Potter and the Chamber of Secrets* (1998); 3: *Harry Potter and the Prisoner of Azkeban* (1999): 4: *Harry Potter and the Goblet of Fire* (2000); 5: *Harry Potter and the Order of the Phoenix* (2003); 6: *Harry Potter and the Half-Blood Prince* (2005); and 7: *Harry Potter and the Deathly Hallows* (2007).

provide one with seemingly supernatural powers, whether they be in the Primary or the Secondary World.

As books about the truth value of the imagination, the *Harry Potter* novels are also books about the truth value of works like themselves. In contrast to Lewis, who was a literary scholar and a Christian apologist as well as a writer of children's stories, Rowling is exclusively a novelist. Her remarks about her *Harry Potter* writings have therefore largely been limited to interviews, web chats, and other informal exchanges, especially with young fans eager to clarify factual details about her Secondary World. In the last volume in this series, however, Rowling makes reference to *The Tales of Beedle the Bard*, a collection of stories for young witches and wizards, similar to "fairy-tales"[121] for "Muggle" (or nonmagical) children, which was supposedly composed by a fifteenth-century Yorkshire wizard. She later published this work as an independent title, with notes to the tales that were allegedly provided by Professor Dumbledore himself. (Indeed, throughout the *Harry Potter* novels, Dumbledore functions as Rowling's authorial voice, explaining how the magical world works and interpreting its events from the inside.) In the course of the final novel, Harry, Ron, and Hermione disagree as to how one should interpret a tale included in this collection known as "The Tale of the Three Brothers" (itself based on Geoffrey Chaucer's *Pardoner's Tale*). According to this tale, three wizard brothers, having thwarted Death at a river where he had expected they would drown, were granted ambiguous gifts from this figure. The oldest brother obtained the Elder Wand, a wand so powerful that it enabled him to defeat any other wizard in a duel. After boasting about this wand in his wine cups, he was slain in his sleep by another wizard who was eager to acquire it for himself. The middle brother obtained the Resurrection Stone, a stone so powerful that it could bring back those who have died. With it, he was able to revive the girl he wanted to marry, but, seeing that she no longer belonged among the living, he killed himself in order to join her among the dead. The youngest brother secured the Invisibility Cloak, a cloak so opaque that it could conceal all who wear it. For many years, he eluded Death by wearing this cloak, but, when he reached an advanced age, he removed it and gave it to his son: *"And then he greeted Death as an old friend, and went with him gladly, and, equals, they departed this life"* (7: 409). On the one hand, as Dumbledore explains in his notes, a small number of witches and wizards believe

121. J. K. Rowling, *The Tales of Beedle the Bard* (New York: Children's High Level Group, 2008), viii.

that the tale is literally true. Xenophilius Lovegood, the eccentric editor of the tabloid *The Quibbler*, for example, maintains that the three brothers were named Antioch, Cadmus, and Ignotus Peverell and that they did, in fact, own the three Deathly Hallows, the possession of which enables one to become the "master of death" (7: 410). Wizards like Mr. Lovegood embark on a quest for the Deathly Hallows in the hope of becoming immortal. On the other hand, other witches and wizards believe that the tale is only figuratively veracious. Ron classes the tale among "kids' stories" (7: 202). He asks, "That story's just one of those things you tell kids to teach them lessons, isn't it? Don't go looking for trouble, don't pick fights, don't go messing around with stuff that's best left alone!" (7: 414) Yet while the Deathly Hallows are not to be sought for one's own gain, as Mr. Lovegood seeks them, it turns out that they are still to be sought for others' benefit. By insisting upon the fundamental reality of the Deathly Hallows, Rowling insists upon the fundamental reality of the "fictional magic"[122] she writes.

Mr. Vernon and Mrs. Petunia Dursley, Harry's uncle and aunt, reject imagination. Even before Harry enters their lives, they try to block out anything out of the ordinary. One morning, while Mr. Dursley is picking out his tie and Mrs. Dursley is feeding her screaming baby Dudley, Rowling writes, "None of them noticed a large, tawny owl flutter past the window" (1: 2). As Mr. Dursley drives off to work, he sees a tabby cat on the corner of the street reading a map and then the sign that says "Privet Drive." "No," he thinks, correcting himself, "*looking* at the sign; cats couldn't read maps *or* signs" (1: 3). Though the owl is a messenger, bearing news from one witch or wizard to another, and though the cat on Privet Drive is a witch, currently in the guise of a cat, Mr. Dursley either does not notice these strange phenomena, or convinces himself that he has not noticed them, or, when forced to acknowledge that he *has* noticed them, becomes troubled. He hopes he is imagining these things, which is unusual for him, we are told, "because he didn't approve of imagination" (3). When Harry is growing up in their family, the Dursleys refuse to answer his questions about his parents and the true circumstances in which they died. One day, when Mr. Dursley is driving them all to the zoo, Harry innocently mentions having had a dream about a flying motorcycle. Mr. Dursley almost smashes his car into the vehicle ahead of them. "MOTORCYCLES DON'T FLY!" (1: 25), he shouts. It is explained, "If there was one thing the Dursleys hated

122. J. K. Rowling, "The Fringe Benefits of Failure, and the Importance of Imagination," http://news.harvard.edu/gazette/story/2008/06/text-of-j-k-rowling-speech/.

even more than his asking questions, it was his talking about anything acting in a way it shouldn't, no matter if it was in a dream or even a cartoon" (26). The problem is not only that "motorcycles don't fly"; it is that such a vehicle would be acting "in a way it shouldn't." When Mr. Dursley condemns the idea of a flying motorcycle, he is establishing not only how motorcycles *do* behave but also how they *ought* to behave, and he is thus linking what is habitual with what is possible and what is possible with what is acceptable. We are told, "Mr. and Mrs. Dursley . . . were the last people you'd expect to be involved in anything strange or mysterious, because they just didn't hold with such nonsense" (1: 1). When they hear someone speaking about things acting as they "don't," "can't," and "shouldn't" act, they believe they are hearing "nonsense," as if the laws by which the world works are no longer operable, and they become as infuriated as they would be if told that up is down or left is right. And when that which does not, cannot, and should not happen happens, they are furious and even terrified.

Not only Muggles but witches and wizards, and even good witches and wizards, at times, reject imagination.[123] Harry's friend Hermione, one of the most beloved characters in these novels, understands much about magic. She is the cleverest student in their year at Hogwarts. When she and the other students take their O.W.L. (Ordinary Wizarding Level) exams during their fifth year, she receives nine "Outstandings" and one "Exceeds Expectations." At the same time, there are aspects of magic that she does not comprehend. In response to Mr. Lovegood's information about the Deathly Hallows, she denies that there is such a thing as an unbeatable wand. Though she admits that there have been stories about extrapowerful wands for hundreds of years, she declares, "Wands are only as powerful as the wizards who use them" (7: 415). She denies that there is such a thing as a Resurrection Stone. When she refers to it, "Her fingers sketched quotation marks around the name, and her tone dripped sarcasm" (7: 427), and she proclaims, "No magic can raise the dead, and that's that!" (7: 427). She does not deny that there can be an Invisibility Cloak, as Harry has inherited one from his father, but she refuses to believe that his

123. Interestingly, in *Harry Potter and the Chamber of Secrets*, it is Hermione who had argued (correctly) for the possibility that the Chamber of Secrets existed, in the face of academic skepticism. When Professor Binns, the history of magic teacher at Hogwarts, dismisses tales about the Chamber of Secrets as "myths and legends" (149), in contrast to the "*facts*" (149) he imparts, Hermione inquires if legends do not have a basis in fact. See also Anne Rubenstein, "Hermione Raised Her Hand Again: Wizards Writing History," in *Harry Potter and History*, ed. Nancy R. Reagin (Hoboken, NJ: John Wiley and Sons, 2011), 309–21.

cloak is the one in the tale. It is not that Hermione is mistaken. In his words to Harry and in his notes to "The Tale of the Three Brothers," Dumbledore confirms the magical principles that Hermione has learned at school and that she uses to guide her interpretation of this legend. But Hermione is unable to grasp the truth of "The Tale of the Three Brothers." "It's just a morality tale" (7: 414), she asserts. "A story about how humans are frightened of death" (7: 426). If Hermione interprets the tale in this manner, it is not because humans are necessarily frightened of death—the youngest brother in the tale exhibits no such fear in the end—but because *she* is frightened of death. When Harry attempts to persuade her that the Resurrection Stone can exists, he sees alarm in her face: "He had scared her with his talk of living with dead people" (7: 427). While Hermione does not go so far as to inveigh against things happening as they "shouldn't," she insists repeatedly, "The Deathly Hallows can't exist!" (7: 415). As she sees it, it is not just that these objects *do not* exist, or that magic *does not* raise the dead; it is that they *cannot* exist, that magic *cannot* do that—"and that's that!" The same magical principles that Dumbledore speaks of tentatively, as provisional conclusions drawn from extant evidence, she speaks of categorically, as immutable laws. After hearing Mr. Lovegood's explanation of the story, she protests, "I never heard such a lot of nonsense in all my life" (7: 426). When she hears someone speaking about these things acting as they "don't" and "can't," she believes that she is hearing "nonsense," as if the laws by which the magical world work are no longer functioning. When that which does not and cannot happen does, in fact, happen, she is "flabbergasted" (7: 496).

Even the very most accomplished witches and wizards, it turns out, may spurn imagination, to their detriment. Voldemort understands much about magic. He was a brilliant student at Hogwarts. In the years since his departure from that school, he boasts, "I have pushed the boundaries of magic further, perhaps, than they have ever been pushed" (6: 443). Yet there is also much that Voldemort does not understand. He does not understand death. It is surmised that having been brought up in a Muggle orphanage, Voldemort would have been ignorant of "The Tale of the Three Brothers," but he imitates the eldest brother in his attempt to obtain the Elder Wand, and he believes himself to be secure from Death once he has succeeded in this endeavor. To the same purpose, he has created a series of Horcruxes, or objects into which he has grafted a part of his soul through the act of murder, so that even if that soul were to be severed from his body (as happens when he attempts to kill the baby Harry), he will survive. In doing so, Voldemort has approached what he calls "my goal—to conquer death" (4: 653). He is convinced that the "master of death" would be the person who would vanquish death by becoming immortal: to die, for him, is to be defeated, and he is too strong, he believes, to succumb to such a fate. Yet like the eldest brother, by seeking "to conquer death," he ensures, ironically, that he will be conquered by it. By seeking to destroy Harry, whom he has heard prophesied may destroy him, he ensures that Harry will have no choice but to try to destroy him. As Dumbledore observes, "Voldemort himself created his worst enemy, just as tyrants everywhere do!" (6: 510). As Voldemort does not understand death, he does not understand love. Because he has never loved anyone, he cannot comprehend other people's love, including the love Harry's mother had exhibited when she had begged him, *"Not Harry, please no, take me, kill me instead—"* (6: 344). Because he assumes that people want to live more than anything, as he does, he cannot fathom what he calls "the woman's foolish sacrifice" (4: 653). Even when Voldemort learns that by dying for her son, Harry's mother cast a protection over him that prevented Voldemort from killing Harry, Voldemort understands this spell cerebrally, not viscerally. As brilliant a wizard as he may be, Voldemort cannot feel, and, because he cannot feel, he cannot understand. Love, like that which Harry's mother displayed, is a magic, Dumbledore explains, "which he despises, and which he has always, therefore, underestimated, to his cost" (5: 835–36).[124] The absence of a moral imagination corresponds to the absence of a literary imagination, especially when it comes to fairy-tales. Dumbledore tells Harry, "That which Voldemort does not value, he takes no trouble to comprehend. Of . . . children's tales . . . Voldemort knows and understands nothing. *Nothing*. That they . . . have a power beyond his own, a power beyond the reach of any magic, is a truth he has never grasped" (7: 710). Self-possessed as Voldemort always is, when that which does not, cannot, and should not happen happens, he is "shocked" (7: 741), and destroyed.

In contrast to his Muggle family, Harry is imaginative.[125] In the

124. As W. H. Auden writes in "The Quest Hero," *Texas Quarterly* 4, no. 4 (1961): 81–93; rpt. in *Understanding "The Lord of the Rings": The Best of Tolkien Criticism*, ed. Rose A. Zimbardo and Neil D. Isaacs (Boston: Houghton Mifflin, 2004), 31–51, about Tolkien's wicked Sauron, "His primary weakness is a lack of imagination, for, while Good can imagine what it would be like to be Evil, Evil cannot imagine what it would be like to be Good" (47).

125. Lisa Hopkins, in "Harry Potter and the Acquisition of Knowledge," in *Reading Harry Potter: Critical Essays*, ed. Giselle Liza Anatol (Westport, CT: Praeger, 2003), 25–34, stresses Harry's tendency to observe what Muggles do not observe.

Dursleys' car, en route to the zoo, he recalls the dream he had about the flying motorcycle because it seemed to him a "good . . . dream" (1: 19). From Harry's perspective, the fact that motorcycles "don't" act in such a manner does not necessarily mean that they "can't" do so, at least in dreams, and it certainly does not mean that they "shouldn't" do so. At the zoo, he accompanies his relatives to the reptile house, where Dudley makes his father tap on the glass of a tank to make the sleeping snake move. When the snake continues to doze, Dudley moans, "This is boring" (1: 27) and continues on. Yet when Harry approaches the tank, Rowling tells us, "Harry . . . looked intently at the snake. He wouldn't have been surprised if it had died of boredom itself—no company except stupid people drumming their fingers on the glass trying to disturb it all day long" (1: 27). Harry is reminded of how his aunt hammers on his bedroom door in the morning to wake him up, and he decides that the snake's fate is worse than his own because at least he can roam throughout the rest of the house. In contrast to his cousin, Harry is able not just to see the snake but also to imagine how the snake sees visitors like themselves. He is able not to feel bored but to imagine that the snake must feel even more bored. He is able not to feel sorry for himself, as difficult as his life with the Dursleys may be, but to feel sorry for the snake, whose life must be even worse. While Harry is having these ruminations, the snake opens his eye, slowly raises his head, and looks at Harry. *"It winked"* (1: 27). After Harry cautiously winks back, we are told, "The snake jerked its head toward Uncle Vernon and Dudley, then raised its eyes to the ceiling. It gave Harry a look that said quite plainly: *'I get that all the time'*" (1: 27). The text continues, "'I know,' Harry murmured through the glass, though he wasn't sure the snake could hear him. 'It must be really annoying.' The snake nodded vigorously" (1: 28). As Harry had imagined what the snake's experience must be like and as he had sympathized with that experience, he expresses interest in his background in Brazil, with a curiosity about something other than himself which the Dursleys would never be capable of. While we will later learn that Harry speaks Parseltongue, the rare wizarding gift to speak with snakes, here, it is clear that he is able to communicate with the snake because of the imaginative investment he has already made in him. As Rowling describes the dialogue, Harry interprets the winks and nods he believes the snake gives him as speech, and he talks to him without being sure that he is being heard. The ability Harry shows to speak with this snake is clearly "magical," yet it is also clearly grounded in his imaginative capacities.

If Harry understands aspects of magic that Hermione does not, it is because he is so imaginative. Whereas Hermione is rational in her approach to truth, Harry is intuitive. He experiences a "feeling" (7: 363) or even "a strong, though inexplicable feeling" (7: 100) of how he must act. "Instinct, overwhelming instinct," even at the expense of "caution" (7: 366), tells him what he must do. The fact that he is guided by "feeling" and "instinct," instead of rational thought, does not lessen the validity of what he knows. On the contrary, we are told that, at one point, "Harry understood without having to think" (7: 698), and, at another, that "understanding was coming so fast that it seemed to have bypassed thought" (7: 698). Whereas Hermione is methodical in her approach to truth, Harry is inspired by flashes of insight. He becomes convinced not only that the Deathly Hallows exist, as Mr. Lovegood has told them that they do, but that he knows where they are. He is sure that Dumbledore possessed the Elder Wand and that Voldemort is flying right now to retrieve it from his tomb. He is sure that Dumbledore possessed the Resurrection Stone and that, before he died, he placed it in the Snitch (the ball used in the magical game of Quiddich) he left to Harry in his will. He is sure that his Invisibility Cloak is *the* Invisibility Cloak of the tale and that he inherited this cloak because he is the last remaining descendant of Ignotus Peverell. Wild as Harry's thought process may seem to be, it is also accurate. As Dumbledore himself acknowledges, there may not be unbeatable wands, but there are wands that absorb the powers of their masters, so that a wand possessed by a long series of dark wizards—like the Elder Wand—would indeed become a formidable weapon. There may not be a stone that can bring back the dead, but there are various ways in which magic can produce simulacra of the departed, including simulacra that speak and move like their subjects and thus convey what Dumbledore calls "the illusion of our loved ones' continuing presence."[126] At one point, after Harry (mistakenly) thought that he saw his father across a lake, casting a spell that ended up protecting him, Dumbledore asks him, "You think the dead we have loved ever truly leave us? You think that we don't recall them more clearly than ever in times of great trouble?" (3: 427) If Harry thought that he saw his father, it was because he saw himself, brought back in time to perform this spell, and he looks remarkably like his father. Finally, there may not seem to be an Invisibility Cloak, like the one in the tale, but that is because, as Dumbledore had suggested, more speculatively than he could have, the youngest

126. "Albus Dumbledore on 'Babbity Rabbitty and Her Cackling Stump,'" in Rowling, *Tales of Beedle the Bard*, 78–86, at 79.

brother's descendants either do not know the origin of their cloak or they refrain from boasting about it. Harry did not at first know that he possessed the Invisibility Cloak of the tale, and, like Ignotus Peverell, he never boasted that he owned such a garment. It is Harry's imagination that enables him to grasp how "The Tale of the Three Brothers" could intersect with his own story, and it is because of this imagination that he stands out from his friends: "Harry's imagination was racing ahead, far beyond Ron and Hermione's" (7: 429).

If Harry is ultimately able to overcome Voldemort, it is because he is so imaginative. In contrast to his powerful antagonist, Harry understands death. It is not clear at what point he realizes that he is the final Horcrux. Even before he is given this information, he seems to grasp that, as Voldemort was trying to kill him years before, a shard of Voldemort's soul entered into him and remained in him all those years; in order for this shard to be extinguished, his life will have to be extinguished as well. One recalls that Ignotus Peverell, "the humblest and also the wisest of the brothers" (7: 408), treated Death neither as someone who vanquishes him nor as someone whom he vanquishes, but as an "equal" and a "friend." After a long life, he put aside his Invisibility Cloak, in recognition that one cannot thwart Death forever, and went off with him. As the last descendant of Ignotus, Harry understands that "the true master of death" (7: 720–21) (which Dumbledore deems him to be) is the person who does not flee death but, on the contrary, accepts it when the time comes. In contrast to Voldemort, Harry understands love. As he heads into the Forbidden Forest near Hogwarts to meet Voldemort, in the expectation that he will die at his hands, he feels the presence of those he loved who had died before him—his parents, his godfather, one of his teachers—as he had not felt it before, and he feels strengthened by their company. The figures he sees are memories, but they are like "memory made solid" (7: 699), and, therefore, no less real or less powerful for that. As unremarkable a wizard as he may be, Harry can feel, and, because he can feel, he can understand, even, we are told, "without having to think." Dumbledore had withheld from Harry for as long as possible the knowledge that he must die, he explained, so that when Harry came to this knowledge, he would be ready to accept and act upon it. "Otherwise how could he have the strength to do what must be done?" (7: 685). When Harry understands, he understands, not because he has actively sought out the truth through the exercise of his reason, but because he has passively awaited the realization of that truth over the course of time. The presence of a moral imagination, which enables Harry to appreciate the sufferings of others under Voldemort, corresponds to the presence of a literary imagination, which enables him to interpret "The Tale of the Three Brothers" correctly.

In the end, the *Harry Potter* novels offer two lessons about how to read products of the imagination. During his first year at Hogwarts, Harry discovers a large mirror that, he learns, is called the Mirror of Erised (or, when the letters of the final word are reversed, "the Mirror of Desire") in a hidden room at Hogwarts.[127] Gazing at the mirror, the lonely boy beholds himself surrounded by his dead parents and other members of his missing, magical family, and he returns the following evening to contemplate again this vision of that for which he most longs. Yet Dumbledore, who sees Harry visiting this mirror, warns him that though it contains "delights," "This mirror will give us neither knowledge nor truth. Men have wasted away before it, entranced by what they have seen, or have been driven mad, not knowing if what it shows is real or even possible" (1: 213). If one seeks mental images of what one desires, he suggests, one will confuse a representation (in a mirror or in a text) with a reality, and one will languish, believing oneself to possess, in one's imagination, what one does not possess, in life. He advises his young charge, "It does not do to dwell on dreams and forget to live" (1: 214). It is dangerous to be enthralled by the images of what one desires, in a way that detaches one from life. Many years later, after Harry has apparently been murdered by Voldemort, he receives another reading lesson from his late headmaster. Waking up from the killing spell, Harry finds himself at what seems to be King's Cross Railway Station in London, and he sees what seems to be Dumbledore near him. They engage in an illuminating conversation that prepares Harry to return to the Forbidden Forest to face Voldemort one last (and ultimately victorious) time. As he takes leave of his old mentor, he asks him about their encounter, "Is this real? Or has this been happening inside my head?" Dumbledore replies, beaming, "Of course it is happening inside your head, Harry, but why on earth should that mean that it is not real?" (7: 723). The image of Harry's dead parents in the mirror did not provide Harry with truth, but the image of the deceased Dumbledore does do so, strengthening him in his resolve to confront

127. Shawn E. Klein, "The Mirror of Erised: Why We Should Heed Dumbledore's Warning," in *Harry Potter and Philosophy: If Aristotle Ran Hogwarts*, ed. David Baggett and Shawn E. Klein (Chicago: Open Court, 2004), 92–104, situates the situates the epistemological issue at the heart of the mirror—the need to distinguish appearance and reality—within the context of Western philosophy.

his nemesis. While those who use their imagination badly are paralyzed by false images, in a way that distracts them from their lives, those who use it well are fortified by real, though mental images, in a way that enables them to soldier on.

In her commencement address to the students at Harvard University in the spring of 2008, Rowling spoke of what she called "The Importance of the Imagination."[128] As a young woman, she recalled, she had worked at Amnesty International's headquarters in London. Based on this experience, she spoke of people who choose not to use their imaginations. These people may be citizens of countries like the United Kingdom or the United States who have never been arrested, imprisoned, or tortured for their beliefs and who do not wish to imagine the experience of those who have not been so fortunate. She said of such people, "They choose to remain comfortably within the bounds of their own experience, never troubling to wonder how it would feel to have been born other than they are. They can refuse to hear screams or to peer inside cages; they can close their minds and hearts to any suffering that does not touch them personally; they can refuse to know." Though the "willfully unimaginative" may not be the ones arresting, imprisoning, and torturing others, she suggested, by refusing to experience vicariously the torments of their fellow men and women, they are colluding with such evil. At the same time, Rowling spoke of people who do use their imaginations. She was struck by Amnesty International's success in mobilizing thousands of such volunteers to advocate for people from other countries—"people they do not know, and will never meet"—who have suffered such privations. These volunteers may also have never suffered persecution for their beliefs, but they are willing to imagine the experiences of others who have done so. While she learned about human evil from working at Amnesty International, she also learned about human goodness, she claimed. "Unlike any other creature on this planet, humans can learn and understand, without having experienced. They can think themselves into other people's places." Though she acknowledged the role that imagination had in bringing about her own career path, she insisted that this faculty constitutes not only the power to envision that which does not exist: "In its arguably most transformative and revelatory capacity, it is the power

128. J. K. Rowling, "The Fringe Benefits of Failure, and the Importance of Imagination," http://news.harvard.edu/gazette/story/2008/06/text-of-j-k-rowling-speech/. All quotations from here on are from this source.

that enables us to empathize with humans whose experiences we have never shared."

In the end, as several philosophers we have considered have made clear, the problem with fantasy, as with romance in general, is that we can imagine far more with our minds than we can observe with our senses. Should we respond to this disjunction in our faculties by reining in our imagination, so that we perceive no more than the empirical world around us? Should we be wary of perceptions of greatness or beauty, lest we project images of reality we have acquired from our reading onto the world—in a word, lest we "romanticize"? Should we insist that that which we read be useful, if not morally or spiritually (as medieval authors might have had it), then ethically or politically (as we might put it)? If the answer to these questions is yes, then the value of literature lies outside literature, in the accuracy with which it represents the world or the effectiveness with which it prepares us to act in that world. Or, on the contrary, should we allow our imagination freedom to gallop where it will? Should we envision a black swan, a golden mountain, a castle in Spain, a griffin, a green sun? Should we allow ourselves to perceive greatness or beauty, confident that they are present in the world and that romance is only alerting us to this fact? Should we insist that the reading of romance is useful, in the sense that it enables us to apprehend a reality, not of the here and the now, but of the past or, possibly, the future? Should we argue that romance is realistic, though realistic in Chesterton's manner of speaking, in that it exposes the fantastical aspect of the most factual elements of our lives? Or should we argue that literature need not be useful or realistic at all, but that, as Frye would have it, it is something to be enjoyed in and of itself, in its resonance with other works of literature? If the answer to these questions is yes, then the value of literature lies in itself, in the freedom it grants our minds to venture beyond our bodies and the world our bodies inhabit. Skeptical as we may be nowadays of anything that exceeds the empirical world, romance is that which promises, counterculturally, a realm beyond this one.

Selected Bibliography

BSGRT	Bibliotheca Scriptorum Graecorum et Romanorum Teubneriana
CCCM	Corpus Christianorum Continuatio Mediaevalis
CCSL	Corpus Christianorum Series Latina
CSEL	Corpus Scriptorum Ecclesiasticorum Latinorum
MGH	Monumenta Germaniae Historica
PL	Patrologia Latina

Primary

Arthur of Britain. Edited by E. K. Chambers. London: Sidgwick and Jackson, 1927; rpt., Cambridge: Speculum Historiale, 1964.

"British History" and "The Welsh Annals." Edited and translated by John Morris. Totowa, NJ: Rowman and Littlefield, 1980.

The Celtic Sources for the Arthurian Legend. Edited and translated by Jon B. Coe and Simon Young. Burnham-on-Sea, Somerset, UK: Llanerch Publishers, 1995.

Chrétien de Troyes. *Le Chevalier au lion (Yvain)*. Edited by David Hult. In *Romans, suivis des chansons, avec, en appendice, "Philomena,"* edited by Michel Zink, 705–936. Paris: Livre de Poche, 1994.

———. *"Le Chevalier de la Charrette" ou "Le Roman de Lancelot."* Edited by Charles Méla and Olivier Collet. In *Romans, suivis des chansons, avec, en appendice, "Philomena,"* edited by Michel Zink, 495–704. Paris: Livre de Poche, 1994.

———. *Cligés*. Edited by Stuart Gregory and Claude Luttrell. Cambridge: D. S. Brewer, 1993.

———. *Cligés*. Edited by Charles Méla and Olivier Collet. In *Romans, suivis des chansons, avec, en appendice, "Philomena,"* edited by Michel Zink, 285–494. Paris: Livre de Poche, 1994.

———. *"Le Conte du Graal" ou "Le Roman de Perceval."* Edited by Charles Méla. In *Romans, suivis des chansons, avec, en appendice, "Philomena,"* edited by Michel Zink, 937–1211. Paris: Livre de Poche, 1994.

———. *Erec et Enide*. Edited by Jean-Marie Fritz. In *Romans, suivis des chansons, avec, en appendice, "Philomena,"* edited by Michel Zink, 56–283. Paris: Livre de Poche, 1994.

———. *Oeuvres complètes*. Edited by Daniel Poirion with Anne Berthelot. Paris: Gallimard, 1994.

———. *"Le Roman de Perceval" ou "Le Conte du Graal": Edition critique d'après tous les manuscrits*. Edited by Keith Busby. Tübingen: Max Niemeyer Verlag, 1993.

———. *Romans, suivis des chansons, avec, en appendice, "Philomena."* Edited by Michel Zink. Paris: Livre de Poche, 1994

———. *The Story of the Grail (Li Contes du Graal)*. Edited by Rupert T. Pickens. New York: Garland, 1990.

The Continuations of the Old French "Perceval" of Chrétien de Troyes. 5 vols. Edited by William Roach. Philadelphia: University of Pennsylvania Press, 1949–83.

The "Didot Perceval" According to the Manuscripts of Modena and Paris. Edited by William Roach. Philadelphia: University of Pennsylvania Press, 1941.

L'Estoire del Saint Graal. Edited by Jean-Paul Ponceau. Paris: Honoré Champion, 1997.

Faral, Edmond, ed. *La Légende Arthurienne: Études et documents*. 3 vols. Paris: H. Champion, 1929.

Geoffrey of Monmouth. *The "Historia regum Britannie" of Geoffrey of Monmouth I: Bern, Burgerbibliothek, MS 568*. Edited by Neil Wright. Cambridge: D. S. Brewer, 1984.

———. *The "Historia regum Britannie" of Geoffrey of Monmouth II: The First Variant Version; A Critical Edition*. Edited by Neil Wright. Cambridge: D. S. Brewer, 1988.

———. *The "Historia regum Britannie" of Geoffrey of Monmouth III: A Summary Catalogue of the Manuscripts*. Edited by Julia C. Crick. Cambridge: D. S. Brewer, 1989.

———. *The "Historia regum Britannie" of Geoffrey of Monmouth IV: Dissemination and Reception in the Later Middle Ages*. Edited by Julia C. Crick. Cambridge: D. S. Brewer, 1991.

———. *The "Historia regum Britannie" of Geoffrey of Monmouth V: "Gesta regum Britannie."* Edited and translated by Neil Wright. Cambridge: D. S. Brewer, 1991.

———. *A History of the Kings of Britain: An Edition and Translation of "De gestis Britonum."* Edited by Michael D. Reeve. Woodbridge, UK: Boydell Press, 2009.

———. *Life of Merlin: Vita Merlini*. Edited and translated by Basil Clarke. Cardiff: University of Wales Press, 1973.

Gerald of Wales. *Opera*. 8 vols. Edited by J. S. Brewer. Edited by James F. Dimock. Rolls Series. London: Longmans, 1861–91; rpt., Nendeln: Kraus Reprint, 1964.

Gerbert de Montreuil. *La Continuation de Perceval*. 3 vols. Edited by Mary Williams. Paris: H. Champion, 1922–75.

Goodrich, Peter, ed. *The Romance of Merlin: An Anthology*. New York: Garland, 1991.

Joseph d'Arimathie. Edited by Gérard Gros. In *Le Livre du Graal*, edited by Daniel Poirion. 2 vols., vol. 1, 1–567. Paris: Gallimard, 2001–9.

Lancelot. Edited by Eric Hicks, Mireille Demaules, Jean-Marie Fritz, and Irene Freire-Nunes. In *Le Livre du Graal*, edited by Daniel Poirion. 2 vols., vol. 2 and vol. 3, 3–805. Paris: Gallimard, 2001–9.

Lancelot: Roman en prose du 13ᵉ siècle. Edited by Alexandre Micha. 9 vols. Geneva: Droz, 1978–83.

Lancelot do Lac: The Non-Cyclic Old French Prose Romance. Edited by Elspeth Kennedy. 2 vols. Oxford: Oxford University Press, 1980.

Lancelot du Lac: Roman français du XIIIᵉ siècle. Edited by Elspeth Kennedy, François Mosès, Laetitia Le Guay, and Yvan G. Lepage. 6 vols. Paris: Livre de Poche, 1991.

The Lancelot-Grail Cycle: Text and Transformations. Edited by William W. Kibler. Austin: University of Texas Press, 1994.

Layamon's Arthur: The Arthurian Section of Layamon's "Brut" (Lines 9229–14297). Edited and translated by W. R. J. Barron and S. C. Weinberg. Exeter: University of Exeter Press, 2001.

Le Livre du Graal. Edited by Daniel Poirion. 2 vols. Paris: Gallimard, 2001–9.

Malory, Sir Thomas. *The Works of Sir Thomas Malory*. Edited by Eugène Vinaver. 3 vols. Oxford: Clarendon Press, 1947.

Merlin. Edited by Irene Freire-Nunes. In *Le Livre du Graal*, edited by Daniel Poirion. 2 vols., vol. 1, 570–805. Paris: Gallimard, 2001–9.

Merlin: Roman en prose du XIIIᵉ siècle, pub. avec la mise en prose du poème de "Merlin" de Robert de Boron d'après le manuscrit appartenant à M. Alfred H. Huth. Edited by Gaston Paris and Jacob Ulrich. 2 vols. Société des anciens textes français. Paris: Firmin Didot, 1886.

Merlin through the Ages: A Chronological Anthology and Source Book. Edited by R. J. Stewart and John Matthews. London: Blanford, 1995.

La Mort du roi Arthur. Edited by Mary B. Speer. In *Le Livre du Graal*, edited by Daniel Poirion. 2 vols., vol. 3, 1179–486. Paris: Gallimard, 2001–9.

La Mort du roi Arthur. Edited by David F. Hult. Paris: Lettres Gothiques, 2009.

La Mort du roi Arthur: Roman publié d'après le manuscrit de Lyon, Palais des Arts 77, complété par le manuscrit BnF n.a.fr. 1119. Edited and translated by Emmanuèle Baumgartner and Marie-Thérèse de Medeiros. Paris: Honoré Champion, 2007.

La Mort le roi Artu = The Death of Arthur: From the Old French Lancelot of Yale 229, with Essays, Glossaries, and Notes to the Text. Edited by Elizabeth Moore Willingham and Nancy B. Black. Turnhout, Belgium: Brepols, 2007.

La Mort le roi Artu: Roman du XIIIe *siècle*. Edited by Jean Frappier. Geneva: Droz, 1936; rpt., 1964.

Novel and Romance, 1700–1800: A Documentary Record. Edited by Ioan Williams. New York: Barnes and Noble, 1970.

Première Continuation de Perceval: Continuation-Gauvain; Texte du ms. L. Edited by William Roach. Translated Colette-Anne van Coolput-Storms. Paris: Livre de poche, 1993.

Les Premiers Faits du Roi Arthur. Edited by Irene Freire-Nunes. In *Le Livre du Graal*, edited by Daniel Poirion. 2 vols., vol. 1, 807–1662. Paris: Gallimard, 2001–9.

La Queste del saint Graal: Roman du XIIIe *siècle*. 2 vols. Edited by Albert Pauphilet. Paris: Honoré Champion, 1923; rpt., 1999.

La Quête du Saint Graal. Edited by Gérard Gros. In *Le Livre du Graal*, edited by Daniel Poirion. 2 vols., vol. 3, 807–1177. Paris: Gallimard, 2001–9.

Robert de Boron. "Le Fragment en vers du *Merlin*." In *Merlin: Roman du XIII*[e] *siècle*, edited by Alexandre Micha, 1–17. Geneva: Droz, 1979.

———. *Merlin: Roman du XIII*[e] *siècle*. Edited by Alexandre Micha. Geneva: Droz, 1979.

———. *Joseph d'Arimathie: A Critical Edition of the Verse and Prose Versions*. Edited by Richard O'Gorman. Toronto: Pontifical Institute of Mediaeval Studies, 1995.

———. *Le Roman de l'Estoire dou Graal*. Edited by William Nitze. Paris: Honoré Champion, 1927.

———. *Roman de l'Estoire dou Graal*. Edited by Richard O'Gorman. Toronto: Pontifical Institute of Mediaeval Studies, 1995.

La Suite du Roman de Merlin. Edited by Gilles Roussineau. 2 vols. Geneva: Droz, 1996.

Ulrich von Zatzikhoven. *Lanzelet: Eine Erzählung*. Edited by Karl August Hahn. Berlin: De Gruyter, 1965.

La Version post-Vulgate de "la Queste del Saint Graal" et de "la Mort Artu": Troisième partie du "Roman de Graal." Edited by Fanni Bogdanow. 3 vols. (1, 2, and 4, part 1). Paris: A. et J. Picard, 1991.

The Vulgate Version of the Arthurian Romances. Edited by H. Oskar Sommer. 8 vols. Washington, DC: Carnegie Institution, 1908–16.

Wace. *Roman de Brut: A History of the British; Text and Translation*. Edited and translated by Judith Weiss. Exeter: University of Exeter Press, 2002.

William of Malmesbury. *Gesta regum Anglorum = The History of the English Kings*. Edited and translated by R. A. B. Mynors, R. M. Thomson, and M. Winterbottom. Oxford: Clarendon Press, 1998.

———. *Gesta Regum Anglorum*. Edited by William Stubbs. London: Rolls Series, 1887.

William of Malmesbury et al. *De Antiquitate Glastoniensis Ecclesiae*. In *Arthur of Britain*, by E. K. Chambers, 265–67. London: Sidgwick and Jackson, 1927; rpt., Cambridge: Speculum Historiale, 1964.

———. *The Early History of Glastonbury: An Edition, Translation, and Study of*

William of Malmesbury's "De Antiquitate Glastonie Ecclesie." Edited by John Scott. Woodbridge, UK: Boydell Press, 1981.

William of Newburgh. *History of English Affairs*. Edited by P. G. Walsh and M. J. Kennedy. 2 vols. Warminster: Aris and Phillips, 1988.

Secondary

Adams, Alison, Armel H. Diverres, Karen Stern, and Kenneth Varty, eds. *The Changing Face of Arthurian Romance: Essays on Arthurian Prose Romances in Memory of Cedric E. Pickford*. Woodbridge, UK: Boydell Press, 1986.

Archibald, Elizabeth, and Ad Putter, eds. *The Cambridge Companion to the Arthurian Legend*. Cambridge: Cambridge University Press, 2009.

Auerbach, Erich. *Mimesis: Dargestellte Wirklichkeit in der abendländischen Literatur*. Bern: A. Francke, 1946.

Aurell, Martin. *La Légende du roi Arthur, 550–1250*. Paris: Perrin, 2007.

Bakhtin, Mikhail M. *The Dialogic Imagination: Four Essays*. Edited by Michael Holquist. Translated by Caryl Emerson and Michael Holquist. Austin: University of Texas Press, 1981.

Barron, W. R. J., ed. *The Arthur of the English: The Arthurian Legend in Medieval English Life and Literature*. Cardiff: University of Wales Press, 1999; rev. ed., 2001.

Barthes, Roland. "L'Effet du réel." In *Littérature et realité*, edited by Tzvetan Todorov and Gérard Genette, 81–90. Paris: Seuil, 1982.

Baswell, Christopher, and William Sharpe, eds. *The Passing of Arthur: New Essays in the Arthurian Tradition*. New York: Garland, 1988.

Beer, Gillian. *The Romance*. London: Methuen, 1970.

Bogdanow, Fanni. *The Romance of the Grail: A Study of the Structure and Genesis of a Thirteenth-Century Prose Romance*. Manchester: Manchester University Press, 1966.

Boitani, Piero. "Romance." In *The Novel*, edited by Franco Moretti. Vol. 1, *History, Geography, and Culture*, 269–82. Princeton, NJ: Princeton University Press, 2006.

Bromwich, Rachel, A. O. H. Jarmen, and Brynley F. Roberts, eds. *The Arthur of the Welsh: The Arthurian Legend in Medieval Welsh Literature*. Cardiff: University of Wales Press, 1991.

Brown-Grant, Rosalind. *French Romances of the Later Middle Ages: Gender, Morality, and Desire*. Oxford: Oxford University Press, 2008.

Brownlee, Kevin, and Marina Scordilis Brownlee, eds. *Romance: Generic Transformations from Chrétien de Troyes to Cervantes*. Hanover, NH: University Press of New England, 1985.

Bruckner, Matilda Tomaryn. *Shaping Romance: Interpretation, Truth, and Closure in Twelfth-Century French Fictions*. Philadelphia: University of Pennsylvania Press, 1993.

Burgess, Glyn, and Karen Pratt, ed. *The Arthur of the French: The Arthurian Legend in Medieval French and Occitan Literature*. Cardiff: University of Wales Press, 2006.

Burns, E. Jane. *Arthurian Fictions: Re-reading the Vulgate Cycle*. Columbus: Ohio State University Press, 1985.

Copeland, Rita. "Between *Romans* and Romantics." *Texas Studies in Literature and Language* 33, no. 2 (1991): 215–24.

Crane, Susan. *Insular Romance: Politics, Faith, and Culture in Anglo-Norman and Middle English Literature*. Berkeley: University of California Press, 1986.

Day, Geoffrey. *From Fiction to the Novel*. New York: Routledge, 1987.

Doody, Margaret Anne. *The True Story of the Novel*. New Brunswick, NJ: Rutgers University Press, 1996.

Dornbush, Jean M. *Pygmalion's Figure: Reading Old French Romance*. Lexington, KY: French Forum, 1990.

Dover, Carol, ed. *A Companion to the Lancelot-Grail Cycle*. Cambridge: D. S. Brewer, 2003.

Dufournet, Jean. *Approches du "Lancelot en prose": Études*. Paris: Librairie Champion, 1984.

Duggan, Joseph. *The Romances of Chrétien de Troyes*. New Haven, CT: Yale University Press, 2001.

Echard, Siân. *Arthurian Narrative in the Latin Tradition*. Cambridge: Cambridge University Press, 1998.

Echard, Siân, ed. *The Arthur of Medieval Latin Literature: The Development and Dissemination of the Arthurian Legend in Medieval Latin*. Cardiff: University of Wales Press, 2011.

Eden, Kathy. *Poetic and Legal Fiction in the Aristotelian Tradition*. Princeton, NJ: Princeton University Press, 1986.

Field, Rosalind. *Tradition and Transformation in Medieval Romance*. Rochester, NY: D. S. Brewer, 1993.

Field, Rosalind, Phillipa Hardman, and Michelle Sweeney, eds. *Christianity and Romance in Medieval England*. Rochester, NY: D. S. Brewer, 2010.

Fletcher, Robert H. *The Arthurian Material in the Chronicles, Especially Those of Great Britain and France*. Boston: Ginn, 1906; rpt., New York: B. Franklin, 1966.

Frappier, Jean. *Amour courtois et Table Ronde*. Geneva: Droz, 1973.

———. *Autour du Graal*. Geneva: Droz, 1977.

———. *Chrétien de Troyes*. Paris: Hatier, 1957; rev. ed., 1968.

Frye, Northrop. *Anatomy of Criticism: Four Essays*. Princeton, NJ: Princeton University Press, 1957.

———. *The Secular Scripture: A Study of the Structure of Romance*. Cambridge, MA: Harvard University Press, 1976.

Fuchs, Barbara. *Romance*. The New Critical Idiom. New York: Routledge, 2004.

Fulton, Helen, ed. *A Companion to Arthurian Literature*. Chichester, UK; Malden, MA: Wiley-Blackwell, 2009.

Furrow, Melissa. *Expectations of Romance: The Reception of a Genre in Medieval England*. Rochester, NY: D. S. Brewer, 2009.

Gallagher, Catherine. "The Rise of Fictionality." In *The Novel*, edited by Franco Moretti. Vol. 1, *History, Geography, and Culture*, 336–63. Princeton, NJ: Princeton University Press, 2006.

Gallagher, Catherine, and Stephen Greenblatt. "The Novel and Other Discourses of Suspended Belief." In *Practicing New Historicism*, 163–210. Chicago: University of Chicago Press, 2000.

Gallais, Pierre. "De la naissance du roman: À propos d'un article recent." *Cahiers de civilisation médiévale* 14 (1971): 69–75.

———. "Recherches sur la mentalité des romanciers français du Moyen Age." *Cahiers de civilisation médiévale* 7, no. 28 (1964): 479–93, and 13 (1970): 333–38.

Ganim, John. "The Myth of Medieval Romance." In *Medievalism and the Modernist Temper*, edited by R. Howard Bloch and Stephen G. Nichols, 148–68. Baltimore: Johns Hopkins University Press, 1995.

Gaunt, Simon. *Gender and Genre in Medieval French Literature*. Cambridge: Cambridge University Press, 1995.

———. *Love and Death in Medieval French and Occitan Courtly Literature: Martyrs to Love*. Oxford: Oxford University Press, 2006.

Genette, Gérard. *Fiction and Diction*. Translated by Catherine Porter. Ithaca, NY: Cornell University Press, 1993.

Green, Dennis Howard. *The Beginnings of Romance, 1150–1220*. Cambridge: Cambridge University Press, 2002.

———. *Women Readers in the Middle Ages*. Cambridge: Cambridge University Press, 2007.

Greene, Virginie. *Logical Fictions in Medieval Literature and Philosophy*. Cambridge: Cambridge University Press, 2014.

Grünkorn, Gertrud. *Die Fiktionalität des höfischen Romans um 1200*. Berlin: Erich Schmidt Verlag, 1994.

Haidu, Peter. "Romance: Idealistic Genre or Historical Text?" In *The Craft of Fiction: Essays in Medieval Poetics*, edited by Leigh A. Arrathoon, 1–46. Rochester, MI: Solaris, 1984.

Hanning, R. W. "The Audience as Co-creator of the First Chivalric Romances." In "Literature and Its Audience." Special number, *Yearbook of English Studies* 11 (1981): 1–28.

Heiserman, Arthur. *The Novel before the Novel: Essays and Discussions about the Beginnings of Prose Fiction in the West*. Chicago: University of Chicago Press, 1977.

Heng, Geraldine. *Empire of Magic: Medieval Romance and the Politics of Cultural Fantasy*. New York: Columbia University Press, 2003.

Jackson, W. T. H. "The Nature of Romance." *Yale French Studies*, no. 51 (1974): 12–25.

Jameson, Fredric. "Magical Narratives: On the Dialectical Use of Genre Criticism." In *The Political Unconscious: Narrative as a Socially Symbolic Act*, 103–50. Ithaca, NY: Cornell University Press, 1981.

———. "Magical Narratives: Romance as a Genre." *New Literary History* 7 (1975): 135–63.

Jauss, Hans Erich. "Theory of Genres and Medieval Literature." In *Toward an Aesthetic of Reception*, translated by Timothy Bahti, 76–109. Minneapolis: University of Minnesota Press, 1982.

Kaeuper, Richard W. *Chivalry and Violence in Medieval Europe*. Oxford: Oxford University Press, 1999.

Kay, Sarah. *The Chansons de Geste in the Age of Romance: Political Fictions*. Oxford: Clarendon Press, 1995.

———. *Courtly Contradictions: The Emergence of the Literary Object in the Twelfth Century*. Stanford, CA: Stanford University Press, 2001.

Kelly, Douglas. *The Art of Medieval French Romance*. Madison: University of Wisconsin Press, 1992.

———. *"Sens" and "Conjointure" in the "Chevalier de la Charrette."* The Hague: Mouton, 1966.

Kennedy, Elspeth. *Lancelot and the Grail: A Study of the "Prose Lancelot."* Oxford: Clarendon Press, 1986.

Ker, W. P. *Epic and Romance: Essays on Medieval Literature*. London: Macmillan, 1926.

Kibler, William W., ed. *The Lancelot-Grail Cycle: Text and Transformations*. Austin: University of Texas Press, 1994.

Knapp, Fritz Peter. *Historie und Fiktion in der mittelalterlichen Gattungspoetik: Sieben Studien und ein Nachwort*. Heidelberg: Universitätsverlag C. Winter, 1997.

Knight, Stephen. *Arthurian Literature and Society*. New York: St. Martin's Press, 1983.

———. *Merlin: Knowledge and Power through the Ages*. Ithaca, NY: Cornell University Press, 2009.

Köhler, Erich. *Ideal und Wirklichkeit in der höfischen Epik: Studien zur Form der frühen Artus- und Graldichtung*. Berlin: Walter de Gruyter, 1956; rev. ed., 1970; 3rd ed., 2002.

Krueger, Roberta L. *Women Readers and the Ideology of Gender in Old French Verse Romance*. Cambridge: Cambridge University Press, 1993.

———, ed. *The Cambridge Companion to Medieval Romance*. Cambridge: Cambridge University Press, 2000.

Lacy, Norris J. *A History of Arthurian Scholarship*. Cambridge: D. S. Brewer, 2006.

———. *Text and Intertext in Medieval Arthurian Literature*. New York: Garland, 1996.

Lacy, Norris J., ed. *The Fortunes of King Arthur*. Cambridge: D. S. Brewer, 2005.

Lacy, Norris J., Douglas Kelly, and Keith Busby, eds. *The Legacy of Chrétien de Troyes*. 2 vols. Amsterdam: Rodopi, 1987.

Lacy, Norris J., and Joan Tasker Grimbert, eds. *A Companion to Chrétien de Troyes*. Cambridge: D. S. Brewer, 2005.

Lancelot-Lanzelet hier et aujourdui: Recueil d'articles assemblées par Danielle Buschinger et Michel Zink pour fêter les 90 ans de Alexandre Micha. Edited by Danielle Buschinger and Michel Zink. Greifswald: Reineke-Verlag, 1995.

Loomis, Roger Sherman, ed. *Arthurian Literature in the Middle Ages: A Collaborative History*. Oxford: Clarendon Press, 1959.

Maddox, Donald. *The Arthurian Romances of Chrétien de Troyes: Once and Future Fictions*. Cambridge: Cambridge University Press, 1991.

McCracken, Peggy. *The Romance of Adultery: Queenship and Sexual Transgression in Old French Literature*. Philadelphia: University of Pennsylvania Press, 1998.

Micha, Alexandre. *De la chanson de geste au roman: Études de littérature médiévale offertes par ses amis, élèves et collègues*. Geneva: Droz, 1976.

Newman, Francis X., ed. *The Meaning of Courtly Love*. Papers of the First Annual Conference of the Center for Medieval and Early Renaissance Studies, State University of New York at Binghamton (March 17–18, 1967). Albany: State University of New York, 1968.

Nykrog, Per. "The Rise of Literary Fiction." In *Renaissance and Renewal in the Twelfth Century*, edited by Robert L. Benson, Giles Constable, and Carol D. Lanham, 593–612. Cambridge, MA: Harvard University Press, 1983; rpt., Toronto: University of Toronto Press, 1991.

Padel, O. J. *Arthur in Medieval Welsh Literature*. Cardiff: University of Wales Press, 2000.

Parker, Patricia A. *Inescapable Romance: Studies in the Poetics of a Mode*. Princeton, NJ: Princeton University Press, 1979.

Pearsall, Derek. *Arthurian Romance: A Short Introduction*. Malden, MA: Blackwell, 2003.

Poirion, Daniel, ed. *Précis de littérature française du Moyen Age*. Paris: Presses Universitaires de France, 1983.

Ramm, Ben. *A Discourse for the Holy Grail in Old French Romance*. Woodbridge, UK: D. S. Brewer, 2007.

Ribard, Jacques. "Aux Origines du roman français: Le roman au XII siècle." *Le Genre du roman, les genres de romans: Actes de Colloque (Amiens, 25–26 Avril 1980)*, 13–23. Paris: Presses Universitaires de France, 1980.

Riffaterre, Michael. *Fictional Truth*. Baltimore: Johns Hopkins University Press, 1990.

Saler, Michael. *As If: Modern Enchantment and the Literary Prehistory of Virtual Reality*. Oxford: Oxford University Press, 2012.

Saunders, Corinne, ed. *A Companion to Romance: From Classical to Contemporary*. Malden, MA: Blackwell, 2007.

Shichtman, Martin B., and James P. Carley. *Culture and the King: The Social

Implications of the Arthurian Legend; Essays in Honor of Valerie M. Lagorio. Albany: State University of New York Press, 1994.

Schmolke-Hasselmann, Beate. *Der arturische Versroman von Chrestien bis Froissart*. Tübingen: Max Niemeyer, 1980.

———. *The Evolution of Arthurian Romance: The Verse Tradition from Chrétien to Froissart*. Translated by Margaret Middleton and Roger Middleton. Cambridge: Cambridge University Press, 2006.

Smith, Joshua Byron. *Walter Map and the Matter of Britain*. Philadelphia: University of Pennsylvania Press, 2017.

Stahuljak, Zrinka, Virginie Greene, Sarah Kay, Sharon Kinoshita, and Peggy McCracken. *Thinking through Chrétien de Troyes*. Cambridge: D. S. Brewer, 2010.

Stanesco, Michel, and Michel Zink. *Histoire européenne du roman médiéval: Esquisse et perspectives*. Paris: Presses Universitaires de France, 1992.

Stein, Robert. *Reality Fictions: Romance, History, and Governmental Authority, 1025–1180*. Notre Dame, IN: University of Notre Dame Press, 2006.

Tatlock, J. S. P. *The Legendary History of Britain: Geoffrey of Monmouth's "Historia regum Britanniae" and Its Vernacular Versions*. Berkeley: University of California Press, 1950.

Todorov, Tzvetan, and Gérard Genette. *Littérature et realité*. Paris: Seuil, 1982

Uitti, Karl. *Story, Myth, and Celebration in Old French Narrative Poetry, 1050–1200*. Princeton, NJ: Princeton University Press, 2015.

Varvaro, Alberto. "Medieval French Romance." In *The Novel*, edited by Franco Moretti. Vol. 1, *History, Geography, and Culture*, 156–80. Princeton, NJ: Princeton University Press, 2006.

Vinaver, Eugène. *Form and Meaning in Medieval Romance*. Cambridge: Modern Humanities Research Association, 1966.

———. *The Rise of Romance*. Oxford: Oxford University Press, 1971.

Vitz, Evelyn Birge. *Orality and Performance in Early French Romance*. Cambridge: D. S. Brewer, 1999.

Whetter, K. S. *Understanding Genre and Medieval Romance*. Aldershot, UK: Ashgate, 2008.

Whitman, Jon, ed. *Romance and History: Imagining Time from the Medieval to the Early Modern Period*. Cambridge: Cambridge University Press, 2015.

Index